The novelist and critic Christine Brooke-Rose reflects on her own fictional craft and turns her well-developed analytic abilities on other writers fictional and critical, from Hawthorne and Pound to Bloom and Derrida, in an attempt to investigate those difficult border zones between the 'invented' and the 'real'. The result is an extended meditation, in a highly personal idiom, on the creative act and its relation to modern theoretical writing and thinking. Like her fiction, Professor Brooke-Rose's criticism is self-consciously experimental, trying out and discarding ideas, adopting others. Her linguistic prowess, her uncommon role as a recognized writer of fiction *and* theory, and the relevance of her work to the feminist and other modern movements, all contribute to the interest of this unusual sequence of essays.

Stories, theories and things

Stories, theories and things

CHRISTINE BROOKE-ROSE

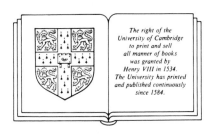

The right of the
University of Cambridge
to print and sell
all manner of books
was granted by
Henry VIII in 1534.
The University has printed
and published continuously
since 1584.

CAMBRIDGE UNIVERSITY PRESS

Cambridge
New York   Port Chester
Melbourne   Sydney

Published by the Press Syndicate of the University of Cambridge
The Pitt Building, Trumpington Street, Cambridge CB2 1RP
40 West 20th Street, New York, NY 10011, USA
10 Stamford Road, Oakleigh, Melbourne 3166, Australia

First published 1991

Printed in Great Britain at The Bath Press, Avon

British Library cataloguing in publication data
Brooke-Rose, Christine
    Stories, theories and things.
    1. Literature. Theories
    I. Title
    801

Library of Congress cataloguing in publication data
Brooke-Rose, Christine, 1923–
    Stories, theories, and things / Christine Brooke-Rose.
        p.   cm.
    Includes bibliographical references
    ISBN 0–521–39181–4
    1. Criticism. 2. Literature – History and criticism – Theory, etc.
3. Creativity in literature.   I. Title.
PN45.B738   1991   801'.953 – dc20 89–20972 CIP

ISBN 0 521 39181 4 hardback

Contents

Part IV. Things?

Preface

This book is about both literary theory and creativity; that is, it mostly contains chapters that were originally asked of me as critic and teacher, but also a few that were asked of me as critic and novelist (1, 3, 10, 11, 18, see Acknowledgements below). I believe they are deeply connected, and have considerably reworked most of them as well as added to them to bring this out, and make a coherent, continuous book.

Novelists are usually indifferent theorists, and possibly this is true of me. Occasionally they are better theorists than novelists. Either way the novelist can often throw an aura of doubt or humour or particular perception upon theory. The book (and particularly Chapter 1, more personal than the rest) is in fact about this connection, about how the critic and teacher reads also as writer and how the novelist writes also as theorist, aware of a fundamental inseparability of elements that critics and teachers have to separate, even rejoice in separating, pin-pointing, for the purpose of this or that type of analysis, though some try to refound them into large universal systems which the novelist knows can only hold in a precarious suspension of disbelief: as with poems and stories, as with ideal definitions of form and formal definitions of ideas, as with statements of position, confessions, autobiographies, greater aims, interpretations, glimmerings of overall themes. All are protean, capturable for brief moments in language, but already changed even into their opposites another brief moment later. That is the excitement, not unique since it is part of the human condition, but more intensely experienced in the critical and creative activities than in the more unreflexive routines of daily life.

Christine Brooke-Rose

Acknowledgements

The following chapters are revised versions of essays originally published elsewhere:

Chapter 1 in *New Literary History* 21/1, 1989, 121–31.

Chapter 2 in *Poetics Today* (to appear).

Chapter 3 in *Psychoanalytical Discourse in Literature*, ed. Shlomith Rimmon-Kenan, London, Methuen 1987, pp. 19–37.

Chapter 4 in *Word and Image* 3/2, April–June 1987, 143–55.

Chapter 5 in *Narrative in Culture – The Uses of Storytelling in the Sciences, Philosophy and Literature*, ed. Cristopher Nash, London, Methuen, 1990, pp. 154–71.

Chapter 6 in *New Essays on the Red Badge of Courage*, ed. Lee Clark Mitchell, Cambridge University Press 1986, pp. 129–46.

Chapter 7 in *Alternative Hardy*, ed. Lance St John Butler, London, Macmillan 1989, pp. 26–48.

Chapter 8 in *PN Review* 55, Vol. 13/5, 1987, 29–37.

Chapter 9 in *Essays in Criticism* 13/3, July 1963, 253–64.

Chapter 10 in French in *Fabula* 3, March 1984, Presses Universitaires de Lille, 121–32.

Chapter 11 as 'The Dissolution of Character in the Modern Novel' in *Reconstructing Individuality*, ed. Th. C. Heller, Morton Sosna and David Wellerby, Stanford University Press 1986, pp. 184–96.

Chapter 13 in *Amerikastudien*, Vol. 30, 1985, 225–33, and in French as 'Chimères de parodie' in *TLE* 4 (*Théorie, Littérature, Enseignèment*), Presses Universitaires de Vincennes, 1986, 9–22.

Chapter 16 in *Poetics Today* 6/1–2, 1985, 9–20 and in *The Female Body in Western Culture*, ed. Susan Suleiman, Harvard University Press 1986, pp. 305–16.

Chapter 17 (title and a few pages only, since this was an opening address at which I had been asked to read from my works as well) in *Comparative Criticism* 10, 121–38.

Chapter 12 was originally a paper delivered at a seminar session following Umberto Eco's Tanner Lectures, Cambridge, March 1990, to be published by Cambridge University Press.

Chapters 14, 15 and 19 were written specifically for the book; Chapter 2 for both the book and *Poetics Today*; Chapters 11, 13 and 18 were the most rehandled for the book.

PART I

Theories as stories

1

Stories, theories and things

The topic of an essay or novel, while I work on it, becomes the most important topic in the world for me, otherwise I couldn't work on it. To write, therefore, about myself as writer, as I have increasingly been asked to do, is very difficult without sounding self-important. Any famous name I may mention by way of illustration will make me seem to be putting myself on the same level, and any statement I may make about anything being unnoticed, on which I spent much thought and time, will sound like petulant complaint, instead of a point about the greatest gap of all, that between intention and effect. Moreover, I have also at times been asked to write about my relationship, as author, to literary theory, which act threatens to quarter or sexter me among all the frailties and fallacies variously attributed to the different functions of Jakobson's diagram.

Nevertheless those two things (myself as novelist and my relation to theory) are what I am going to write about in this opening chapter, not just to get rid of it, but to give a certain personal, author's perspective on the critical, that is, supposedly more 'objective' (but see Ch. 2) chapters that mostly make up this book.

This preamble is an attempt at a distancing disclaimer. I think I can honestly say that my attitude to my own creative work has become (or has been made to become) quite wise. On the sweet success side, I have long thought that to promote or protest, to scramble and scheme, is a waste of my precious energy because, either my work is of value and will therefore be more widely appreciated one day even if I am dead, or it is not, in which case, *pourquoi me fatiguer?* I have had little enough time to write what I wanted as it is. My only concern has been to be at least available in print, a bottle in the sea, and it is quite troublesome enough to have to protest behind the scenes to the bottle-throwers about their occasional malpractices.

The canon

Similarly, on the question of my relationship to theory, I know that nothing I may say about it will be of the slightest interest or value unless my work should enter into what Frank Kermode, in his admirable book *The Genesis of Secrecy* (1979), calls the canon, reviving the term from religious exegesis and showing how it functions the same way in literature. Only works that are considered, on whatever criteria and at whatever time, part of a canon, receive the (to an author ambiguous) blessing of interpretation. The term caught on, and the concept of canon was further finicked since Kermode's book (for example, the curious division between 'canon' and 'classic', see Gumbrecht 1988), but I am using it here in its generally accepted sense. And although Kermode would perhaps not go as far as Stanley Fish (1980), the implication is clear: outside the canon no interpretation, rather as one (now abandoned) dogma had it: outside the Church no Salvation. Fish would add: therefore no existence.

In other words, I am one of the many authors who have a brief existence at what Hirsch (1967), as opposed to Fish, calls the interpretation level (the 'meaning' or simple reading of the text as syntax, for instance by reviewers), but who have little or no existence at what Hirsch calls the critical level (the 'significance' or what others call interpretation, that links the text to other things/realms of thought: the world, that is, other stories, other texts). This can only begin to happen, for better or for worse, when an author enters a canon, however shifting, and I have a knack of somehow escaping most would-be canonic networks and labels: I have been called '*nouveau roman* in English' and *nouveau nouveau*, I have been called Postmodern, I have been called Experimental, I have been included in the SF Encyclopaedia, I automatically come under Women Writers (British, Contemporary), I sometimes interest the Feminists, but I am fairly regularly omitted from the 'canonic' surveys (chapters, articles, books) that come under those or indeed other labels. On the whole I regard this as a good sign.

To talk about one's own work is therefore peculiarly hazardous, since to talk about is already to interpret, and therefore to bring my work into an existence, for me as interpreter, which it does not apparently have much for me as writer, except in so far as the act of writing is also already an act of reading and therefore of interpretation. Perhaps I should emborgesize my work and talk about it as if it did not exist save as a fiction (Tlön?) merely alluded to, which everyone knows they can't go and look up, let alone look up to, look down on, look through and into or look wise by, in other words interpret. But then, Borges is himself an author, not a theorist.

Stories as theories

Yet is he not? There are more stars in heaven and earth, Horatio, than are dreamt of in your philosophy ... There are more stories in heaven and earth, Horatio ... For 'story' has now become a star word in critical theory for theory, for the representation of 'things': history, criticism, chemistry, physics, sociology, psychoanalysis or philosophy, all are stories we tell ourselves to understand the world, all quite meta (-phorical, -linguistic, -historical, if there is a meta-), the Matter of Britain, of France, of the World, of Me. Not only institutional agreements, or languages, or language-games, but also the Fact of the Matter, which the realist philosopher insists on, has itself become meta, that is, 'story' for the Pragmatist: 'His own technique in philosophy is that same Homeric, narrative style which he recommends to the literary critic [...] a narrative whose details he hopes the literary critic will help him fill in' (Rorty 1985, 5, see also 1979; 1982).[1]

George Steiner once told me that my books weren't novels but language-games: the context was so friendly I still don't know whether this was simple categorizing, or praise, or dismissal, but on present terminology it would mean 'story'. Could literature, so long outcast to the backyard of philosophy, be making a comeback through the front-door?

Novelists are usually indifferent theorists, I said at the beginning, or regarded as such. For example Brian McHale, in examining John Barth's 'story' of late modernism as a 'literature of exhaustion' (1967) and postmodernism as a 'literature of replenishment' (1984a), finds that it doesn't fit the facts, and prefers the 'story' of Dick Higgins (1984) whereby, before 1958, 'innovative artists and thinkers had typically been preoccupied with the process of cognition', characterized by the questions 'How can I interpret this world of which I am part? And what am I in it?' whereas 'postcognitive' artists and thinkers ask 'Which world is this? What is to be done in it? Which

---

[1] See Brian McHale 1988 for a similar constatation and use of the fact that 'theory' is more and more recognized as 'story'. The original essay on which this chapter is based was written in 1985, but not published until after McHale's. It is always pleasing to see that one's ideas are independently confirmed by others.

of my selves is to do it?' (1978, 10, quoted McHale 1988, 560). This distinction is the basis for his own impressive study of postmodernism as concerned with 'ontological' rather than with 'epistemological' questions and effects (see Ch. 14). Whatever the case, he considers Barth's theory as a less good 'story'. But novelists are usually good story-tellers, and their stories sometimes survive theories. But that, too, depends on the canon-makers.

So 'story' has replaced 'philosophy', 'model', 'paradigm', 'theory', and may even swallow up the supposedly non-paradigmatic Fact of the Matter: It is the case, say the philosophers, it is a case-history, say the psychoanalysts, it is a model, say the scientists, it is a story say the poets and some philosophers, it is the repetition of an absent story, say the post-Lacanian deconstructionists. Let us play: There are more theories in heaven and earth, Horatio. There are more models in heaven and earth, Horatio. There are more paradigms in heaven and earth, Horatio. There are more absences in heaven and earth, Horatio. But no, it won't do, since it is all our philosophies that dream up the paradigms, models, interpretations, stories, scenarios, matters, things, absences, and there cannot, on much present theory, be more than are dreamt up, only more to be still dreamt up. Let's try another way in, *medias res*.

A metastory, with metacharacters

Chapter 1 (draft). Once upon a time, in 1968, there appeared a novel called *Between*, by Christine Brooke-Rose, hereafter in this metastory or story-matter referred to as the author, author of *Out, Such*, and earlier novels. *Between* deals with (?), explores (?), represents (?), plays around with (?), makes variations on (?), expresses (?), communicates (?), is about (?), generates (?), has great fun with the theme / complex experience / story / of bilingualism. The I / central consciousness / non-narrating narrative voice / is a simultaneous interpreter who travels constantly from congress to conference and whose mind is a whirl of topics and jargons and foreign languages / whose mind is a whirl of worldviews, interpretations, stories, models, paradigms, theories, languages. Note that in this metastory the simultaneous interpreter has no sex.

But [analepsis to explain origin of facts presented *in medias res*] during the writing of the first draft in 1964 the author became totally blocked until, some three years and another novel later, this simultaneous interpreter became a woman. Why? Obviously not because the author had ever been a simultaneous interpreter, but presumably [author-comment] because other themes / experiences (worldviews, interpretations, stories) became entangled with the notion / imagined experience / theory / story that simultaneous interpretation is a passive activity, that of translating the ideas of others but giving voice to none of one's own, and therefore a feminine experience. Yet, apart from the initial idea of bilingualism, none of this had been the author's personal experience either as woman or as author, at least, not consciously. It was a cliché, which was nevertheless true enough generally (like all clichés) for the purpose of creating the language of the novel and getting, as I. A. Richards used to say, the 'tone' right. Thus two non-experiences of the author (simultaneous interpretation, woman as passive transmitter) fused with genuine experiences of worldviews (stories, etc.) to produce an imaginative experience that rang true, at least to the author. Clearly these two non-experiences must have repeated an absent story. [This is where the analepsis catches up on the *in medias res* presentation. Yet it is *hors-texte*. Yet there is no *hors-texte* that is not really in.]

The novel is written in what Bakhtin (1929a) calls 'free direct' discourse, that is, there is no separate narrative voice from that of the character, yet the character is not narrating, the distinction between hetero- and homodiegetic is collapsed, as in most Beckett. The syntax of *Between* is free-ranging in that a sentence can start in one place or time, continue correctly, yet by the end of the sentence one is elsewhere. The novel is also written entirely without the verb *to be*. [I'll skip the writing difficulties of this and the *hors-texte* proleptic analepsis in which after such practice the author went on doing without the verb *to be* for months, out of habit, even anonymously in the *Times Literary Supplement*.] There were reasons, for all this, which fall into two groups: (i) at the source of writing, the self-imposition of constraints; (ii) for the intended effect of the writing, mimetic 'realism' (yes! see Chapter 14 on anti-realism) – in brief, perpetual motion in my central consciousness, and loss of identity due to her activity. The point, however, is that (i) was more important in that these constraints produced a specific style; and that, although the novel received much praise at the time, no one ever noticed either: the novel was by no means received as 'realistic' but as 'experimental' (*nouveau roman*, 'no story', etc.). But more on realism vs. experimentation elsewhere (Chs. 14, 17).

As to the verb *to be*, there is no reason why anyone except a deconstructionist should notice the lack of something, unless it is

announced in the blurb, all the less so because the novel is not part
of a canon and thus doesn't exist. Another author might come along,
and maybe has, announcing that he has written a whole novel without
the verb *to be*, and it would surely be either acclaimed as a *tour
de force* or dismissed as a mere *tour de force*. But it would at any
rate exist in a minor canon of books written without this or that
verb. Others would then start writing without auxiliaries or modals
– and indeed a French author did shortly after but without having
heard of me write a whole novel without the letter *e*, and later another
with only the letter *e*, but said so, and was much written about,
and interpreted, and thus existent (Georges Perec, *La Disparition*,
1969, *Les Revenentes*, 1972, see Ch. 14).

Chapter 2 (introducing a new character), Thru. *Thru* was conceived in
1970 but for obstetrico-typographical reasons did not appear until
1975. This was the only novel in which two selves, actual author
and theoretical critic, came together. It was [author-comment] a
novel about the theory of the novel, that is, a narrative about narrativity, a fiction about fictionality, a text about intertextuality and
[*hors-texte* analepsis] it took four summers to get 'right'. The author
had enormous fun with it and was duly rapped on the typographic
knuckles for it – typographic because by the time it came out it
all seemed pretty external to him. She had stuck her neck out and
his neck knew what it would get. [Conclusion in proleptic analepsis:
the external harm this book did to her reputation as incomprehensible
and pretentious was lasting and profound. He was dismissed and
had a long *traversée du désert*.] It was, at that point [author-comment],
her best and most daring book in the self-reflexive genre. Concluding
moral: this chapter is a metaphoric metaparadigmatic model meta-
story of my relationship to theory.

Chapter 3. A new character called *Amalgamemnon*, by the same author,
was started in 1978 and appeared, after trials and tribs, in 1984.
It is written in the future and conditional tenses, the subjunctive
or imperative moods. [*Hors-texte* analepsis of origin: there were also
reasons, partly technical (see Genette) and partly sociopsychopoliti-
cophilosophical, that is, 'realist' (skip); and many difficulties and
rewritings to avoid the oracular tone of the future, as well as a real
(fictional) ontological problem of how the characters should speak,
since they are made to speak there and then on the page; this was
eventually resolved by various suggestions that they do not do so,

and the necessary 'naturalness' was obtained by a compromise (cheating, as indeed does Perec in his hypogrammic novels): present and past allowed in dialogue, but as interrogative and negative only, thus preserving the notion that nothing can be said to have happened or be happening. End of analepsis, now *en-texte* but metatextual.]

Despite strong hints in the blurb this time, the author was praised or blamed or commented for things undreamt of in her philosophy, and his text, after briefly becoming quite other, ceased, like the previous ones, to exist for a while, though now it is actually being 'taught' in some American universities, but that's another story.

This neglect can be received as all to the bad: the act of reading (Hirsch's 'interpreting') has been lost, except for the canon, those boom-books of any one historical literary moment, where reading gets so 'close' it becomes interpretation (Hirsch's criticism) and self-perpetuates itself to exhaustion. Or it can be received as all to the good: at least the author's gigantic tussles with language, or their results, do not stick out like a sore thumb [Metalinguistic/Poetic/Phatic/Subjective play: medium has become a sore thumb, as for a sculptor. Thor sum? Fore sum? Or sum? Awesome foursome].

Chapter 4. While *Amalgamemnon* was doing the rounds (my previous publisher having sacked me on economico-typographic grounds), the author cheered herself up by writing a science fiction story. He wrote it in as mainstream a way as possible, with every narrative cliché in use (hetero- and extradiegetic narrative voice, change of focalization in each chapter – to each focused character his psychological problems – a classic title *The Alphaguys*, etc.). She had decided to show he could do 'story' [plot], which she was said to be weak on, and who knows, perhaps to write a best-seller? It was read by a publisher who had just turned down *Amalgamemnon*. He said 'it's very mainstream, isn't it? Why didn't you write it in your own way?' The author said (with a smile/an ironic laugh/her heart sinking a little, etc.) 'But you've just turned down my own way.' At least the publisher didn't say 'style'. She meant, the author supposed, why couldn't I mingle this nice clear plot with 'my own way'?

And that is what the author did, once *Amalgamemnon* had been accepted, she turned back to the science fiction, jettisoned the mainstream technique and rewrote it entirely, to produce *Xorandor* (the title change came from the rewriting, which had meant working much harder inside computer-languages). In fact it was still remarkably straightforward but without the earlier attempts at familiar modes. The only experiment he allowed himself was the narration wholly in dialogue, by two kids dictating into their computer, i.e. learning how to tell their own story as they go, and with the concomitant invention of a children's slang out of electronic and physics jargon, for the simple reason that he had no idea (generation gap + living abroad) how kids talk. The reason was practical, the result, again, a particular style. (Though as to inventing a slang Burgess had already done much the same and no doubt better with Russian words in *A Clockwork Orange*, 1962.) *Xorandor* was indeed more successful than the author's previous 'experimental' novels. And yet it was a distinct compromise: more plot, less play. I then went on to write *Verbivore*, a 'sequel' or rather a playing both with the realistic technique of sequels and with shifting narrative levels which demolish that technique. Then *Textermination*, the whole four from *Amalgamemnon* forming one 'Intercom' Quartet.

Chapter 5 (author reflections). If a text (centre of Jakobson diagram) does not exist until attended to and interpreted, according to one story (East of the diagram), then according to another the *hors-texte* West of the diagram does not exist either, the myth of origin, the *always already there* which makes nonsense of the preceding ('Chapters' 1–4). And since the preceding is a form of interpretation, and since interpretation is metalanguage (South), and since, according to yet another story (Lacan's) there is no metalanguage, the interpretation that brings a text into existence doesn't exist either. What is left? The Phatic function (South but less far down), largely ignored by criticism, presumably because it's merely taken to mean the more perishable aspect of contact, such as paper, or even reading aloud, although clearly there are many texts which exploit this Phatic function more fully and textually. Oh, and the Referential (North), the world.

Chapter 6. Scrap the six chapters, try another way in, not as meta-author. End of meta-story.

Story (of theory), theory (of story), story of story

In my parallel professions, I have often been asked the same question in two different versions. It is a naive question, but each generation of students from seventeen to seventy-seven years old seems to have to ask it.

The question is (a) addressed to me as a teacher, for example, in a class: but does the author think of, intend, is he aware of all these structures (of significance, etc.) that you read into the text? and (b) addressed to me as author, for instance, after a reading: when you write, do you think of, intend, are you aware of, all the theory you write and teach?

Now (b), my relationship to theory as author, is the topic I am trying somewhat digressively to tackle in this opening chapter, so as maybe to find some answer to it, but clearly it's the same question as (a). Or, to quote Hillis Miller (1982) on repetition in *Lord Jim*: 'The question the novel asks and cannot unequivocally answer is "Why is this?" To say it is because Conrad designed his novel in recurring patterns is to trivialize the question and to give a misplaced answer to it' (36).

But I should here (at last) distinguish between two current notions of 'literary theory'. As these questions show, most students, at least to begin with, think of 'theory' as a set of magic techniques that will give them access to the arcanum of the text, that is, enable them to do their assignments in the way the teacher expects. Over and over again, in a freshman class, I have been discouraged by the silence, or at very best the vaguest one-word paraphrase, that greets my request for reactions to a text, until I give them some clue as to how it is possible to read it. Then they busily take notes (but maybe this is a comment on French secondary school teaching, which the university has to spend much time in unteaching). And a technique for reading implies a reading of the technique for writing: theory as *technique*. Represented, at its best and worst, by rhetoric and poetics, the study of literary devices and conventions.

The other notion of theory, which deals with ultimate aims and the very status and conditions of meaning (to put it at its simplest) is represented, also at its worst and best, by philosophy in all its many aspects from hermeneutics to logical analysis, from aesthetics to epistemology, from the philosophy of science or history to the history of philosophy, from traditional metaphysics to the decon-struction of same and the beyonding of that. This much wider and more far-reaching notion of theory seems at the moment to be replac-ing or to have replaced the other, but both are at the root of the 'naive' question in both its aspects, and both exist and function within my consciousness, no, more, as part of my passionate interests and curiosity without which I cannot write, and both make the split into author and theorist particularly painful and exhilarating.

To take the rhetorical sense first. Some authors do seem less self-conscious than others. There is a sliding-scale that goes all the way from those, at one end, who reflect little on the conventions of their craft and take them over happily as a sort of ready-made net to catch a not too slippery fish called reality; to those, at the other end, who painstakingly examine and remake every knot in that net, only to find that a harpoon or a beowulfian wrestling-match under water would have been better (more efficient? or more exciting?), and then that the monster was imaginary anyway. Being extremes, both these tend to be marginalized. The naive writer who takes over the conventions of his craft when they have already become cliché, is sooner or later relegated to pulp (but sells meanwhile, or, nowadays, is sociologically and patronizingly studied as popular culture); while the over-technically conscious are dismissed as over-technically conscious. Which means: sooner rather than later they are relegated to pulp (but do not sell meanwhile, nor are they studied as popular culture).

And yet I find it hard to believe that all writers at all points of that scale are *not* to some degree technically conscious, despite the peculiar and recurring prejudice against technical competence in writing (the very word 'competence' after 'technical' becomes derogatory – but I shall return to this in Ch. 2). More important, however, I find it impossible to discuss the rhetorical aspect of theory without at least reaching out to if not reaching the philosophical.

Obviously it is possible to 'do' rhetoric, analyse a text, a genre, a device, without touching on philosophy (or even, for that matter, on the 'significance'). But the moment one discusses the implications of rhetoric, or even simply of technical consciousness, from any viewpoint whatsoever, one also touches on philosophy. Oh, not in the way philosophers discuss their problems, I would not presume. But as has often been observed, those poets who have also written as critics and theorists have all written in a way that passionately defends their own practice (Du Bellay, Ronsard, Sidney, Wordsworth, Coleridge, Shelley ...) or even exemplifies it (Boileau, Pope). And behind their practice lies their philosophy, their contradictions, their seachanges, their readings and misreadings. Pound's *Don'ts* are addressed to what he once did. Conventions, like disconventions, are transmitted by writers with minds that touch ours, not by rhetoricians, who merely observe, categorize, and directly or indirectly prescribe, post-factum. To give the most technical example: how is it that for six centuries poets wrote perfect and perfectly varied iambic pentameters without a single rhetorician having ever formulated its one and only unbreakable rule as discovered by Halle and Keyser (1971) and then refined by Kiparsky (1977)?

But I am falling back into the second of my parallel professions and (still) not answering the personal question so often addressed to me as author and critic. As (at least) two people I am prone to these evasive tactics. Yet not as one: as author I face the white page alone.

Not true.

Both theorists, rhetorical and philosophical, accompany me. We are what we read and do (but are we what we do when we write?). I do not, when writing, put away the literary theory I have absorbed and used. It is true that during my teaching career I could only write a novel in the summer (if I wasn't doing research and criticism), with a longish stretch of time in my head, rather than a week or weekend with a meeting on Tuesday. It is true that materially, I went away or pretended to have gone away. It is true that when I write a novel I close all books of theory and open a foolscap-size exercise book and work with what seems another brain, foolscap-size with jingle-bell. But it is not another brain. It is permeated with consciousness of what I am doing, if not before or while I do it, then very soon after as angry or delighted recognition. The intensity of super-consciousness guides my pen and also paralyses it. Theory has released an immense hidden strength in me, but it has also made writing more and more difficult, because more and more demanding.

What do I mean specifically by that? Not merely the outward fact that my early novels used to take me one summer to write and my later ones (from *Out*, 1964, onwards) anything from two to seven. It is impossible really to put my finger on why. Shelley said that 'when composition begins, inspiration is already on the decline, and the most glorious poetry that has ever been communicated to the world is probably a feeble shadow of the original conceptions of the poet' (*A Defence of Poetry*, 1840). The 'probably' implies that the original conception was not conscious or remembered, and that it represents at most a glimpse of a platonic pre-existent perfect idea. That may well be so for poets, or for Shelley, but I do not work like that at all, I never have a perfect idea or even a perfect original conception, of which my text is but a feeble shadow. Or if I do it is an absence (but then so in a way are platonic ideas). For me, the idea is formed out of the writing, the text *is* (generates) the idea, perfect or imperfect. I do not mean that I start with no idea at all, but it barely deserves to be called 'idea', even less a glorious original conception. It is sometimes a mere thematic single notion, such as writing about a simultaneous interpreter, or reversing the colour-bar (*Out*), and sometimes a technical notion, such as writing in the future tense. But that is all. Thousands of people who have never written a word can have such ideas, and so can those who write, and the texts that might arise from such ideas would all be totally different. The writer's work begins here.

Witness: when *Between* (as yet untitled) wouldn't get going in the summer of 1964, I dropped it in despair. The hotel where I was staying at that moment, somewhere in Portugal, had creaking stairs, and a notice saying Silence. So I opened a new exercise book and wrote: 'Silence says the notice on the stairs and the stairs creak.' Is that an 'idea' or a sentence? It is certainly a sentence in the present tense, already a choice, but there was nothing remarkable about that even then. Which led me to a coffin-lid creaking open, and faces like moons hanging above it. The eventual result was *Such*, taken up again in the summer of 1965 and published in 1966. It was not until 1967 that I went on a long journey which opened up my mind for *Between*. All this is anecdotal, but the point is that *Such*, the least 'mimetic' of the novels I had yet written, grew out of a mimetic sentence and out of what was neither a technical nor a philosophical idea. Nevertheless, once the text had got going and the 'idea' had emerged, it needed much more background reading in (popular) astrophysics, which was its guiding metaphor for psychic space and communication. Hence a year between that first sentence and the 'real' or final writing of it. That, surely, is 'using' theory, if not literary theory then a scientific 'story' or model, in my (feeble but poetic) understanding of it: I had discovered that scientific language, when taken 'literally' (non-scientifically) becomes metaphoric. In fact, the very distance between astrophysics and literature, the very type of metaphor used, is probably itself another model 'story', a way to explain how literary theory has released certain creative forces from within me. One starts with a sentence *ex* almost *nihilo* (since the *toujours déjà* is not *nihil* or, to quote from one of my novels, I forget which, 'are not all *idées reçues*?'); and even with a specific idea like simultaneous interpretation I still start *ex* almost *nihilo* with a sentence, the words suggest another sentence, and so on until a very specific 'idea' (story, model, paradigm, theory) begins to take form. Sometimes this story needs checking or even filling

out against the 'correct' or provisionally official version of it, sometimes on the contrary it's all there, at the back of my critical and
teaching creative mind, ready to help or block, to excite and urge
on or to crush and censure, out of which censure the excitement
will nevertheless emerge elsewhere in some other form, as the psychoanalytical story tells.

I had hoped we wouldn't get back to that one (see Ch. 3). Is
theory for me, then, simply the Mentor, the Law-Giver and Forbid-
der, the opening and shutting door, the magic sesame accompanied
by strict conditions, the mastery of the absent Master (or of the
Master of the absent story), the lure of constraints and difficulties
all artists need, if only to break the rules? But then, so is grammar.
So are the conventions of whatever world one ventures into. Perhaps
then, I merely need more constraints than those who scoff at theory
and do (they think) without. Or, to put it more precisely, I first
have to produce a text, as author, and then, as its first reader, I
interpret it, in other words rewrite it. That is where theory should
in theory come in, but that is also when it really becomes 'story'.

All this, however, is merely my side of things, and although that
was the point of this opening chapter, I have fallen back into the
myth of origin, or at least into the intentional function, fallacy, fra-
gility, the fore-sum, fore-warning or fore-cast. That of course is what
I have been trying to write about. But the further back one goes
in that direction the more, paradoxically, one ceases to exist as
author, I mean as text. Have I written only another story? As plotless
as my novels are said to be, usually by those who can't even attribute
dialogue correctly or who otherwise betray lack of reading attention.
And without such attention they do not exist either. They belong
to Tlön. But Tlön, having been made public, is also in my mind.
And there, for the present, I am content to let the Meta rest.

2

Whatever happened to narratology?

It got swallowed into story seems the obvious answer, it slid off the slippery methods of a million structures and became the story of its own functioning. Like mathematics, which has never claimed to speak of anything but itself, or even to speak at all.

But was it a good story? Did narratology ever have that air of a neo-divine activity in which to formulate is to function and to function is to self-verify? Even in physics, there are always differences and disturbances, escape-hatches which mean that, however minute the particles or the units observed, the system has to adjust, to cheat ever so slightly, in order to present a good theory, to tell a coherent story. Reality is a scandal, it never quite fits.

Discourse, texts of all kinds, purport to represent the real, but what does this mean? Is the representation in excess of the real (Aristotle), or less than the real (Plato), or does it merely reorganize the real? These are ancient questions, but we are still asking them, not just of representations (stories) in general, but also of the very discourses (stories) that purport to analyse stories, stories of people, stories of people reading stories of people, stories of people reading stories of the world.

East is East but sometimes West

The initial excitements and fairly rapid disappointments of narratology must have had to do with the early high claims of universality. But the laws discovered, though often couched in learned words, severe analyses and diagrams, even mathematical or logical formulas, often turned out to be over-general, and so rather trivial. Above all, there was no constancy of terms or basic method, as there is in mathematics, or in modern linguistics.

Structures were 'discovered' that every poet and writer knows or learns, simple structures of agents and patients, movements and quests, more complex structures of modes of telling, structures of reading activities with more and more *ad hoc* rules and personal idio-syncrasies, all meticulously, sophistically coded and named, until the chief problem came to be seen as arising not from inherent univer-sal structures but from reading, as if analysers had a profound need to experience, not a text or even a story, but their own mental pro-cesses when faced with a poem or story that perhaps did not give them the immediate and unalloyed pleasures that its renown, its place in the canon or histories of literature had led them to expect.

The shift from belief in the text as 'object', with 'inherent' analys-able structures, to belief in the reader who has internalized and learnt to recognize these structures is always interesting. For the reader (East of the Jakobson Communications diagram) is historically the least often taken into account in critical shifts from the Author (West), the World (North), or the Text (Centre), the 'Phatic' South being almost totally ignored and the 'Metalinguistic' South being in theory the language of criticism.

Plato is concerned with origins, divine madness (Author, West); with art's relation to the 'truth' (World, North), which he regards as false on two counts, philosophical and technico-realistic. His only concern with the receiving end is that of corruption (with fictional 'lies'). Aristotle ignores the divine madness, the two removes, corrects the technico-realistic objection (there can be errors in art), and resolves the 'corruption' via catharsis. Above all he's interested in the text (Rhetoric and Poetics, Centre).

In general criticism has concentrated chiefly on the Author (West, say Traditional nineteenth- and twentieth-century criticism); the Text (Centre, for instance The New Criticism and early Structura-lism, both insisting on 'scientific', that is, 'objective' methods); or the World (North, say the classic theory of the Imitation of 'Nature' or later of 'Reality', or modern sociorealist and Marxist criticism). The Reader was in fact also taken into account in some New Criti-cism, notably by I. A. Richards in *Practical Criticism* (1929) and in his use of early psychology in the effects of a poem; also by Empson and his followers who stressed multimeanings in words as read by the reader, not necessarily as existing at the time of the text or as intended by the author (this was later denounced by Wimsatt and Beardsley as 'The Affective Fallacy', 1949). In earlier tradition, how-ever, one of the few voices who reintroduces the reader is Sir Philip Sidney, to answer the revived platonic argument that poetry 'abuseth man's wit': 'yet think I [...] their sentence may with good manners, put the last words foremost: and not say, that poetry abuseth man's wit, but that, man's wit abuseth poetry' (*An Apology for Poetry*). It is all in the reader, not in the text, nor in the author.

So the massive return to reader-oriented analysis that followed early Structuralism (beginning with Stanley Fish's 'Affective Stylistics' in 1970) is itself (together with the beginning of deconstructionism in 1967) a condemnation of methods that rejected all considerations of the Author and the World (and indirectly the Reader) as irrelevant. Not that Structuralist narratology collapsed thereby; on the contrary, it incorporated the notion of the reader, but as 'decoder' of structures really presented and thought of as in the text.

For it is a good deal easier to name and chart and systematize rhetorical conventions as 'inherent' to the text (even if this inherence represents, as in linguistics, structures in OUR mental processes) than to name and chart and systematize the mental processes of THE reader, who in practice often represents the analyser in any one system proposed. But let's look at those structures and conventions, whether inherent to the text or to our minds.

The poetry of poetics

It would be easy to say that both Chaucer and Shakespeare (and others) mocked rhetoric, that artists have always gone beyond the rules and categories of rhetoricians, subverting them and creating others so that rhetoricians have to return and recodify. Yet both Chaucer and Shakespeare (and everyone) also used and observed these rules. The disclaiming of rhetoric is itself a figure of rhetoric. Perhaps this is why they mocked it, for its manic naming of everything it is possible to do, consciously or not, when putting words together and making utterances. All, all, has been used before, and named.

However, I doubt whether this ancient dichotomy (poetics vs. poetry) is so easy to handle today. Our 'postmodern' situation, of which as writer I have been here and there and willy-nilly a more or less conscious participant, has been defined by Lyotard (1979, 7; 1988) as one of 'incredulity with regard to metanarratives' (in the sense of universalist Big Ideas, such as the emancipation of man, of reason; from ignorance, from inequality; the Hegelian or the Marxist metanarratives, etc.) and a recommended preference for 'little' narratives. It has also been interpreted in more and more complex and differing ways. Postmodern artists are said to write metafiction, that is fiction about fiction; to accept the aporia of significant form; or to use 'suspensive' irony as opposed to the Modernist 'disjunctive' irony; or to be facing ontological (or 'postcognitive') questions as opposed to an epistemological (Modernist) crisis; or again, what they have given up is all idea of achieving overall meaning or 'totalization', and both these versions are clearly if not explicitly linked to the fracture of the subject as stable interpreter of the real; to write 'neocosmic' and 'anticosmic' fiction as opposed to 'cosmic'.[1] Lyotard's latest definition (my translation):

I suggest that the postmodern is that which, in the modern, pleads for (*allègue*) the unpresentable in the presentable itself, [...] that which inquires into new presentations, not for enjoyment, but the better to convey that there is something unpresentable (*de l'imprésentable*).

(1988, p. 31).

Above all, and very familiar by now, is the view that critical and creative writing have become one and are indistinguishable. (This view is in diametrical opposition to the Structuralist metalanguage, diagrams, logical formulae, and so on, vs. the text.) On the one hand, the modern novel read 'as act of cognition supersedes the aesthetics of plot and repetition' (Richard 1985, p. 22). On the other, the best theoreticians and philosophers are read as literature, not (as before and always), for their 'fine' style, but (like all good authors) for their more or less shattering defamiliarization of familiar modes of thought and world visions. They are read as narratives about the text of the world and the world of texts. Moreover the essays of certain novelists (William Gass for instance) can read like fictions. As I observed in Chapter 1, philosophers and literary theorists frequently refer to theories as stories (in this story we have to accept that ...). Or even scenarios. It is as if phiction and filosophy had changed places.

Story of theory

Perhaps a brief retelling of the story, or rather a story of the story (by me), a re-presentation, can exceed or shadow or reorganize the reality (if any) of that story. And I shall start with another story, a more or less historical detour via the New Criticism, the detour itself an anecdote.

I say 'more or less' historical because it was only a few months ago that I read, by chance, a fairly recent essay on a seventeenth-century poem, by an intelligent and articulate critic who had clearly

---

[1] The views in this paragraph are attributable to Linda Hutcheon, Ihab Hassan, Dick Higgins, Brian McHale, Alan Wilde, Mas'ud Zavarzadeh, Cristopher Nash (see References), but there are others.

not gone through (in the sense of assimilating, teaching, reflecting on, contributing to) either Structuralism or Poststructuralism. The essay talked of tension, paradox, resolution, as if we were still in the New Criticism. As New Criticism, it was good, and of course had to find resolution and global meaning (as the 'real' seventeenth century had to?). The experience was odd because, although myself brought up on the New Criticism and its close reading of poetry, I had since moved very far from it indeed (towards fiction, towards narratology, towards the postmodern sensibility) and yet had to admit that if such criticism (or the original New Criticism) is still readable today it may be precisely because the great shift of interest at the turn of the mid-century went towards narrative and its structures, on which the New Criticism and earlier schools had been peculiarly unsophisticated and barren, whereas pure Structuralism, however fascinating on narrative structures, evolved a particularly clumsy machinery for the analysis of poetry, uneconomic, inelegant, text-destroying – and the New Criticism certainly wasn't any of those.

Poetry was too subtle for early Structuralism, and indeed it could be argued that the early Structural analysis of narrative, like its Formalist forbear, modestly tested out its theoretical models (when it did so at all) on what Frye (1957) called 'naive romance', which reveals its structures easily, and that most of these early 'grammars' of narrative turned out to be inadequate to the more complex novel, save at the cost of sheer reduction to a general and very bare structure it shared with all narrative (and universality was the point).[2] Nevertheless, Structuralism did evolve more complex models for more complex narratives, but failed to do so for poetry. It wasn't until the seventies that poetic analysis took off again, and this chiefly in the United States, where the good habits of the New Criticism (notably close reading) had taken deep root, rather than in Europe where schools even today still apparently teach future students no more than the extraction and summary of a main theme (love, death ...). Something remains of older 'stories' (scenarios, theories, models, paradigms), as the above reading anecdote shows.

Another reading anecdote, from Stanley Fish this time and well-known, though it will bear retelling, will round off this detour via the New Criticism. Fish relates how at the end of a linguistics-and-stylistics class he put up a reading assignment on the board:

---

[2] See Pawel 1988b for an account of the debate on, together with his own criticisms of, the Greimasian model. Also Pawel 1988a.

Jacobs-Rosenbaum
Levin
Thorne
Hayes
Ohman (?)

(The query was because he couldn't remember if there were two
n's.) When his next class on seventeenth-century English poetry
trooped in, Fish had drawn a frame round the list, written 'p. 43'
at the top, then told them it was a poem and asked them to interpret
it. The result was hilarious (Jacob's ladder as cross and Christian
ascent, cross as the Virgin Mary as rose-tree, the crown of thorns,
Christ as the fulfilment of the priestly function of the tribe of Levi,
hence Exodus, Oh Man/Omen, and so on. Fish's main concern in
this essay ('How to Recognize a Poem When You See One', 1980a)
is not to mock his students but to ask: how were they able to do
what they did? His analysis does not concern me here, but clearly
part of the answer is that recognition of the Christian symbolism
and typological patterns is what they were learning in that class
and, I would add, the forty years of New Criticism that had slowly
reached down to school or first-year college level still pertained.[3]
And what interested me, and abashed my postgraduate students
in Paris when I discussed the Fish essay with them (not as similar
test but as part of a seminar on Interpretation), is not only that
none of them would have coped with such a long reading assignment,
but, more important, none of them would have produced, nor had
the background to produce, any of these significances. But perhaps
they would not have believed that it was a poem, bereft as it was
of syntax, but also bereft as they were of associated meanings for the
names. They might, perhaps, have found a 'main theme' (death? love?).

Something remains, then, when critical fashions pass. It may seem
strange, looking back on the days of Structuralism, that so many
should have made high reputations on models that were so clearly
or turned out so rapidly to be unusable, or merely to translate into
mathematical or logical formulas what could easily or had already
been said, on the opposite page, much more readably in discourse.

---

[3] I gather there has been, and still is, a power struggle in American academia
between the 'literarians' (exponents of New Criticism, close reading) and the
'textualists' (theory). See DeKoven 1988 (76–7) where she examines the problem
of why Feminine Writing, however 'avant-garde', refuses to acknowledge the
'avant-garde' (predominantly male) and vice versa, and how this problem also
relates to that power-struggle. See also Chapter 15 where I return to DeKoven.

But these were 'representations', just like fictions. And quick jettisoning can hardly be a reproach in a high consumer society where ninety-nine per cent of both criticism and artistic production also gets jettisoned after barely a decade. The few models that survived, on the contrary, became so second-nature as to make their very use in detailed analysis almost unnecessary, their codes and categories leaping to the naked eye in a sad professional deformation of reading for pleasure (to which indeed the chief protagonists of Structuralism later turned with a sigh of relief).[4]

Meanwhile, however, generations of students had been taught to pick out these codes and categories, exactly as the disciples of the New Criticism had learnt to chase through dictionaries for multiple meanings and through scholarly tracts for symbols, icons, emblems, myths. Few could go further than this recognition process, the naming of a category. Elements that 'mere' critics (as early narratologists tended to dismiss them) would consider as artistic weaknesses were flattened out with elements that might be considered as strokes of genius, both vanishing under the same name. An immense relief that one need no longer make critical judgments, that is, commit oneself, swept through certain academic communities. Naming (right or wrong) was enough. As in ancient and mediaeval rhetorics. Hence Chaucer's laughter.

But this was a choice, even a dogma, of many Structuralists, whose dream of a 'science' of literature with universal rules had caused them to evacuate (a) the diachronic dimension, (b) traditional thematics, (c) interpretation, (d) evaluation. Those were the tasks of 'traditional' criticism and literary history, while the science of literature had the task of (1) discovering and describing how a narrative text functions, and (2) evolving a universal system. In practice, the scientific dream was quietly abandoned and (a), (b), (c), (d) have crept back, together with other taboos such as author intention.[5]

For it soon became clear (among other things) that all four are present, if not explicitly, the moment one speaks of a text, even in the barest plot or theme summary. This applies also to narrative

[4] Clearly I cannot name all those who developed from early Structuralism, but the two I am obviously thinking of in this paragraph are Gérard Genette and Roland Barthes. The last sentence applies to Barthes' *The Pleasure of the Text*, 1972; 1976.

[5] In 'Texts and Lumps' (1985), discussed for other reasons in Chapter 1, Rorty even suggests that the author's intention should be regarded as a 'lump' (piece of reality), which has the same relation to 'text' as external reality in science has to a scientific 'text'. See Darrel Mansell (1988) for refutation. See also Chapter 14, p. 210.

categories, and hence to the relations between them. For example, one must move from mere naming to a consideration of how and why a category functions in any one text or group of texts, and of course this was done, in studies of realism, of 'parody', and so on.[6] Interpretation begins, according to Ricoeur (1971), where structural analysis stops. On the other hand mere naming is already a critical activity, as indeed Barthes had said already in his early 'pyramid' stage (1966) and again in *S/Z* (1970), into which the subjectivity of the analyzer enters at every stage. Indeed I defy anyone to apply Barthes' pyramids (or any other model) even to a simple short story in a class, and not get multiple versions of micro- and macrosequences. And since the mere picking out of these to construct the pyramids is only the assembling of the elements with which one should come to 'critical' conclusions about the structure, it is only too easy to 'arrange' these pyramids towards a preconceived and desired result.

But naming of a textual feature is also an unavowed way of returning to the so-called 'intentional fallacy': if this or that feature is used, then it is part of 'narrative strategy', that is *intended*, which more often than not lets the critic out of having to 'evaluate' a successful or unsuccessful use of such a strategy. I shall return to this aspect in Chapter 14. Often, indeed, critics of contemporary literature forget all about the 'ideal author' as construct and use interviews with the 'real' author as part of their criticism.

But more: all naming is itself a story. When as child or immigrant we learn the nouns of a culture, says Lyotard (1988, 53), as well as its units of measurement, space, time, exchange, they signify nothing but can be charged with diverse meanings by attaching them to different types of sentences (descriptive, interrogative, ostensive, evaluative, prescriptive) and including them in different discursive genres (persuasive, cognitive, tragic): 'Names are not learnt in isolation, but lodged in little stories' (53). Names, units of measurement, space, time, exchange, already form a story, that is, things in relation, in other words a structure.[7]

Did Adam tell himself stories when he named the animals? An

---

[6] See n.4. I cannot name everyone, but in this sentence I am thinking of Barthes' *S/Z*, Hamon's 'Un discours contraint', Genette's *Palimpsestes*, Ricoeur's *Temps et récit*, the 'and so on' covering psychoanalytical and deconstructive analyses such as those by Shoshana Felman and Barbara Johnson, or Hillis Miller and Deleuze (differently) on repetition, or Bakhtin's work on the polyphonic novel and all studies engendered by him (see References). But with the last five names we are out of narratology as understood by the Structuralists.

[7] See Ronen 1988, 501–2 for the polemic on names and descriptions.

indifferent pentameter from a lost early poem of mine (from the days when I still wrote poems every day, instead of a novel every five to eight years) returns to me: When Adam named the beasts he started hell. I wonder what I meant, and what the poem was 'about'? Does naming really solve, and cure, or kill? The question is adamic, endemic, academic.

Thus every name, every category, is in practice itself a story, and by discovering it the theorist tells a story, not only about textual practice but about himself and his place in his culture, as does the writer who exploits the feature named. And since the categories thus produced are not innocent of subjectivity, they can be 'wrong', or at any rate arbitrary, as arbitrary and convention-formed as words. An early postmodernist, John Barth, has always been fascinated by formalism and by systems of every kind, chiefly to represent them fictionally since his characters are themselves manic systematizers who consistently discover that narrative systems hardly guarantee their own stability as interpreters. In *The Friday Book* he says: 'I take the tragic view of categories, that they are, though indispensable, more or less arbitrary', and he insists that the novel is the least categorizable of genres (Barth 1984b, 257). Are not Harold Bloom's strange categories arbitrary? (See Ch. 3.) Or again, I have heard (orally so I need give no refs) one judgment of Brian McHale's theory of Postmodernism as ontological in concern, versus Modernism as epistemological (see above, p. 19) that it is exactly the other way about. I don't agree, and shall later use his theory and the interpretations based thereon. I only mention this other view to show how the arbitrariness of categories can work: the thesis of an entire book may (rightly or wrongly) be inverted.

Phictions and filosophy

Did narratology, then, bring us any further than we were before that unfulfilled dream of objectivity? In the sense that it *was* unfulfilled, clearly not, nor would even its staunchest then-protagonists make the claim today, all the less so since the scientist is now recognized to be working under subjective constraints and in a tropical discourse similar to those of the historian and literary critic. But in the sense that those illusions *were* wisely jettisoned, yes, it brought much understanding of how texts work and work on us. It could even be said, in a superficial way, that with the return of much that Structuralism had jettisoned, Poststructuralism is a kind of complex return to, and sophisticated inversion of the New Criticism: paradoxes are not 'resolved' but deconstructed and called aporia, disturbances in the system are revelled in and even created. The notion of mastery is no longer tenable.

In *Le Mirage linguistique* (1988a), Thomas Pawel traces the Structuralist scientific claim through all its stages, and there is no point in my doing it here. What interests me about that illusion (which I partly shared) is precisely that the scientific dream (itself a story, a fiction, about a lack of humility) was achieved via linguistics, the only 'science' in the humanities; and that when this turned out to be (in most cases, but especially in the case of Structuralist linguistics) maybe a science but not humanist enough, literary theory turned 'back' to its oldest rival and ally, philosophy. Yet it did so considerably strengthened by the rigour it had learnt from linguistics (as philosophy had been by its own kind of linguistic analysis).

For it is philosophy, not linguistics, that from Nietzsche on slowly but thoroughly undermined our set notions about universality, truth, reality, representation, metanarratives (in the Lyotard sense), which permeate all criticism in various forms from Plato to the mid twentieth century.

Part of the difficulty is that a fictional text is only fictional as a whole, each sentence separately has exactly the same form as a 'true' sentence, which is what makes the problem of irony, or the poet's 'lies' according to Plato, or (to take a more specific instance), the problem of 'voice' in free indirect discourse (see Ch. 5) so difficult to analyse. It is also what caused Austin (1962) to exclude all fiction from his philosophical analysis of the performative, although all his examples are (necessarily) fictions.

Narratology was important in accounting for the exact mechanisms through which these various illusions are achieved, as linguistics accounts for the unconscious grammar we are fabricating or following when we utter sentences. All, all is language, even the reader. But linguistics seemed unable to go much beyond the structure of the sentence and remain significant, despite attempts at discourse analysis. For in fact all, all is text, and textuality is a far richer concept than is syntax or lexic, including as it does intertextuality of many kinds, secret polemic, or the aporetic but powerful notion that any text does the opposite of what it says it does.

As a narratologist, I believe I contributed little to the wide movements I have been (briefly and inadequately) describing in this scenario – and this summary description is also a story, 'my' fiction.

I was good at manipulating other people's scenarios in my criticism, and I'm a good critic. But I have never considered myself a theorist, not, at any rate, in the sense of 'having' a theory or theories I would defend against all comers, or revise and accommodate, as a fulltime job and work of a lifetime.

As a novelist, I went through all stages of apprenticeship, as any writer must, and I believe that the scorn of some writers and critics for theory and what they call 'mere' technique is a purely literary and semi-literate phenomenon. As far as I know people do not regularly argue that a painter or sculptor or composer should not thoroughly understand and master, and be seen to master, the technique of his art. But because we can all hold a pen and cover paper since school the myth of 'look in thy heart and write' dies hard. The linguistic mirage was a learned illusion but the belief that anyone who has learnt to write can WRITE is a popular one. The classic tradition (say Horace, Jonson, Boileau) stresses work and technique more than does the Romantic tradition (Longinus, Wordsworth, Coleridge, Shelley), which goes all the way to Plato's divine madness for the poet, but we have long been still in a post-romantico-realist period and one still hears the opinion, expressed by Kingsley Amis in the fifties, that the poet should not be seen to be 'doing his stuff' (the Realist myth of language as a transparent window on the world). 'Postmodernism' has veered to the extreme opposite practice with metafiction and the self-reflexive novel (where the writer shows himself 'doing his stuff') but the Amis view returns constantly in various guises, perhaps to swing back the pendulum or check metamadness when it goes too far. To transgress intelligently, one must know the rule. I benefited immensely from understanding in every tiny detail how a narrative text functions. I obviously know that this isn't enough. '*Il ne suffit pas pour être un grand poète de savoir à fond la syntaxe et de ne pas faire de fautes de langue!*' says the painter Frenhofer in Balzac's *Le Chef d'oeuvre inconnu* (1839, rev. 1939; 1986, p. 46 my translation: To be a great poet, it is not enough to know the syntax and not to make errors of language), and '*le dessin n'existe pas* [...] *la ligne est le moyen par lequel l'homme se rend compte de l'effet de la lumière sur les objets; mais il n'y a pas de lignes dans la nature*' (p. 56: drawing does not exist [...] the line is the means by which man becomes aware of the light's effect on objects; but there are no lines in nature). But then, Frenhofer was mad (his masterpiece is meaningless to Poussin, who sees 'nothing' and calls it '*une muraille de peinture*'), although he is interesting modern critics more and more as forerunner not only of Cézanne (who identified with him) or Picasso, but of Pollock or Kooning (see Anthony Rudolf's Introduction to his translation, 1988).

It is the old quarrel, not only between line and colour, but between genius and work (Longinus), the genius whose errors of 'taste' (a changeable concept) or of, say narrative 'rules' are forgiven or explained away as strokes of genius because he is a genius (a circular argument proper to the canon), and the plodding poet or writer who knows all the rules but whose text lies dead on the page. Things are never quite so simple. Nevertheless most good writers do understand form, which (and this is the point of Balzac's story) is 'protean', 'godlike'. Narrative 'syntax' is not enough, yet being protean it can make or break the spirit of the story, it *is* the spirit of the story. And I am often surprised to discover that many a modern novelist seems, not transgressive but naively unconscious of this 'mere' technique. Indeed, if one sinks very deep to the level of soap operas, their authors seem to know neither line (syntax) nor colour (protean form, transmuted), neither technique (work) nor genius. If technique isn't enough, it is nevertheless essential, and the more one knows the implications of every word one writes, every change of tense or mood or voice (to name only three categories) the more difficult it is to write, because more demanding.

Narratology was thus immensely useful. But in the end, it couldn't cope with narrative and its complexities, except at the price of either trivialization or of becoming a separate theoretical discourse, rarely relevant to the narrative discussed, *when discussed*. In other words, it became itself a story, or set of stories, of narratives not only extradiegetic, metalinguistic, transtextual, paratextual, hypotextual, extratextual, intertextual, but also, yes, sometimes, textual, all at the same time. And so, yes, a 'good' story. Nevertheless, the study of narratological phenomena, as happens so often, turned into an endless discussion about how to speak of them. The story of narratology became as self-reflexive as a 'postmodern' novel. But after all, every age has the rhetoric it deserves.

3

Id is, is id?

The Concise Cambridge History of English Literature, 1942 edition, which I read assiduously long before going up to Oxford and being taught not to rely on such summaries but to read the texts, contained a paragraph that made a great impression on me:

> As the physicians had explained temperament to be dependent on the predominance of one of the four 'humours' or moistures – phlegm, blood, choler and melancholy – it became fashionable to dignify any eccentricity or pose with the name of 'humour', and to deem the most miserable affectations worthy of literary comment. Hence arose a literature of 'humours', and 'humour' became as tiresome a word in that age as 'complex' is in this.
>
> (Sampson 1942, 219–20)

In those unformed days, it never occurred to me to question whose view this was or how the tiresomeness of a word 'in that age' could be gauged, and I similarly accepted that 'complex' had become as tiresome 'in this'. And, in fact, humours were also called complexions.

My point in recounting this is that I also remember wondering as corollary whether the explanations of modern psychology would seem as quaint and unscientific in a century or so as the humours do today. In other words, that facile and perhaps dismissive comparison had one important effect: it instilled into me a solid dose of healthy scepticism about all scenarios (stories), however useful, that purport to explain human behaviour and, by the same token, their extremely curious byproducts.

Over forty-five years later, that healthy scepticism has remained, and I still ask myself practically the same question, though it now concerns the knotty problems of hermeneutics in general. For although criticism of any school continues to make assertive statements ('what this means is'), we nevertheless keep declaring that we have lost our innocence at last and no longer believe in truth as something out there, to be discovered and then stated, independent of our many systems of perception including language. Even history is now considered to be a product of our tropes (Hayden White 1978).

Truth, troth, trope

And a trope is a lie based on the copula, even if the verb *to be* is not actually used: 'love IS a *fire*' can also be said 'love [...] THAT *fire*, SUCH A *fire*' or 'love [...], the *fire*', or 'love [...] O *fire*' or 'X made my love a *fire*' or 'the *fire* OF love', 'the *fire* WITHIN my heart' or '*fiery* love' or 'love *burns* me', and so on. And although banal metaphors like the above seem gratuitous with a grammatical link as strong and dogmatic as the verb *to be,* the verb *to be* allows, and is usually necessary, for outrageous metaphors such as 'She's *all States*, and *all Princes*, I' or 'And her who is *dry corke*' (see Brooke-Rose 1958, 105ff). This, however, is a matter of individual style: whichever grammatical link is used, the copula (or concept of identity, the equation $A = B$) underlies the metaphor (or other trope).

Plato exiled the poet from his republic because (a) he tells lies and (b) he tells beautiful lies that corrupt: the Referential function and the Conative function already problematic. What Plato meant by Truth, however, was itself a beautiful scenario. He merely happened to believe it *as* the truth – and the 'happened' is a neutral way of saying that belief is always based on desire.

There, I have used the copula dogmatically myself. I shall no doubt do so again. We all do. We can't avoid it, unless we become mathematicians and use equations, which are copulas, but methodically demonstrated. And even there another demonstration might and has in the past upset a whole paradigm. Scientists cheerfully admit this and have to work within current paradigms, or nothing would be done at all and whole societies would grind to a halt on philosophic doubt. Indeed, when one reads modern deconstructions of 'the metaphysics of presence' that is said to have founded our beliefs for twenty-five centuries, one sometimes wonders whether philosophers have done anything for civilization except *suivre leur idée, et comme elle était fixe, ils piétinaient*. However, between philosophers and scientists it is perhaps a moot point which have done more harm, those who have argued about Truth and Beauty and Being, or those who have helped to produce our comfortable and fearful civilization.

The eternal divisions start early: the poet knows less about charioteering and potions and flutes than a charioteer or a doctor or a

flute-player (*Ion*, *Republic*), and even less about Truth, that 'real'
(= ideal) bed, model for the carpenter's bed (*Republic*). For Plato
the poet fails the Referential function (World) on two grounds, the
first technico-realist: he cannot have the technical knowledge of char-
iots, potions and flutes as we know them in the world (poetry versus
science); the second philosophical: he does not have access to the
'true', the 'real' (the ideal) models of these things, since no man
has, except, apparently, Plato who postulates their ideal existence
and even produces scenarios (for instance in the *Phaedrus*) of superior
souls (philosophers) who in their transmigration 'remember' more
of this inaccessible truth than others do (poetry versus philosophy).
Or, in mediaeval versions, poetry versus theology: for Aquinas, the
poet was way down below the seven disciplines of the Trivium and
Quadrivium, among the saddle-makers, though Boccaccio in his
Genealogia Deorum Gentilium later insisted on making them equal: 'I
say that theology and poetry can be called almost the same thing,
when they have the same subject; I even say that theology is none
other than the poetry of God' (quoted in Brooks & Wimsatt 1957,
p. 152).

These divisions, as we know, have pursued us through the ages,
in various versions of a two-truths theory, poetry later rejoining religion as against science in the nineteenth century: one truth for religion and one for science, or, in I. A. Richards earlier this century,
an emotive language for poetry, a scientific language for science.

Meanwhile, there had arisen that shadowy area of the *ersatz* or
'human' sciences: *ersatz* because they cannot observe even the elementary rules of science such as, for instance, the exact reproduci-
bility of an experiment in identical and controlled conditions. Thus
they have it both ways: they can speculate about relationships and
structures and identities as scientists do inside their systems; but
they can state these speculations as dogmatically and without proof
as poetry and metaphysics always have: in the name of the principle
of non-contradiction which produces the principle of identity A is
A (Aristotle) you could also state that A is B or Z, as does the
poet. These modern 'scientists' sometimes strangely resemble (or
did before they perfected their systems with jargon, 'laws', perequa-
tions and the like) the pre-Socratic philosophers, one of whom
equated the First Principle of Being with fire, another with water,
another with air, another with earth. These early philosophers (or
what we know of them through fragments and later accounts) were
ALSO physicists, and eventually produced Democritus, and Aristotle,

so perhaps our *ersatz* sciences are also becoming more 'exact', unless our exact sciences are becoming more metaphorical. The splits, however, between poetry and philosophy as representing two kinds of truth seem to start with Plato (who was pure philosopher and mathematician, not scientist).

Doubts and dogmas

In a passage quoted by Derrida, Nietzsche questions even our right to say '"the stone is hard", as if "hard" were known to us otherwise than through a subjective excitation' (Nietzsche, quoted in Derrida 1972c, in 1972e, 213). Derrida notes:

l'illusion diagnostiquée porte sur la valeur du 'est' qui a pour fonction de transformer 'une excitation subjective' en jugement objectif, en prétension à la vérité. Fonction grammaticale? Fonction lexicologique? C'est une question qui se déterminera plus loin.

The diagnosed illusion rests on the value of the 'is' whose function transforms 'a subjective excitation' into objectified judgement and claim to truth. Grammatical function? Lexicological function? This question will be dealt with below.

(213)[1]

The essay is called 'Le supplément de copule' and Derrida is discussing the venerable problem of whether philosophical concepts are constrained by language, in this instance whether the concept of identity (copula) is constrained by the verb *to be* in any one language, notably Greek for Aristotle's *Categories*.[2] He does this chiefly by criticizing philosophical naiveties in Benveniste's 'Catégories de pensées et catégories de langue' ([1958] repr. 1966, 63ff.). The 'supplément' turns out to be all the other ways languages with or without the verb *to be* can express identity (as indeed I had less philosophically analysed them, 1958, and see my simplistic examples above, p. 29). And, disappointingly, after much close argument over long quotations from Benveniste, the essay ends on a string of questions that more or less repeat that contained in the above quotation. To return to which, it could be argued that Nietzsche's example is badly chosen

---

[1] Translations from Derrida in this chapter are my own, not out of disrespect for existing translations but because it is very hard to obtain or consult English translations of French books in France.

[2] 'La catégorie est une des manières pour l' "être" de se dire ou de se signifier, c'est à dire d'ouvrir la langue à son dehors, à ce qui est en tant qu'il est ou tel qu'il est, à la vérité' (1972e, 218). ('Category is one of the ways for "being" to say or signify itself, that is, to open out language to its outside, to what is as it is and inasmuch as it is, to open language to truth.')

since science can in fact define hardness in molecular and other terms, whereas philosophy can't.

Paul de Man, that other great deconstructor of our time, has also paid much attention to Nietzsche on this point: in Section 516 of *Der Wille zur Macht* Nietzsche says (de Man's emphases):

> Supposing [*gesetzt*] there were no self-identical A, such as is presupposed [*vorausgesetzt*] by every proposition of logic (and of mathematics), and the A were already mere *appearance*, then logic would have a merely *apparent world* as its precondition [*Voraussetzung*] [...] The A of logic is, like the atom, a reconstruction [*Nachkonstruktion*] of the 'thing' [...] In fact, *logic* (like geometry and arithmetic), applies only to *fictitious truths* [fingierte Wahrheiten] that we have created. Logic is the attempt to understand the actual world by means of a scheme of being posited [*gesetzt*] by ourselves, more correctly; to make it easier to formalize and to compute [*berechnen*].
>
> (Nietzsche, 1968, 279, quoted in de Man 1979, 120–1)

Later de Man comments:

> The unwarranted substitution of knowledge for mere sensation becomes paradigmatic for a wide set of aberrations all linked to the positional power of language in general and allowing for the radical possibility that all being, as the ground for entities may be linguistically 'gesetzt', a correlative of speech aspects.
>
> (de Man 1979, 123)

We cannot assert that logical axioms are adequate to reality without having previous knowledge of entities, says Nietzsche, who adds, 'which is certainly not the case'. De Man points out that while this last sentence has not been proved explicitly, neither can we prove it is not so. Nietzsche is drawing our attention to the possibility of unwarranted substitution (for instance of identity for signification) and hence puts into question the postulate of logical adequacy. Indeed:

> Nietzsche seems to go further than this and concludes: '[The law of contradiction] *therefore* [de Man's italics] contains no *criterion of truth* [Nietzsche's italics] but an *imperative* concerning that which should count as true.' The conclusion seems irrevocable. As is stated at the beginning of the passage (in the form of a thesis), the inability to contradict – to state at the same time that A is and is not A – is not a necessity but an inadequacy, 'ein Nicht-Vermögen'. Something one has failed to do can become feasible again only in the mode of compulsion; the performative correlate of 'I cannot' is 'I [or you] must.'
>
> (1979, 123–4)

And de Man goes on to ask:

> Can we consequently free ourselves once and forever from the constraints of identity by asserting and denying the same proposition at the same time? Is language an act, a 'sollen' or a 'tun', and now that we know that there is no longer such an illusion as that of knowledge but only feigned truths, can we replace knowledge by

performance? The text seems to assert this without question. [...] But in so doing it does not do what it claims to be entitled to do. The text does not simultaneously affirm and deny identity but it denies affirmation.

(1979, 124)

But de Man had begun his essay by noting that 'value-seductions are tolerated (even admired) in so-called literary texts in a manner that would not pass muster in "philosophical" writings', and that one of the first difficulties of Nietzsche's texts is their patent literariness, although they make 'claims usually associated with philosophy rather than with literature. Nietzsche's work raises the perennial question of the distinction between philosophy and literature by way of a deconstruction of the value of values' (119), of which the most fundamental is the principle of non-contradiction, ground of the identity principle. And de Man confronts the passage about 'tun ist alles' in *Genealogy of Morals* ('there is no "being" behind "doing" [...] the "doer" is merely a fiction added to the deed – the deed is everything', Nietzsche 1922, vol. 15, p. 295) with another from Section 477 of *The Will to Power:*

The 'Spirit' [*Geist*, better translated as 'Mind'], *something that thinks* ... here we *first* imagine an act that does not exist, 'thinking', and *second* we imagine as substratum of this act a subject in which every act of thought and nothing else originates: this means that *the deed as well as the doer are fictions* [*sowohl das Tun, als der Täter sind fingiert*].

(Nietzsche 1968, 264, de Man 1979, 127)

The parallel that concerns us is the symmetry between this fictitious doing [*fingiertes Tun*] and the fictitious truths [*fingierte Wahrheiten* in authorized edition, not *Wesenheiten* or 'entities', as in earlier editions] that appear in the previously discussed passage on the principle of identity ['logic ... applies only to fictitious truths']: here, in Section 516, truth is opposed to action as fiction is opposed to reality. In the later passage (Section 477) this conception of action as a 'reality' opposed to the illusion of knowledge, is, in its turn, undermined. Performative language is no less ambivalent in its referential function than the language of constatation.

(de Man 1979, 127)

Hence, presumably, the now 'literary' language of philosophers like Nietzsche (or Derrida, Deleuze, Serres and others), and of 'human' scientists like Freud or Lacan. Perhaps, after all, as poets have always 'known', the formula of the identity principle A is A is just as fictitious as the tropic formula A is Z. And since 'love burns' says the same as 'love is a fire' but in a different way, any action can be attributed to any entity, both being fictions anyway. Thus may we assert any dogma, any lie, any scenario. Equally, we may affirm that these are 'wrong', because the 'facts' are otherwise.

It is indeed amazing how we continue to assert personal opinions as equations. Even those who have done most to deconstruct illusions of language use the copula liberally. 'L'indécidabilité est une "preuve" d'écriture', says Barthes at a critical moment of *S/Z* though clearly many must have disagreed and perhaps still do, and Derrida's readings move splendidly from copula to copula, from metaphor to metaphor.

What is a dogma? A dogma is a scenario elaborated from one premise to be taken on trust, whether that trust be ideological or epistemological (and some would equate the two). This is the second of my dogmatic statements based on the copula (and of course such statements can *also* be platitudes – that's part of the trouble: who one is addressing).

To avoid overt politics let's take a harmless Roman Catholic dogma – relatively recent as declared dogma (1950) though much older (fourth century at least) as feast and apocryphal tradition: that of the Assumption of the Blessed Virgin Mary (BVM), which functions on pure logic, given the initial assumption (with small 'a'): Christ is the Son of God. Elaboration: therefore He is free of Original Sin (another dogma); therefore He is born through a body also free of Original Sin (the Immaculate Conception of the BVM, another dogma, not proclaimed as such till 1854, and often confused by non-Catholics with the Virgin birth). That's for the Immaculate Birth. But the process must logically extend to an Immaculate Death. Christ's body could not rot in the earth, hence the Ascension; and, quite soon, the same applies to the BVM, hence the Assumption – without evangelical 'evidence', but theologically, psychologically and structurally satisfying. (See also Kristeva 1977 for meditations on the Virgin Birth and other elaborations.)

All ideology works this way, and the transparence we feel here only appears with historical perspective when passions on the topic have become dead letter. Hence the impossibility of arguing (or even discussing) any ideological point without maybe dislodging the one article of faith on which the structure is erected. And this we cannot do, have learnt or are still learning not to do, out of respect for others' articles of faith if tenaciously held. Nevertheless, there are sufficient millions of people throughout the world who are still prepared to conquer and kill each other, usually on orders, for such articles of faith – at least as given reason, the real drive being power (this is my third dogmatic statement based on the copula). Thus a tentative answer to the earlier moot point about who has done most harm (see p. 29) would be that ideologies relying on a metaphysics of presence (the only one available so far) have not hesitated to use the means that science has put at their disposal to destroy each other.

The non-scientific 'human' sciences, that were supposed to cure us of all our libidinal acquisitive and aggressive instincts, seem to function in the same way, by creating dogmatic scenarios, *Nachkonstruktione* (from symptomatic events) of other events that have occurred only once (or not at all, absent stories post-reconstructed) and are supposed to be recurring in the very symptoms from which they are reconstructed, but not in exactly reproducible conditions; these scenarios have become the paradigm of the systems. The most familiar are the Freudian scenarios which we have all studied, accepted in fascination, rejected and mocked, analysed or been analysed through. Religion having failed, the family romance was better than no romance at all, and if family continues to fail, presumably romance *tout court* in the form of video comic strips will continue to take over. But the most curious aspect of the Freudian scenarios was the detailed topology of the psychic system that 'writes' the romance. With the verb *to be* and other assertive forms:

The ego is not sharply separated from the id, its lower portion merges into it.
But the repressed merges into the id as well, and is merely part of it. The repressed is only cut off sharply from the ego by the resistance of repression; it can communicate with the ego through the id.

(Freud 1961a [1923], 14, with a diagram)

So Descartes placed the soul in the pineal gland, so Bunyan and Langland and de Lorris and Dante variously topologized vices and virtues. Examples of such topology abound in Freud's work. Freud is, however, always careful to point out that he is only trying to 'represent pictorially' (14), or that 'what follows is speculation' (1955b [1920], 24, on the neurological position of 'the System Pept-Cs [Perception-Consciousness])'. And in his incredible search for a mechanical analogy to the psychic memory, from the 'Project for a scientific psychology' (1966 [1885]), through the *Traumdeutung* (1955a [1900]) to the 'Note on the "Mystic writing pad"' (1961b [1925]) as traced by Derrida (1967), the analogy has to represent the permanence of both the trace and of the virginity of the substance that receives the trace. A virgin birth in a way.

'The machine doesn't function by itself', says Derrida, 'it is a mechanism without its own energy. The machine is dead, it is death.' (1967, 335).

It would be interesting to know how Freud would have used, rather than his waxen *Wunderblock*, the analogy of the computer, with its Read-Only Memory (ROM), called in French *mémoire morte* – or how would Derrida, for that matter, with his verb *to be*: 'it is death'. Or again: 'Mais ce qui devait marcher tout seul, c'était le psychique et non son imitation ou sa représentation mécanique. Celle-çi ne vit pas. La représentation est la mort.' (335, 'But what should have functioned by itself was the psychic, and not its imitation or its mechanical representation. This does not live. Representation is death.') And Derrida goes on to show that Freud's concept of writing is essentially platonic, opposing hypomnesic writing to writing 'in the psyche', itself woven of a truth present out of time (336). And later (the long bracket between subordinate clause and main clause is Derrida's):

Here in the Freudian thrust, we can perhaps discern both sides [*l'au-delà et l'en-deçà*] of the closure that could be called 'platonic'. In the moment of world history that appears under the name of Freud, and by means of an incredible mythology (neurological or metapsychological: for the metapsychological fable could never be taken seriously, except in the sense that disorganises and disturbs its literality. Its advantage, as regards the neurological stories told in the *Project*, is perhaps slim), a relation of the historico-transcendental writing-scene to the self has been said without being said, thought without being thought: metaphorised, self-designated through indications of intra-worldly links, *represented*. This can perhaps be recognised [...] by the fact that Freud [...] also made us a writing-scene. As do all those who write.[3]

Elsewhere, Derrida attributes more consciousness to Freud's use of metaphor. Freud, Bergson and Lenin, he says in 'La mythologie blanche', who were all attentive to the metaphoric activity in theoretical or philosophical discourse, 'ont proposé ou pratiqué la multiplication de métaphores antagonistes afin de mieux en neutraliser ou contrôler l'effet' ('proposed or practised the multiplication of antago-

---

[3] 'Ainsi s'annoncent peut-être, dans la trouée freudienne, l'au-delà et l'en-deçà de la clôture qu'on peut appeler "platonicienne". Dans ce moment de l'histoire du monde, tel qu'il s' "indique" sous le nom de Freud, à travers une incroyable mythologie (neurologique ou métapsychologique: car nous n'avons jamais songé à prendre au sérieux, sauf en la question qui désorganise et inquiète sa littéralité, la fable métapsychologique. Au regard des histoires neurologiques que nous raconte l' *Esquisse*, son avantage peut-être est mince) un rapport à soi de la scène historico-transcendante de l'écriture s'est dit sans se dire, pensé sans s'être pensé: écrit et à la fois effacé, métaphorisé; désigné lui-même en indiquant des rapports intra-mondains, *représenté*.

Cela se reconnaît peut-être [...] à ce signe que Freud [...] nous a aussi fait la scène de l'écriture. Comme tous ceux qui écrivent' (Derrida 1967a in 1967b, 337–8).

nistic metaphors in order the better to neutralise or control their effect', Derrida 1972b, 255).

The effect, nevertheless, of Freud's scenarios on many disciples has been a certain literalness, and the creation of a new theology, which works on exactly the same principle of faith as do theology and political ideology, except that the unconscious has replaced eternal and dogmatic truth: any individual refusal must come from a repression of a truth that is there unrecognized, and this will be analysed as resistance, just as it will be prayed for as a faltering of faith or 'amicably' (with luck) discussed as revisionism or other ideological heresy.

Scenarios are for poets, for paranoiacs, for schizophrenics; and for those who want to believe in the scenarios in the first place, people of faith, sectarians and ideologists of all kinds. We all know the outrageous use of static scenarios in politics. Poets, paranoiacs and schizophrenics have one great advantage over the ideologists in that they frequently change scenarios, they get tired of the old ones and invent new ones, equally convincing. Freud himself was a poet in this respect, and as poet and doctor he gave an explanation of the functioning of the unconscious on an (as yet then unelaborated) model of human languages, an explanation which was both neurologically and linguistically more satisfying than he perhaps fully understood at the time, or at any rate stated in the elaboration of his scenarios.

Similarly, the most poetic and creative literary critics – those one reads for their own texts rather than to learn about the texts they discuss – have produced enchanting scenarios: Barthes on Balzac, Derrida on Rousseau or Plato, or Lacan on Poe, Barbara Johnson on Derrida and Lacan and Poe, Shoshana Felman on James and Poe, and many others – they are themselves poets in prose, critics as writers. But are their beautiful statements 'true?' 'The poet nothing affirmeth, and therefore never lieth', said Sir Philip Sidney four centuries ago. Poets are liars but say so, unlike politicians, unlike scientists whether *exact* or *ersatz*. Dogmatic statements (and this is my fourth conscious one) are turned into tropes.

But is it always so? No, of course not. For we also know the outrageous use of static scenarios for flat, pointless, tropeful but unmagical criticism. Perhaps these do no harm because no one takes them seriously? I believe they do harm in the classroom, and therefore in future adults, but that is another problem. Between these and the best, however, lies a curious zone of Freudian critics who *are* taken seriously and who to my mind fall into the very dogmatic pseudo-equation trap I have tried to point up. I shall end this chapter by discussing only one of them, Harold Bloom.

Anxieties of apophrades

In *The Anxiety of Influence*, Bloom proposes 'a theory of poetry by way of a description of poetic influence, or the story of intrapoetic relationships' (Bloom 1973, 5). By which, he has to re-insist in *A Map of Misreading*:

> I continue not to mean the passing on of images and ideas from earlier to later poets. Influence, as I conceive it, means that there are *no* texts, but only relationships *between* texts. These relationships depend upon a critical act, a misreading or misprision, that one poet performs upon another, and that does not differ in kind from the necessary critical acts performed by every strong reader upon every text he encounters.
>
> (Bloom 1975, 3)

Through his theory of influence Bloom offers 'instruction in the practical criticism of poetry' (he too: like I. A. Richards, who also tried to use the psychology of his time).

In Chapter 5 of *A Map of Misreading* he says:

> After Nietzsche and Freud, it is not possible to return wholly to a mode of interpretation that seeks to *restore* meanings to texts. Yet even the subtlest of contemporary Nietzschean 'deconstructionists' of texts must *reduce* those texts in a detour or flight from psychology and history [...] A semiological enigma, however prized, is generally an elaborate evasion of the inevitable discursiveness of a literary text. Latecomer fictions must know themselves to be fictions [...]
>
> We can prefer Freud as a clearer-away of illusions to his chief competitor, Jung, who offers himself as a restorer of primal meanings but discredits almost all possibility of such restoration; but we will remain uneasy at the Freudian reductiveness. [...] And we have discovered no way as yet to evade the insights of Nietzsche, which are more dangerously far-reaching even than those of Freud, since Freud would not have told us that rational thought is only interpretation according to a scheme we cannot throw off. Yet Nietzsche's 'perspectivism', which is all he can offer us as an alternative to Western metaphysics, is a labyrinth more pragmatically illusive than the illusions he would dispel. One need not be religious in any sense or intention [...] still to conclude that meaning, whether of poems or dreams, of any text, is excessively impoverished by a Nietzsche-inspired deconstruction, however scrupulous.
>
> (1975, 85–6)

Thus Bloom's chief objection to deconstruction, whether Freudian or Nietzschean-inspired or both, is its reductiveness ('reduced', 'reductiveness', 'excessively impoverished'). His own system, however, though excessively rich and immensely complicated, seems equally reductive through arbitrary rigidity of categorization (and the mere act of reading texts through one system alone is reductive).

On the one hand, he describes six stages, called misreadings or misprisions or revisionary ratios, in the latecomer's relationship to his precursor or 'Father' (I summarize from Bloom's own synopsis, 1973, 14–15):

Clinamen: The later poet swerves from the precursor. This is a corrective movement in his own poem.

Tessera: He antithetically completes his precursor by retaining the terms but meaning them differently.

Kenosis: He seems to humble and empty himself, but in such a way that the precursor is emptied out also.

Daemonization: He opens himself to a power in the parent poem that belongs to a range of being beyond the precursor.

Askesis: He yields up part of his own endowment to separate himself. Self-purgation, solitude.

Apophrades: He opens his poem again to the precursor's work, but the result is as if the later poet had himself written the precursor's most characteristic work.

Each of these revisionary ratios is then arbitrarily equated with a trope – and Bloom adds two to the 'Four Master Tropes' of Kenneth Burke out of Vico (irony, metonymy, metaphor and synecdoche): hyperbole and metalepsis (metalepsis here not in Genette's sense of transgressing narrative levels, see Chapter 14, but meaning fusion of times). Obviously, he has to have six. And he justifies it by appeal to authority: 'following Nietzsche and de Man in needing two more tropes of representation to go beyond synecdoche in accounting for Romantic representations' (Bloom 1975, 94):

A trope as I define it is [. . .] more Vichian than Nietzschean, 'poetic monsters and metamorphoses', [. . .] necessary errors about language, defending ultimately against the deathly dangers of literal meaning, and more immediately against all other tropes that intervene between the literal meaning and the fresh opening to discourse.

(94)

Each revisionary ratio is *also* equated with a psychic defence (against the precursor), and here he *reduces* Anna Freud's ten defences (themselves a mechanical schematization of highly complex interrelated activities) to six. Indeed, Bloom gives priority to psychic defences over tropes (a trope is practically a defence); and each revisionary ratio is *also* equated with types of images; and *also* with terms in the 'dialectic of revisionism' or 'tropes of limitation and tropes of representation' (84, see col. 2 in Table 1); and each category has already been pre-equated (in 'The primal scene of instruction' 51ff.) with six biblical notions of development: election, covenant, rivalry, incarnation, interpretation, revision. Later, Bloom in fact reduced these six inter-equated categories to three with each a dialectical movement, equivalent to three kinds of psychic defence, so that in fact Clinamen and Tessera go together (as do the others) in a contracting away and reopening movement, repeated three times (Bloom 1977). This can all be reconstructed in a chart as shown in Table 1.

Table 1. *Summary of Bloom's 'revisionary ratios'*

Biblical	Dialectic	Images	Tropes action	Tropes desire	Psychic defence	Ratio
election	limitation/ substitution	presence/ absence	irony		Reaction-formation	Clinamen ↕
covenant	represent-ation	part/ whole		synecdoche	reversal (turning against Self)	Tessera
rivalry	limitation/ substitution	fullness/ emptiness	metonymy		regression (undoing, isolation)	Kenosis ↕
incarn'n	represent-ation	high/ low		hyperbole/ litotes	repression	Daemon'n
interp'n	limitation/ substitution	inside/ outside	metaphor		sublim'n	Askesis ↕
revision	represent-ation	early/ late		metalepsis	introj'n/ projection	Apophrades

It must be understood that this is not a biographical theory: it is not the poet who *in his life* goes through all these equivalent stages, but *a poem*, and this is clearly a great advantage.

This is a rich system, and pure Structuralists would object that it is *too* rich and arbitrary to *be* a system – as Todorov in his Structuralist days objected to Frye's categories on the same ground (Todorov 1970). And Bloom's readings are clearly not meant to be reductive as Structuralist, and, in his view, Deconstructionist, readings are.

Yet, as often with Structuralist readings, the practice either cannot follow the theory (if it *is* rich and interesting), or follows it too obediently (if it is reductive or arbitrary). In Bloom we have both. His best readings do enrich us through the diagram's perspective, but often seem to fall away into personal assertions. Conversely, the temptation to invert the critical procedure and refer a passage back to the diagram through its 'images' and tropes is very strong. Thus any image of presence/absence belongs to *clinamen* (and to irony, and to reaction-formation, etc.); while any image of earliness/lateness belongs to *apophrades* (etc.). The result is sometimes hilarious.

Wordsworth's *Ode*, for instance, 'sets or follows the patterns of our map of misreading' (Bloom 1975, 146) – the precursor being Milton's *Lycidas*. Thus 'images of absence dominate only the poem's first stanza' (145):

> From stanza V through VIII there are a series of images showing different aspects of emptying out of a prior and valuable fullness. These include trailing clouds, shades, journeyings westwards, fading of a greater into a lesser light, imitation of the lesser by the greater, darkness and, finally, weighing down by frost. As images of reduction, they show subjectivity yielding to a world of things, of meaningless repetition, the 'realistic' world of metonymies.
>
> (146)

Traditional thematics at a spanking pace? And on to the final stage, where 'The acceptance of belatedness at first seems complete' [quotation: 'What though the radiance ... / We will grieve not']. But the final stanza proclaims freshness and earliness:

> The innocent brightness of a new-born Day
> Is lovely yet ...
>
> (147–8)

Je veux bien, as the French say to express doubt. But it does seem rather strange (and to me unacceptable) that this 'final' stage, described in such splendid theoretical terms and receiving the greatest focus of Bloom's hermeneutic machine (for he is only interested in 'strong' poets who reach this final stage), should be illustrated by Wordsworth at his flattest and most bathetic (this is my fifth personal and dogmatic statement).

Would the terrible father-figure, the precursor, have pre-cursed his son, the belated newcomer, to suffer so and come through all these deep defences but for this?

This model of poetic creation, moreover, 'works' (is of interest) only for what he calls 'strong' poets; it celebrates heroic struggles of will between a poet and his precursors. And (as it happens?) his strong poets are male poets, for although Marianne Moore (once) and Emily Dickinson (thrice) figure in lists (pp. 6, 162, 163), they are not discussed. Feminist critics have oddly enough shown interest in Bloom because, according to Culler, 'it makes explicit the sexual connotations of authorship and authority' (Culler 1983, 60n) and therefore also the problematic situation of a woman poet in relation to the tradition – an interest by omission as it were. As Leitch observes, 'Presumably, one could take a weak poem and pinpoint its stages of failure' (Leitch 1983, 135). I thought this was irony, but he goes on:

> And one might be able to characterize schools and periods of literary history by their practice of a dominant ratio. Poets of mid-eighteenth-century sensibility, for example, favour hyperbole-daemonization. To practice such criticism would be to employ a diachronic rhetoric, which Bloom has lately started to do.
>
> (135)

(Perhaps it *is* irony?)

But as Bove has shown, tradition (which for Freud represented what the individual represses), is itself a trope, a defence mechanism, because:

> it is the rhetorical centre upon which the entire Bloomian critical structure depends in its *circular* effort to *demonstrate* the absolute necessity and value of *tradition as centre*. This is the classical example of the vicious circle: critical language turns back upon itself, against the author's intent, to reveal its own blindness and unexamined rhetoric.
>
> (Bove 1980, 19)

And tropes, Bloom says, are 'necessary errors about language'. It would indeed seem, as Bove concludes via other arguments, that Bloom:

> has proven what he set out, in opposition to Nietzsche, Derrida and de Man, to disprove. The anxiety of influence is necessarily a linguistic structure because the unexamined pressure of what Heidegger calls the ontotheological and Derrida the logocentric language of tradition bring him to demonstrate unwittingly, the fact that to some extent, it is language which thinks, reads, and writes.
>
> (19)

My own necessary but absurd 'reduction' of Bloom is unfair, which is why I quote the comments of others who have examined him in more generous detail than I could here, yet nevertheless end up in this negative way. It is one thing to say that 'after Nietzsche and Freud it is not possible to return wholly to a mode of interpretation that seeks to *restore* meanings to texts'. It is quite another to read tropes via Freud, whose concepts, Derrida (among others) maintains, one should

> use cautiously and in quotations: they all belong without exception to the history of metaphysics, that is to the system of logocentric repression organised to exclude

or lower the body of the written trace, to shove it out and down as a didactic and technical metaphor, as servile and excremental matter.

(Derrida 1967a, 294)

Derrida adds that Freud is of course not exhausted by this logocentric inheritance:

witness the precautions and the 'nominalism' with which he manipulates what he calls conceptual conventions and hypotheses [...] But the historical and theoretical sense of these precautions was never truly enough thought out by Freud. Hence the need for the immense work of deconstruction.

(294)

If all reading is misreading, as Bloom insists, this presupposes, as many have pointed out, a correct reading. But Culler goes further than this simplistic objection and turns the proposition round to mean that all understanding can be seen as a special case of misunderstanding (Culler 1983, 176).[4]

It is always tempting to deconstruct a text and to show that the author has in his practice done the opposite of what he claims or seems to claim. I shall be showing it myself in a few subsequent chapters, and no doubt also doing the opposite of what I claim, since every text deconstructs itself. There is a certain post-Freudian glee in showing the unconscious contradictions, and even those who have deconstructed texts by Derrida himself (for instance Barbara Johnson) do not escape this. Bloom, though against deconstruction, does precisely that, though briefly, to a passage from Nietzsche, by affirming that 'Nietzsche, like Emerson, is one of the great deniers of anxiety-as-influence, just as Johnson and Coleridge are its great affirmers' (Bloom 1973, 50). Since the concept is Bloom's, not theirs, the suggestion is clear that they are denying or affirming it despite themselves. But in Derrida and de Man and Johnson and the best deconstructors the intention is generous and the result enriching: for Derrida a text deconstructs itself and one only has to find out how; for de Man the greatest insight comes at the moments of greatest blindness.

---

[4] Naturally I am not suggesting that arbitrary equations are acceptable only in poetic metaphors by poets and not acceptable in literary criticism or philosophy. Equations of apparently unrelated things are inherent to the language we think in. Derrida is clear when he says that Bergson, Freud and Lenin were attentive to metaphor, as he is himself. Bloom's notion of tropes as 'necessary errors about language' puts the point neatly. Metaphors shift our perceptions and fixed concepts and so create new meaning. But Derrida is equally clear when he recommends we use them cautiously in reading both the world and the language of the world. 'Il faut interroger inlassablement les métaphores' (1972a, 87).

Nevertheless, I feel that these problems form part of the post-Freudian status of the analyst versus analysand (who in literature is not there to 'help' the analyst or, in more aggressive terms, to 'defend himself' – which defence would itself be analysed as part of a highly significant pattern, and so on). However subtly we go about it (thus protected by the 'patient's' absence), we fall into the traps of language and notably of the copula and its protean forms, behind which is desire and dogma and mastery. Our very institutions of learning encourage 'mastery' of the arts. And these traps of language and desire belong to the mythological scenarios of mastery.

One profound difference between psychoanalysis and philosophy, however, is that the former claims to be a science and behaves like a science: (1) it supersedes itself, at least in theory (the scientist, unless he is a historian of science, is not interested in earlier states of knowledge); (2) it acts in the world – but with rather less success than sciences like, say, medicine or even psychiatry, by which I mean that wholly successful repressions (the most dangerous cases) are inaccessible to its methods, as Freud himself admitted (Freud 1957 [1915], 153). Like Christianity which relies on recognition of sin, it preaches to the converted.

Thus it seems to me more dangerous, more 'dating', as the system of 'humours' is dated, to 'use' psychoanalysis in literary criticism, at least in its purely Freudian though simplified form, but fascinating and enriching to consider it, at its best, as a literary text, as Nietzsche's texts are literary texts. Perhaps after all we *should* accept the joyful wisdom and ambiguity of Nietzsche's own position: 'Art treats appearance as appearance; its aim is precisely *not* to deceive, it is therefore *true*' (Nietzsche 1922, Vol. 6, 98), which says exactly what Sidney said four centuries ago (quoted p. 37). And the artist who accepts illusion and lie for what they are gains a special kind of *Heiterkeit* or serenity that 'differs entirely from the pleasure principle tied to libido and desire' (de Man 1979, 114). De Man, however, goes on to deconstruct even that: 'Philosophy turns out to be an endless reflection on its own destruction at the hands of literature' (115).

And isn't that, in the end, what we have all secretly wanted for a hundred years since Arnold? Or for twenty-five centuries since our exclusion as writers from that written Republic?

PART II

Stories and style

4

A for but: Hawthorne's 'The Custom-House'

Antithesis has much in common with metaphor in that it brings together, by juxtaposition, two entities normally separated by an opposition like a wall, and Barthes describes it just so in his analysis of what he calls the rhetorical entry into his Symbolic Code: the Symbolic is the magical moment when the wall crumbles, when for example age and youth, the monstrously effeminate male and innocently strong female have briefly come together to form a chimerical creature, then spring apart at a touch (1974, 65). We may compare this notion of a wall with the metaphor of the ruined wall towards the end of *The Scarlet Letter*, where the soul is a citadel once breached by guilt, well guarded 'so that the enemy shall not force his way again [...] But there is still the ruined wall, and, near it, the stealthy tread of the foe that would win over again his unforgotten triumph' (144).[1] This metaphor can also extend from good and evil to the way antithesis functions.

The soul as citadel is a very old metaphor, though usually the building is rather the body that houses the soul. The psyche as house is familiar to psychoanalysts. Many critics have remarked on the novel's opening, where Hester Prynne emerges from the prison in seventeenth-century Boston, and its prefiguring by the author in his nineteenth-century Custom-House in Salem. What has not been explored is the unusualness of having a Custom-House at all in this opening role of hostel for the psyche, for the author's imagination.[2]

The use of the Custom-House as Introduction to *The Scarlet Letter* is ingenuously presented by Hawthorne, and understood by critics, as purely autobiographical, and thus fortuitous. But a Custom-House is a frontier, a mediation between goods coming in from outside

---

[1] All page references to the text of *The Scarlet Letter* are taken from the Norton Critical edition of 1961, see References.
[2] See Baskett, Baym, Stouck, Van Deusen in Norton Critical Edition, and Cox, Eakin, McCall, Ziff elsewhere, see References.

and going out from inside. It is a public, institutional place, a place of law and order, where custom and excise must be paid on goods (on pleasure, as cost). It is a threshold, the threshold of the narrative, and this very phrase is used at the end of the first chapter, called 'The Prison-Door', thus linking the two buildings.

Custom and forking paths

And custom is also human behaviour institutionalized, social habit both good and bad, public as opposed to private or secret thought. It is the declared, the formalized, the outer world, as opposed to the undeclared, unformalized, inner world. And one of these public customs is the custom of narration, which is also, at least for Hawthorne as he describes it, an exaction of excise, a cost, a toll upon the telling, as well as a consideration of his customers, or readers. And it is with this custom or convention of narration that 'The Custom-House' opens, forking continually right and left in antithesis (see Fig. 1).

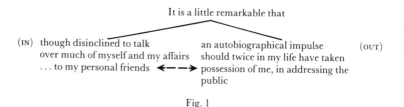

Fig. 1

This antithesis (disinclination/impulse) is a particular aspect of more general ones such as IN/OUT, PRIVATE/PUBLIC, SELF/SOCIETY. But inside that antithesis there is another one, that of personal friends and the public, and this acts as a link (marked by the broken line) between the two oppositions; on either side there *is* a public, but one is small and intimate, the other is larger and unknown. The opposition is qualified: not a wholly silent, secret self versus society but a communicative, though private self.

In the next sentence the OUT or PUBLIC branch splits off again into past and present (see Fig. 2).

Here again both reader and author are linked again by 'could imagine' (both can imagine). But the upper left node also branches out (see Fig. 3).

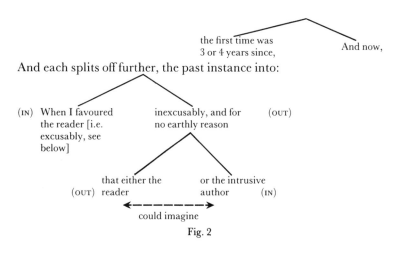

And each splits off further, the past instance into:

(IN)   When I favoured   inexcusably, and for   (OUT)
       the reader [i.e.   no earthly reason
       excusably, see
       below]

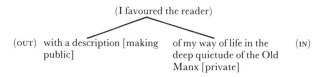

Fig. 2

(I favoured the reader)

(OUT)   with a description [making   of my way of life in the   (IN)
        public]   deep quietude of the Old
                                           Manx [private]

Fig. 3

While further up still, the 'And now' (present) node, which had been left in suspense, is caught back and further split (see Fig. 4).

For we may formalize antithesis, unlike metaphor, as a forking path. And when we do this Hawthorne's style, particularly in its concentrated version in 'The Custom-House', appears as a very forest of forking paths, or Chomskian trees.[3] In these forking paths, the left and right branches frequently link up again, either by a mediating notion (marked by the broken line), or by constant reversals of the opposition (marked by IN/OUT as also representing the concepts of PRIVATE/PUBLIC, SELF/SOCIETY and so on, which annuls their forking path. Antithesis, in other words, can be shown to function emblematically like the latter A.

---

[3] These of course are used here to represent, not the deep structures of grammatical elements inside a sentence, but the surface structures of semantic units which divide, either as clauses of superordinate sentences, or as new sentences.

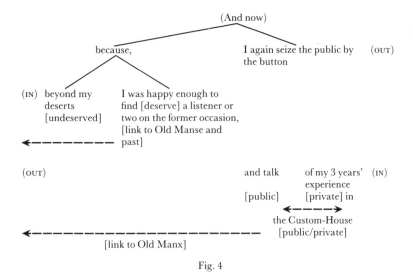

Fig. 4

Metalinguistics and metanarrative

Some may be scandalized by my thus equating an abstract, outside representation of an inside, stylistic feature with a symbol which has its concrete fictional existence inside the text. And indeed it would scandalize a pure Structuralist. But so much interesting work has been done since on iconicity and spatio-temporal representation in fiction, that I am allowing myself this metaleptic leap in order to bring out Hawthorne's poetic mind more clearly.

Jean Paris (1978) for instance, in analysing what he calls Balzac's writing-machines, or the repeated antithetical mechanisms in Maupassant, has in effect proposed a kind of semantic generative grammar of narrative, with disjunction and its reversal into conjunction of oppositions as first generative principle of narrativity. And in a fascinating number of *Poetics Today* on Representation, there is an essay entitled 'Figures in Novelistic Description' by Raymonde Debray-Genette (1984), who shows that nineteenth-century novelists, including Scott, whom Hawthorne admired, and Balzac, were particularly conscious of formal description, and that 'models of documentary discourse refer to models of the idea we have of science and scientific exposition'. The names Buffon and Geoffroy Saint-Hilaire were constantly referred to by theorists and writers. She goes on:

The crossing of the scientific model and the pictorial novel – in brief, the tabular as well as the taxonomic play of description – confuses analysis and masks processes that are properly literary, scriptural – or 'plastic' in Flaubert's sense. For example, when Zola surrounds a landscape with 'in the distance', 'closer', 'to the right', 'below', we do not know whether the enumerative clarity or the pictorial effect is more important, which refers to the analysis and which to the picture. In fact we have gone from the Homeric 'and then' … and then' to the 'up … down' of the fresco, with optic variations, depth, movement, and temporal reiterations. But these devices are eternal transpositions. In contrast, there is the play of writing, which no longer retains the traces of plastic mimetic illusion, but produces an effect designated variously as realistic or 'artistic', and is in fact figural.

(680)

Debray-Genette's essay chiefly concerns the figures of metonymy and synecdoche, but her remarks can clearly apply to any figure, and all the more to antithesis which is a form of metonymy, and which, according to Jean Paris, generates narrative.

It may still be felt, however, that my use of Chomskian trees goes beyond this and represents a conflation of metalinguistic into poetic function, a transgression of levels, a metalepsis as Gérard Genette calls the transgression of narrative levels. So be it. Or rather, with many writers I might agree, but not with Hawthorne, who made a very particular and metaphoric use of narrative space. Does he not, in any case, himself give us a narrative metalepsis of a Shandean kind at the end of Chapter 1?

But, on one side of the portal, and rooted almost at the threshold, was a wild rose-bush, covered, in this month of June, with its delicate gems, which might be imagined to offer their fragrance and fragile beauty to the prisoner as he went in, and to the condemned criminal as he came forth to his doom, in token that the deep heart of Nature could pity and be kind to him.

This rose-bush, by a strange chance, had been kept alive in history […] Finding it so directly on the threshold of our narrative, which is now about to issue from that inauspicious portal, we could hardly do otherwise than pluck one of its flowers and present it to the reader. It may serve, let us hope, to symbolize some sweet moral blossom …

(40)

If this is not exactly on a comic par with Tristram begging the reader to help him get his father to bed, it is nevertheless a metalepsis, and a complex one. A rose, much insisted on as inside the narrative, is brought down through history and offered to the reader outside both story and history, exactly as it was said to offer its fragrance and fragile beauty to a prisoner – with whom the reader is thus briefly identified. What is about to issue forth from 'that inauspicious portal', however, is not that generalized prisoner but the narrative, and what in fact comes out is another prisoner, Hester Prynne. A quadruple identification is thus effected between the anonymous historical prisoner, the reader, the narrative, and its heroine. Moreover, the prison is the threshold of the narrative where the rose-bush grows, and the threshold of the narrative is also the authentifying preface we have just read, called 'The Custom-House', which describes another building, from which the narrating author, a Civil Servant and prisoner has also emerged, free at last to tell his story.

And although the rose offered to the reader is at once turned into a symbolic moral blossom, so it was offered to the prisoner, 'in token that the deep heart of Nature could pity and be kind to him'. Both the narrative rose and the symbolic rose have the same verbal status. It's all done with words, that is, with letters. And the letter A, which looks like a building, is also a threshold, to other letters.

The text of 'The Custom-House', after an allusion to an eighteenth-century mock-autobiography (past), then continues with the custom of narration, but now as a maxim, or rather as a speculation about 'the author' in general, rather than as personal account (pp. 6–7) (see Fig. 5).

This first paragraph on the author/reader relationship forks constantly between IN (less in) and OUT (less OUT), SELF and SOCIETY, with frequent reversals and links that rejoin the forks. The narrating author then returns to the particular autobiographical text in question. This Custom-House Sketch, he says, will be seen to have a certain propriety (and propriety is due to custom), 'of a kind recognised in literature, as explaining how a large portion of the following pages came into my possession' (7).

The word 'large' turns out not to be wholly true, since by the end of the Sketch he admits that he has not confined himself to the limits of Surveyor Pue's half a dozen sheets of foolscap. 'On the contrary, I have allowed myself [...] nearly or altogether as much licence as if the facts had been entirely of my own invention. What I contend for is the authenticity of outline' (29).

The propriety, in other words, is wholly that of a recognized genre, the mock-authentifying preface, which traditionally introduces either a narrator who can vouch for the facts (like Conrad's Marlow), or a manuscript, in the form of letters (the epistolary novel) or a narrative (the governess's manuscript in *The Turn of the Screw*, but this too is a kind of 'letter' to Douglas). Here we have a curious combination of both, since the author introduces himself, at great

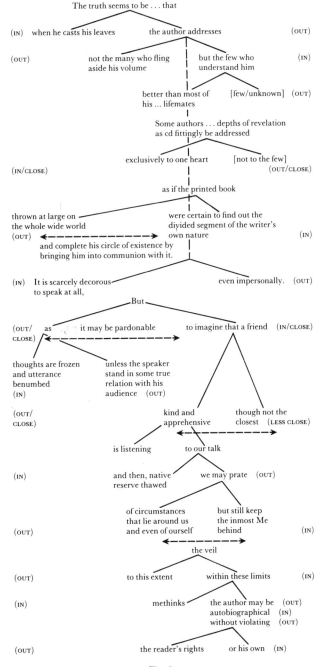

Fig. 5

length, as the one who finds the manuscript which, felt as Surveyor Pue's moving appeal to posterity, is also a letter to him, who will narrate the story yet not as witness or participant. As for the 'facts' vouched for, we even get, not just letters written on paper, but a concrete piece of embroidered stuff, somewhat tattered, that once was the scarlet letter.

And yet the narrating author claims no more than his 'true position as editor, or very little more', and this only is his true reason for assuming a personal relationship with the public. But this true position manages to reinclude the author already at the very start of the Sketch, for his true position as editor *is* his job as Customs Officer, and his personal relation with the public therefore entails a description of this. And so, 'In accomplishing the main purpose [telling his story] it has appeared to be allowable, by a few extra touches, to give a faint representation of a way of life not heretofore described' – just as he had earlier described his way of life 'in the deep quietude of the Old Manse'. In other words, this is a link back to the second node of the whole tree, the 'And now' (versus 'three or four years since'). And this way of life includes 'some of the characters that move in it, among whom the author happens to make one' (7). The Custom-House Sketch is not only an authentification of the story's source but an authentification of the author as 'editor'/narrator, and by the same token an introduction, to the reader, of himself as author. Thus the tree ends (7) (see Fig. 6).

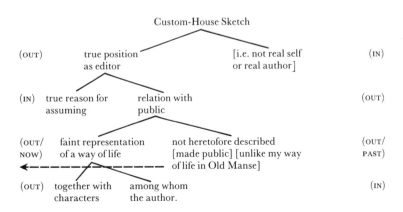

Fig. 6

As we can see, throughout these complex forkings, the Author in the sense of the 'inmost Me' remains always hidden behind the public persona, but with constant reversals, shy peerings forth, movements towards and away from the outer relationship, sentence by sentence and phrase by phrase.

For as has been said, *The Scarlet Letter* is not a story of adultery, it is a story of concealment (Brownell 1909). Notably by Dimmesdale, but also by Hester and Chillingworth, each for different reasons, but who in this sense all resemble the Surveyor of the Custom-House. As 'editor' he reveals, as author he conceals the inmost Me, and a good deal more, behind the persistent antitheses. This concealment and revelation is itself concealed in the title: the scar *let letter*. The very letter stammers itself into revelation of the scar, but in doing so also says *let* the letter speak. Letting things speak, or be, is also custom, or anti-custom according to the period. Hence the importance of this curiously blocked, hesitant style in 'The Custom-House'.

After these two opening paragraphs on the custom of narration, the Author goes on to describe Salem and the Custom-House, and the oppositions become (as already hinted in the first trees) those of the past (alive and bustling) versus the present (decayed); of past aggressive boldness versus present softness and security; of ancestors versus descendants; of the first emigrant versus himself; of the Old versus the New World; of vessels from Africa or South America versus the granite steps of the port (OUT/IN); of his aged officers versus his relative youth; of Surveyor Pue versus himself. And so on. Thus if we shrink and summarize the trees of the opening paragraphs on the custom of narration as the apex of a much larger tree, the beginning of 'The Custom-House' is as shown in Figure 7.

It would be fastidious to show here and in the same detail that the style of the entire Sketch functions exactly like that of the opening paragraphs, but I have analysed it and ask to be believed that it is so. Indeed the oppositions become so enmeshed below the surface rhetorical order that the 'scientific' Chomskian tree-symbol should really be abandoned and replaced by the anti-order (unrepresentable) image of the rhizome, which Deleuze (1976) prefers for dealing with the variously demential aspects of human discourse. Hawthorne's style is not demential, and does have that surface rhetorical order. But my point is this: if it were materially and legibly possible to present, on one page, a tree of the whole Sketch called 'the Custom-House', it would look like a huge letter A, richly embroidered with smaller, reiterated A's.

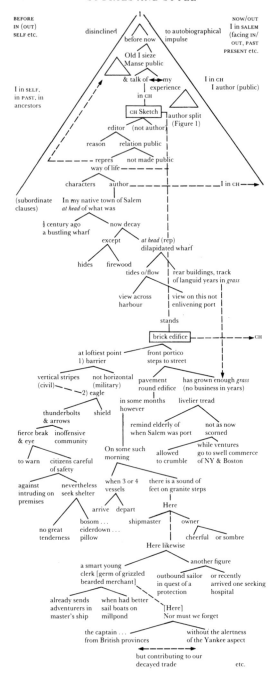

Fig. 7

The Letter

Lacan has written most eloquently about letters – not only in the famous Seminar on 'The Purloined Letter', deconstructed by Derrida and further deconstructed by Barbara Johnson – but also, and more importantly for me here, in 'L'Instance de la Lettre dans l'inconscient' (1957, in 1966, 493–528), on the letter as signifier that 'insists', that moves from signifier to signifier without ever revealing a vulgarly definite signified. It is we who do this when we try to interpret the dream, the symptom, the action, the poem, or other signifying chains. Serge Leclaire (1968, 1972) has gone further and linked the letter with the earliest inscriptions of caresses on the human body, the creation of erogenous zones around a scar or dimple or any part marking a distance between two lips or ridges. He uses the word 'letter' as metaphor because of its abstract quality, and here I quote from Jean-Jacques Lecercle, who has written about this in English:

it is the mark of an absent object, defined by differential significance. It is both there, in the erogenous zone, as a trace, and distinct from it, detached from the body on which it is inscribed. It is this abstract quality which allows it to persist [...] The term that links the two aspects of the letter is 'different' [a physical distance and a temporal difference between primary satisfaction and present unsatisfactory fulfilment]. The letter [...] is both material and abstract, physical and ideal. It is the first element in the system which, according to Leclaire, constitutes the unconscious. The second element is the object. Desire is produced by the illusion of a missing primary object – marked and disguised by the letter.

(1985, 147)

And Lecercle reminds us in a footnote that the primary experience is an event, rather than an object, that is to say, it is unrepeatable.

This physical inscription of the letter, primarily on the body but insistently as a trace in the unconscious, reminds us also of all that Derrida has been telling us about *écriture* as a trace, or architrace, of both difference and deferral. And also, here, of Hawthorne's style in 'The Custom-House'. And of the concrete piece of stuff sewn to Hester's breast, which she had to pick up and resew on after her one gesture of defiance in the forest, and which she kept for life, long after its meaning had been forgotten by the outside world. This physical inscription is also foreshadowed in the author's gesture as he puts the piece of stuff to his own breast, and feels a burning sensation.

'A' as entry into the story, into the strange alphabet of *The Scarlet Letter*. Just as the Custom-House, both as building and as fictional portico, opens onto the Prison and its Portal, from which emerges

Hester with the letter embroidered on her breast, so the style of 'The Custom-House' represents that letter which, as symbol, 'stands for' a story other than and previous to the one we are about to read, which is the story of the scarlet letter itself and its effect – an effect of reading the letter – and not the story behind the scarlet letter, which is an absent story, referred to but never told.

Language-games

In one of the most interesting essays I have read about *The Scarlet Letter*, Gabriel Josipovici (1971) argues that the letter is not a natural but a conventional sign, and is thus dependent on what language-game we play with it. It is true that Hawthorne is deliberately elusive about it, and reduced the crude Puritan 'Ad' for Adultery to 'A', thus allowing for multi-meaning. Hester, says Josipovici, accepts the conventional nature of the letter and is therefore able to transform its meaning, and to behave in such a way as to cause its meaning eventually to be transformed by the society which has forgotten its original meaning.

The task of Chillingworth, on the other hand, is to turn the silence of nature into discourse, nature into allegory and meaning. Out of Dimmesdale's resistance art is born, between the silence of nature and the verbalization of allegory. But, Josipovici goes on, the silence of nature can only be conveyed in a wholly natural language. A conventional language must fail to convey it. What is required then is a language that is both natural and conventional: the hieroglyph. But for a language of genuine hieroglyphs the world would have to be absolutely meaningful in itself. All the writer can do therefore is to articulate the conditions for a hieroglyphic language. This is what Hawthorne does in *The Scarlet Letter*.

Pearl, herself a living hieroglyph, is what Dimmesdale would suppress. Once acknowledged, there is nothing more to write. The novel is built out of the suppression of its own origin, it steers between the silence of Dimmesdale and the knowledge of Chillingworth, as does Pearl. The book, according to Josipovici, is like Pearl, but the author is like Hester (that is, he knows that the letter is a conventional sign). *The Scarlet Letter* is more than the story of Hester and her badge, it is also the story of how Hawthorne settled on his theme, finding not just the manuscript but the letter itself, a physical object. And rather than write what he shows he could have written, describing the characters of the Custom-House 'with the freedom of a

Dickens or a Hardy', he 'submits to the letter's reality: it is in a room, in a building, but there is nothing *in* the letter, it just is'. Yet the narrating author feels it has deep significance:

The book which grows from this meditation, then, is Hawthorne's scarlet letter, living, like Pearl, and evading the deadly probing of those who, like Chillingworth, would pluck out its secret. But it can only do this because, like Hester Prynne, it recognizes that the letter is not a natural sign whose meaning must be unearthed. Yet it is more than the first letter of the alphabet.

(1971, 176; Norton, 428)

I have quoted and summarized Josipovici in some detail because his thoughtful essay confirms my intuition about Hawthorne's style as itself a 'hieroglyph'. As style ideally should be – at least in a 'romance' as opposed to a realistic novel.

In that perspective, however, I am not sure that the so-called realistic narrative of 'The Custom-House', always discussed as Hawthorne's attempt to show what he could do in that vein if he chose, is all that 'realistic'. Or rather, it is more like hyper-realism to kill a certain type of realism. The great illusion of realism was the delirium of plenitude: to capture it all, to put it all in, to explore both terms of every opposition. But as against that, the text had to be 'readerly', transparent as a window on the world, and the whole art was to balance this and other contradictions (Barthes 1970, Hamon 1972, Brooke-Rose 1981). Hawthorne does not 'explore' both terms of every opposition as the realistic novel does (oppositions of character, event, and so on), nor does he 'balance' them. He touches them lightly and intertwines them completely. In this sense his language is not 'readerly'.

As I have indicated, the whole of 'The Custom-House' is written in the forking antithetical style that I analysed for the first few paragraphs. There is hardly a word – whether physical feature or abstract notion or both – that is not followed by its opposite: youth and age, past and present, haleness and sickness, sailing in and sailing out, risk and protection, sensuous attachment to Salem and the moral quality of that sentiment, dirt and a magic broom, good and evil, knowledge and ignorance, curse and prayer, the sword and the bible, and so on, each item copresent yet each also annulling the other in antithesis, which is itself annulled through a mediating notion or a reversal.

The result has a referential density quite at odds with the supposed transparence of realistic writing which, when too exhaustive, can turn into a 'metonymic overkill', as has been said of Robbe-Grillet's

descriptions (Lodge 1977a, 237–9), and that of course is the undermining point by then. But the density here is not in fact wholly
referential, it is also and mainly rhetorical. The descriptions and
portraits remain obstinately static behind the obsessionally forking
style. It would be difficult to imagine the characters of 'The Custom-
House' at any moment sufficiently 'alive', as they say of realistic
novels, to become characters of any fiction to come (indeed the present, for Hawthorne, is decayed and dull). For all the supposed
attempt at realism, the style belongs to what Barthes calls the Symbolic Code (not the Referential or even the Hermeneutic), through
its rhetorical entry, Antithesis. And the editor/author of the Sketch
soon forgets about these 'real' characters and leaves them in the
limbo of dead letters when he reaches his real subject at last: his
'decapitation' or replacement by another Surveyor after a political
change, which frees him, and his finding of the half dozen pages
and a piece of stuff, the tattered but still embroidered and burning
letter A.

    This densely complex style naturally loosens out in the story itself,
for a story must advance, and 'take life' from this motion, it cannot
afford the static *piétinement* of 'The Custom-House'. In fact, *The Scarlet
Letter* has to be extremely selective, since it spans the years of Pearl's
childhood and eventually that of Hester's whole life, chiefly, of course,
in summary and ellipsis. But the obsessional exploitation of oppositions is still there, not only in the characters and events, but also
in the static scenes, themselves antithetically structured, and these
oppositions have often been noted, particularly those between the
heart and the head, the tribal promise of love and the tribal promise
of death, the natural and the institutional, the hidden and the
revealed, the silenced and the said. And they are also there in the
detail of each scene, from the opening paragraph, in the hooded
and the bared heads waiting outside the prison, in the necessity
for all Utopian founders to allot virgin soil to a cemetery on the
one hand, and to a prison on the other.

    In addition, there are many visual echoes of the forking image,
if only in the number of focusing scenes, of which Chapter 1 is the
most immediately striking. James (1879) complains that the word
'sphere' occurs too often, yet it too links 'The Custom-House', where
we hear of 'the circle of existence' and its 'divided segment of the
author's nature', to the prison-door where the observers in a circle
all focus upon Hester. And any two radii of a circle, together with
the arc, form a letter A.

The peculiar intensity of the story is, I suggest, due to this antithetical structure projected from 'the Custom-House' by the editor/author and his own split/private personality. For as commenting narrating author, he is constantly both there and not there, discreetly limited by and filtered through one point of view at a time: that of the crowd, that of Hester, that of Chillingworth, that of Dimmesdale. But that of the crowd is only the implicit link between any two of the three main characters, and soon merely hovers like background embroidery as we focus on each of them in turn. For it could more aptly be said that each of the three is also the link between the other two. Thus Dimmesdale originally came between Hester and her absent husband, Chillingworth comes between Dimmesdale and Hester in their silent pact, and Hester comes between Dimmesdale and Chillingworth in their supposed friendship. If A is like a human figure, so it is like the eternal triangle: Donne's compasses, with a measuring hinge as hyphen.

'Letters in the shape of figures of men', Hawthorne wrote in his Notebooks in 1839. 'At a distance, the words composed by the letters are alone distinguishable. Close at hand, the figures alone are seen, and not distinguished as letters. Thus things may have a positive, a relative, and a composite meaning, according to the point of view' (1932, 183).

The forking style of 'The Custom-House' also represents all the ambiguities in the story that have caused so much spilling of ink in the innumerable interpretations I shall not rehearse here. But in addition, I suggest, it re-presents the very hieroglyph that symbolizes that ambiguity.

Josipovici argues that Hawthorne is not primarily interested in theology or in psychology but in conveying experience by means of a *map of the journey* (Josipovici's italics). And what are forking paths, even rendered as Chomskian trees, but a sort of map?

F. O. Matthiessen, writing on Symbolism and Allegory in Hawthorne, tells us that Hawthorne 'seems sometimes to have started from a physical object – the minister's black veil, the Faun of Praxiteles', but that he could also start with noting an idea, 'and then working up an embodiment to fit it' (1941, 244). The idea, he says later, 'might itself be hardly more than a nervous *tic*, some freakish notion that possessed him in his solitude'. And he quotes an example of this from the Notebooks: 'To personify If – But – And – Though etc.' Matthiessen adds: 'To be sure, this proved too insubstantial even for Hawthorne, and got no further than his notebook' (242).[4]

I submit that in *The Scarlet Letter* it got a good deal further, and is far more than a freakish notion or a nervous tic, but the very stuff of poetry. I submit that as an idea it in fact rejoined the physical object, the piece of cloth, to form the antithetical style to 'personify If – But – And – Though', a style itself representing the signifier A and all its protean forms along the signifying chain, the human shape, openings both physiological and abstract, the threshold of the narrative, the prison-door, the alpha and omega of the human soul, the house of custom.

---

[4] Part of this chapter is also in Norton as 'From Allegory to Symbolism', 293–300, corresponding to 242–82 of the original book. Matthiessen gives no reference for the quotation from the Notebooks but it occurs in *The American Notebooks, 1841–52*, ed. 1932 (see References), p. 242, item [70].

5

Ill locutions

This century seems to have relived, with greater intensity and sophistication, all the ancient quarrels, and none more than the quarrel between literature and philosophy. For although this has often taken the form of a quarrel between literature and science, basically it's the same quarrel, since ancient philosophy included science, both being searches for the truth, whereas poets, as everyone knows, told lies.

Today, however, we have been brought curiously back to that age in antiquity when philosophy could embrace not only science but politics and metaphysics and literature, even if poets lied and writing was a threat to pure thought. We seem, at any rate, much closer to those times, and notably to pre-Socratic times, than we did earlier this century when, as I suggested in Chapter 3 (30), science and poetry were still deeply opposed in a two-truths theory, one for poetry and one for science, which was only a refurbished version of the nineteenth-century two-truths theory, one for religion (a 'higher' truth) and one for science.

Today literary critics have apparently come out of their entrenchment and in various ways have stopped, or think they have stopped, hiding behind a higher truth. Nevertheless, they have done this by opening out onto other disciplines which are often considered scientific, or which at least claim to use scientific methods, such as psychoanalysis, sociology, linguistics, different kinds of logic or even mathematics. And all these, like philosophy, more or less still claim to seek truth. We thus have a curious double situation.

On the one hand, the movement which led Plato to exclude poets from his Republic, and writing from his notion of the truth is, according to Derrida, regularly repeated in the logocentric tradition to which we belong, recurring for example in the work of J. L. Austin and that of his disciple John Searle, whose texts, as Derrida shows, deconstruct themselves exactly in the same way as do those of Plato or Rousseau or Saussure, or even, as others have shown, those of Derrida himself, in the sense that the author repeats the very gesture which he has criticized in his predecessors.

On the other hand, and largely thanks to this deconstructive activity, philosophy and literature have moved closer together in the work of many scholars, who have come round to proclaim, or to admit, sometimes regretfully, that the language of all the human sciences without exception, and indeed all language, is literary through and through, rather as one might say rotten through and through.

There is an ingenious reading of J. L. Austin for instance, by Shoshana Felman (1980), who tries to turn Austin into Derrida, partly in order to show that Derrida has misread him. His famous act of exclusion of the 'non-serious' (the literary) from his performative (such as promises uttered by actors in a play, or jokes, or poetry), is read as itself non-serious. His sentence defining the performative, which says 'I must not be joking, for example, or writing a poem' is read by Felman as itself a joke (188), on the well-demonstrated and delightful grounds that Austin has such fun with language, takes such pleasure in it, and transforms his whole performance into a performative, which in the end, through his vocabulary of desire and excitement, itself represents promise, while the constative represents constancy and the difficulty of remaining faithful to a text.

Jonathan Culler comments:

Still, to treat the exclusion of jokes as a joke prevents one from explaining the logical economy of Austin's project, which can admit infelicities and exploit them so profitably only by excluding the fictional and the non-serious. This logic is what is at stake, not Austin's attitude or his liking for what Felman calls 'le fun'.

(1983, 118n)

I shall not enter here into the quarrel between Derrida and Speech Act Theory. What I want to do is to look at some of Austin's examples in *How to do Things with Words* (1965; 1971), and relate them to narrative technique, or rather, to one very particular aspect of narrative technique, namely a type of sentence which represents two different kinds of perception – reflective and non-reflective – which philosophers have recognized, even if they have had some difficulty in representing the latter, except in long-winded descriptions about automatically side-stepping puddles (Russell) or counting cigarettes (Sartre), and becoming conscious of this only if asked about it afterwards. The type of literary sentence which does this much better is a pure invention of narrative and cannot occur outside narrative.

It is usually referred to as 'free indirect discourse' (formerly 'free indirect speech') but for reasons to be explained I wish to avoid the word 'discourse', and shall follow Ann Banfield (*Unspeakable Sentences*, 1983), whom I shall be discussing in some detail, and who calls it 'Represented Speech and Thought', precisely because she opposes this type of sentence to 'discourse' in the sense of speech, or speech act in the communications model. This opposition between *histoire* (history, not story, best translated here as narration) and *discours* (the communications model or 'system of person', with deictics etc. as in speech) is that established by Benveniste (1966), and will become clear below. It is not to be confused with the now more familiar narratological opposition between *histoire* (story) and *discours* (treatment, *agencement*) established by Genette (1972), which derives from the opposition 'fabula/sjuzhet' of the Russian Formalists.

Swans on Mars

As a non-philosopher I am often surprised at the sentences that philosophers think up to make their points. With Austin in particular, it is amusing to see how many of his examples are cast in fictional narrative form – which is odd for someone who claims to exclude fiction as non-serious. Linguistic philosophy is full of fictional suppositions such as this one:

> Suppose that before Australia is discovered X says 'All swans are white'. If you later find black swans in Australia, is X refuted? Is his statement false now? Not necessarily: he will take it back but he could say 'I wasn't talking about swans absolutely everywhere: for example, I was not making a statement about possible swans on Mars.
>
> (Austin 1962, 143)

Under our eyes, X has become a peculiarly complex fictional character. A novelist might want to continue the dialogue to see how neurotically X might develop.

In Lecture VIII we get the odd distinction between phonetic, phatic and rhetic acts – the first not illustrated since 'it is merely the act of uttering certain noises'. The phatic act, however, turns out to be our old friend 'direct speech' or *oratio directa* (now called 'direct discourse' but I am avoiding that word):

He said 'I shall be there'
He said 'Get out'
He said 'Is it in Oxford or Cambridge?'

While the rhetic act turns out to be our equally familiar friend
oratio obliqua or 'indirect speech':

> He said he would be there
> He told me to get out
> He asked whether it was in Oxford or Cambridge

Now indirect speech is always summary: we are not given the
words uttered, and this can even lead to ambiguity, as in the sentence
analysed by Quine (1976, 185–96), 'Oedipus said that his mother
was beautiful', which can be read in two ways (see Banfield 1982, 17).

Austin later drops these terms, which have not survived, and calls
the phatic act *Locution*, giving more examples:

> He said to me 'Shoot her!'
> He said to me 'You can't do that'

While the rhetic act can be either *Illocution*:

> He urged (advised, ordered . . .) me to shoot her
> He protested against my doing it

Or *Perlocution* (*effect incorporated, two degrees*):

(a) He persuaded me to shoot her
     He pulled me up, checked me
(b) He got me to (made me) shoot her
     He stopped me, brought me to my senses

The accuracy of and the philosophical reasons for these distinctions
are not in question here, but formally the three types correspond
to the traditional narrative distinctions that Genette (1972) classifies
under *Distance* (distance between what he calls the narrator's voice
and the character's actual words): 'direct' being the least distant
(language imitating language), 'indirect' more so (the character's
words summarized or even interpreted), and 'narrativized' (a new
refinement) being the most distant, the character's words transformed into an action and thus even more irrecoverable than in
indirect speech, as in for instance 'I informed him of my decision
to leave.'

Clearly language has developed these different registers for specific
reasons that have to do with distancing of the speaker's perception
from that of the person whose words he is reporting, and hence
with the indirect manipulation of his interlocutor.

But what *don't* we find in Austin's examples? Obviously, since he excludes fiction as non-serious, what is missing is the type of sentence specific to narrative, invented by narrative and impossible in the speech situation as opposed to that of narration. What is missing is the type of sentence Banfield calls *Represented Speech and Thought*, traditionally called Free Indirect Speech, and now called Free Indirect Discourse, *discours indirect libre* (previously *style indirect libre*), *erlebte Rede* . . .

Experienced Speech and Thought

'Experienced' (*erlebte*) is perhaps the best of the traditional terms, for it is less abstract than 'free indirect' and reminds us that 'experience' is being expressed. But for reasons that will become clear, Banfield's is even clearer: *Represented* Speech and Thought. This is the type of sentence which gives the vocabulary and idiom characteristic of direct speech, that is, expressive elements such as exclamations and questions, as well as the deictics of the speaking/thinking person in his situation (*now*, for instance, although in a narrative past); but it retains the shift of tense and (when necessary) the change of person from first to third which are characteristic of indirect speech. It is like indirect speech but without the impression of summary, since we get the actual words and expression of the character. Here is an invented example:

> (1) He was walking down the street. Would he find the courage to tell his father? Yesterday, there had been nothing but trust. But now, yes, oh God, he was afraid.

The presence of the thinking or perceiving character is given. We get the tense-shift and change of person of indirect speech rather than those of direct (Shall I find the courage to tell dad), but we also get the deictics and personal vocabulary and often the characteristic syntax of direct speech (question-form, exclamation, the deictics *yesterday* and *now* although we are in the narrative past). We shall see later why 'dad' cannot be inserted into this sentence.

Because of these dual characteristics this type of sentence – which appears spontaneously in all European narrative with the rise of the novel, but which was not recognized or formally analysed until the end of the last century – has been regarded as 'mixed', and the traditional view has been and still is that the character's thought or speech is given in his own words but that the 'narrator's voice' is also heard, in the narrational tenses and in the distancing third person, thus creating an ironic distance and indirect comment.

This is certainly the way most people have come to read this type of sentence, which is often used for comic effects, and these are automatically attributed to an ironic over-voice. The first example, from George Eliot, is Represented Thought, the second, from Zola, is Represented Speech:

> (2) A wild idea shot through Mr Chubb's brain: could this grand visitor be Harold Transome? Excuse him; he had been given to understand by his cousin that ...
>
> *(Felix Holt)*
>
> (3) En tout cas, Monsieur était prévenu, elle préférait flanquer son diner au feu, si elle ratait, à cause de la révolution.
>
> *(Germinal)*

But we can get a represented letter or a represented conversation, as in these two examples from Forster's *A Room with a View*:

> (4) Of course Miss Bartlett accepted. And equally of course, she felt that she would prove a nuisance, and begged to be given an inferior spare room – something with no view, anything. Her love to Lucy.
>
> (5) A conversation then ensued, not on unfamiliar lines. Miss Bartlett was, after all, a wee bit tired, and thought they had better spend the morning settling in; unless Lucy would rather like to go out? Lucy would rather like to go out, as it was her first day in Florence, but of course, she could go alone. Miss Bartlett could not allow this. Of course she would accompany Lucy everywhere. Oh, certainly not: Lucy would stop with her cousin. Oh no! that would never do! Oh yes!

By the time we get to Virginia Woolf and Joyce we have this changing viewpoint highlighted, and the supposed ironic voice seems a little louder and more intrusive, indeed in Joyce the device is already part of the parody of narrative styles displayed in *Ulysses*:

> (6) 'I met Clarissa in the Park this morning', said Hugh Whitbread, diving into the casserole, anxious to pay himself this little tribute, for he had only to come to London and he met everybody at once; but greedy, one of the greediest men she had known, Milly Brown thought, who observed men with unflinching rectitude.
>
> *(Mrs Dalloway)*

(7) Cissy Caffrey caught the two twins and she was itching to
give them a ringing good clip on the ear but she didn't because
she thought he might be watching but she never made a bigger
mistake in all her life because Gerty could see without looking
that he never took his eyes off her.

(*Ulysses*)

Despite the traditionally clear 'Milly Brown thought' in (6), there
is a blurring of Represented Thought and what Banfield calls narration *per se*, or Narrative Sentence, which *can* carry authorial comment (for example 'who observed men with unflinching rectitude'
could be authorial comment or part of Milly's consciousness). In
(7), what looks here like a changing viewpoint from Cissy to Gerty
is not so in context, but we do have to reread. The main ambiguity
I shall be discussing, however, is that between Represented Thought
and the Narrative Sentence.

In practice both Stylistics and Linguistics treat a Narrative Sentence as Represented Thought as long as a character is clearly present
as perceiving:

(8) Emma mit un châle sur ses épaules, ouvrit la fenêtre et
s'accouda. La nuit était noire. Quelques gouttes de pluie
tombaient.

(*Madame Bovary*)

Formally there is no distinction here between a Narrative Sentence
in the progressive, that tells us that the night was dark, and that
rain was falling, and a sentence of Represented Thought that represents what Emma was passively perceiving (as opposed to consciously thinking). One test (apart from the presence of a perceiving
character) would be to see whether one can insert a deictic such
as *now* into that past: 'the night was now dark', where a Narrative
Sentence can have (but unnecessarily): 'the night was then dark'.

This is Benveniste's famous distinction between *discours* (or speech
as part of a communications model, which he calls 'the system of
person') and *histoire* (narration), which he clearly envisaged as both
historical and fictional (history and story). For the difference between
so-called truth and fiction is not linguistically marked (a lie uses
the same syntax), any more than is irony, since irony is saying something and meaning more, or even the opposite, or letting a character
say something that has a clear meaning for him while another

interpretation is also possible for another character or for the reader. But it is made possible contextually and culturally. Parody, too, is culturally determined (see Ch. 13).

I have on purpose given examples from Banfield, because her ideas caused quite a rumpus among literary critics. I cannot go into the detail of it here, but I do want to take up its main thesis as something that clearly interests philosophy, something that should convince literary critics more than it has so far succeeded in doing, and something that ought to make writers think.

Banfield calls this type of sentence Represented Speech and Thought because it *represents* (as opposed to imitating, as does direct speech) the words or perceptions of characters, and the spontaneous development of this device has had two consequences: one in the way the device has been interpreted by analysts of it, which is what I shall mostly deal with here; another in the way it has come to be used by writers, and this I shall touch on at the end of the chapter.

Two voices or one?

Literary critics, then, have persisted in seeing a dual-voiced device, and this is because they remain in a communication model of addresser-addressee.[1]

Certain linguists, however, make a distinction, like Benveniste, between the 'discourse' (or speech) of the communication model, and the language of narration (*histoire*), which is, literally, unspeakable: 'No one speaks here, the events seem to narrate themselves', says Benveniste (1966, 241; 1971, 206). This language of narration cannot use the pronouns *I/you* without passing into the speech situation, or the deictics that go with these (*here, now, tomorrow, last week*, etc.), and it has its own tenses. It cannot use the present tense or the present perfect, for instance, or the future, which belong to the speech situation.

The tense-system of narrative is particularly clear in French, where the *passé simple* or aorist is wholly restricted to literary narrative and unusable in speech except in mock-quotes. Contrary to what some may think, it is still very much alive in narrative and necessary to it, though not, interestingly, in the second person, for the Narrative Sentence does not belong to the communications model and thus

---

[1] I am using the anonymous 'literary critics' because I do not wish to enter into the controversy and praise or blame specific discussions. Bibliographical references can be found in Banfield and in McHale 1978; 1983.

excludes the second person and all its deictics (such as the imperative). Indeed, publishers' editors insist on the *passé simple* in translations of the English past, which has no such 'literary' vs. 'speech'
style. The exclusion of the *passé simple* from speech can be dated
very precisely in the sixteenth century, says Banfield, and it is not
by chance that Represented Speech and Thought, which is based
on the Narrative Sentence but allows certain deictics, can first be
found in La Fontaine (poetic narratives) and develops with the novel,
a form specifically associated with writing, as opposed to the mediaeval taking down of essentially oral narratives (Banfield, Ch. 6).

Benveniste's theory, as well as Käte Hamburger's work on the
'epic preterite' and *erlebte Rede* (1973), are used by Banfield to analyse
these two types of unspeakable sentences that are Narrative Sentences and Represented Speech and Thought. She takes as her cue
Kuroda's discovery of a literary style in Japanese that 'transcends
the paradigm of linguistic performance in terms of speaker and
hearer' (Banfield, 11) and involves an epistemological distinction
between two forms of language, one used to indicate fact, the other
to express the speaker's state (even an emotive adjective like *sad*
can indicate a fact or express a state). This distinction seems roughly
equivalent to that between *énoncé* and *énonciation*, sometimes translated as 'utterance' vs. 'uttering' (Todorov 1970; transl. 1973) or,
by me (1981) as 'statement' vs., 'utterance'. But Kuroda also distinguishes between reflective and non-reflective consciousness. These
elements enable Banfield to develop several hypotheses in a way
that accounts linguistically for the types of sentences in question.

Let us go back to sentence (4), Miss Bartlett's letter. Banfield
stops the quotation at 'Her love to Lucy'. But the text goes on:

(4a) Of course Miss Bartlett accepted; and equally of course, she
felt sure that she would prove a nuisance, and begged to
be given an inferior spare room – something with no view,
anything. Her love to Lucy. And equally of course, George
Emerson would come to tennis on the Sunday week.

Clearly the last sentence cannot represent Miss Bartlett's letter,
since she is away and unaware of the arrangements at the Honey-
churches. We have passed from Represented Speech (or Writing)
in the mind of the reader of the letter, to Represented Thought (in
the same mind), which takes over the 'and equally of course' from
the reader's reactions to Miss Bartlett's letter. The traditional view
would be that the 'of course' and 'equally of course' come from

the 'narrator'. In Banfield's theory however, both these would 'represent' Miss Bartlett's way of writing (just as Sentence 5 represented her way of talking) as reflected in the letter-reader's mind. Another of Banfield's examples, from Jane Austen, is even more revealing, since it can in itself be read as a Narrative Sentence on first reading, but must be read as Represented Thought on second reading:

(9) He [Frank Churchill] stopped and rose again, and seemed quite embarrassed. He was more in love with her than Emma had supposed.

(*Emma*)

Banfield discusses this, and other examples that contain the proper name or kinship names like *dad* or *papa*, or even a title and surname ('Miss Bartlett'), under what she calls non-reflective consciousness. It would be too complicated here to rehearse the details of this essential chapter in her book, but clearly one doesn't think of oneself by one's name. Here the sentence from *Emma* must be read as character's perception second time round, since we know by then that Emma was wrong, and a realist novel's Narrative Sentence by convention cannot lie (in the sense that it must be coherent with the rest of that fictional world). The use of the name or kinship-word is thus an extra convention that marks non-reflective consciousness. This is why one could not insert *dad* in Sentence (1), which represented reflective consciousness.

Banfield's theory has been attacked, not by linguists but by literary critics who cling to various versions of the dual-voiced theory, and above all to the notion of a narrative *voice*. Banfield on the other hand insists that the word 'narrator' has become a hold-all substitute for the evacuated and taboo word 'author', so that we now have 'two competing theories about the text's unity, one which assigns all the sentences of the text to a single narrating voice and another which sees author and narrator as distinct constructs of literary theory, restricting the latter to [here she cites Hamburger] "cases where the narrating poet actually does 'create' a narrator, namely the first person narrator of the first person narrative"' (185). Clearly she defends the second theory. And she adds that 'since the thesis of the author's silence ultimately touches the language of the text it is fair to ask whether linguistic argumentation can enable us to decide between these two theories'.

On the mere question of constructs and terminology we would have to ask what useful function is fulfilled by simply substituting 'narrator' where critics used to say 'author', which then forces further distinctions between explicit/implicit, reliable/unreliable narrators and all the other terms inherited from Booth (1961).[2]

But beyond the terminology, Banfield seems to have hit somewhere below the belt of reflective consciousness, at the question of 'authority'. Her theory essentially draws a distinction between 'optionally narratorless sentences of pure narration and sentences of represented speech and thought', both 'unspeakable' but representing two poles of narrative style, narration and the representation of consciousness (17, 18). And in Chapter 5 she deals with the type of 'ambiguous' sentence I have been talking about, which can be read either at one pole or at the other (but, like Gombrich's duck-rabbit, not both at the same time, and so not *really* ambiguous). It is this type of sentence which has become the centre of the controversy, precisely because 'it seems to combine features of both narration and represented speech and thought', and it has been used as 'counter-evidence' for a supposed 'merging' of two voices, and as proof of 'the constantly shifting data of literary style' (12) or the mysterious inaccessibility of literature to scientific analysis, in the kind of argument which, like religion before the onslaught of science, attacks the very attempt to define narrative style linguistically.[3]

Banfield's thesis is presented through extremely rigorous linguistic argumentation that shows, for example, why indirect speech cannot be derived from direct (28ff.) or, more generally, that extends Chomsky's grammar to account for these 'unspeakable' sentences of Narration and Represented Speech and Thought, by adding a top node E (Expression) to Chomsky's $\bar{S}$ (pp. 40ff.), from which expressive elements such as exclamations descend directly and announce subjectivity, rather in the same way as Ross (1970) posited an introductory performative to all declaratory sentences; whereas

---

[2] Clearly the 'author' is behind *all* the sentences of the novel, including those of 'direct speech' in dialogue. But we need a construct to distinguish this 'author' from that of Narrative Sentences, and 'narrator' won't do. F. K. Stanzel (1979) suggests 'authorial narrator'. In this book I have preferred 'narrating author', to get away from the tiresomely ambiguous word 'narrator'.

[3] These are her terms. As I indicated in Chapter 2, I do not myself believe in all 'scientific' analysis of literature, for instance, in the (often metaphoric) borrowing of linguistic terms in the analysis of broad narrative structures. But in so far as Banfield is dealing with sentences, as opposed to broad structures, her highly knowledgeable use of linguistics is fully operative. It is also important to know that she is a literary critic who has mastered linguistics, not a linguist who applies linguistics to literature, often without the sensitivity of a literary critic.

deictics and evaluative words are embeddable within the S which wholly represents the announced subjectivity or character's viewpoint. She does not invent sentences the way philosophers and linguists do, but goes through, element by element and literary example by literary example, all the formal differences between sentences that are uttered in a context of the communication model (first and second person, addressee-oriented adverbs, subject/object inversion in parentheticals, echo-questions and so on), and shows that direct speech in a narrative naturally belongs to this system of person since it imitates communication, whereas Narrative Sentences and sentences of Represented Speech and Thought (reflective and non-reflective) do not imitate but represent, in words, what does not occur in words (actions, gestures, expressions, objects, landscapes, and so on, for Narrative Sentences) or what does not necessarily occur in words (consciousness for Represented Speech and Thought).

For this she posits a formula with both a SPEAKER and an ADDRESSEE/HEARER, and a PRESENT for the communication model (the SPEAKER being one with the E of Expression); but a SELF for the Unspeakable Sentences, a SELF who is separate from the SPEAKER. Her first rule, which has naturally received the brunt of the attacks, is 1E/1 SELF (and of course there can be many Es, and hence SELFS, in one TEXT, however brief, as we have seen from the Forster and Woolf examples). That SELF perceives in its own PRESENT which is past in the narrative (NOW = PAST) is her second rule.

In discourse [what I have called speech], the speaker's telling cannot be separated from his expression. But in narration, a sentence exists whose sole function is to tell. Alongside this sentence is another whose sole function is to represent subjectivity. When a NOW is invoked in narration, language no longer recounts: it represents. This is as true for first person narration as for third person narration.

(178)

The language of narration, she goes on to show, has no 'voice', no accent, no dialect (otherwise it becomes 'discourse', or what I have called speech, as in, say, *Huckleberry Finn*, or Russian *skaz*):

If narration contains a narrator, this 'I' is not speaking, quoted by an author; he is narrating. If it does not, then the story 'tells itself', as Benveniste has it. Rather, it is of its nature to be totally ignorant of an audience, and this fact is reflected in its very language.

(179)

She goes on to say that it is the language of narrative that 'realises most fully in its form and not only in its intent the essence of the literary which has for long been taken to be the achievement of

poetry', and quotes J. S. Mill's contrast between poetry and elo-
quence, likening it to that between narration and 'discourse' (speech
or 'personal system' of addresser/addressee).

So far I have seen no convincing reply to Banfield's arguments,
though perhaps they might one day be improved on by other
linguists. Literary critics tend to think that the mere production
of supposed counter-examples (assuming they are such and do not
in fact prove Banfield's case) can demolish a linguistic argument,
whereas, as in science, only a better linguistic argument can do so.
As Banfield puts it:

For a sentence to qualify as a syntactic counter-evidence to 1E/1 SELF , it must
be either (i) a single E containing both a first person and a third person SELF
or (ii) a single E containing more than one expressive construction, where all are
not interpreted as the expression of the same SELF .

(188)

For instance, I myself thought I had found counter-examples from
Jane Austen, but they do not fulfil these conditions and therefore
illustrate Banfield's thesis. Emma is imagining Jane Fairfax married to
Knightley, and she wickedly imitates Jane's companion Miss Bates:

(10) 'If it would be good to her, I am sure it would be evil to
himself; a very shameful and degrading connection. How
would he bear to have Miss Bates belonging to him? – To
have her haunting the Abbey, and thanking him all day long
for his great kindness in marrying Jane? – "So very kind and
obliging! But he always had been such a very kind neighbour!"
And then fly off, through half a sentence, to her mother's
old petticoat. "Not that it was such a very old petticoat either
– for it would last a great while – and indeed, she must
thankfully say that their petticoats were all very strong."'
'For shame, Emma! Do not mimic her!'

I quote Mrs Weston's reproach to show that we are in dialogue
(direct speech). Of course we hear another voice here, which assumes
responsibility for the Represented Speech of Miss Bates exactly as
an *author* does, but it is Emma's voice, and the Represented Speech
is only that of Miss Bates as 'experienced' by her. It has been embedded in the direct speech, exactly as the 'narrativized' speech of 'thanking him all day long' or 'flying to her mother's old petticoat' are
further embedded within it. For Represented Speech, although
'unspeakable' (and this Banfield does not say), can be used inside
direct speech, even in 'real life', but only in narration, when we

are telling a story and unconsciously using literary devices. And I suspect that this only occurs among fairly literate speakers, whereas non-literate speakers tend to retell with direct speech ('And I said to him ... And he said "Oh!"').

Or Mrs Bennett bidding farewell to Mr Bingley in *Pride and Prejudice*:

(11) 'Next time you call', said she, 'I hope we shall be more lucky.'
      He should be particularly happy at any time, &c &c; and if she would give him leave, would take an early opportunity of waiting on them.
      'Can you come tomorrow?'
      Yes, he had no engagement at all for tomorrow; and her invitation was accepted with alacrity.

Who says '&c &c'? It is very easy to hear 'narrator' irony about polite formulas. But in Banfield's theory, the '&c &c' would represent the character's own awareness of them, though at a non-verbalized semi-conscious level (formulas he could add but does not, or formulas he is adding and still uttering, while thinking '&c &c', but which we are not given). We thus have a passage from Represented Speech to Represented Thought (perhaps non-reflective). Such passages are swift in Jane Austen: here we pass from direct speech to Represented Speech to Represented Thought and back to Represented Speech, then to direct speech and back again to Represented Speech, ending with a Narrative Sentence that names the acceptance without giving the words ('narrativized' discourse in Genette's system).

We have a situation, then, in which a linguist has shown the grammatical evidence for one viewpoint only, the character's in Represented Speech and Thought, while non-linguists cling to a narrator's viewpoint as well, to which certain bits and pieces of the sentence are attributed on the ground that the character would be incapable of 'thinking' in those terms. Thus the whole subtlety of the device, which represents the complexity of non-verbalized consciousness and even flashes of self-awareness a character may have for a split second, is lost, with value-judgments parcelled out to a narrator (often *also* confused with the author despite the 'taboo', e.g. the view of 'Flaubert' or 'James'). 'But what grammatical evidence of a narrator's point of view do we find?' Banfield asks. 'This is what is problematic in the dual voice claim. The second voice of the dual voice position is always the narrator's, never another character's [for example, Emma's in my Sentence (10)]. The logic behind the claim [...] is a case of *petitio principii*.' Certain words of narration in a sentence

of Represented Speech and Thought cannot, it is said, represent
the character's point of view, therefore they represent the narrator's.
'But the missing premiss is none other than the conclusion' (189).[4]

The incapacity to argue in rigorous linguistic terms is understand-
able, if regrettable, in literary critics who attack a linguist. But what
is so strange – and this will be my small contribution to the debate
– is their self-deconstruction, their insistence, by way of the supposed
richness and unaccountability of Literature in scientific terms, on
pushing narrative into 'discourse', on pushing the type of sentence
that is unspeakable and thus absolutely specific to the novel, into
the merely speakable; on pushing the type of sentence that uniquely
represents two levels of perception that have long fascinated philosophers, into a banal 'narrator'/character dichotomy that merely
replaces the author/character dichotomy and harks back to the
author as God, present and authoritative and omniscient in his text;
on pushing such sentences, which distinctively result from the
achievement of writing, back into a communications model. And
this last of course repeats the very gesture that Derrida has revealed
as phonocentric and logocentric, from Plato to Austin and Searle,
as privileging voice and speech over what he calls *l'écriture*, that 'writing in general' of which writing and speech are but particular cases.
L'écriture, or differentiation and deferral and the trace of an origin
that is never there, is once again rejected here.

The novelists

That's for the critics, and ultimately unimportant, although it has
necessarily received the most space in this chapter and this sort
of book. What is sadder has been the misunderstanding of Represented Speech and Thought by writers. Invented spontaneously,
almost unconsciously, unreflectively, then developed very reflectively
indeed, Represented Speech and Thought, like most artistic devices,
eventually became unconscious again, that is, it was not only used
as a cliché (already parodied by Joyce), its subtlety wasted on trivia,
but it was also misused because misunderstood.

Formally, as we have seen, the sentence of Represented Speech

---

[4] Cristopher Nash (1987) perpetuates the notion: 'Once again, by one of the great
sophisticated strategies in literary history, Realism masters that sleight of hand,
of word, *free indirect discourse (style indirect libre)*. The narrator becomes so defoca-
lized that we think there's no "voice" but the character's; standing at the window
peering at the scene, we fail to see the source of the whisper at our ear.' (30)

and Thought can be similar to the Narrative Sentence, indeed identical with it when deictics and other signs of E are not linguistically present, but only the perceiving character. This formal similarity led, inevitably, to these two distinct poles being fused, and the sentence of Represented Speech and Thought being used as narration, to tell, to give narrative information – whole summaries of a situation, for instance, or analepses (flashbacks) of a whole past, which are clearly there to inform the reader and not to represent a character's perceptions, save at the cost of making them rather gross, or at best wholly artificial. This can go on for pages. Such misuse is extremely frequent in the average modern neo-realist novel, including most classical Science Fiction that imitated the worn-out techniques of the realist novel in an attempt to be respectable. This misuse is a direct result, not only of the post-Jamesian (and Aristotelian) condemnation of 'telling' in favour of 'showing', but also of the concomitant attempt to eliminate the author: and since narrative information must be given, the easy solution was to 'filter' it all through a character's mind, however implausibly, thus thoroughly weakening the device into its opposite.

Consequently – and writers on the topic rarely say this – the device at its best belongs wholly to the classical realist novel, and a reaction to its weakening had to come. It came with Camus' *L'Etranger* (1942), written in the present perfect of ordinary speech (as in a journal); and especially with Beckett, who used direct speech as narrative; and with the *nouveau roman* in the fifties.[5] Robbe-Grillet (1962) loudly dismissed the *passé simple* as the hallmark of the traditional novel, and adopted (after Dujardin and Joyce in *Finnegans Wake*) the present tense, which he used in a brilliantly unsettling manner (since time-shifts are necessarily unmarked), though this was soon more weakly imitated. What Robbe-Grillet did not mention as sign of the traditional was Represented Speech and Thought (which he would have called *style indirect libre*), but its jettisoning

---

[5] This isn't always recognized, even by experts, e.g. Stevick (1988) on Ann Quin's supposed 'set of conventions largely of her own devising, and that is why the representation of consciousness in her fiction seems so different from that of anyone else [...] It is not the inner monologue of a character in Virginia Woolf [...] registering sensation, conflating past and present, musing on other people [...] It is not the inner talk of Joyce, as Bloom or Stephen observe the phenomenological world and interrogate themselves' (232). In fact Quin uses either straight narrative sentences ('She thought a woman held her hand', *Passages* 72) or, as more often in *Berg*, direct speech, straight from Beckett and ultimately from Molly Bloom's monologue in *Ulysses*. These are formal remarks, not intended to detract from Quin's originality in other ways.

was implicit in his rejection of the past, as it was in his rejection of *le mythe de la profondeur* (psychological exploration in depth).

At any rate, the device disappeared, together with the traditional narrative sentence in the past tense. The novel passed for a while into 'discourse', a voice speaking (but not two at once) in Beckett, or, in Sarraute, many voices (but one at a time) speaking, thinking, perceiving, in direct speech, or what Voloshinov (Bakhtin 1929b) has called 'free direct speech' (direct speech but not in dialogue). In Robbe-Grillet it was less a voice speaking than a consciousness perceiving, but in present tense deictics. And in Butor we even got the second person plural as central consciousness. And in the trail of this 'avant-garde' writing of the fifties and sixties, Represented Speech and Thought also vanished from the work of individual writers who were not at the time specifically avant-garde, for instance and partially in Doris Lessing, who prefers rich variations of direct speech (in diaries and notebooks). But naturally it still persists in the modern neo-realist novel.

It was a necessary purge, and parallel in a way to the critics' pushing of the 'unspeakable' into the 'speakable', except that the critics remain in the old dispensation of the dual-voice theory which merely replaces the ancient author/character dichotomy with the 'narrator' as ironic God; whereas the modern novel truly dispenses with both narrator and his irony and lets the character speak direct, in 'free direct speech'. As Sontag said long ago (1967), irony, after Nietzsche, is no longer possible, has exhausted itself, and similarly Barthes (1970) insists that classical irony is merely the power of one discourse over another, merely another bit of the Referential Code. Postmodern irony is far more complex than this dual-voiced model (see Wilde 1981). None of the critics writing on Represented Speech and Thought cite many examples after Woolf and Joyce.

It was a necessary purge, and certainly brought new ways of perceiving. Many 'postmodern' writers have adopted this 'free direct' mode, though a few continued at first with 'free indirect' as if it were still alive (see Ch. 13), others play with all literary devices but to explode or undermine them. But Represented Speech and Thought has not been renewed. Perhaps because, according to Derrida, representation is death (see Ch. 3, p. 36). Yet mankind cannot not represent. If it were renewed, it would have to be renewed through some other development, perhaps unimaginable as yet. But where there are artists nothing is unimaginable.

We can, however, understand why Austin and other Speech Act

Theorists after him do not deal with this kind of sentence. First, it is fictitious and therefore non-serious – though that also applies to Austin's swan story (which, however, and I can say it now, is in direct speech, and so not in a traditional narrative mode); but second, and more important, the sentences of both Narration and Represented Speech and Thought are too literary, a biproduct of writing, unspeakable, ill locutions.

6

Ill logics of irony

In the light of the previous chapters on metaphoric thinking and on Represented Thought, I now propose to show how unstable the major concepts in Stephen Crane's *The Red Badge of Courage* keep turning out to be – how, in fact, they deconstruct themselves as we read, so that the irony, which has been the element most resistant to new modes of understanding this text, is bound to be unstable.[1]

I have found four major oppositions: *the hero/the monster, running to/running from, separation/membership, spectator/spectacle*. All these deconstruct themselves, but not simply in a series. Intertwined with each other, they are also caught up in another, subsuming opposition, that of *courage/cowardice*. And the whole of this swallowing act is itself part of a more basic *in/out* opposition that comes into play throughout the narrative in the outsideness or the insideness of the author, in other words, in irony.

Many critics who have disagreed about Crane's irony take the term for granted, and in two ways: they evaluate it positively, assuming that the author's attitude toward his character is clear; and they do not go into its technique, assuming that if something they do not approve of seems to come from the author it must be ironical. Now the positive evaluation of irony has been questioned since Nietzsche (see Ch. 5, p. 79), and reversed by Bakhtin (1929a), for whom irony is typical of the 'monological' novel (as in Tolstoy), where, however complex the viewpoints, the author is always in control and has 'the last word' on his characters, as opposed to the 'dialogical' (as in Dostoevsky), where the hero is always resisting the control that tries to determine him and which includes irony. Yet irony, like interpretation, never ends: even when we are watching

---

[1] This study is based on the Binder edition from Crane's manuscript (1982), which restores many deletions of the Appleton text, including the original Chapter 12. All Chapter references after 12 will thus be double (e.g. 16/17), the first figure representing the Appleton text, the second the Binder text (both Norton, see References).

a character struggle against all definitions of himself, including his own, we are still interpreting ironically.

The techniques involved in irony make it one of the major achievements of the nineteenth-century realist novel, which perfected a unique device to bring us inside a character's mind. This device is the one I discussed in the last chapter, Represented Speech and Thought. In *Red Badge* we get almost no Represented Speech, only Represented Thought which, as we saw, can be close in form to Narrative Sentences and even identical. As I suggested in Chapter 5, Represented Thought has, through misuse, become somewhat of a narrative cliché since the nineteenth century, and disappeared in the mid-twentieth, which phenomenon may support Barthes' contention that irony too had disappeared by then. But these views should not prevent us from analysing the way Represented Thought functions in a traditionally ironic text, especially one in which its distinctiveness is already beginning to get blurred. I shall use the following abbreviations throughout: NS (Narrative Sentence), RT (Represented Thought), RS (Represented Speech – rare), DS (Direct Speech, that is straight from characters, in dialogue). RT/NS will mean an unclear case, NS→RT a Narrative Sentence that slides into Represented Thought.

Distance: Crane and Fleming

The question of viewpoint has too often been taken for granted in criticism of *Red Badge*. It is generally assumed to be that of the hero from the beginning, who is often called 'Fleming' by critics discussing these early passages although we do not learn his surname until Chapter 11. In fact the opposite is the case: two distinct points of view, the narrating author's, in NS, and the character's in RT, are established from the start. For the interpretive convention of the scene filtered through RT, well established in the classical novel, is that the perceiver must be described or stated as present. The 'youthful private' is not introduced until after the introductory scenes (dawn and the camp scene), and when he is, it is in external focalization (except for the word 'eager', but Crane was not a purist with focalization, as we shall see):

There was a youthful private who listened with eager ears to the words of the tall soldier and to the varied comments of his comrades.

(Ch.1)

Moreover, the external nomination 'the youth' is maintained throughout, which not only expresses the anonymity of the army, but establishes the author's distance. Similarly, it is the author who refers to 'the loud soldier' and 'the tall soldier' (the youth has known the latter, Jim Conklin, 'since childhood', Ch. 2). Names are given only by characters (in DS), and we learn the youth's first name, Henry, from his mother in the flashback scene of Chapter 1, soon after the 'youthful private' has been introduced. In other words, it is technically incorrect to say that the reader sees through Fleming's eyes from the opening paragraph. The reader has not yet heard of Fleming, or even of 'a youthful private'. The distance established in the first two pages between the narrating author and the character's RT is particularly marked, even if it is later blurred.

And yet this distance is far less great than that between the character's thoughts and his own direct speech. An obvious analogy is *What Maisie Knew*, about which James explicitly stated that he was representing complex movements in Maisie's development which she could not express – hence a particularly interesting use of RT as Maisie's childish vocabulary is caught up in James's syntax. Maisie, however, was much more articulate than the youth. We are rarely given, in DS, an idea of someone who could verbalize the complex, sophisticated and metaphoric thoughts the youth is described by the author (in NS) as having. Even when he harangues the troops in Chapter 20/21 we are not given the words, only summary: 'He harangued his fellows [...] he made frantic appeals' (NS). There is, however, one exception in Chapter 16/17, after an enemy advance, where 'he exploded in loud sentences: "B'jiminy, we're generaled by a lot 'a lunkheads"', followed a little later by 'He presently began a long and intricate denunciation of the commander of the forces' [not given], answered by his friend. The youth replies '"Well, don't we fight like th'devil? Don't we do all that men kin?"', which sentiment secretly dumbfounds him (this is after his flight). Later, he is twice fairly loquacious, and even figurative ('"bein' chased around like rats!"' and '"It makes a man feel like a damn' kitten in a bag"'). I believe that the reader, used to his silence and tongue-tied or brief direct speech, feels the difference here, and would interpret this as irony: the youth talks most of their courage after his shame and before he has 'proved himself' to himself. My point is not of course that he does not express himself much or could not, only that he is not represented as doing so.

None of this means that he cannot have complex thoughts, only that the author is verbalizing these confused impulses for him, as a novelist should. Moreover, the very consistency of the appellation 'the youth' shows that NS/RT is being used to represent half conscious or unarticulated thoughts: one does not think of oneself by an appellation (see Ch. 5, 72).

What we have then are two distinct viewpoints from the start. The first is clearly that of the narrating author, who uses Narrative Sentences, both descriptive ('The cold was passing . . .') and evaluative ('he said pompously', both Ch. 1). The author can also tell us that the youth was *un*conscious of something he then proceeds to describe, and what the youth was *later* to think, or that he and his friend 'had a geographical *illusion* concerning a stream' (my italics, Ch. 18/19), or even that the lieutenant '*always un*consciously addressed himself to the youth' (Ch. 17/18); he can make judgments about the youth's 'tupenny fury' or 'the cloak of his pride' (Ch. 10, 20/21). He can see the youth in external focalization and often does, as in: 'a scowl of mortification and rage was upon his face' (20/21). He can shift to the collective viewpoint of 'the men', and this happens during many of the battle-scenes or rest-periods. And with the death of Jim Conklin he suddenly enters Jim's conscience although the scene is described from the watchers' viewpoint (though this does jar and may be a lapse): 'He [Jim] was invaded by a creeping strangeness that slowly enveloped him' (9).

The other distinct viewpoint is that of the youth, whose thoughts are given in RT, first in flashback (with his mother's monologue inside it) but then simultaneous (Ch. 1), and whose speech is of course in DS. In other words, the really complex movements are either in NS, where the irony is clear and sometimes heavy; or in RT, left to betray themselves in an irony that operates metatextually. There is no 'narrative voice' or 'whisper at our ear' (see Ch. 5, p. 77n): we the readers provide (or not) the ironic reading. Hence the innumerable interpretations. To do this, as well as to deconstruct the oppositions, *il faut interroger inlassablement les métaphores* (Derrida 1972a, 87).

The hero and the monster

It is, then, the narrating author who first presents us with the monsters in the novel's famous opening paragraph, though they are metaphorically implied rather than stated. The image of 'An army stretched out on the hills [. . .] awakened [. . .] and cast its eyes [. . .]'

is echoed by other implied monsters of liquid mud [roads] and a river, 'amber-tinted', 'purling at the army's feet'; and a second, rival monster on the other side: 'across it the red, eye-like gleam of hostile campfires set in the low brow of the distant hills'. Both armies are monsters, as is the space between them, the no-man's land, the battle-ground, and both are neutrally likened to the 'brown and green' landscape they are on. Yet we also soon learn that the youth had chatted across the stream with an enemy soldier and been called by him 'a right dum [damn] good fellow', and that this incident 'had made him temporarily regret war' (Ch. 6).

The concept of hero is so easily read as irony (at the beginning of the early flashback and, inside it, in his mother's attitude), that it can be considered as not even constructed, let alone deconstructed. Those 'greeklike' and 'Homeric' dreams serve chiefly to remind us, extratextually, that Homeric heroes were always great chieftains, who had names, who killed other noble and named heroes in indivi-dual combat after an exchange of identities and genealogies, often helped *in extremis* by their protecting god. There is little sense of an army of common soldiers in Homer, Virgil, or the later *Chansons de Geste* or Romances. Thus the very contrast between the conven-tional notion of 'hero' and the anonymous youth is strongly and intertextually suggested from the start – in fact he rapidly forgets these notions which are presented in flashback as already in the past. When they return, they are totally deconstructed, by the events of course, but more especially by the multi-levelled irony from the end of Chapter 17/18 (see later), or by the extraordinary show of moral cowardice and self-deception at the end of Chapter 15/16, followed by the youth imagining himself back home telling wartales to 'the consternation and the ejaculations of his mother and the young lady at the seminary as they drank in his recitals. Their vague feminine formula for beloved ones doing brave deeds on the field of battle without risk of life would be destroyed' (NS→RT).

The extratextual irony of this notion of a hero (from our modern viewpoint) is that it is a man's view of a woman's view. Inside the text, the youth's mother gives him two contradictory messages: (1) 'Don't go a-thinkin' you kin lick th'hull rebel army at th'start, b'cause yeh can't', and (2) 'yeh must never do no shirkin' child, on my account. If so be a time when yeh have t'be kilt or do a mean thing, why, Henry, don't think of anythin' 'cept what's right' (Ch. 1). In other words, 'don't try to be a hero' and 'be a hero', all wrapped up in more sober realism. His own disappointment and impatience at her speech, which said 'nothing whatever about returning with his shield or on it', makes the later intertextual irony of the man's view of a woman's view particularly strong.

What then is a hero? In this early flashback, he is legend, *legenda* or things to read, or, in more heroic times, hear about or say. In fact he can only be clearly defined by what he has to fight against: the monster.

Yet by Chapter 2 the monsters have considerably changed their signifieds. They are no longer two armies lying in wait, they are, first, the enemy (NS or RT), italics mine throughout:[2] 'From across the river the *red eyes* were still peering' (NS). But this is at once cut in with a monster-word for parts of the youth's own army: 'loomed the *gigantic* figure of the colonel on a *gigantic horse*' (NS/RT), followed by an ambiguous reference: 'From off in the darkness came the trampling of feet. The youth could occasionally see dark shadows that moved like *monsters*' [enemy or own side? it seems the latter], followed by a clearer reference to the enemy: 'Staring once at the *red eyes* across the river, he conceived them to be growing larger, as the *orbs of a row of dragons advancing*' (NS). This is cut in again by the giant colonel, though ironized with a realistic touch: 'He turned toward the colonel and saw him lift his *gigantic* arm and calmly stroke his moustache' (NS→RT). A dozen lines after this fluctuation the monster has finally become attached to parts of the youth's own army: 'A moment later the regiment went swinging off into the darkness. It was now like one of those *moving monsters wending with many feet*' (NS). This meaning remains for several paragraphs: 'two long thin black columns [...] They were like two *serpents* crawling from the cavern of night [...] the long *serpents* crawled' (NS/RT).

This shift from the initial objective monsters (author's viewpoint) to the youth's fear of his own side occurs partly because he is already concerned with 'his problem' (will he run?), a problem that even as early as Chapter 2 separates him from the others. He keeps trying to discover whether they too are troubled, and constantly projects his fear of running away onto the fear of what 'they' will think of him, which rules him throughout, and through which they become

---

[2] Because of the ambiguity of RT which can be formally identical with NS, individual readers may disagree with my notations after this or that sentence. I have counted as RT all sentences with value words like *gigantic* or *monsters*, unless they are clearly literary (*as the orbs of a row of dragons advancing*). But many could be noted NS/RT, so thoroughly does the narrating author adopt the character's viewpoint, while not depriving himself of comment.

monsters. By the end of Chapter 2 'he saw visions of a *thousand-tongued* fear that would babble at his back and cause him to flee [...] He admitted that he would not be able to cope with this monster' (RT). This paradox is metaleptic (in Bloom's sense, see p. 39): what will babble *if* he flees will *cause* him to flee. And, after his flight, when he returns to camp at last: 'Of a sudden he confronted a black and *monstrous* figure', which turns out to be his friend Wilson (Ch. 13/14, RT). The monster has become not only his own fear projected onto others, that might cause him to flee, but the fear of what they will say when he has.

Soon after the own-side monsters of Chapter 2, however, the metaphor has shifted again: 'The youth looked at the men nearest him [...] They were going to look at war, *the red animal*, war, *the blood-swollen god*' (Ch. 3, RT). The identical phrase is repeated in Chapter 12/13, and an image of *the infernal mouth of the war god* has occurred in Chapter 6, all in RT. The adjective *red* is associated so regularly with war that it alone can evoke the monster: 'the *red*, formidable difficulties of war had been vanquished' (Ch. 6, RT). By the novel's final lines, however, the red animal has moved within: 'He had rid himself of the *red* sickness of battle' (RT). Meanwhile in Chapter 4 the monster is refocused as the immediate enemy: 'the composite *monster*, (RT), 'redoubtable *dragons* [...] the *red and green monster* [...] He seemed to shut his eyes and wait to *be gobbled*' (Ch. 6, RT).[3]

In other words, from the narrating author's objective monsters (the two armies) we have moved to the character's monsters as (1) the enemy, (2) elements of his own army, representing (3) his own fear of his comrades' opinion, projected onto (4) war, then (5) the enemy again, and finally reinteriorized as (6) the red sickness of battle.

After his flight the dragons seem less terrible:

he had been out among the *dragons*, he said, and he assured himself that they were

---

[3] See Barthes (1966, 19) and Genette (1972, 210) for the impropriety of using *sembler* for personal reactions, as in 'he seemed to shut his eyes' above. It is true that this sounds more absurd in French (Barthes' example is 'le tintement de la glace contre le verre sembla donner à Bond une brusque inspiration', clearly translated from English, and which alone puts Bond in external focalization, and James uses 'I/he seemed to feel' and such phrases continually). Genette's example, picked up by Proust, is from Balzac: 'la vallée et ses coteaux, dont je parus un admirateur fervent', which is indeed absurd, since we are in internal focalization. In the Crane sentence, 'seemed' alone puts the youth in external focalization (NS), where we would otherwise be in RT. The two narrative poles have fused, but this is simply bad writing, and does not alter Banfield's theoretical separation.

not so hideous as he had imagined them. Also, they were inaccurate; they did not
sting with precision. A stout heart often defied; and defying, escaped them. And furthermore, how could they kill him who was the chosen of the gods?

(Ch. 15/16, RT)

This is one of the many self-justifications of his flight, and as
paradoxically aporetic as the 'thousand-tongued fear' image: the dragons missed him because he ran, therefore he is a hero. This kind
of self-betrayal is always expressed in RT. As the tale progresses,
however, and as the youth becomes more familiar with the monsters,
they get curiously defabulated: 'wagons like fat sheep', 'like ungainly
animals' (Ch. 11), men charging down upon him 'like terrified buffa-
loes' (Ch. 12/13). So do the author's typifying comparisons ('dog-like
obedience', 'yokel-like eyes', 'like sheep', 'the dominant animal',
'wolf-like temper', 'like a mad horse', 'as a panther at prey' (Chs.13/
14, 19/20, 20/21, 23/24). The army itself, however, and its mysteriously inefficient hierarchy (including the regiment) are more and
more often compared to a machine: the animal monster has become
mechanized. But the men remain animals.

Thus the author classifies and is theoretically objective, but judges:
both armies are monsters, there is a dominant animal in man, men
fight like animals. The youth whose thought he represents, however,
rehandles every signifier according to his desires and fears. The monster is the youth, it is also every man in every army. And every
man, including the youth, can be a hero or a coward. The monster
in the youth, that represents his fear of what others will say about
his running, suggests that cowardice, like heroism, is for the youth
what people *say*: the monster and the hero are one.

Running to and running from

The process of constant shifts and reversals in the notion of running
resembles that of the hero/monster opposition, and is of course
involved with it, as it is with the other oppositions: running away
involves separation which involves watching.

Clearly there are many different kinds of running, but when the
youth ruminates his 'problem' at the beginning, there is only one
meaning: would he 'run'? Would they run? Would Jim run? But
when in Chapter 3 'he found himself running down a wood-road
in the midst of men [...] he felt carried by a mob', running has

reversed its meaning: running *to* battle, *with* men, in a mob.[4] And in practice the running into battle is not positively valued, but wrapped in notions of inability to do otherwise: 'he instantly saw it would be impossible for him to escape from the regiment. It enclosed him. And there were iron laws of tradition and law on four sides. He was in a moving box' (NS/RT). Throughout, going into battle is presented as unconscious, wild, primitive behaviour.

There is also a clear distinction made between the treatment of *others* running away (handled as objective acts by the narrating author, or with scorn by the youth after his flight), and the treatment of *himself* running away (handled first in NS as he yells with fright and turns, but afterwards in RT as a world-shaking event). The description that 'he was like a proverbial chicken. He lost the direction of safety', which is NS, shifts to external focalization: 'His unbuttoned coat flapped in the wind [...] on his face was all the horror of those doings which he imagined [...] He ran like blind man' (Ch. 6, NS). His later shame and self-justification (RT) are too well-known to be detailed. Here I shall merely stress the shifts in evaluation:

(1) *Running from battle*: envisaged with terror (RT + DS); described externally (NS, as above), then with a shift to RT that contains strange ideas indeed:

Since he had turned his back upon the fight, his fears had been wondrously magnified. Death about to thrust him between the shoulder-blades was far more dreadful than death about to smite him between the eyes [...] As he ran on, he mingled with others [...] He thought that all the regiment was fleeing, pursued by these ominous crashes [...] In his flight, the sound of these following footsteps gave him his one meagre relief. He felt vaguely that death must make a first choice of men who were nearest; the initial morsels for the dragons would be, then, those who were following him. So he displayed the zeal of an insane sprinter in his purpose to keep them in the rear. There was a race. As he, leading ...

(Ch. 6, RT)

Thus running *from* death is worse than running *to*, yet behind him are men of his own side, also running away and so in apparent *pursuit*, and he runs faster so that the dragon death will take them first. He is winning a race. The entire experience is highly conscious, yet remembered later as animal-like, un*manly*.

Running to battle: also experienced as animal-like and un*manly*

[4] Cp. Sherburn in *Huckleberry Finn* (1977, 118–19): 'The pitifulest thing out is a mob. That's what an army is – a mob; they don't fight with courage that's born in them, but with courage that's borrowed from their mass, and from their officers.'

(RT and NS): 'He became not a man but a member' (Ch. 5, NS/RT). But also as a race: 'The flying regiment was going to have a catapultian effect. The dream made him run faster among his comrades, who were giving vent to hoarse and frantic cheers' (Ch. 22/23, NS). This contradictory experience is well brought out in two strange comparisons: (1) 'He went instantly forward, like a dog, who, seeing his foes lagging, turns and insists on being pursued' (Ch. 17/18, NS) – the 'foes' being in fact his comrades and, figuratively, the dog's master in a joyful game; (2) 'The youth was pushed and jostled for a moment [...] and he ran desperately as if pursued for a murder' (Ch. 19/20, NS). Here the youth rushing into battle is suddenly a criminal, and his comrades the police. Both comparisons describe running into battle in terms of flight, as if one were pursued by one's own side. And this irony (for the reader who spots it) comes from the author.

There are also variations such as running for cover or for an aimed spot (Chs. 19/20, 23/24, RT); running out of curiosity (Ch. 3, RT); running back to battle after flight: 'Then he began to run in the direction of the battle [...] But he obstinately took round about ways' (Ch. 8, NS); and running to battle as walking: 'The youth walked stolidly into the midst of the mob, and with his flag [...]' (Ch.20/21, NS).

Running by others: described dispassionately in NS and not devalued, although this is at first witnessed with horror by the youth in RT. When the youth later learns that others of his regiment have also fled, he reluctantly decides that he is not unique, yet can restore his pride by scorning them, since 'he had fled with discretion and dignity' (Ch.15/16, RT).

Running by him: sometimes meditated in shame and usually in fear of what others will say (Chs. 2,3,4,7,11, RT); projected onto others (Nature, generals, the Universe etc.), rehandled as superior strategy, compared favourably with that of others, and finally minimized (RT).

Running from a defeat or from a victory: 'The youth cringed as if discovered at a crime. By heaven, they had won after all' (Ch. 7, NS → RT). In other words, his running away is made worse by victory, since a defeat would have been a 'salve', and he later hopes for it as 'a roundabout vindication of himself' (Ch.11, RT).

Running as ordered retreat: fast (the whole command, Ch.4) or slow (the march of the wounded in Ch. 8 and other collective retreats, one of which is described as 'jaunty', Ch. 22). Usually in NS.

Running from the tattered soldier's searching questions: 'he turned away suddenly and slid through the crowd. His brow was heavily flushed' (Ch. 8, NS).

Running with the tattered soldier after the tall soldier: 'He and the tattered soldier began a pursuit. There was a singular race' (Ch. 9, Jim Conklin's death agony, NS).

Running from or towards death: he imagines death behind him when he runs away, but still figuratively as a dragon. His first concrete sight of death comes early: 'The ranks opened covertly to avoid a corpse. The invulnerable dead man forced a way for himself' (Ch. 3, a striking image of men avoiding death which still seems to move live among them, NS). Later the horrifying spectacle of the dead soldier he stumbles on after his flight puts the youth to flight again, but slowly, backwards, for 'he feared, that if he turned his back, the body might spring up and stealthily pursue him' (the above image reversed) and he is, in his mind, 'pursued by a sight of the black ants swarming greedily upon the grey face and venturing horribly near to the eyes' (Ch. 8, NS/RT). Yet much earlier, before battle, death had seemed preferable to the idea of running away, a solution to his 'problem', and much later he desires it as personal revenge on the officer who had called them mule-drivers and later mud-diggers (Ch. 22/23). More dramatically, he and the tattered soldier are amazed to see Jim Conklin running into a field to die: 'Gawd! he's runnin'!' says the tattered soldier (Ch. 9, DS).

Running as an illusion in space and time: 'His mind flew in all directions' (Ch. 9, NS). This phrase sums up much of the novel. More particularly: 'He discovered that the distances, as compared with the brilliant measurings of his mind, were trivial and ridiculous' (Ch. 21/22, NS). It soon ceases to be as clear as it was at the beginning in which direction he is running. The most dramatic instance of this occurs when fleeing troops meet those who have already fled and who are returning, pursued by a new enemy group (Ch. 20/21, NS).

No doubt other configurations can be found, since the word 'run' is extremely frequent, along with variants such as skedaddle, sweep, rush, scatter, scamper, charge, and so on. But the interpretations can vary enormously, especially since Narrative Sentences are sometimes clearly distinct from Represented Thought and sometimes blurred into it in the modern way. Moreover, all the meanings are caught up in the idea of separateness and spectacle. The youth's running has apparently not been observed (strangely, since so many fled at the same time), at least as far as he knows. There are in fact several subtle indications to the reader that he may have been observed: the lieutenant was very near him when he fled (NS), and both Wilson and the corporal comment on how many were thought lost and keep returning, which we may read as either ironical (by them) or naive surprise (DS). Similarly the corporal's remarks on his wound can be read both ways (DS). For the youth, however, because he thinks his flight has been unobserved, it ceases to count.

In the end, neither author nor character (for different reasons and after the youth's shame) puts a particularly negative value on running from battle, or a particularly positive one on running into it.

Separateness and membership[5]

Separateness and membership are not simply manifestations of the more abstract opposition absence/presence. Even in the opening chapter, the youth feels separate from his companions while in their presence, and in Chapter 2 he 'continually tried to measure himself by his comrades', for traces of fear and courage (NS). Moreover, phrases of separateness, such as 'took no part' and 'kept from intercourse with' are frequent throughout. This separateness does not merely stem from his fear of being a coward, but also and paradoxically from the conviction that he is superior. Then, after fighting well for the first time, he even becomes separated from himself: 'Standing apart from himself, he viewed the last scene. He perceived that the man who had fought thus was magnificent' (Ch. 6 NS/RT).[5]

Because it involves loss of membership, the separation caused by his running away is hard to bear. It has to be rehandled, first as superior strategy, then as a personal affront when he learns that the enemy's attack has been repulsed, then as a mixture of both: 'The imbecile line had remained and had become victors' (Ch. 7, RT). His conviction of superiority is particularly strong in the original Chapter 12.

Before this, he is separated through envy, as when he watches a column marching into battle, and 'felt he was regarding a procession of chosen beings. The separation was as great to him as if they had marched with weapons of flames and banners of sunlight' (Ch.11, brief echo of legendary heroes, but with exclusion, NS/RT).

---

[5] Cp.: 'Join the army, meet interesting people, and kill them' (*Graffiti*, Coll. Rees 1983, in Calendar form, Jan. 2)

His separateness is complex enough to warrant a point-by-point summary presentation (in chronological order):

(1) he fears he is unlike those he believes to be heroes, and although relieved to hear Jim admit he might run if others do, he feels that the separation of death is nonetheless preferable (Chs. 1–3, RT)

(2) he is brave but in 'battlesleep' and part of a mob, having learnt that fighting means being 'not a man but a member' (Ch. 5, NS/RT)

(3) he separates himself by running away, so (a) he has been wronged, (b) he is superior to those who fought and won (Ch. 7, RT)

(4) he envies the brave and feels separate, but also envies the wounded, and feels an intruder among dead men (Ch. 8, RT)

(5) he is different from the others, case in a unique mould, yet also wants revenge on nature and the universe (original Ch. 12, RT)

(6) he feels different from others in being protected by the gods, and his flight is a sign of this (Ch. 15/16, RT)

(7) when he hears that others of the regiment fled he is at first relieved, then scorns them and needs to distinguish himself as one who fled 'with discretion and dignity' (Ch.15/16, RT)

This complicated, self-cancelling separateness is then reversed in his apparent later bravery. Yet even in communal battlesleep, he effectively reseparates himself by being, in the first episode, 'not aware of a lull' (NS) and continuing to use his rifle after everyone has stopped. 'He returned to his comrades and threw himself on the ground. He sprawled like a man who has been thrashed' (NS/RT, he feels punished). He realizes that his fellows are staring at him and regard him as 'a war-devil' and soon, 'It was revealed to him that he had been a barbarian, a beast' (all Ch.17/18; NS/RT). After this, he remains separate to the last, not only from his friends but from his author as well (see ' *In/out*' below).

Spectator and spectacle[6]

All the concepts so far discussed are caught up in that of the spectacle, since the youth is perpetually the spectator who watches his comrades, the battles, and himself. Indeed, he often makes a spectacle of himself, and turns himself into a spectacle when separated and alone. Crane emphasizes this role by introducing Narrative Sentences with verbs of perception, so that they half shift to RT: he saw, he stared, he observed, he viewed, he watched, he gawked, it was

---

[6] Cp. *Graffiti*, Rees 1983 (for Feb.13): 'Supposing they gave a war, and nobody came.'

revealed to him, and more oddly, 'from this glimpse [...] it was derived' (Ch. 20/21).

But the theme is far more explicit than this, as the soldiers constantly become spectacles for each other, whether new recruits are mocked by the veterans, or cowards watched by those still advancing, or the youth himself stared at when he goes on shooting unnecessarily. The youth watches far more than he acts, out of a curiosity that seems even to overcome his fear: 'he felt an unconscious impulse of curiosity. He scrambled up the bank with a speed that could not be exceeded by a bloodthirsty man. He expected a battle scene' (Ch. 3, NS, RT).

Time after time, when one is led to feel he has no alternative but to fight, the youth becomes a spectator. Even on one of the rare occasions when he is actually said to shoot, he pauses: 'He slowly lifted his rifle and catching a glimpse of the thick-spread field he blazed at the cantering cluster. He stopped then and began to peer as best he could through the smoke' (Ch. 6, NS). And after his flight there is much peering, spying and staring at other units still fighting, which culminates in his horrified stare at the dead soldier. Back with his regiment he watches the soldiers who likewise seem dead, but who are only asleep by the fire. When the officer calls them mule-drivers to the general he and his friend have become watchers and eavesdroppers, and later, instead of fighting, he runs toward a clump of trees and stares 'like an insane soldier [...] it seemed to the youth that he saw everything' (Ch. 19/20, NS).

The spectator/spectacle collocation becomes more complex when he yearns for the flag and seizes it from their dying colour-bearer, fighting his friend for it and pushing him roughly away (Chs. 19/20, 20/21, RT, NS, DD). When the regiment falls back, the youth is in a rage of mortification, having 'pictured red letters of curious revenge' (NS) on the officer who had called them mule-drivers, and he harangues his fellows to fight (reversing his much earlier urge to harangue them not to). And then he suddenly sees the enemy flag: 'The youth peering once through a sudden rift in the cloud, saw a brown mass of troops interwoven and magnified until they appeared to be thousands. A fierce-hued flag rushed before his vision' (Ch. 20/21, NS). When fleeing troops are met by others panicking back, 'The youth walked stolidly into the midst of the mob and with his flag in his hands, took a stand [...] He unconsciously assumed the attitude of the colour-bearer of the preceding day' (Ch. 20/21, NS). But as the lieutenant bawls out again 'Here they

come! Right onto us b'Gawd!', the youth seems immobile: 'The
youth's eyes had instantly turned in the direction indicated [...]
They were so near that he could see their features [...] He strained
his vision to learn [...] and achieved a few unsatisfactory views
of the enemy [...] He seated himself gloomily on the ground with
his flag between his knees' (Ch. 20/21, NS).

The Narrative Sentences then switch to a collective viewpoint,
during which the charge is repulsed, and the men 'made an ungainly
dance of joy at the sight of this tableau' (Ch. 20/21, NS). The youth,
who has apparently done nothing, takes time to 'appreciate himself'
(NS), and only now do we learn, back in a collective viewpoint,
(a) that the officer who had called them mule-drivers is furious and
tells their colonel 'what a lot of mud-diggers you've got anyway!'
(Ch. 21/22, NS, DS), and (b) that the colonel has singled out the
youth and his friend for praise. The fact that the reader has not
seen this spectacle, but only hears about it afterwards, at second-hand
and in comical DS from the soldier who reports the colonel's words,
suggests that it may be wild exaggeration. In the next charge, the
youth is still colour-bearer, but to spite the officer he has 'resolved
not to budge' (Ch. 22/23, RT): 'he was deeply absorbed as spectator'
(NS). Yet he is galvanized into action by the regiment's weakening
defence (a reversal of his flight *because* they were losing), and in
plunging forward at the enemy flag (which his friend obtains this
time) he becomes a spectacle again (Ch. 23/24, mostly NS).

A reversal has thus taken place in the presentation: during the
first action he first adopts a heroic pose then merely sits and watches,
yet is singled out afterwards as a hero, a 'jim-hickey', in an action
we have not been allowed to follow (Ch. 21/23, NS, DS). In the
second action he resolves not to budge, and yet we see him in action,
not killing the enemy but vainly coveting the enemy flag as well
as his own.

Early in the story (Chs. 3–6), the joint themes of spectator and
spectacle are linked in terms of watching the flag. In these later
battles, the presentation of the youth is so deconstructed as to turn
the flag into a figure of bitter irony, the very metaphors for it shifting
from sentimentality (a woman) to comedy: 'the youth could see the
two flags shaking with laughter amid the smoke-remnants' (Ch. 22/
23, NS).

The role of colour-bearer that the youth so desires was the equivalent of cheer-leader, but more importantly, that of a man who did
not fight. At the very worst it meant exposure: 'Each felt satisfied

with the other's possession of it but each felt bound to declare by an offer to carry the emblem, his willingness to further risk himself (Ch. 22/23, NS). Of course the youth does shoot, and perhaps kills, on his first day, but this aspect is curiously muffled. When he later becomes a 'wild-cat', it is as the inheritor of his own side's flag, and his bravery is thus presented as useless exposure. That posture was twice ridiculed (in NS) when the lieutenant stands with his 'forgotten back' towards the enemy and curses. The youth's plans to *get* killed – once early as the only answer to his 'problem', later as revenge on the officer – are part of the same ironic reversal, as was the notion of heroism that the youth attributed to women at the end of Chapter 16/17: beloved ones should do brave deeds but not die. And also, implicitly, not kill.

Finally, the idea of the youth redeeming himself as colour-bearer deconstructs itself. He is said to have been brave again, but we are not allowed to witness it as spectators and can only see him watching. The rest is the spectacle of the flag-bearer, in which the spectator and spectacle have become one.

Courage and cowardice

There would seem to be nothing left to say about courage and coward-ice, since the concepts are so intricately woven into the others, already deconstructed, and into one another. The fact that Crane called his book a study of fear adds little to this deadlock, for fear is not the opposite of courage but another given: courage and cowardice are opposite ways of dealing with fear. Yet *Red Badge* offers a constant shifting and reversal of values, for both the youth and the reader, which culminates in the reversals of Chapters 17 to 23. The steady build-up towards these reversals, however, deserves our attention.

During this build-up, courage is associated with: calculation, cur-iosity, harangues, over-valiant airs, a death-wish, selflessness, mem-bership, battlesleep, an absence of heroic poses, red rage, acute exasperation, ecstasy, wounds, envy, war-desire, the expectation of success, the observation of a weak defence.

Cowardice during this same period is associated with: calculation, fear of ignominy, a death-wish, revelation, an act made worse by victory, crime, shame, fear of questioning, his superior strategy, uniqueness, discretion and dignity.

More importantly, courage is hardly ever valued positively or treated other than ironically. Conversely the youth's running away is never valued negatively, except by himself, and this not consistently.

From Chapter 17/18 on, cowardice seemingly disappears, and yet the reversals of the concept of courage continue: 'It was revealed to him that he had been a barbarian, a beast. He had fought like a pagan who defends his religion [...] he was now what he called a hero. And he had not been aware of the process. He had slept and, wakening, found himself a knight' (Ch.17/18, NS/RT). Courage now becomes: hatred for the foe, for his own generals, for the officer, for the universe; rage, unconsciousness, determination, a run with a dog, shooting alone, a sickness, barbarism, beastliness, paganism, waking up a knight, being pushed, being pursued for a murder, insanity, frenzy, mad enthusiasm, foolhardiness, indignation, love of the flag, a heroic pose, personal revenge, pride, despair, insane fever, a race, and so on to the 'red sickness' of the last page.

The only positive evaluation of courage seems to come from the narrating author in the present tense, and can only, in all that context, be ironical: 'There was the delirium that encounters despair and death. It is a temporary but sublime absence of selfishness' (Ch. 19/20, NS).

But what is the value of courage if it is punished in the author's irony of event? The seeming reward for the youth's first bravery is another attack (and his flight): that for his second (firing for nothing) is mockery and being made to feel a barbarian, and later to hear his unit described as mule-drivers: for his third, the mockery of the veterans and the general's fury. The colonel's distantly transmitted praise, not guaranteed either for him or for the reader, can hardly be said to compensate.

Soldiers in battle, then, are animals and savages, no better than 'a dog, a woman an' a walnut tree/Th' more yeh beat 'em the better they be' (Ch.17/18, with double meaning of 'beat').

Moreover, the use of the words 'man' and 'manhood' as apparent equivalents for courage also deconstructs itself (my italics):

He became not a *man* but a member (5, NS/RT, courage as *not* man)

He feels below 'the standard of traditional *manhood*', but since his lies are believed he is 'returned to his comrades unimpeached' (14/15, RT, manhood as apparent non-cowardice)

'he had performed his mistakes in the dark, so *he was still a man*' (15/16, RT, manhood as *hidden* cowardice)

'Since much of their strength [the men's] and their breath had vanished they returned to caution. They were *become men again*' (19/20, NS, manhood as caution)

After despair at their impotence things change and the men 'gazed about them with looks of uplifted pride, feeling new trust in the grim, always-confident weapons in their hands. *And they were men* (20/21, NS, manhood as pride and revenge on earlier impotence)

'Yet gradually he mustered force to put the sin at a distance [...] At last, he concluded that he saw in it quaint uses [...] It would become a good part of him [...] And he would be taught to deal gently and with care. He *would be a man*' (24/25, RT, manhood as gentleness and as 'use' of sin toward moral consciousness)

'he felt a quiet *manhood*, non-assertive but of sturdy and strong blood [...] He had been to touch the great death, and found that, after all, it was but the great death and was for others. *He was a man*' (24/25, RT).

The youth's self-ignorant satisfaction, confirmed here in the restored original phrase 'and was for others', thoroughly undercuts the notion of 'manhood'. Manhood has been equated in NS with courage as not man, with caution, with renewed pride after impotence; and in RT as apparent non-cowardice, hidden cowardice, gentleness and moral consciousness, and (at the very end) as loss of fear because the great death is for others.

Henry Binder in his Introduction has conjectured that the ellipsis at the end of Chapter 14/15, caused by lost manuscript pages, must have included a guilty recollection by the youth of his desertion of the tattered soldier. The argument is that 'Henry commits three acts that cause him to be ashamed: his flight from battle, his rebellions against nature, and his desertion of the tattered soldier – only two of which are recalled. Yet Binder neglects the youth's other misdeeds, precisely because they do not 'cause him to be ashamed'. It is part of the self-deconstructive process noted by Felman (1977) and myself (1977) whereby the condition of a fictional character becomes contagious, so that critics now and again behave in some ways like the character. Of the three misdeeds mentioned by Binder, the desertion of the tattered soldier is indeed the most serious, but the youth does remember it, with acute shame, to the point of crying out loud, at the very end of the story; the rebellion against nature, on the other hand, which critics have made so much of, seems trivial and no more than a minor instance of other projections by the youth.

In contrast, far more shameful acts are presented, which seem to have attracted little attention because the youth also represses them. He lies about his desertion and wound in order to pass himself off as a hero, and then plans to blackmail his friend Wilson, 'rejoicing in the possession of a small weapon [Wilson's letters] with which he could prostrate his comrade' should he question him (Ch.15/16, RT). Of course this second act could not have been included in the balance-recovering operation at the end of the *previous* chapter (14/15), but the former (the lying about his flight and wound) could and should have been, had the flight itself not been immediately 'buried'. Both these acts result from the fear that his flight (the first shame) would be discovered, and although the first deception briefly and mildly embarrasses him, the blackmail never does. On the contrary, when Wilson's candour prevents it, the youth even considers his non-action as 'a generous thing' and disdains Wilson for his shame at having entrusted his letters to another in a moment of weakness: 'He [the youth] had never been compelled to blush in such a manner for his acts, he was an individual of extraordinary virtue' (Ch.15/16, RT).

The irony is savage but metatextual, that is, not in NS. Having so soon forgotten his own shifting furies and humiliations, he is incapable of recognizing the most shameful act of all. He is prepared to blackmail his loyal friend out of sheer terror at being questioned, in much the same way as he had deserted the tattered soldier. Both actions, the blackmail and the desertion, go back to his flight. And both are suppressed, they are part of the 'mistakes in the dark' that he thinks enable him to be 'still a man'. They are the means, however, by which the first mistake, the flight, remains in the dark. And only one of them, the desertion of the tattered soldier, will come back and torment him much later, after the battles and before the idyllic end.

These two straightforward scenes of moral cowardice are embedded in a narrative that everywhere inverts the concepts of physical courage and cowardice. As Paul de Man says: 'A narrative endlessly tells the story of its own denominational aberration' (1979, 162).

The youth's quiet suppressions, then, compound the irony of events presented throughout with an irony of silence about events. Physical courage? Physical cowardice? The concepts are almost meaningless in battle, where men become savages. But moral courage and moral cowardice are oppositions latent under the manifest ones – under the 'little red badge of courage' and 'the sore red badge of his dishonor'. These cannot be inverted or fused, precisely because they are not talked of, not turned into legend.

In and out: Fleming and Crane

The author's viewpoint and narration is clearly outside that of the youth's, and seems to define him at every turn. Self-revealing as is the youth's Represented Thought, it is always controlled and sometimes doubled by the author's irony. The style is thus basically monological. The text is an early example of the fused poles NS and RT which eventually turned the RT device into cliché (see end of Ch.5), but here the tension is still highly effective, if often misleading to critics.

Yet the very instability of the irony brings it occasionally and for brief moments close to the dialogical. The youth's constant worry, especially, about what 'they' will think forms a considerable in/out tension that governs all the other oppositions. Not only does the youth project his ills onto those responsible outsiders the generals, nature, the universe, but sometimes his comrades, the 'they' whose opinion he so fears, could even include the author who defines him:

> He imagined the whole regiment saying: 'Where's Henry Fleming?[7] He run did't 'e? Oh, my!' [...] Wherever he went in camp, he would encounter insolent and lingeringly cruel stares. As he imagined himself passing near a crowd of comrades, he could hear someone making a humorous remark in a low tone. At it, the others all crowed and cackled. *He was a slang phrase.*
>
> (Ch. 11, RT, my italics)

He is, in Bakhtin's terms, the other's word on him, and in a restored passage of Chapter 17, he even blames the whole 'snivelling race of poets'. For the other's word on him is also the author's word.

Chapter 11 in particular fluctuates his attitudes, and the suppressed Chapter 12, the centre of the novel, interestingly continues this faint trace of what Bakhtin calls the dialogical process. It is reminiscent of the way a Dostoevskian hero answers and anticipates the word of the other, except that here this imagined word is given, it is not what Bakhtin called 'hidden polemic', which replies to an unstated discourse.

The hidden polemic of *Red Badge* is in fact that which is never said by either author or character. Instead, it is latent in the very self-deconstruction of every stable opposition, in the swallowing of

---

[7] This is the place I mentioned at the beginning, where we first learn the youth's surname. As with other names, it is given in Direct Speech, but it is remarkable that it should be the DS of others as imagined by the youth and hence in his mind.

each concept by its opposite as the monster war swallows the soldiers. The latent polemic is not about running away or lying about it or redeeming oneself or even about 'growing' as the critics call it. It is about the rhetoric of war – the legend, the spectacle, the bullying and galvanizing of men into action and death. It is also about what this does to them, turning them either (for courage) into savages, animals, unconscious creatures, sentimental symbol-lovers, voyeurs, spies and show-offs; or (for cowardice), into self-pitying children, liars, braggarts, self-deceivers and blackmailers. 'The red animal, war' not only gobbles men, but makes them insignificant when left ungobbled: 'And the most startling thing was to learn suddenly that he was very insignificant. The officer spoke of the regiment as if he referred to a broom [...] it was war, no doubt, but it appeared strange' (Ch.18/19, RT).

All the author's ironies about the youth thus escape into another irony, shared perhaps with the youth and certainly with us, about war as told and recreated in legend. That story undermines itself in its very failure to denominate, as the constant deconstructions keep shifting the perspective. If the last two paragraphs of *Red Badge* have caused so much critical discussion over the sentimentality of (a) the author, or (b) the character, it is largely because of this final irony, about the way war turns men into either brutes or lost kids. The author, having swallowed the youth in his irony, spills him out again on another less explicit level in the central Chapters 11 and 12, and then in the last two paragraphs of the book he leaves him free and selfish but still 'unfinished', separate to the last, unable as Bakhtin puts it to 'coincide with himself'.

Or so it would seem, right up to the original ending of the novel (at 'walking-sticks'). But the three sentences the author added to the Appleton text enclose him again in one final controlling irony:

He had rid himself of the red sickness of battle. The sultry nightmare was in the past. He had been an animal blistered and sweating in the heat and pain of war. He turned now with a lover's thirst, to images of tranquil skies, fresh meadows, cool brooks; an existence of soft and eternal peace.

(Ch. 24/25, RT)

The youth may feel he has earned this contrast, but clearly he is deluded. For as a practical truth, one local battle does not end a war, and he will go back into the red sickness which, like all sickness, lies within. Or as Gertrude Stein (1937, 139) puts it: 'You must remember that in a battle or a war everything has been prepared which is what has been called begun and then everything happens at once which is called done and then a battle or a war is either not or won.'

7

Ill wit and sick tragedy

Thomas Hardy has been called 'innovative' in his attempts to fuse 'narrator' and character (see below), but in this respect he is much more traditional than Crane, where the fusion of the poles NS and RT leads to unstable irony, as we saw in the last chapter. In Hardy the problem lies more with the handling of representation, and notably of viewpoint, and this is involved with questions of knowledge and understanding.

In an interesting essay (1979) John Goode analyses Hardy's most controversial character, Sue Bridehead, as an image in Jude's life, whose function is to open a gap between what she says and the way she is understood, and he argues that we go seriously wrong in treating *Jude* 'in terms of a representation which we then find "incomprehensible"', for it is the incomprehensibility that constitutes the novel's effect' (108).

What is interesting about Goode's essay is that while insisting that representational readings (sexist, feminist, or whatever) are wrong, he inverts, to show this, the type of representational reading that blames Sue: in a naturalistic interpretation, he says, we would question the absurdity of Jude's lack of understanding:

Sue is driven round the country by prejudice and poverty, stuck in Christminster by Jude's obsession, and her children are killed by Jude's son whom she had made her own [...] But we don't consider it naturalistically because we never ask what is happening to Sue, it is Sue happening to Jude. So what matters is where this reaction puts her, rather than why it came about.

(108)

By 'representational' Goode seems to mean ideological, in which case he simply shifts the emphasis to Jude. By 'naturalistic' he seems to mean sound common sense or fairness, rather than the Naturalism of Zola, but in either sense I do not feel we have to be feminists to 'question the absurdity of Jude's lack of understanding'. It is not 'we' who 'never ask what is happening to Sue', it is Hardy.

J. Hillis Miller (1982) takes up Hardy's insistent question 'why
does Tess suffer so?', which has led critics to assume that they must
find a cause (and a single one), whereas, although Hardy's work
is over-determined, 'the problem is not that there are no explanations
proposed in the text but that there are too many [...] incompatible
causes [...] There is no "original version", only an endless sequence
of them [...] always recorded from some previously existing exem-
plar' (140–1). Hillis Miller is exploring the functioning of two different kinds of repetition, as proposed by Deleuze (1969a), the Platonic
(representations, or the world as icon) and the Nietzschean (simu-
lacra, or the world as phantasm).

It is this kind of functioning in *Jude the Obscure* that I would like
to explore, not so much with reference to Sue vs. Jude, nor to repetition, but with reference to the problem of knowledge, in fiction generally, in Hardy, in *Jude*.

'Books and other impedimenta' (I.i)

That Hardy, deprived of university education, became obsessed with
the acquisition of knowledge and methodical note-taking for incor-
poration of 'items' into his novels, is particularly stressed in Gittings'
biography (1975), as well as his general conviction that everything
could be learnt, even the writing of poetry, by consulting the right
books. It is this last aspect which is so savagely treated in *Jude*.
That he also became a well-educated man 'in a way that Dickens,
Trollope and James were not', as argued by Rehder (1977), is no
doubt true but irrelevant to my purpose. What interests me here
is the peculiar intensity and the intense peculiarity of Hardy's use
of knowledge in *Jude*, not only as narrative theme but as narration
itself.

As narrative theme, it has been amply (and of course contradic-
torily) treated, and I shall merely summarize my reading. There
is the clear equivalence of intellectual knowledge and carnal knowledge, each proving evasive and illusory, each killed by the 'letter'
of the epigraph. Knowledge is desire and Christminster is clearly
female: 'like a young lover alluding to his mistress' (I.iii); or female
fused with God the Father: 'my Alma Mater, and I'll be her beloved
son, in whom she shall be well pleased' (I.vi); the recurrent image
of the wall that keeps him out (e.g. II.ii) is paralleled by Sue's behaviour, both inviting and refusing, and by: 'Now that the high window-
sill stood between them, so that he could not get at her, she seemed

not to mind' (IV.i); and when he has lost both, it is Sue who becomes a ghostly presence in Christminster, replacing that of poets and divines of earlier days (III.viii). As Rehder puts it: 'The tragedy in Hardy's novels is often the end of a dream. The awakening is a prelude to destruction, as if knowledge were forbidden [...] knowledge comes with the force of a blow' (1977, 24).

The two types of knowledge are also antagonistic, and Jude is perfectly aware, both during and after the early relationships, that two women have prevented his studies (I.ix, II.iv, IV.iii). At the same time the reader is made aware that Jude falls, with varying degrees of blindness, into every trap (a facile Freudian reading would say that he doesn't *really* want to study), and that his problematic love for Sue replaces, at least in the narration, his single-minded project of 'reading most of the night after working all day' (II.ii).

There are also complex polarities in types of knowledge, first and very early (I.v) between knowledge as classics and knowledge as theology, a tug incarnated by Sue herself as 'pagan' versus Jude as Christian, with the parallel reversal which is the basis of the novel's structure. But both these unite against other knowledge, as when Jude 'reads', as craftsman, 'the numberless architectural pages round him' (II.ii), and has 'a true illumination, that here in the stone yard was a centre of effort as worthy as that dignified by the name of scholarly study' – though the narrating author steps in: 'But he lost it under the stress of his old idea' (II.ii). And after the crash of his dream he discovers for a moment, though as mere spectator still, 'the real Christminster life', the town life, which 'was a book of humanity' (II.vi). A deal of 'reading', but of what might be called 'ordinary' knowledge. It is thus rather odd to find him opposing Divinity as 'ordinary' knowledge to classics, and a moment later also reducing the classics to 'the ordinary classical grind'.

It was a new idea [...] A man could preach and do good without taking double-firsts in the schools of Christminster or having anything but ordinary knowledge [...] It would be necessary that he should continue for a time to work at his trade while reading up Divinity, which he had neglected at Christminster for the ordinary classical grind.

(III.i)

What is 'ordinary' knowledge? In Tinker Taylor's words: 'I always saw there was more to be learnt outside a book than in' (II.vii). But knowledge, whatever it is of, is always a taking IN what is OUT, in order to pass it OUT again, in teaching, in bringing up, in communicating, in living: like money or other acquisitions, it circulates, but you can't take it with you.

And yet, though Jude has read and experienced much, he does not die with greater self-knowledge, or even with the deep knowledge of the other that he thought he had. It is news (event) rather than knowledge as such that 'comes with the force of a blow' (Rehder), and his bookish quotation from Job as he dies seems abysmally pathetic and irrelevant, as does that from *Agamemnon* after the children's death, and Sue's reaction to the latter is amazingly condescending in the circumstances:

My poor Jude – how you've missed everything! you more than I, for I did get you! [he got her too, so she must mean he didn't to the same full extent] To think that you should know that by unassisted reading, and yet be in poverty and despair!

(VI.ii)

In no novel that I have ever read do words of knowledge seem to occur quite so frequently. The plot manipulations depend on it (knowledge as secrecy and revelation), as do all the thematic elements: knowledge as books ('books and other impedimenta' says the narrating author, of Phillotson's baggage in the first chapter, and we need knowledge that the Latin plural means baggage, to see the full irony); knowledge as common sense, as craftsmanship, as superstition, as misleading items from ignorant others; knowledge like money, as access to knowledge ('to get ready by accumulating money and knowledge', II.ii); knowledge as self-awareness, as knowledge of the other, perpetually contradicted, or as fear of the other's knowledge, or as self-assurance (Phillotson in VI.v, 'they don't know Sue as I do' or Sue in VI.iii, 'I am convinced I am right'); or as public knowledge of private facts: for their troubles, too, are largely due to the paradox that their illicit union gets 'known', so that they have to keep moving to where they are 'unknown', while inversely, the theme of their legalistic marriage depends also on the knowledge (or non-knowledge) of consummation: 'if the truth about us had been known' says Sue on getting a divorce under 'false pretences'. It seems that only the vulgar Arabelle reads life correctly, from her viewpoint of survival, and she is gifted with quite an animal knowledge: she can tell, not from 'knowing' Sue but simply from looking at her, that her marriage had not, and has now, been consummated (V.ii), and naturally imparts this knowledge to Phillotson.

'But nobody did come because nobody does' (I.iv)

What about knowledge in the narration itself?

When the boy Jude has at last obtained his Latin and Greek Grammars and learnt, as his first great shock, that a grammar is not a simple prescription or rule or 'secret cipher, which, once known, would enable him by merely applying it, to change at will all words of his own speech into those of the foreign tongue', the narrating author (after giving us extraneous information about Grimm's Law to show that he knew better), ends the chapter:

> Somebody might have come along that way who would have asked him his trouble, and might have cheered him by saying that his notions were further advanced than those of his grammarian. But nobody did come, because nobody does, and under the crushing recognition of his gigantic error Jude continued to wish himself out of the world.

> (I.iv)

Nobody does, except the narrating author, who tells us (wrongly as it happens, Grimm's 'Law' not being a law in the sense needed here), but withholds knowledge from him. And all his life, Jude will seek 'a secret cipher' to life, and end up wishing and getting himself out of the world.

Knowledge circulates incessantly in any narrative, which depends on it, and the proper questions are how much, what kind, and whether external or internal to the fiction; and, within the fiction, whether external or internal to a character.

In the nineteenth-century Realist novel, especially in its Naturalist version (Zola), a vast amount of knowledge about the world circulated in various ways, and since the ideology of Realism (to show, to teach, a rich, pre-existent but capturable world) was inhabited by the basic contradiction of all pedagogy (a plethora of information vs. the need for readability, see Hamon 1973 and Brooke-Rose 1981), all sorts of disguises had developed.

Hardy had presumably mastered all these, though he is often accused of clumsiness, notably with point of view. Taking it rather as mastery, two modern critics, Penny Boumelha and David Lodge, each treat Hardy as highly innovative.

Boumelha (1982) discusses the 'formal experimentation' with genre, voice and structures of perceptions that were explored by the 'New Woman' novels of the eighties and nineties, but which had already marked Hardy's earlier career, and were now 'given a significant contemporaneity by the practices of these lesser-known writers' (93). These structures attempted a dissolution of the boundaries between author and character, as opposed to the 'objective', 'scientific', authoritative 'narrator' of the Naturalisitic novel. *The Woodlanders*, she says, is Hardy's 'most experimental' novel, with a 'continuing multiplicity of generic elements almost to end', so that in

> the crucial figure of Grace Melbury, for whom no coherent personality [...] is con-
> structed [...] the full play of ambiguities and tensions is enacted in the shifts and
> vacancies of her role as narrative centre. It is not by accident that Grace is also
> the focus of Hardy's most radical attempt so far to confront the issues of sexuality
> and marriage in his fiction.
>
> (113)

Here two ways of writing emerge, the attempt to give a 'scientific authoritative encompassant that will shape the narrative of Tess Durbeyfield, and the deflected and overtly partial mode of narration that will grant to Sue Bridehead an inaccessibility pushing beyond the emptiness of enigma' (114). *Jude*, she says later,

> is a novel that threatens to crack open the powerful ideology of realism as a literary
> mode, and throws into question the whole enterprise of narrative. 'The letter killeth'
> – and not only Jude [...]. Sue is progressively reduced from a challenging articulacy
> to a tense and painful silence that returns her to the fold of marriage – a conclusion
> which ironically duplicates the death of Jude. Writing comes increasingly to resemble
> an instrument of death.
>
> (146)

I am not sure that generic mixture as such (by which she means re-using traditional elements from other genres, popular ballads, theatricality, and so on is 'experimental', but the word has become pretty meaningless (and at the time was used by Zola of the Naturalistic novel, 'objective' and well documented, which Hardy's 'experiment' opposed). As for the 'cracking open' of Realism's ideology, it is treated (as the quotations from Boumelha show) much more thematically, so that 'writing' (and 'experiment'?) as instrument of death seems rather a sleight of hand. Her 'overtly partial' mode of narration simply means that the narrative adopts mostly Jude's point of view in what is today called 'internal focalization', but this is hardly innovative and, as we have seen with Crane, this does not efface the distance between narrating author and character, nor does the notion of 'partial' mode prove their fusion, as Boumelha appears to think. However, without basically disagreeing with Boumelha in other respects, I want to show that it is paradoxically through misuse of traditional elements that a novel so concerned with knowledge should turn out to be, in the modern sense, so unknowable.

Inversely, David Lodge (1977b) has stressed Hardy's modernity by showing how cinematic his treatment of perspective is: aerial shots of diminutive figures on a huge landscape (= vulnerability of human creatures and the indifference of nature) or the illuminated figure inside observed by the unobserved observer outside (= imperfect understanding and defective communication). Or the 'hypothetical or unspecified observer', a sort of 'second narrator' who 'might have seen' which (though strictly speaking impossible in the cinema which would have to show such a figure) Lodge argues is like a different camera-angle that needs no such explanatory supposition (but then of course any 'narrator' can switch viewpoints, for instance in dialogue, without need for a 'hypothetical' observer). Lodge adds that what is so original in Hardy is commonplace in film, which must narrate in images only, so that transposition of a Hardy novel into film is difficult.

Here too, I doubt whether Hardy's treatment of perspective is all that new. Balzac was doing it in the first half of the century (see Ch. 4, pp. 50–1), as were Hawthorne, Melville, Scott, and Dickens. Indeed it could be argued that the cinema inherited all the by-then clichés of the novel except the 'narrative voice', and took another quarter-century to free itself.

Balzac's fascination with visual treatment has been well analysed by Jean Paris (1986) and by Le Huenon and Perron (1984), notably for the descriptive aporia it often entails. The knowledge imposed is both postulated and concealed. 'Every reader of Balzac is familiar with those introductory descriptions set into play by an image, a picture, a vision that is immediately indexed as lack of knowledge' (LH & P, 716). This refers specifically to Balzac's many 'hypothetical observers' (already in Stendhal), and similarly Jean Paris shows that Balzac's use of this device produces indetermination.[1] In Balzac, 'this veiled indexation of knowledge results in a shift from descriptive to a narrative programme', but also in a reversal of function, because it is still necessary 'to demonstrate that the narrator can effectively take over the function of guarantor [of knowledge known to him but not to the character]' (LH & P, 719).

'But what is the nature of knowledge?' the authors ask, and reply by quoting Balzac on the *Comédie humaine*, on knowledge moving from effects to causes, and then to principles. 'The customs are the spectacle, the causes are the wings and the machinery. Principles, that's the author' (*Pléiade* 1967, 270). They comment: 'This, taken

---

[1] Poe uses it also for the ambiguity of the fantastic, for instance in *The Fall of the House of Usher* (1845): 'Perhaps the eye of a scrutinizing observer might have discovered a barely perceptible fissure ...'

literally, postulates a sharp dissociation between the realm of representation and the realm of knowledge' (722).

Above all, it postulates the place of representation as the place of accident, chance, and the subject of knowing as 'principle'. The 'author' will, for instance, interpret an obscure inscription on a house (his technical knowledge), while the idle passer-by (the hypothetical observer) stays at the level of appearance. Where Jameson (1980, 69) sees in this ordered visual topos the constitution of the bourgeois subject and narrative strategies that block development, Le Huenon and Perron suggest on the contrary another space of knowledge:

These interminable comings and goings are final moments in the constitution of a new space, a new knowledge where the subject cannot find a place; they are the end terms of transformation processes that take archaic spaces of knowledge originally inscribed in the text, redistribute them, and re-present them according to an incoherent and incomprehensible logic.

(728)

One might almost be reading about Hardy. Doesn't Sue rearrange the books of the New Testament in the order in which they were written, which shocks Jude, but makes it 'twice as interesting'? (III.iv). Except that, for Hardy, there were (ultimately) no 'principles'. And therein will lie the contradiction.

'The same womanly character' (III.vi)

Hardy, to be sure, achieves his indetermination in other ways. When Balzac uses the hypothetical observer it is to create a mystery, an as-yet-unknown, a 'veiled indexation of knowledge'. In Hardy it has already become an empty tic, which can even abolish the hypothetical observer:

An hour later his thin form [. . .] could have been seen walking along the five-mile road to Marygreen. On his face showed the determined purpose that alone sustained him but to which his weakness afforded a sorry foundation.

(VI.viii)

The external focalization necessary to a hypothetical observer is contradicted by information only the author can know, whereupon the hypothetical observer, already weak, textually vanishes. Similarly the device of the 'pretended unknown', already a cliché in Balzac, is used for pointless exclusion of the reader who nevertheless knows from immediate context:

[previous paragraph about Sue]
On an afternoon at this time a young girl entered the stonemason's yard [. . .] 'That's

a nice girl [...] Who is she [...] I don't know [...] Why yes' [identification by the craftsman] Meanwhile the young woman had knocked at the office.

(II.iv)

Meanwhile a middle-aged man was dreaming a dream of great beauty concerning the writer of the above letter [whom we know to be Sue]. He was Richard Phillotson [whom we already know, and know to be interested in Sue], who [description and analeptic information ...] These were historic notes, written in a bold womanly hand at his dictation some months before [...] the same womanly character as the historic notes [...] frank letters signed 'Sue B' [...] written during short absences with no other thought than their speedy destruction [...] forgotten doubtless by the writer [...] In one of them [...] the young woman said ...:

(III.vi)

The viewpoint of the craftsman is taken in the first passage, though there is no particular narrative point or realist interest in this. The viewpoint of the second passage becomes aporetic. Who speaks? Both the narrating author and Phillotson know who wrote the letter, as does the reader. Only the first can know the 'thought', and Phillotson could be said to guess ('doubtless') the forgetting. There is an uncertain hovering between the 'pretended unknown', Narration and Represented Thought. The 'pretended unknown', frequent still in *Jude*, has become a pointless trick of pseudo-exclusion of the reader for its own sake, pseudo-suspense.

Elsewhere however, readers are, on the contrary, as in melodrama, let *in on* the terrible traps that are preparing for Jude, and this with ultra-simplistic shifts of focalization derived from popular forms, almost of the 'little-does-he-know' type, usually signalled by 'Meanwhile Arabella', 'Meanwhile Sue' and so on; like cutting in the cinema, where it is a fundamentally popular technique but also, as Lodge does not say, authoritarian as to camera angle for limitation or revelation. Today the trick has become mechanical and meaningless in soap opera. And what the readers are and are not told can seem visibly arbitrary. In *Jude* for instance (to remain with trivial items), we are let in on Arabella's false dimples (and so watch Jude discover them), but not on her false hair, which has been elided (we discover it with him). Similarly the frequent voyeuristic or overhearing scenes sometimes tell us something new (Sue walking close to Phillotson, II.v) and sometimes not; Jude overhearing Arabella's friends on their 'advice' to her (I.x) – and even then he only surmises, so that some readers may feel exasperated at his stupidity, as throughout his courtship.

Thus, on the level of plot, readers are ostentatiously manipulated, as Jude is (Hardy said Jude was a 'puppet') and made to enter

a crudely ironic structure rather like that of a Punch-and-Judy show
where the children cry 'look out!', and not an identifying one that
makes them share the experience (as in, say, *Red Badge*).

With other elements of knowledge, however, such as self-awareness
(wisdom), or knowledge of the other (insight), we are on the contrary
drawn into an identifying structure, but in a peculiar way, through
a similar dialectic of the hidden and the revealed but on a different
scale, a dialectic as cock-teasing as Jude's 'ever-evasive Sue'. And
this is achieved through:

> (1) a skilful use of dialogue to conceal what it suggests (and this is rather modern)
> (2) a heavy-handed use of narration
> (3) a blurred use of Represented Speech and Thought.

'You don't know how bad I am, from your point of view' (III.i)

By definition the most mimetic parts of a narrative are in Direct
Speech ('Language can only imitate language', says Genette 1972).
Hardy is a master of dramatic form, and *Jude* has perhaps more
dialogue than any of his other novels. Dialogue has a revealing/
concealing structure since we reveal ourselves through utterance,
but only to the limits of what can be articulated. It thus draws
us IN and keeps us OUT, guessing. It is not by chance that Sue and
Jude are interesting chiefly in dialogue and when they are talking
about the *problems* of their relationship (and of the book): 'You must
take me as I am', says Sue, twice, the first time meaning one thing
(non-consummation, V.i), the second time another (she is about
to leave him, VI.iii): there too she says 'Ah – you don't know my
badness!' and he exclaims vehemently 'I do! Every atom and dreg
of it! You make me hate Christianity, or mysticism, or whatever
it may be called, if it's that which has caused this deterioration
in you.' A big IF. And much earlier she had said 'Only you don't
know how bad I am, from your point of view', meaning her paganism,
but also perhaps 'The Ishmaelite' (III.i, III.ii), and later she repeats
'I said you didn't know how bad I was', meaning (apparently) what
'people say', that 'I must be cold-natured – sexless' (III.iv).

Not all the dialogue is so 'writerly' (the readers fill in, see Barthes
1972; 1974). More often it is punctuated by author-comment: 'with
the perverseness that was part of her' (III.i), 'with a gentle seriousness that did not reveal her mind' (III.vi), 'in the delicate voice
of an epicure of the emotions' (III.vii), or her 'tragic contralto' (IV.i).
And even here all these perceptions might be Jude's, in RT, since

we are in dialogue and he is present as perceiver. As we saw, the late realist novel does not distinguish clearly between narration in internal focalization and RT, but comments after dialogue usually still come from the narrating author. Either way the perceptions are outside Sue, even though she is speaking. The blurring of author-comment and Jude's perceptions is important to understand Jude. But the viewpoint of Sue, and above all the nature of their relationship, its quality, its texture (what attracts two such different people apart from loneliness, especially on Sue's side), this is treated much more bizarrely, from regular distancing to total occultation, whereas we are given all the scenes with Arabella straight – a much simpler affair.

'A chronicler of moods and deeds'

At their first meeting, Jude and Sue at once go off to see Phillotson, and any conversation they might have had on the way is elided. When they arrive, Jude's interest shifts at once to Phillotson, then the walk back is distanced by narrative summary in internal focalization on Jude (II.iv). This is followed by a practical discussion about why she has to leave and Jude's fatal suggestion that she should go to Phillotson as pupil-teacher. And this sort of occultation will mark the whole development: desperate dialogue, desperate messages, internal focalization on Jude, author-comment on both, or ellipsis of Sue, although Hardy is by no means averse to the classical-viewpoint change for other characters.

We do, of course, have separate access to Sue, but only in dialogue or letters with Phillotson, or in dialogue with Arabella or with Mrs Edlin, and hardly at all in internal focalization.

The most remarkable occultation is that of their happiness. The kiss which 'was a turning point in Jude's career', for instance, is elided, then hinted at by a hypothetical observer (who however has authorial knowledge) as he returns from the station: 'in his face was a look of exultation not unmixed with recklessness', then told in summary analepsis: 'An incident had occurred' (IV.iii). And when Sue at last comes to live with Jude they merely have another intense conversation about their situation, then a scene about Arabella, then we switch to Phillotson and Gillingham. The next section starts:

How Gillingham's doubts were disposed of will most quickly appear by passing over the series of dreary months and incidents that followed the events of the last chapter.

(V.i)

The same happens after the consummation, finally achieved through Jude playing on her jealousy and followed after the normal Victorian ellipsis by a sad absent-mindedness on Sue's part and immediate departure, out of guilt, to see Arabella, and a switch to the arrival of Jude's son. Then:

> The purpose of a chronicler of moods and deeds does not require him to express his personal views upon the grave controversy above given. That the twain were happy – between their times of sadness – was indubitable. And when the unexpected apparition of Jude's child in the house had shown itself to be no such disturbing event as it had looked . . .
>
> (V.v)

The sleight of hand is obvious: the reader's desire is not for the chronicler's personal views but for the moods and deeds. And after the incident which makes them decide to leave Aldbrickham the narration resumes:

> Whither they had gone nobody knew, chiefly because nobody cared to know. And anyone sufficiently curious to trace the steps of such an obscure pair might have discovered. . .
>
> (V.iii)

Nobody knows, chiefly because the author, momentarily hiding behind 'nobody', does not care to tell us, though as usual the hypothetical observer does tell us at once, but in summary. And suddenly we're at the Kennetbridge Fair, in dramatic form again, but between Sue and Arabella, and Sue has two children of her own. As Patricia Ingham says in her excellent introduction to the Oxford edition: 'The joy is looked forward to and back, but it is never actually there' (xx), at least, when evoked, it is always as 'veiled indexation of knowledge', as vanishing-point in the narrative technique, the narrating author heavily marking or not marking his ellipses and sudden shifts.

The reason is the *author's* knowledge: what matters to Hardy is desire (male), while marriage is death: hence the allowance we have to make, not for Sue's (and Hardy's?) horror of sex (a Victorian commonplace no odder than the post-Freudian treatment of sex-refusal as abnormal), but for her horror of *legalized* marriage, three times endorsed separately in author-comment and clearly a euphemism for the death of desire through familiarity, or knowledge possessed and therefore undesired, since desire is by definition for something absent. The equally obvious fact that it is sometimes not so, that some rare people have the ludic art of love – another form of 'knowledge' – does not interest Hardy, or indeed most novelists, since narrative is based on desire, yet for this of all relationships, where so much depends on that mysterious quality called companionship (which is what Sue wanted), the imaginative effort should have been made. It is a serious lack, for it pushes the reader further OUT, and alienates him from both Jude and Sue.

'A voice whispered that, though he desired to know her ...' (II.iv)

Author-comment pulls us OUT, as does narration in external focalization. Narration in internal focalization gives the viewpoint of the character but as told by the narrating author, in summary for instance, or in what Genette (1972; 1976) calls 'narrativized discourse', which summarizes a character's words (spoken or thought) without giving them. Represented Speech and Thought (here almost entirely Thought, RT) draws us much further IN, since it gives the character's idiom, but still in narrative sentences. It has now become an extremely blurred narrative cliché of average realist fiction, where it is often used to pass narrative information that could not be going through the character's mind in that form (see Ch. 5). And this we already get in Hardy.

The distinction is very clear when the knowledge is author-knowledge extraneous to the fiction: information about Roman Britain is passed through Jude's mind in RT (I.viii), but the history of Shaston comes from the author in IV.i (transferred from III.vi where it presumably formed part of Phillotson's interests). But when the knowledge is the content of a consciousness the distinction is much less clear. This blurring seems to me to begin with Hardy and is, together with simple occultation, largely responsible for the indetermination, the (later fashionable) 'ambiguities and tensions', the 'shifts and vacancies' (Boumelha) or the 'incomprehensibility that constitutes the novel's effect' (Goode). No doubt this is what Boumelha means by 'fusion' of 'narrator' and character. Hardy constantly shifts from narrative sentences to RT, and it is often impossible to discern 'who speaks':

To be sure she was almost an ideality to him still. Perhaps to know her would be to cure himself of this unexpected and unauthorized passion. A voice whispered that, though he desired to know her, he did not desire to be cured.

(II.iv)

We start in RT ('to be sure', 'Perhaps', 'would be'). But does one think to oneself 'a voice whispers'? Does not that voice also 'represent' author-comment? Here it is unimportant, but there are strange moments of aporia with Sue:

> Sue paused patiently beside him, and stole critical looks into his face as, regarding the Virgins, Holy Families, and Saints, it grew reverent and abstracted. When she had thoroughly estimated him at this she would move on and wait for him before a Lely or Reynolds. It was evident that her cousin deeply interested her, as one might be interested in a man puzzling out his way along a labyrinth from which one had oneself escaped.
>
> (II.ii)

Evident to whom? Who says 'her cousin'? Until then we could be either in narration (internal focalization) or (less likely) in RT (the 'would' as future, but more convincingly as iterative), then suddenly we veer, not just to narration but to an implied hypothetical observer, followed by author-comment. Or:

> to keep him from his jealous thoughts, which she read clearly, as she always did
>
> (IV.i)

> But Sue either saw it not at all, or, seeing it, would not allow herself to feel it
>
> (IV.ii)

Grammatically both could be RT. But who says 'as she always did'? Since Sue is rarely treated in RT we must assume that it is narrational, but then it is either untrue, or Sue must be interpreted (elsewhere) as consciously cruel. And in the second example the narrating author is explicitly not telling.

One of the rare instances of RT with Sue immediately veers to author-comment:

> Meanwhile Sue [...] had gone along to the station [NS], with tears in her eyes for having run back and let him kiss her [NS/RT]. Jude ought not to have pretended that he was not her lover, and made her give way to an impulse to act unconventionally, if not wrongly [RT]. She was inclined to call it the latter [NS/RT]; for Sue's logic was extraordinarily compounded, and seemed [... NS]
>
> (IV.iii)

These various unclarities naturally happen all the time with Jude, who is treated regularly in RT, which critics do not always distinguish from narration (or even from their own comments). In fact it will be easier to show the blurring by quoting one good critic producing just that confusion. Patricia Ingham writes:

> Rather disconcertingly for the reader, the narrator, whose sympathy with Jude has been acute so far, now berates him for 'mundane ambition masquerading in a surplice' and rebukes him for that social unrest, that desire for upward mobility, which from

the 1870s had been an explicit reason for Oxford in particular holding back the spread of adult education to the working class in order to protect 'the over-crowded professions'. The narrator's volte-face sets the future pattern. He may condemn Jude sometimes but elsewhere, for instance in Jude's speech to the crowd at Christminster, he will support his attempt to 'reshape' his course and rise into another class [...]

(xiii–xiv)

The 'narrator' does not 'berate' Jude for mundane ambition, Jude berates himself, since the passage is in RT (III.i, opening, 'It was a new idea ...' partly quoted p. 108). Nor *a fortiori*, does he rebuke him for 'that social unrest' and all that follows, since all that follows is the critic's language (outside the text), whereas the text says, more vaguely, 'a social unrest which had no foundation in the nobler instincts; which was purely an artificial product of civilization'. Nor for that matter does the 'narrator' 'support' Jude during his speech at Christminster since it is given by Jude in Direct Speech, with no author-comment but plenty of disapproval from Sue as well as irony of event: she keeps saying they ought to find a room first, and Jude's ignoring her leads to their difficulty in finding a room and the boy's disastrous reactions.

Ingham also says first that 'the narrator makes clear from the start the delusory nature of the boy's [Jude's] quest, *and*, later, that 'Jude and the narrator are seized with the desirability of the learning that the university offers', and then again (after dealing with the irony of the quotations): 'What Jude only learns of life's cruelty the narrator knows from the start: he is already aware of the ironic irrelevance of the literary text.'

This seems to be having it all ways, and like the previous example, comes from a misreading of narrative techniques, which are much clearer than this reading implies. The 'delusory nature of the boy's quest' refers to his seeing or perhaps not seeing Christminster from Marygreen as a boy, but this is told in internal focalization and dialogue without author-comment, and to say 'the narrator makes clear from the start' is to mistake narration in internal focalization for author-comment. Nor is the 'narrator' at any point seized with the 'desirability', and so on; only Jude, and the ghastly irrelevance of the bits of classical knowledge and theological authors he tries to study on his own is not commented, it can only be *at once* clear to the reader (as opposed to later) from a shared cultural code (knowledge again, but outside the text), which varies in time and space and from reader to reader, irony being culturally determined. Ingham's last statement fuses what she calls the 'narrator' with the author, which shows (once again) how misleading the term 'narrator' can be (see Ch. 5).

It is probable that in Hardy the narrating author only speaks clearly as such when he is giving us information unknown to the characters, and this he does a great deal (he didn't know, didn't notice, had an illumination ... but forgot it etc.), sometimes heavily and oddly, as when he tells us that Jude (then a boy), 'was the sort of man who was born to ache a good deal before the fall of the curtain upon his unnecessary life should signify that all was well with him again' (I.ii); sometimes wrongly, as when he says that 'Sue did not for a moment, either now or later, suspect what troubles had resulted to him [Phillotson] from letting her go' (IV.vi – later? she obviously learns it eventually); or dogmatically: 'He did not at that time see that mediaevalism was as dead as a fern leaf in a lump of coal' (II.ii – which is the author's view). All the internal focalization on Jude, however, hovers between narration and RT. And much of the 'ambiguity' lies here. But 'ambiguity' can also lie in careless critical reading.

'Or is it the artificial system of things?' (IV.iii)

John Goode (1979) quotes Jude asking what Goode takes 'to be the fundamental ideological question posed by the novel' and found unforgivable by the critics who cannot take Sue:

> What I can't understand in you is your extraordinary blindness now to your old logic. Is it peculiar to you, or is it common to woman? Is a woman a thinking unit at all, or a fraction always wanting its integer?
>
> (VI.iii)

If this question (Goode continues) is asked in the novel, it is surely naive to ask it of the novel.

> What is important is that this question should be asked; it poses for Sue only one of two possibilities – that the nature of her blindness to her own logic must be explained either by her 'peculiarity' or by her belonging to womanhood. Either way, she is committed to being an image, and it is this that pervades the novel. Nobody ever confronts Jude with the choice between being a man or being peculiar. The essential thing is that Sue must be available to understanding. We might want to deduce that Hardy feels the same way as Jude at this point, but I think to do so would go against the consistency of the novel and against Hardy's whole career as a writer [his theme being woman as the object of male understanding].
>
> (103)

The point is excellent, but I am not so sure of his last arguments for the author not sharing Jude's feelings. Jude had of course already expressed a similar view before, in ambiguous RT then in DS to himself, when he reflects on two women blocking his aspirations: 'Is it that the women are to blame; or is it the artificial system of things, under which the normal sex-impulses are turned into devilish domestic gins . . .'? (IV.iii). But a few paragraphs later it is unambiguously the author who says 'for Sue's logic was extraordinarily compounded'. And after all it is the author who makes Sue change her logic. The 'artificial system of things' is of course made by men but neither Jude nor the author seems aware of that. Elsewhere Jude exclaims that he is not against her, 'taking her hand, and surprised at her introducing personal feeling into mere argument' (III.iv). This is narration not RT, and a gender-image, for Jude himself takes her arguments personally all the time. There is, moreover, Jude's own blindness to his 'old logic' (his reverence for the classics and Divinity, or his own past belief in legalistic marriage, which allowed him to sleep with Arabella and then be horrified to learn of her bigamous remarriage: 'why the devil didn't you tell me last night?' (III.ix); or his total unawareness that his speechifying was as much the cause of the tragedy as were Sue's careless answers to the boy, whereas it is Sue's awareness of these (her long habit of apparently neurotic self-reproach) that destroys her:

'Why did you do it, Sue?'
'I can't tell. It was that I wanted to be truthful. And yet I wasn't truthful, for with a false delicacy I told him too obscurely. Why was I half wiser than my fellow-women? and not entirely wiser! Why didn't I tell him pleasant untruths, instead of half realities! It was my want of self-control so that I could neither conceal things nor reveal them!'
(VI.ii)

As always. And like the author. But if her self-imposed penance seems excessive, at least she is given to know that it is for this 'half' wisdom, and whatever the readers feel about her description they must surely know during the scene with the boy (and think 'look out!') that the boy is being wholly misled. Jude however talks here of 'our peculiar case', and his only apparent self-reproach is that he 'seduced' her, and 'spoilt one of the highest and purest loves that ever existed between man and woman' (VI.iii). This shows a very peculiar logic and a very limited self-awareness, for it is no more than the simplistic Victorian dualism of purity vs. sex, and his own remarriage and self-imposed penance of death seem far blinder than hers. Thus Sue, whose complex inner feelings are occulted throughout, turns out, in dialogue, to be far more self-aware and less blinded than he is, while the gender-images of Jude, despite constant internal focalization, are left for some readers to see and some not to see. Sue must be pin-pointed for Jude as image of guilt and blindness.

'Good-bye, my mistaken wife. Good-bye!' (VI.iv)

The multi-meaning of 'mistaken' is painful: *she* has been mistaken all along: *he* has been mistaken in marrying her: *he* has mistaken her for someone else (an ideal); *he* has mis-taken her. The debit is on his side. And all because of 'the artificial system of things'.

Lance Butler (1977b) has argued that Hardy is one of the rare writers who does not have a 'world-view', whereas for most literary texts we do a 'doublethink' and 'make allowances' for cosmological orders that are 'frankly ludicrous' (for example, Dante, Dickens' innocent children, George Eliot's providential endings). He takes the endings of six major Hardy novels and shows a clear progression from various compromises (there is a providential structure) to *Jude* where Hardy finally achieves 'an ending that isn't false'. Since the novels are minutely planned and orchestrated, the paradox is that the order imposed 'implies that there is no final order [...], that in this rich patterned universe, there is no ultimate meaning. Whatever happens in Hardy's major fiction, however much he manipulates and controls it, he finally finds out how to prevent it from falling into a contrived moral or supernatural order' (125).

But we are not told how, apart from the endings, which are summarized. This leaves us with one highly reductive content (the absence of plan), which could also be said of many books including Voltaire's *Essais sur les moeurs* (and Jude twice accuses Sue of being Voltairean); and it seems to me in the 'how', in the meaning-production differentials of language, that the difficulties arise. Butler says that Hardy has received too much formal attention, so that his supposed 'faults' have excluded him from the company of the great. I have had the opposite impression that traditional attention had been thematic, and formal attention superficial, often falling back on the famous descriptions, and that Hardy is now being revalued in many exciting ways, while Boumelha's formal study turns the 'faults' into high experiment and Lodge's turns them into anticipations of film. I have tried to go further and point up, within the 'experiment', basic contradictions that in no way belittle Hardy (as deconstruction is not demolition) but seem deeper than that of careful (literary) structure revealing absence of (cosmological) structure.

For the attempt to blur the gap between the narrating author's discourse and the character's discourse is already traceable in *Daniel Deronda* twenty years earlier, together with an attempt, more radical than anything in Hardy, to disrupt the determinism of sequence and plot, and these will not fully flourish until Virginia Woolf (see Gillian Beer 1979). Hardy is part of that struggle, but his endings, like those of George Eliot, still 'exceed the book's terms' or 'strive structurally for a unity its perceptions will not fully permit' (Beer on Eliot), if for inverse reasons: a clinging to providential structure in Eliot, a rejection of providential structure in Hardy. And I see little difference between 'making allowances' for Dickens' innocent children and doing so for (among other things) a concept of tragedy that depends so heavily on organized stupidity, that is, on limitation (a secular version of a theological stance, the orthodox Augustinian one), while the characters blame institutions and faintly hope for a change (a Pelagian stance, whose secular version was liberal social-ism). I agree with Lance Butler about the 'doublethink' we bring to literature (though that is part of the pleasure, unless we read only for our own period 'truth'), but I do not agree that Hardy is as exempt from these allowances as he claims, or that he 'speaks to us today, as Shakespeare does and Beckett does, because he faces the ultimate penury of the world' (119).

For Shakespeare wrote plays, and Beckett wrote either plays or novels in what Bakhtin calls 'free direct discourse' (see Ch. 5), that is, one voice, but wholly dialogical, indeterminable. Hardy's indeter-minacy seems addressed to different readers (which is why I have been using the plural rather than THE reader of theory, see Pratt 1986): readers whose relation with the text may be submissive and coerced, readers whose relation with it may be subversive or conflict-ing or resisting. This may well explain his universal appeal despite the 'allowances' we have to make, which can thus be regarded as internal to the period fiction, like the 'allowances' we make for, say, the divine right of kings in Shakespeare.

Formally however, I suggest that Hardy's *poetic* indeterminacy, the feeling of a meaningless chasm behind the very precision, comes from his handling of direct speech, while the *pointless* indeterminacy and compensating pinpointing come from his handling of traditional narrative devices, which he has if anything weakened rather than enriched, and which have largely vanished except as fatigued stereotypes. They may of course return, if the present philosophy of 'ultimate penury' is succeeded by another period of firm beliefs, as Voltaire (and the concomitant eighteenth-century games with narrative authority) was succeeded by Victorian faith and its crises. But then, like the faith and authoritarian certainties, they would surely return in a refreshed and more energetic form.

Sentimentality, says Butler, 'is not simply an error of taste but the inevitable product of a world-view in which man comes into the world trailing clouds of glory' (118). I wholly agree, but would add: the blurred and empty use of old ironic devices is not simply an error of taste but the inevitable result of a world-view in which, however 'not false' one's endings, someone controls things, but indifferently and unfairly. A double-think world-view. Hardy stands between the two centuries, a great traditional figure.

For the treatment of knowledge, in narrational terms, wraps up all the fundamental ideological questions, telling us, like the cinema, too much when we would rather not know and, like the cinema, blurring the very origin of knowledge when we want to know 'who speaks' (or why that camera angle). This, so stated, can be interpreted as highly modern, but it can also be said to mean that, in the practice of reading, the narration still mimes God.

For example, if Jude's quotations are 'ironic' because incomplete, he may or may not know this, and the readers depend on outside knowledge, a cultural code. On the other hand, Jude doesn't know that the epigraphs frame his story. Or *does* he? He quotes that of the book to Sue: 'Sue, Sue, we are acting by the letter, and "the letter killeth"' (VI.viii). Is Jude, after all, a dialogical character carrying on a 'secret polemic' with his author or any other defining entity? In whom he loses faith.

But no. The quotation is 'ordinary' knowledge, available to authors and characters and readers alike, and he quotes it only about their legalistic marriage, not about the deathly and lifely power of language to say the opposite of what it says. We are still too much in traditional, ironic, monological modes, however indeterminate, the author manipulating the very indeterminacy before our eyes: now you see it, now you don't. There is Christminster, there it maybe isn't. There is knowledge, there it isn't. There is desire, there it isn't. There is the voice that utters, there it isn't, it was only Jude, the obscure.

8

Cheng Ming Chi'I'd

By dealing in detail with three traditional male novelists, and more particularly with the problem of Represented Thought, I have in this Section tried to show how important apparently minor elements of style can become in the interpretation of Story. But there are other ways of telling stories than the prose novel, and although I shall be returning to this (my main theme), in the next Sections, I would like to end this one by considering two texts by two Modernist poets, Pound (here) and Auden (Ch. 9), also from a very particular stylistic point of view.

The Cantos tells a story too, but in a very different, non-narrative way, although there are narratives in them. And the Pound story is itself a huge and complex one, which includes the story of a style that was a lifetime developing towards adequacy to its vast material, a style, moreover, that altered the English poetic language more profoundly than any other in the twentieth century.

Critical interpretations sometimes misread, misrepresent, misunderstand stylistic features, but nothing can do this as thoroughly as translation does, especially for poetry, which uses language in a very specific way. Poetry is what gets lost in translation, said Frost, and style is the man, said Buffon; these two statements together are the best affirmation that language is of the essence. And yet the French translation of *The Cantos* that marked the centenary of Pound's birth in 1985 is nothing short of a scandal. I would like to show how.

'There is no substitute for a lifetime' (C.98)

So wrote Pound in *Thrones* and *The Cantos* are the work of a lifetime. To translate such monumental work poses monumental problems, and to translate it into French seems to pose even more.

Naturally one cannot expect a translator to be as single-minded

as the poet himself and to devote his entire life to translating one
such text, unless he or she is as possessed with it as the poet was.
Clearly this was so with his daughter, Mary de Rachewiltz, who
did devote a large part of her already busy life translating *The Cantos*
into Italian (de Rachewiltz, 1985) and who, be it said in passing,
also produced it in a bilingual and annotated edition, giving the
only reliable English text available so far, as well as the two missing
'Italian' Cantos. Similarly Eva Hesse devoted many years to her
German translation of Pound.[1] This translation is alas incomplete,
Ms Hesse having turned to other things, but two criticisms that
cannot be made against either of these translators are (1) lack of
tonal unity and (2) ignorance of Pound. They are both, for different
reasons and in different ways, Pound experts through and through.

The French story is very different. The deliberate decision was
made (because of lateness in the field) to share out blocks of Cantos
among five translators. The poet Denis Roche had already translated
The Pisan Cantos (L'Herne 1966), and this was regarded by Jacques
Darras as a 'historic' text, not to be touched – a curiously elitist
decision since other Cantos had been translated by various hands,
and were not considered too sacred to be redone by others here.
The decision to share out was rational but not without its consequences, which could have been avoided through constant consultation and a more humble acceptance of Jean-Michel Rabaté's
careful work of overall supervision. Rabaté is a Poundian in a way
the others are not, but this work of correction was filtered, either
by the publisher or by one of the contributors. Nor was my own
last-minute offer to save the text accepted, or perhaps even transmitted. Only Philippe Mikriammos had the creative humility to come
and work with me. The result is that the first forty-one Cantos by
his hand, which are among the best translations anyway but which
contained some errors of English reading, are now free of them.
It is therefore the very uneven rest that I shall be discussing here,
as, on the one hand, a curious case of French vanity not pulled
down, and, on the other, as an illustration of just what language
can do and undo.

---

[1] '*Cantos I-XXX, Pisaner Cantos, Letzte Texte – Entwurfe und Fragmente zu Cantos CX-
CXX, Arche Verlag 1964; 1956, rev. 1969; 1975*, all bilingual editions.

'These are distinctions in clarity' (C.84)

Most theorists of translation agree that it is better to be a poet in the language of arrival and not know the language of departure very well (providing one accepts help), than to know the original and not be a poet (if there must be a choice). One of the recurring problems in poetic translation, which Pound knew only too well, is that of 'creative' mistakes, for he was often accused of 'howlers' by classicists, sinologists and others, while Poundians defended these as pure poetry, truer equivalents than a more 'correct' version would have given.

So here, although Denis Roche has more howlers than all the others put together, some could certainly be defended in this way. Pound for instance did not say *travail à la chaine* (production line) in C.74 but 'canal work' (Hesse: *Kanalarbeit*). Perhaps Roche confused 'canal' with 'channel', and the French word for TV channel is *chaine*. Whatever the case, *travail à la chaine* used to mean chain-gang work and gives a vivid image, except that the making of canals, one of Pound's recurring themes in the American Cantos, disappears. Or again, I was tripped up by *De grands seigneurs la terre se gave [. . .] La terre se gave d'eux* in the same Canto, for 'Great lords are to the earth o'er given [. . .] are to the earth o'er given', which is a quotation from Pound's translation of the Anglo-Saxon poem *The Seafarer*. Here Roche may have misunderstood 'o'er given' as 'over given' (given too much) instead of 'given over' (given up), and this gave him *la terre se gave*, literally overfeeds itself. The result is splendid, and produces a phonetic echo as well. This is not the kind of 'mistake' I shall be criticizing.

Two other recurring problems in poetic translation are: (1) those inherent to the structures of the two languages concerned, so that specific solutions must be found; (2) those relating to knowledge of the translated poet, knowledge beyond the actual lines being translated: beyond in space (in the rest of the poem – the orchestration) and beyond in time (the 'sources', textual, biographical or cultural – the archeology).

These problems are particularly important here. Pound's English idiom – from archaism to slang – is highly individual in every way, and obviously a translator must find constant equivalents and not fall back on classical literary French, nor for that matter on non-literary but banal French. Similarly, *The Cantos* are partly structured on echoes, not just of themes but of specific syntactic structures, and partly on a very individual archeology: it is what Pound does with his sources which is so enriching, so full of 'hilaritas', and sometimes it would have helped the translators to have known or consulted these sources.

I shall discuss the French translation (on a detailed check of three or four Cantos per translator) in the order of problems rather than of people, adding only the initials of each translator after the reference of any quotation given.[2] The order will be:

(1) comparative linguistic structures
(2) misreadings of English
(3) lack of coordination (orchestration and archeology).

'It can't be all in one language' (C.86)

'Sono tutti eretici, Santo Padre,
    ma non sono cattivi'
It can't be all in one language
    'They are all prots YR HOLINESS,
        but not bad.'

(C.86)

Pound was deeply aware that some things go better in one language than in another, and is here expressing the fact with a joke translation (botched by Roche's *mais ils ne sont pas méchants*). Hence his use of so many languages in *The Cantos* – notably French for wit, vulgarity and sentiment (*J'ai eu pitié des autres/Pas assez! Pas assez!* C.93), but also (for love and beauty), Old French and Provençal; for philosophic clarity and comedy, Italian; for political and social ideas, Chinese, and so on (this is over-schematic of course).

In the Middle Ages French was a light and concise instrument, much closer to English (which it transformed) than it is now. It had a dynamic present participale (*s'en allait cheminant*), it could take short cuts with a verb or a strong preposition, it could elide articles and even subjects. *Enfin Malherbe vint* (Boileau's *art poétique*) and (I simplify) the language became unusually abstract and cluttered, so that even its best poets can sound grandiloquent and rhetorical. Today, after many 'naturalizing' movements from the Romantics

---

[2] Philippe Mikriammos (PM) for Cantos 1–41; Jacques Darras (JD) for Cantos 42–51 and 62–71; Yves di Manno (YM) for Cantos 52–61; Denis Roche (DR) for Cantos 74–84 (Pisan) and 85–95 (Rock-Drill); Francois Sauzey (FS) for Cantos 96–109 (Thrones) and 110–17 (Drafts and Fragments).

to the Surrealists, the literary language remains at a far greater distance from the spoken than it does in English.[3]

There is thus a primary problem of tone to surmount. Of course a translator cannot wrench his own language out of shape to render the original. But he should consider the original's own such wrenchings.

What do I mean by abstraction and clutter? Simply that although French is often called a more *precise* language than English, it is far more rigid and less *concise*, it takes more words to say the same thing. So before we have even read anything, the look of *The Cantos* in French is very different, the lines are much longer and often go over, and the policies of each translator are different: Darras recreates convincing French poetry by altering the line-pattern to shorter (but more) lines, others follow Pound regardless.

English, like all Germanic languages, has a system of strong prepositions, which are dynamic and directional (out of, into, from, through, over, up, down, off, till etc.) where French has weaker ones (*de*), and often needs several (*à travers, par dessus, jusqu'à ce que*) or a verb, or a noun to help out or replace. Pound makes his prepositions work hard, often omitting the verb (my italics in English): '*Out of* Syracuse' (*Quittant Syracuse*), '*from* Florence' (*provenance Florence*), 'thou must sail *after* knowledge' (*ta voile/quêtera la connaissance*), 'gnawed *through* the mountain' (*grignoté la montagne*), 'Hauled *off* the butt of that carcass, 20 feet *up* a tree trunk' (*traine hors la butte de cette/ruine, 20 pieds en l'air tronc d'arbre*) (Cs.43, 47, 48). These are all from Darras, and good solutions. As Professor of English and poet he understands the problem, though the last two also show up its nature; *grignoter* means 'to nibble', and loses *through*, while *en l'air tronc d'arbre* is a bold, unFrench use of an adverb as preposition – poetic licence where Pound's phrase is normal English. That of course is what translation is about, to do what the poet does but not necessarily in the same place. Roche too, as poet, is aware of the problem, and finds happy solutions.

Others seem far less conscious of Pound's prepositional and adverbial force, especially YM: 'that *when not against* the interest of Empire' (*Que si ca n'allait pas à l'encontre des intérêts de l'Empire*, C.52); 'and

---

[3] I remember a curious experience when the first few translations of Pound came out in *Les Cahiers de l'Herne* (1966): they all seemed unreadable except one, which rang true. Then I realized that it was Pound's own two pages in French in C.16, very slangy, and perhaps unnatural for a Frenchman (despite Queneau, Céline, etc.), but alive.

the tower half ruin'd/*with* a peasant complaining that her son' (*et la tour à demi en ruine/au pied de laquelle une paysanne se plaignait que son fils*, C.52); 'No wood burnt *into* charcoal' (*brulé par la fabrication du charbon*) and so on. The length and heaviness seem part of the French language, but di Manno is the one who does the least to avoid this, and loses the Pound tone.

Similarly Pound's chronicle-like strong use of 'was' in the Chinese Cantos is not (cannot be?) rendered by di Manno: 'And that year was a comet in Scorpio' (*apparut*, C.52): 'and HAN was after 43 years of TSIN dynasty' (*les Han arrivèrent*, C.54); 'HIA's fortune was in good ministers' (*la chance des HIA avait été d'avoir de bons conseillers*, C.54). Inversely Darras and Roche sometimes use the rather literary historic present for Pound's normal narrative past, but rightly I think, the alternative being the dead aorist, preferred by Mikriammos (*nous boutâmes*), who also likes the even deader imperfect subjunctive that sounds absurd for Pound's colloquial idiom: 'not that I could sing him the music' (*Non que j'eusse pu lui chanter la musique*, C.20).

English can also cut across a periphrase with a compound noun, as well as drop the article, where French cannot: 'Ching Quang kept lynx eye on bureaucrats/lynx eye on currency' (*Ching Quang ne perdit pas un instant de vue les bureaucrates/ne perdit pas de vue la monnaie*, C.53, YM); 'There is a partridge-shaped cloud over dust-storm' (*Ce nuage en forme de perdrix sur un vent de poussière*, C.113, FS). An attempt to reproduce a verbalized noun-metaphor as a noun-compound is distinctly unfortunate (my italics in English): 'mules are *gabled* with slate on the hill road' (*Ici on bâte les mules d'un faix faîte d'ardoise sur la pente*, C.47, JD). The following line from Roche shows all the difficulties:

squawky as larks over death-cells

(C.74)

criaillant autant qu'alouettes survolant les cellules de la mort

The comparison with adjective + 'as' becomes present participle + *autant que*, though the unFrench dropping of the article compensates; the preposition 'over' becomes the present participle *survolant*, and the two-syllable compound 'death-cells' has to become *les cellules de la mort*.

Pound also likes to turn a foreign noun into a past participle, which is impossible in French: 'the lake waves Caneletto'd' (*vagues du lac à la Caneletto*, C.110, FS, a good solution). When he does this with Chinese, and puns as well, French gives up altogether

(Pound's italics): 'and he *ch'i'd* 'em or *shed* 'em', the first of which means 'abandon', the second 'reject', followed by the two ideograms. Sauzey has clearly inquired, but merely puts *à n'en savoir que faire* (C.98).

Obviously the general abstractness of French is sometimes inevitable, and even effective, as in 'neap-tide' (*l'eau d'équinoxe*, C.47, JD), French having no archaic equivalent to 'neap', and '*marée*' being too mundane. Similarly, *le sphinx franchit la crête* must I suppose accepted for 'Moth is called over mountain' (C.47, JD), despite the learned *sphinx*, since *mite* has a purely cloth-eating connotation. Other times the abstractness is at least questionable: 'the arts gone to hell by 1750' (*décadence artistique, 1750*, C.50, JD), though this does get the telegraphic, verbless style Pound has elsewhere. Less acceptable is the shock, after the fifth decad by Darras (light and speedy, whatever one's minor disagreements) of plunging into the clumsy administratese at the opening of the Chinese Cantos:

> And I have told you of how things were under Duke Leopold in Siena
>
> (C.52)

> *Et je vous ai dors et déja parlé de l'état des choses à Sienne sous le règne du Duc Léopold*
>
> (YM)

Why *dors et déja*? – a pompous phrase even the French use in vocal joke-quotes. And surely *sous le règne de*, though inherent to the problems of rigidity under discussion, could have been avoided? My spot-check revealed di Manno as the worst offender here: 'showeth the places of heaven' (*qui représentent les demeures des immortels*, C.53); 'he wished to carve up the empire' (*son seul souhait était de démembrer l'empire*, C.54 – what's wrong with *il voulait*?). But even English abstractness is more punchy: 'rule out irrelevant evidence' (*ne prononcez / aucune accusation si vous n'avez pas de preuve*, C.54), which is not only heavy but misses 'irrelevant'. French by the way has no word for 'evidence', as distinct from 'proof', except *pièce à conviction*, which I find revealing of the French legal system.

Darras and Sauzey are perhaps the least averse to dropping articles, verbs, auxiliaries and subjects where Pound does, thus reproducing in French something close to his style:

> *Direz-vous que ce conte enseigne . . .*
> *leçon, ou que le Révérend Eliot*
> *use d'une langue plus naturelle . . . vous*
> *qui croyez franchir l'enfer en hâte . . .*
> *Ce jour-là sur Zoagli nuages*
> *nuées de neige trois jours durant*

Tassées comme crêts de montagne

(C.46, JD)

Avec navires donjonnés et images Dei Matris,
HERACLIUS, six, zéro, deux
imperator simul et sponsus,
   trouve les affaires de la 'rep' en lambeaux
– les Avars, transformé l'Europe en désert.
les Perses, exterminé toute l'Asie

(C.96, FS)

All these are minor problems of comparative linguistics, but as they (1) accumulate, (2) vary from version to version, they can give a very blurred notion of Pound's poetic idiom. If this were the only point it would be very minor indeed, one would impute all unease to linguistic differences and give the translators the benefit of all doubts. Unfortunately there are far more serious flaws.

'The text is somewhat exigeant' (C.98)

'Parents naturally hope their sons will be gentlemen'
    [ideo-   cheng
    grams]   king
The text is somewhat exigeant, perhaps you will consider the meaning of
    cheng   [ideo-
    king   grams]

(C.98)

Pound is having fun with a translation of *The Sacred Edict* by one W. J. Baller, named several times and with text-references throughout the Canto. A page earlier he had exclaimed: 'And as Ford said: get a dictionary/and learn the meaning of words.'

But there are far too many instances here, especially in Roche, where this clearly has not been done, and for which no conceivable 'poetic' justification can be found, which look, in other words, like straight misreadings of English. Sometimes they don't matter too much, as with Darras' *soixante-dix sacs de café* for 'five score' (C.48). Perhaps he disliked *cent sacs*, but then why not *quatre-vingt*, which is as inaccurate but feels closer since 'score' meant twenty? This is all the odder because elsewhere he skilfully resolves a syntactic problem by using an old French measure where Pound doesn't: *quatre outres de graisse les Georges* for 'greased fat were four Georges' (C.50). But occasionally even Darras produces nonsense:

grass nowhere out of place

(C.43)

grass; nowhere out of place

(C.51)

(1) *Jamais de manque d'herbe* [never lack of grass]
(2) *L'herbe; partout lieu d'être* [grass; everywhere reason for being]

De Rachewiltz has *ogni filo d'erba al suo posto*, and I don't see what is contributed by not translating *chaque brin d'herbe en place*. But even if a 'poetic' case can be made for one of these, the echo is lost.

Darras in fact is usually more careful than this, but sometimes neglects meanings concealed in the rhetoric, as in certain lines of the otherwise successful rendering of the Usura Canto, a sort of negative litany. Usura is never in direct object position, acted on by men, it acts directly or indirectly on men. The first half repeats 'With usura', the second has usura briefly as subject, then back to indirect object position but with 'came not by' ('Pietro Lombardo / Came not by usura') and variations without 'came' or without 'by'. Darras chooses to drop this phrase for a filial metaphor (*n'est pas fils d'usura*) which is his right, but the ambiguity of 'came not by' (did not come across / did not succeed through) is lost. Then later he *drops* a powerful engendering metaphor: 'azure hath a canker by usura', which to any English reader is calqued on 'to have a child by', thus suggesting that the canker is engendered by usura (Latin feminine) on azure (French masculine) and announcing the perversion of nature on which the litany ends. Darras reads 'canker' at one level only and translates as *L'azure se chancre par usura*, a nice verbalization of verb + noun, but it misses a great deal.

With di Manno there are few and trivial errors, but they sometimes produce a wrong visual image:

and they still know where his tomb is
by the high cypress between the strong walls

(C.53)

et l'on connait encore l'emplacement de sa tombe
aux murs épais, au pied d'un grand cyprès
[strong walls attributed to tomb]

or a wrong connotation:

seek old men and new tools

(C.53)

occupez-vous des hommes du passé et des outils nouveaux
[look after the men of the past and the new tools]

Hope without work is crazy
(C.53)
L'espoir sans le travail, conduit à la folie [leads to madness]

because of fool litterati [stupid]

(C.54)

à cause de ces fous de litterati [crazy]

But these are perhaps not serious flaws. François Sauzey is similarly accurate on the whole, with only minor errors:

> seem to be foreign importers
>   are to stay 3 months only

(C.96)

> *les importateurs étrangers, semble-t-il*
>   *ne séjourneront pas plus de 3 mois*
> ['seem' attached to 'stay', not to 'foreigners']

or a syntactic muddle:

> & that Nicephoras
>   kolobozed the tetarteron
> need not have applied to the aureus
> or caused Nicole to understand token coinage

(C.96)

> *& ce Nicéphoras*
>   *prokstua le tetarteron*
> *n'était pas forcément applicable à l'aureus*
> *ou de faire comprendre à Nicole la monnaie fiduciaire*

We are in 'The Eparch's Book' or Edict of Leo the Wise (ninth century), edited in Greek and Latin by Professor Jules Nicole, and Pound is having textual fun again: '& that' is his favourite opening for introducing events in chronicle style, and means 'the fact that', subject of the verbs 'need not' and 'caused' (*et le fait que* or *et que*). This is frequently either ignored or understood as a demonstrative (as here, but also by others), which leads di Manno to a syntactic impossibility in French: *n'était pas* has no subject, and although Pound often drops the subject, it cannot be done here, and further leads to *de faire* being attached to nothing. Pound's grammatical ellipses are never of this sort, nor are there any in this passage. Pity, as *prokstua* (prostitua) is an amusing attempt for 'kolobozed'.

The really serious misunderstandings of English are mostly in Denis Roche, often several per page. A mere selection shows that irony may be missed, or weakened:

> so the total sweated out of the Indian farmers
>   rose in Churchillian grandeur

(C.74)

> *si bien qu l'intérêt total est venu de la sueur des fermiers indiens*
>   *épanoui dans la grandeur churchillienne*

which alters the emphasis of the first line and separates the sentences so that the Churchillian grandeur sounds like fact. Or a meaning is missed:

> and the greatest is charity
> to be found among those who have not observed regulations
>   not of course that we advocate –

(C.74)

> *et le plus beau est de trouver la charité*
> *parmi ceux qui n'ont pas observé les règlements*
>   *ce n'est pas qu'on plaide bien sûr*

Not only has the familiar Pauline source of the charity quotation not been recognized (a permanent problem in this translation, here unforgivable), but the lack of recognition leads to a different syntax and meaning, with the howler *plaide* for 'advocate' (*recommander*) thrown in. For a poet, Roche is often peculiarly literal with English syntax: *chacun dans le nom de son dieu* for 'each in the name of his god' (C.79) is simply ignorant, though this correctly becomes *au nom de son dieu* in later echoes; 'As it were to dream of / morticians' daughters' becomes *Comme s'il s'agissait de rêver des / filles de croque-morts* (C.74), 'as it were' turned into 'as if it were a question of'. Moreover the infinitive 'to dream' leads straight into the famous passage translated by Pound from Confucius, syntactically garbled by Roche:

> To study with the white wings of time passing
>   is that not our delight
> to have friends come from far countries
>   is not that pleasure
> nor to care that we are untrumpeted?

(C.74)

The three infinitives are in parallel structure, as are the two 'is not that' questions ('étudier ... n'est-ce pas là notre joie ... avoir la visite ... n'est-ce pas là notre plaisir ... sans s'inquiéter ... '). Roche seems to have understood 'that' as 'it' so that 'is not that our delight' now goes with the second infinitive phrase 'to have friends', as does 'is not that our pleasure' (this apart from the heaviness):

> *Etudier alors que passent les blanches ailes du temps*
>   *n'est-ce pas notre joie*
> *d'avoir la visite d'amis de lointains pays*
>   *n'est-ce pas notre plaisir*
> *ni de s'inquiéter de n'être pas reçu en fanfare?*

Inversely, a generalized English 'it' has been read as anaphoric where Pound uses it cataphorically (referring forward) for one of his sudden juxtapositions to a new topic (despair, San Juan's *noche oscura*), which obliges Roche to alter *elle* to *ce*:

> grass worn from its root-hold
> is it blacker? was it blacker? N☲ animae?
> is there a blacker or was it merely San Juan with a belly ache writing ad posteros
> in short shall we look for a deeper or is this the bottom?

(C.74)

> *l'herbe usée jusqu'à la racine*
> *est-elle plus noire? était-ce plus noir? N☲ animae*
> *y a-t-il plus noir ou était-ce simplement San Juan avec un mal de ventre*
> *écrivant ad posteros en bref faut-il creuser plus profound ou est-ce le fond?*

Of course Pound's ellipsis is misleading, and Roche is entitled to interpretation, which, in a French way, opts for linking back at all cost, with a subsequent sliding, rather than for a sharp juxtaposition. But Pound's juxtapositions are sharp, that his 'ideogrammic' method, and elsewhere Roche blurs it with less justification, when he changes Pound's 'as for', so frequently used to introduce a new topic or a sudden aside ('and as for those who deform thought with iambics', C.98) into 'as if to' (*comme pour*):

> and the medallions
>   to forge Achaia
> and as for playing chequers with black Jim

(C.74)

> *et pour que les médaillons*
>   *fassent l'Achaie*
> *et comme pour jouer aux dames avec Jim le noir*

The syntax is twice wrong: the first *pour que* needs a subjunctive (instead of *les médaillons/pour forger*) and *comme pour* makes a link that isn't there. This merely produces nonsense, but sometimes his misunderstanding of English makes Roche limpidly say the opposite:

> But Miss Norton's memory for the conversation
>   (or 'go on') of idiots
> was such as even the eminent Irish writer
>   has, if equalled at moments (?sinthetic'ly)
> certainly never surpassed

(C.76)

> *Mais la mémoire de Miss Norton pour la conversation*
>   *(ou le 'train-train') des idiots*
> *était presque celle de l'éminent écrivain irlandais,*
>   *si elle l'égalait par moments (?synthétiq'ment)*
> *elle ne la dépassait certainement jamais*

Or something else:

Awareness restful and fake is fatiguing

(C.76)

La vigilance véritable repose et l'hypocrisie fatigue
[true vigilance is restful and hypocrisy tiring]

Prince of Kano [ideograms]
Risked the smoke to go forward

(C.86)

La fumée risquait de se propager

Here the distant subject (before the ideograms) was not seen, but in addition the predicate has been wholly misread.

There is in fact a great laziness about simply asking a native speaker, or getting a dictionary and learning, not just the meaning of words or their grammar, but all their semantic possibilities: 'a copy of the Gedichte of Heine's [poems, plural] becomes *de la Gedichte de Heine* [singular, which ought then to be *Gedicht*, and makes one wonder which, C.74); 'Beauty is difficult . . . the plain ground [meaning background] / precedes the colour' becomes *La Beauté est difficile . . . la terre franche* [arable soil!] *précède les couleurs* (C.74); 'cornflower, thistle and sword-flower / to a half metre grass growth' becomes *de maïs en fleur* [for *bleuet*], *de chardon et d'herbes coupantes* [for *iris des marais*] / *fleuries à une moitié de mètre de hauteur* [C.76, hardly astonishing if you translate maize]; 'England [. . .] sold down the river' [idiom. orig. from slave trade English] becomes *vendue au fil de l'eau* (C.86); 'Jury trial was in Athens' [Pound's strong use of 'was' for 'already existed'] becomes *Le tribunal siégeait à Athènes* [C.85, the court was sitting in Athens].

The famous passage at the end of C.81. heavily rendered, is also marred by carelessness:

> *Rabaisse ta vanité, je dis rabaisse-la*
> *Apprends du monde verdoyant quelle peut être ta place*
> *Dans l'echelle de la découverte ou de l'art vrai,*
> *Rabaisse ta vanité,*
>> *Paquin rabaisse-le!*
> *Le casque de verdure l'a emporté sur ton élégance [. . .]*
> *Mais d'avoir fait au lieu de ne pas faire*
>> *ce n'est pas là de la vanité*
> *D'avoir, par décence, frappé à la porte*
> *Pour qu'un Blunt ouvre*
>> *D'avoir fait naître de l'air une tradition vivante*
> *ou d'un vieil oeil malin la flamme insoumise*
> *Ce n'est pas là de la vanité*

Ici-bas toute l'erreur est de n'avoir rien accompli.
toute l'erreur est, dans le doute, d'avoir tremblé

Originally Roche had *orgueil* (pride) for vanity, and was persuaded by Rabaté to alter it, but one masculine *le* was not corrected (creating a *le/Le* with the next line). *L'échelle de la découverte* makes little sense, for Pound is playing on 'scaled' in 'the green world' ('scale' as *échelle* perhaps but more as *écaille*), the inventive world of nature being here *opposed* to that of man so that *découverte* is also wrong:

Learn of the green world what can be thy place
In scaled invention or true artistry

And *par décence* is misleading for 'with decency', as is *Ici-bas*, with its religious tone, for simply 'Here' (in these cases), the echoing 'done' and 'not done' is botched (*fait/pas fait/fait naître/accompli*), and the last two lines are completely off: it is not in 'to have achieved nothing' but 'in the not done' that error lies, and it is not man that falters (*trembles?*) but, much more ambiguously, his diffidence:

Here error is all in the not done.
all in the diffidence that faltered
[*dans la modestie qui trébuche*]

'So that' C.1, C.17, and so on

It is by now well known, and obvious to any reasonably attentive reader, that Pound's *Cantos* are constructed on a system of echoes that resound down the text, part of the 'ideogrammic' method of recalling the same words in new contexts, creating a new 'chord'. Any translation that does not attend to this is seriously banalized.

I have quoted 'So that' here because it points up the method: there is (apparent) reason in the apparent madness. Thus Canto I, the Homeric *nekuia* rendered via a Latin translation by one Divus ('lie quiet Divus') but in a splendid evocation of *The Seafarer* in Anglo-Saxon rhythm (well captured by Mikriammos), ends, famously, with 'So that:' and Canto 2 starts (famously) with 'Hang it all, Robert Browning'. We then go through many layers of European culture before picking up 'So that the vines burst from my fingers' at the beginning of Canto 17. Mikriammos knows all this and renders both very well as *Et donc*. But other instances of 'so that' are never echoed, and rendered each time differently (*ainsi que*, *de sorte que*, c'est ainsi que ...), just as the constant '(and) that' (*et que*, see p. 132) is constantly misunderstood as a demonstrative, or rendered *et comme, et comment*, or dropped.

Or, to go back to Pound's strong use of prepositions, his favourite 'out of', which marks his style, is rendered differently each time, not only according to context (linguistic structures) but also according to translator (individual solutions), from the multipurpose *de* to *hors de* or verb. Each solution or even omission is good in isolation, but the Pound tone is lost. And often the same translator is unaware of the echoes: 'out of dark, and toward half-light' (C.113) becomes *du noir en route vers le demi-jour* (FS), but 'out of dark, thou Father Helios, leadest' (same Canto) is rendered *C'est toi. Père Helios, qui nous montre la voie.* This happens *a fortiori* between translators: 'under Fortuna' is wisely left as *sous Fortuna* by Sauzey (C. 96, 97) but verbalized as *soumis à Fortuna* by Roche (C. 88). Similarly San Juan's 'belly ache' (C.74), comically echoed for Plotinus in C.98, is *mal de ventre* for Roche, which is closer, and *mal d'estomac* for Sauzey.

More seriously, it is the key phrases that are not echoed, and not only between translators (coordination) but within the work of one translator (attention). Thus the 'no man' image for Odysseus-Pound, which comes from the Homeric incident when Odysseus tells Polyphemus his name is OὐΤΙΣ (no man, no one, or *personne* in French), and alluded to in C.74, occurs much earlier, throughout the Usura Canto ('With usura hath no man a house of good stone'), which Darras translates catastrophically as *n'ont pas les hommes ... les hommes n'ont*: nor are the echoes of C.45 reproduced as they should be in C.51 (with a loosening, through usury, of C.45's close syntactic effects). The opening of the idyllic C.49 ('For the seven lakes, and by no man these verses') is rendered *Pour les sept lacs, ces vers écrits par nul*, which is effective in itself but annuls all echo. Yves di Manno and Denis Roche both 'correctly' translate *personne*: 'No man was under another' (*Personne n'obéissait à personne*, C.51, YD); 'I am noman, my name is noman' (*Je ne suis personne, mon nom est personne* (C.74, DR)), but François Sauzey has *Nul grec en Grèce* for 'No man in Greece' (C.98). Coordination would probably have given *nul homme* in all cases.

Similarly the phrase 'Keep the peace, Borso!' in C.20 is translated by Mikriammos *Protège la paix, Borso!*, then as *Maintiens la paix, Borso* in C.21, and as the phrase 'keep the peace' is re-echoed throughout, we would expect one of those verbs to be chosen, but we get *préservez la paix* (twice) by di Manno in C.53 and *resta en paix* by François Sauzey in C.91. The phrase 'that hath power over wild beasts' at the end of C.47 is echoed at the end of C.49 as 'And the power over wild beasts', but each is differently rendered by Darras, first as a [...] *puissance de maîtriser la bête sauvage,* then *Pouvoir de maîtrise sur la bête sauvage.* Neither is very good, *puissance* or *maîtrise* alone would have sufficed, but either way the echo is weakened.

Similarly the 'smoke hole' in Pound's tent at Pisa is rendered as *le rond de ma fumée* (smoke ring) by Roche, then by *le trou de ma tente* on the opposite page (C.76). The beautiful 'meteyard' from Leviticus XIX (reference given in text at first occurrence, C.74) is translated each time differently, as is the 'with justice' that goes with it, meaning 'fairly' but also 'accurately' (*avec justice* OR *avec justesse,* not *avec la justice,* nor even *justement*): 'with justice shall be redeemed ... in meteyard in weight or in measure' becomes *justement sera racheté ... en métrage en poids ou en mesure* (C.74, DR), but later *avec la justice en yards et en mesure* and in C.76 *pas d'injustice dans le yard et la mesure (des prix).* None is quite wrong but the echo is blurred. Or again the ordinary word 'span' or 'handspan' is nicely rendered *coudée* by Roche but *l'empan* (much rarer) by Darras.

There is, too, the important word 'process', which Roche keeps in *The Pisan Cantos* (*la pluie est du procès* [...] *le vent aussi est du procès* [...] *la racine du procès,* C.74), although it more usually means 'trial' in French and *processus* might have been clearer; but changes in *Rock-Drill:* Mais si vous suivez cette méthode (+ideogram for 'process') and *La Loi céleste* for 'Heaven's process' in C.85. The equally important word 'awareness' is rendered as *vigilance* by Roche but as *conscience* and *clairvoyance* by Sauzey. The ringing 'this is not vanity' is rendered as *ce n'est pas là de la vanité* by Roche but as *là nulle vanité* by Sauzey when it recurs in C.114. As for Pound's own famous motto MAKE IT NEW, from Tching Tang, it is sensibly left in English by di Manno in C.53, but translated as *Renouvèle* by Sauzey when it is recalled at the opening of C.98.

There are innumerable more trivial examples of echoes lost and it would be fastidious to note them all. Within the same author it seems due to lack of attentiveness to what he has previously translated. From author to author it is sheer lack of consultation and coordination.

Neither is there any coordination about francizing proper names or not: we get *Gonzague* but *Firenze, le roi Charles* for 'Carolus' but also *Carolus,* though *Pippin* is left in English. We even get *Bretagne* (Brittany) for 'Britain' (YM) where others more historically have *l'Angleterre.* Nor is there any coordination of what English words are acceptable. Thus Darras has *vendu au-dessous de son prix / du pétrole* for 'dumping' while Roche less academically says *se livraient au dumping*, and di Manno has *le racket* (for 'vendetta') and *bluffa les tartares*, which would be inconceivable in Darras yet perfectly Poundian.

This lack of coordination can sometimes produce serious (and comical) errors. The phrase 'of no fortune and with a name to come' in C.74. throws us right back to C.1, to Elpenor talking to Odysseus in Hades and begging for burial, with the inscription 'A man of no fortune, and with a name to come'. This is succinctly translated by Mikriammos as *Homme infortuné, et au nom à venir*. But in C.74 Roche translates on his own: *malchanceux et dont le nom est à venir*. Then, when the phrase recurs later in the Canto he doesn't recognize it and links (with the French mania for linking where Pound suddenly juxtaposes) to *les trois dames*:

> et les trois dames attendaient
> 'et leur nom était à venir'

(C.76)

Of course Pound's ellipsis *could* mean that, but every Poundian knows that it does not, and the quotation marks might have warned him. Indeed more juxtapositions follow immediately.

A deeper understanding of the ideogrammic method and a better knowledge of the echo-system, not to mention a better memory for the phrases one has just translated, and failing all that, automatic checking sessions with a Poundian, would have avoided this kind of nonsense.

'These fragments you have shelved (shored)' (C.8)

Canto 8 opens with that phrase which, as every literate English reader knows, is a quotation from Eliot's *The Waste Land*: 'These fragments I have shored against my ruin'. He may or may not know that the first draft of *The Waste Land* was ruthlessly cut and altered by Pound (MS later published by Faber, V. Eliot 1971), for which service Eliot dedicated the poem to him as *il miglior fabbro*, the best craftsman. The original version of this line was 'These fragments I have spelt into my ruins', corrected by Pound to 'shored against'. Pound is here misremembering the original. Or again, everyone knows Eliot's lines 'This is the way the world ends / Not with a bang but a whimper' (*The Hollow Men*), the phrase having passed into the language. And Pound recalls it in C.74:

Yet say this to the Possum: a bang not a whimper.
 With a bang, not with a whimper.

No doubt one cannot expect translators to go into all this, though the lines are so famous one could expect *anglicistes* at least to use the same Eliot translation. But no. In C.8 Mikriammos has *Ces fragments tu les as remisés (étayés)*, which isn't quite right but passes. Then when the phrase re-echoes in *Drafts and Fragments* at the other end of the poem:

From time's wreckage shored,
 these fragments shored against ruin

(C.110)

Sauzey has:

*Réchappés des décombres du temps
 ces fragments qui bravent la ruine*

which doesn't even get the repetition of 'shored'. And Roche in C.74 doesn't seem to understand the childish 'horridness' of 'bang' (*boum*) and puts *fracas* (din), and botches the syntactic repetition:

tout de même dites-le à l'Opossum: un fracas et non une plainte, avec fracas et pas de plainte

Nor does Roche know how Pound has fused Dante's *directio voluntatis* with Confucian concepts, which the word *directio* then alone evokes, so that his translation suggests 'in this direction': '"brew up this directio, tchéu"' becomes *brasse le tout dans cette directio, tchéu* (C.85).

Or again in the Usura Canto there is the triple repetition (but with 'seeth' for 'hath' the third time): 'With usura / hath no man a house of good stone [...] With usura hath no man a painted paradise on his church wall [...] With usura seeth no man Gonzaga his heirs and his concubines' (C.45). This last refers to a famous fresco by Mantegna in the ducal palace at Mantua, of the lord Gonzaga and all his heirs and concubines that is a painting not as yet affected by usura, like the painters who 'came not by' usura in the second half of the Canto. It has nothing to do with Gonzaga's reproductive potential, yet Darras continues the 'hath' and translates flatly: *n'aura Gonzague d'héritier concubine*, which is not only cryptic but wrong.

This sort of thing simply won't do. There is a perfectly adequate Index to the Cantos which explains all the allusions and gives all sources, and there are many books on Pound, each itself with an index (unlike, alas and disastrously, French scholarly books). Yet time and again meanings are not looked up, quotations are not recognized or checked back, either with Pound's sources or with more generally accessible ones such as the Eliot, or the charity quotation mentioned earlier. Not even *French* sources, such as Mailla for the Chinese Cantos or Couvreur for C.85:

> not water, ôu iu chouèi
> > [ideogram]
> there by thy mirour in men

> *Là sera le miroir que tu auras des hommes*

The English is clear, but Roche has misundertood it. Here a consultation of Pound's source, Père Couvreur's translations of the *Chou King* (all references given in the Canto as we go through the text, and the fact added in a French footnote to this Canto) might have helped: *ne prenez pas pour miroir le cristal des eaux, mais les autres hommes*, that is, men are the mirrors, not water the mirror of men. But clearly no one has consulted any sources, not American, not Italian, nothing. And *within* the text, Sauzey doesn't seem to recognize Pound's acknowledgement to Baller's translation *as* an acknowledgement:

> Thought is built out of Sagetrieb
> > and our debt here is to Baller
> and to *volgar'eloquio*

> (C.98)

> *Pensée née droit du Sagetrieb*
> > *et c'est à Baller qu'on le doit*
> *comme au* volgar'eloquio

which makes Baller and Dante sound responsible for thought and Sagetrieb, whereas Pound is acknowledging *his* debt (with the first person plural that should be only too familiar to French critics and thesis-writers). Pound has in front of him F. W. Baller's translation of *The Sacred Edict* of K'ang Hsi, originally written in a high literary style then redone in simplified form by K'ang Hsi's son Iong Cheng (Yong Cheng in C.61). But Uang-iu-p'uh, who was Commissioner of the Salt Works in Shensi, felt it was still too inaccessible for simple people and translated it into more colloquial Chinese, just as Dante wrote *De Vulgari Eloquentia*. And this is the story Pound is telling us, in a comical, interrupted way, giving his sources.

It is also what Pound himself is *doing*: for however arcane his sources may be, and however abrupt his transitions, his English is a highly individual but simple and contemporary vernacular, with brief excursions into archaism or foreign languages for specific reasons (and the foreign languages do not affect the translation – indeed they become the best part of it). The 'difficulty' in reading Pound is not in his language, but in his orchestration and archeology. It is this dimension which the French translators so frequently miss: the forceful but light, simple language is often unduly learned, abstract or heavy (no Commissioner of the Salt Works here), while the much more complex system of echoes (intratextual and intertextual) is wholly ignored, and lines are translated as they come, as surface phenomena. This, of course, is also how many novelists WRITE.

Cheng ming

This beautiful ideogram is the first to appear in *The Cantos* (end of C.51) and expresses all of Pound's effort of a lifetime, his story. It means exactitude, accuracy, what Pound for a long time thought of as *le mot juste*, so hard to find ('his true Penelope was Flaubert' – *Hugh Selwyn Mauberley*). But here (and too often elsewhere) Cheng ming has been *chi'i'd* (abandoned) and *shed* (rejected). Betrayed. Beauty is difficult, in translation as in creation.

9

Notes on the metre of Auden's *The Age of Anxiety*

Five years have now elapsed since the discovery, in 2192, of the almost unique Old British poem called *The Age of Anxiety*, by one W. H. Auden. It is being carefully edited, and a description of the volume itself, together with an outline of its contents, has already appeared in *Teen-Age Studies* (Cass.9, Prog.2, April 2191). In spite of some apparent Americanisms, the dialect is distinctly twentieth-century British, and the poem is in fact dated for us, since it was recovered relatively undamaged in book form, in a Californian cave: it was published in London in 1948. The question of emendation thus does not arise. I propose here to give a preliminary account of its metre.

As readers will know, almost nothing of the apparently copious poetry in the English language survived the two Semi-Nuclear Wars. Some early manuscripts in the Anglo-Saxon tongue were evidently considered precious, for they were hidden in a vault in the Himalayas before the first of these wars, and are thus fortunately extant. There is, however, ample external evidence of a continuous poetic tradition throughout the ten centuries between these early records and the newly discovered *Age of Anxiety*. We have numerous references to poetry in the little English prose which survived, as well as in foreign literatures (for instance in India and Peru). And there is the famous Bantu translation of a verse-play called *Hamlet*, though it is difficult to determine from this what the original metre may have been: the laxity of barely discernible rules may be due to the translator. A few extant poems in the French language, found in Canada, have led scholars to believe that the common European metre was syllabic and end-rhymed, but the Bantu *Hamlet* would seem to belie this assumption.

It is therefore all the more intriguing to find that *The Age of Anxiety* uses the same alliterative measure as that found in the Anglo-Saxon epic poetry of over ten centuries earlier. This at first sight appears to support those who have argued against the existence of a syllabic rhymed verse, and although it may seem curious that during all this time no change was found to be necessary, we know from other sources that British tradition died hard. And yet, when one examines the poet Auden's metre in greater detail, one finds many interesting signs of decadence. I shall discuss some of these, pending a more exhaustive analysis in the forthcoming edition.

The alliteration

First I shall consider the alliteration, which is the most regular feature, being also the easiest technique to master. The Anglo-Saxon half-line consisted of two lifts (or stresses) and two dips (unaccented syllables varying in number). In the first half-line either both lifts, or one lift only, could carry the alliteration; in the second half-line, only the first lift could do so, the last lift being unalliterated, as neutral ground on the way to the new alliteration in the next line. So in Auden:

> My *d*euce, my *d*ouble, / my *d*ear image,
> It is *l*ively there, / that *l*and of glass . . .

Occasionally the poet alliterates on the fourth lift, but such lapses are comparatively rare, though they might support the suggestion I shall make below that the poet tends to over-use alliteration rather than avail himself of the means to give relief from it.

The rules of grammatical precedence are also well observed on the whole. In Anglo-Saxon poetry, nouns and adjectives, participles and proper adverbs regularly carry the alliteration; verbs and other adverbs (such as *then*, *there*, and so on) do so sometimes, while pronouns and prepositions rarely do so. In Auden we find the unimportant words carrying the alliteration rather too often, such as *now*, *all*, *not*, *them*, *there*, *this*, *these*, *if*, *no*, *was*, *is*, *in*, but they are not made to take precedence over nouns and adjectives. They occur, naturally enough, either with verbs, or with words as unimportant as themselves, so that although the line seems trivial and the emphasis of the lift unwarranted, at least no more important word is pushed into the dip: *does your self like mine*, or *as if it were done*. Interestingly, there is no alliteration at all on any of the lifts in either of these half-lines. Perhaps a new rule had come about, allowing no alliteration when the words on the lift were unimportant, as it were to emphasize the triviality of the line. Such a rule might reflect, for all we know, a conscious reaction against the over-rich concision of the more majestic epic line, rather than lack of inspiration or even mere lapse into the poverty of language which, from the prose remains, seems to have been the chief weakness of this pre-war managerial society. Indeed, such light lines may have been the poet's only way of affording some relief from his obsession with regular alliteration.

The most notable feature of this twentieth-century poem is the alliteration inside the word, on the stressed syllable (for example, canal alliterating on *n*). In Anglo-Saxon certain prefixes could be discounted in this way (*a-*, *for-*, *ofer-*, etc.), while others on the contrary took the alliteration (*and-*, *after*, *fore-* and so on) according to their natural stress in the word. The poet Auden goes far beyond this and simply alliterates on the stressed syllable of any word; romantic, silhou*e*tte, cre*a*tive, her*o*ic, ma*r*ine, Thi*b*etan, po*l*ice, fa*r*ouche, noc*t*urnal, patri*o*tic, Val*d*ivian, fa*n*atical, arc*h*aic, suc*c*essive (= s), bra*v*ura, and so on. This seems reasonable enough, and no doubt reflects the exact stressing of the time, so that the poem should be extremely useful to the phonologists: clearly the words taking alliteration in Anglo-Saxon were mostly much shorter than the many Latin words taken into the language later. Moreover, the disyllabic words tended to take the stress on the first syllable (Hróthgar, Béowulf, for instance), as in all Germanic languages, whereas the natural rhythm of English later became basically iambic, possibly under French influence after the Norman Conquest. This alliteration on the iambically stresed inner syllable might be adduced to support the theory that an iambic syllabic metre had developed between the Anglo-Saxon remains and *The Age of Anxiety*, from which, perhaps, the poet Auden was trying to free himself.

Occasionally, however, we get a few discrepancies:

(i) inter*n*ational, inter*f*ere; but *in*terjection
(ii) fore*c*ast (the natural stress seems from other evidence to have been on the first syllable, or at least equal stress)
(iii) the prefix *ex*:
　　　　With *p*ower to *p*lace, to ex*p*lain every ...
　　　　Ex*p*osed by the *sp*ade, *sp*eaks its warning ...
　　　　E*x*aggerate to e*x*ist, po*ss*essed by hope ...

In the first line of (iii) *ex* is altogether discounted, *p* alliterating with *p*. In the second only the [ek] part of it is discounted, the [s + p] part alliterating with *sp*. Similarly in the third only the [eg] part is discounted, the [z + vowel] alliterating with the *z*-sound in *possessed*.

Another curious feature is the regular alliteration of *h* with a vowel (as well as with itself), which may point to a South Eastern dialect and a humble origin. All in all, however, the alliterative technique seems to be highly sophisticated rather than lax or decadent.

It is all the more disconcerting therefore to find that the poet's handling of prosody is far less assured.

The prosody

Anglo-Saxon metre was quantitative as well as stressed, that is to say, a lift had to consist of either one long stressed syllable or of one short stressed syllable plus one unstressed. The latter is called *resolution*, and is rarely used by the poet Auden, a fact which suggests either that he had no ear for this variation, or that the feeling for quantity in the language had already died out. But it was the total weight of the line which mattered, and the line could not be too light. There were thus five possible combinations of the two lifts and two dips in one half-line:

Type A (falling): ´ ⌣ ´
Type B (rising): ⌣ ´ ⌣ ´
Type C (two lifts together in centre): ⌣ ´ ´ ⌣
Type D (two lifts together beginning or end;
      this requires a half-stress): ´ ´ ⌣ ⌣̀ or ´ ´ ⌣̀ ⌣
Type E (lift at either end; + half-stress): ´ ⌣̀ ⌣ ´ or ´ ⌣ ⌣̀ ´

The theoretically possible combinations are of course more numerous, but since the dip could consist of more than one unstressed syllable – indeed any number, within reason – it follows that in practice the two dips could not come together, or they would simply become one dip (instead of two dips separated by a lift) and the line would become too light. This is why the two dips together in D and E *must* be reinforced by a half-stress. In other words, the following three combinations do not make up a correct half-line: ´ ´ ⌣ ⌣; ´ ⌣ ⌣ ´; ⌣ ⌣ ´ ´.

Yet all three occur profusely in *The Age of Anxiety*. The first two (´ ´ ⌣ ⌣ and ´ ⌣ ⌣ ´) are really defective D and E types, that is, they are only permissible on condition that one of the unstressed syllables can be distinctly half-stressed. The third (⌣ ⌣ ´ ´) is not possible at all, even with half-stress, since unstressed syllables at the beginning of a half-line were permissible (anacrusis) counting as the dip, however, but not two stresses together at the end.

Some of Auden's defective half-lines can be forced into a correct D or E by half-stressing one of the unaccented syllables, if a little unnaturally according to phonological evidence:

Wrý rélatìves	D (even so, second lift on 're' too short)
Vágue végetàble	D (with resolution of 2nd lift)
Próud on thàt pláin	E

Many, however, cannot even be forced. The poet is particularly fond of what I have called above defective E, the pattern ∠ ∪ ∪ ∠ without the necessary half-stress: *Lacks a surround, Perilous leaps, singular then, Undulant land, Crowded with lives, phantoms who try,* and so on. And he even adds a syllable to the dip: *Hiding in your heart, darted at our will, Wanted by the waste, Anxious into air, Bullets were about,* and many others.

This curious phenomenon seems to me to suggest the possible influence of a syllabic 'pom-petty-pom' rhythm (or anapaest) from which the poet could not get away, but I shall return to this later.

The defective D type, ending most irregularly on two unstressed syllables (∠ ∠ ∪ ∪) is much less frequent, but its occurrence may also suggest the influence of a syllabic metre (here a dactyl, though I am not sure that the use of the surviving Greek terms is really helpful, Greek poetry having apparently also been quantitative rather than syllabic).

Apart from these defective D and E types, the third wrong combination of dips and lifts mentioned above as impossible (∪ ∪ ∠ ∠) is also very frequent in Auden:

The liquor you lift	*with your léft hánd . . .*
They brood over being	*till the bárs clóse . . .*
Which her Adam is	*till his Éve dóes . . .*

And many others.

These are not permissible half-lines at all. But not content with wrong combinations of two lifts and two dips, and poet even uses ultra-light half-lines with one unstressed syllable only, either between two lifts (∠ ∪ ∠): *cool as this, Thinks it thinks, Fire and fear;* or with two lifts together (∪ ∠ ∠ and ∠ ∠ ∪): *the calm plant, have ghosts too, sound logic, small tradesmen* (the latter possibly taking half-stress on *men*). We even get half-lines without any dip at all: *Knees numb; more will* – the latter in a line which is repeated four times: *Many have perished: more will.*

Admittedly some of these very defective types (not those just quoted) occur in the remarkable passages where the radio breaks into the thoughts or conversation of the protagonists, and may perhaps be intentionally faulty, satirizing journalistic insensitivity to the nobler epic metre. The poet catches the rhythm of what must have then been radio headlines (half-lines separated by me, those in italics do not scan):

Now the news.   Night raids on
Five cities.   Fires started.
Pressure applied by pincer movement
In threatening thrust.   Third Division
Enlarges beachhead.   *Lucky charm*
Saves sniper [...]
                    Rochester barber
Fools foe.   Finns ignore
Peace feeler [...] etc.

And we get similar satiric echoes of publicity slogans:

Buy a bond.   Blood saves lives.
Donate now.   Name this station.

Nevertheless, there are far too many such defective lines elsewhere for us to give the poet the benefit of the doubt as to his satiric purposes. Moreover, one radio passage echoing the crude publicity of the period, which ought to have given him even more scope for scoffing at insensitivity, is comparatively correct in its scansion (lines marked for later reference):

A	Definitely different. Has that democratic	A an.
A rare	Extra elegance. *Easy to clean.*	—
A2	Will gladden grand-dad *and your girl friend.*	—
A2	Lasts a lifetime. Leaves no odour.	A
B	American made. A modern product	A an.
A2 an.	Of nerve and know-how *with a new thrill.*	—
B	Patriotic to own. Is on its way	B
A an.	In a patent package. Pays to investigate.	A
A2	Serves through science. Has something added	A an.
A an.	By upper classmen and Uncle Sam.	B
C rare	By skilled Scotchmen. Exclusively used	B
—	*Tops in tests* by teen-agers.	B
A an.	Just ask for it always.	

Four unscannable lines in twenty-five is a good average for this poet.
So much then, for non-existent lines and lines which can just be forced into a D or E type by half-stressing an unstressed syllable.

But even the easier and more common types A, B and C are used with unwarranted licence, unwarranted because it does not relieve the poet's basic monotony, as licence should, a point to which I shall return.

The licence taken by the poet with A, B and C types is chiefly with unstressed syllables. For example in A (falling: ´ ˘ ´ ˘), he over-indulges anacrusis (one, very occasionally more, unstressed syllables before the first lift, marked 'A an.' above: ˘] ´ ˘ ´). Anacrusis was on the whole avoided in Anglo-Saxon, the fundamental A-type being falling, but it was useful to make up the weight if the first lift consisted of a short syllable:] ´ ˘ ´ ˘). But this is precisely where Auden does not use it: in *Seven selfish / supperless ages*, the stressed syllable of seven is short and should be given anacrusis (e.g. *For seven selfish*).

On the other hand, he uses both simple and double anacrusis in half-lines containing polysyllabic dips, which was rare in Anglo-Saxon since it made the line rather heavy: *His] greenest arcadias*; *Bra] vura of revolvers*; *the e] normous disappointment*. A trisyllabic dip in an A type was in any case rare and extremely dubious. We may note that in the above examples [g] alliterates with [k] of *arcadias*, and the third has no alliteration at all.

Similarly he uses anacrusis quite often with a strengthened dip (Type A2 with a half-stress on the dip, for variation). Anacrusis with a strengthened dip was avoided in Anglo-Saxon, for it made a heavy-half-line: *Is it] cold by contrast*: *The] lie of my lifetime*. Such over-weighting again suggests a lack of feeling for quantity and the influence of a 'tim-pom-petty-pom' rhythm.

Another, more serious licence is the use of A with a disyllabic second dip (´ ˘ ´ ˘ ˘ , marked 'rare' above), which is extremely rare in the classical poetry because the half-line should not end on several unstressed syllables (cp. the D type ´ ´ ˘ ˘ , where the dip *has* to be strengthened for this same reason). In the whole of *Beowulf* there are only twenty-two such lines and many of them are doubtful, but the 448 lines of Auden's Part I have seventeen. For instance: *Showed their shapeliness. Simply insists upon*. Here again, as with the defective D's, we may see the influence of a syllabic line with dactylic ending.

The use of the B type (rising: ˘ ´ ˘ ´) is also a little unorthodox. For example, the basic rising type just given is not very common in Anglo-Saxon. The first dip was nearly always given two or three unstressed syllables (˘ ˘ ˘ ´ ˘ ´), to avoid confusion with anacrusis and perhaps to emphasize the rising rhythm with a 'run-in'. Yet out of 210 B lines in Auden's Part I, 115 are of this over-simple basic type, rare in classical epic. It is, of course equivalent to iambic metre.

Again, when the second dip was disyllabic, a monosyllabic first dip was avoided (⏑ ´ ⏑ ⏑ ´), the types ⏑ ⏑ ´ ⏑ ⏑ ´ or ⏑ ⏑ ⏑ ´ ⏑ ⏑ ´ being preferred for balance. Yet Auden uses ⏑ ´ ⏑ ⏑ ´ sixty-five times, and frequently gives even a trisyllabic second dip (⏑ ´ ⏑ ⏑ ⏑ ´), which is extremely rare and dubious in a B, since it upsets the steady rise and fall of a B and gives a tim-pom-tim-petty-pom effect. Two examples even have four unstressed syllables: *Exaggerate to exist*; *Security at all costs*.

Auden's use of the C type (⏑ ´ ´ ⏑) is the most correct, and varied occasionally within its legitimate possibilities. For instance the C1 half-line, with disyllabic first dip: *Till our deaths differ; though the wrong question*. Nor do we find any faulty C types with a disyllabic second dip (⏑ ´ ´ ⏑ ⏑), as we did frequently with the A type and defective D types (a half-line should never end on several unstressed syllables). On the other hand, the splendid 'run-in' C types with polysyllabic first dip do not occur at all (⏑ ⏑ ⏑ ⏑ ´ ´ ⏑).

The monotony

Apart from faulty lines and free play with unaccented syllables, the poet's chief flaw is lack of variation, as I have already had occasion to note. This has two aspects: the failure to exploit legitimate variations of any one type (and here I shall consider both prosody and alliteration): and the repetition of the same metrical types from one half-line to another, or even for several lines.

Variation by resolution of one of the lifts, though it does occur, is rare in Auden, especially in A and B. However, it may not be the poet's ear which is to blame, but the state of the language, in which the feeling for quantity seems to have died out. Any stressed syllable, even when short, is apparently regarded as a full lift (e.g. *Seven selfish*, quoted above as over-light A).

Yet the poet does seem to have had some notion of quantity, since some of his lines can only be correctly scanned if we assume conscious resolution: *He looks natural: by grass corridors* (both C2, with resolution of the second lift: ⏑ ´ ´⏑ ⏑). But it is difficult to determine today whether the second syllable in 'natural' and 'corridors' was pronounced or not. Perhaps we have to conclude that Auden did feel quantity, but rarely availed himself of resolution as legitimate variation.

Similarly he hardly exploits the various means for giving relief from alliteration. For example, the A2 type, with a strengthened (half-stressed) first dip, should take alliteration on the first lift only, to avoid over-emphasis. But this correct A2 type occurs once only: *The horse-shoe glaciers curled up and died.* And here there is no alliteration at all on the first three lifts ([h] [gl] [k]). All other A2 types with strengthened first dip have double alliteration (e.g. *Lasts a lifetime* in marked passage). On the other hand the poet is extremely fond of the A2 type with the *second* dip strengthened where alliteration *can* be double: *Of cooks at key holes*, and many others.

Again, the legitimate relaxation, for relief, of alliteration on the first lift in an A type (A3) occurs only twice:

| A | limitates *n*othing. *N*othing rewards [...] | — |
| A rare | incompre*h*ensible compre*h*ensive dread [...] | B |

And in both the repetition of the same or similar words gives the opposite effect of richness, particularly in the second example, where the first *lift* (com-) unfortunately *also* alliterates with the first *dip* of the second half-line, giving a superficial effect of two sets of alliteration. This in itself is a legitimate device for added richness, but it should be the four lifts which cross alliterate, as in the double B line: *The night's odours, the noise of the El on* [...]

Similarly Auden's chief fault in his otherwise correct use of the C type is his almost constant double alliteration, which is rare in C, even in the first half-line. The two lifts coming together make the alliterating words too close, and usually only the first lift carried the alliteration. But in Auden double alliteration is almost the rule (e.g. *By skilled Scotchmen* in marked passage).

All this seems to me to suggest a self-conscious use of alliteration, as if the technique had died out and the poet was somewhat grimly determined to force it back.

The second flaw is repetition of the same types. Not only does Auden hardly vary each type, but he uses A and B much too repetitively, and often together in one full line. Anglo-Saxon poets avoided two A's ($\acute{-} \smile \acute{-} \smile / \acute{-} \smile \acute{-} \smile$) or two B's ($\smile \acute{-} \smile \acute{-} / \smile \acute{-} \smile \acute{-}$), but Auden does not, and too frequently juxtaposes A (often with anacrusis) and B ($\smile] \acute{-} \smile \acute{-} \smile / \smile \acute{-} \smile \acute{-}$), C and E being his only reasonably frequent variations, and most of his E's are defective. The subtle D-type ($\acute{-} \acute{-} \breve{\smile} \smile$) and its many variations are hardly exploited at all. One of the few exceptions shows how effectively a D can be used to vary the rhythm. A protagonist has stopped his silent thinking, and the next one echoes the D1 type (´ ´ ⌣ ⌣) with a D4 (´ ´ ⌣ ⌣):

C	Till our deaths differ; drink, strange future	D1
B	To your neighbour now.	
	No chimpanzee	D4
–	Thinks it thinks. Things are divisible	A

The presence of a defective line in this subtly varied passage is a pity. Elsewhere the rhythm is monotonously repetitive. One might argue that the many defective lines were Auden's only way of varying this, as if he were conscious of his own monotony and wrote a half-line like *Knees numb* out of sheer defiance or despair.

Conclusion

The foregoing notes seem to me very strongly to suggest the influence of a syllabic metrical verse: the use of two A's or of an A and a B so frequently, and many defective E's (´ ⌣ ⌣ ´) alone point to the existence of a 'tim-pom-tim-pom' rhythm, varied with 'pompetty-pom', from which the poet could not free himself.

There are two hypotheses:

(1) the original Anglo-Saxon metre had lasted but was in decadence, in a period of transition towards a syllabic metre, basically iambic, which was already influencing the otherwise fiercely conservative poet.

(2) the original Anglo-Saxon metre had already died out and been replaced by a syllabic, basically iambic metre (precisely when is difficult to determine), and the poet was trying to revive the old technique, though himself entirely conditioned by the syllabic metre.

The existence of the French syllabic verse found in Canada does not in itself support the second supposition, since it is in French, but there is one valuable piece of evidence in Auden's own book. Before each 'Part' of his long poem he quotes some verse, and most of it is syllabic and end-rhymed:

The quotation heading the whole work seems to be in some sort of Latin:

Lacrimosa dies illa
Que resurget ex favilla
Iudicandus homo reus.

                                     Thomas a Celano (?) *Dies Irae*

Part I (*Prologue*) is headed:

Now the day is over,
Night is drawing nigh,
Shadows of the evening
Steal across the sky.

S. Baring-Gould

Part II (*The Seven Ages*):

A sick toss'd vessel, dashing on each thing:
    Nay, his own shelf:
  My God, I mean myself

George Herbert, *Miserie*

Part III (*The Seven Stages*), probably Italian:

O Patria patria! Quanto mi costi.

A. Ghislanzoni, *Aida*

Part IV (*The Dirge*):

His mighty work for the nation,
Strengthening peace and securing union,
Always at it since on the throne,
Has saved the country more than one billion.

Broadsheet on the death of Edward VII

Part V (*The Masque*): prose
Part VI (*Epilogue*):

Some natural tears they drop'd, but wip'd them soon;
The world was all before them, where to choose.

John Milton, *Paradise Lost*

These precious quotations, which I must leave to others to analyse, definitely support my conclusions, based on Auden's deficient measure, that a syllabic and end-rhymed verse of some sort had existed in Europe, though they are unfortunately too short for us to determine its metre, which seems lax to say the least. Nevertheless they do show the sort of thing which had existed between the older epic and the poet Auden's brave attempt at rebellion against such new-fangled devices, with a return to the more traditional native measure. And, as often happens, the rebel owed a little too much to that which he was trying to overthrow. Even without these valuable fragments, however, Auden's metre shows that something had gone seriously awry with the noble epic line.

You have been reading a spoof scholarly essay. Its aim, after a few somewhat technical chapters, was to show that however much I deplore anti-technique attitudes, I am not for the kind of formal analysis that kills the text.

PART III

Theories of stories

10

Fiction, figment, feign

Feign, fiction, figment: all from *fingere* (to form). To form, to fashion, to forge, that is (isn't it?), to imitate 'Nature', or later, 'Reality'. To impose a form, therefore to change. To invent, to fabulate.

But *fabula*, in its origins, meant discourse, from *fari* (to speak): it seems a little disconcerting that *fabula* should originally mean *sjuzhet*, that *story* should originally mean *discourse*, that the *what* (which can be and is in practice summarized, reduced) should originally have meant the *how*. But is it so disconcerting?

Labels and etymology

For the further back one goes in etymology (in the 'myth of origin' as Derrida would say), the more often one finds this fusion, this ambiguity in literary terms, and even a clear tendency towards the signifier (the *how*) rather than towards the signified (the *what*):

What	How
	myth (*mythos* : word, discourse, other senses later)
	poem (*poiesis* : action of making, fabricating)
	lyric (which is sung with a lyre)
	satire (*satura* : mixture)
	eclogue (*ekloge*, from *eklegein*, to select)
threnody (*threnos* + ode, song of lamentation	parody (*para* + ode, *parodein* : to sing out of tune)
	idyll (from *eidos*, form, image)
	iamb (*iambos*: foot, leg); trochee (from *trechein*, to run, stumble); dactyl (*dactylos* : finger, 3 joints);

What	How
	anapaest (*anapaistos*: hit in reverse, reversed dactyl)
	spondee (*spondeios*, from *sponda* : solemn drink hence manner)
	sonnet (*sonetto*, dimin of *sono*: sound)
	sestina (poem of 6 stanzas of 6 lines + envoi)
	mimesis (imitation)
narration (*narrare*, prob. from **gnarare*, cogn. *gnarus*, know)	diegesis (way of telling, summarizing)
story (from *historia*, *istor-* to know, one who knows, wise man, judge)	fable (*fabula*, from *fari*, to speak)
	legend (*legenda*, to be read)
	tale (cogn.tally, counting, cp. teller in banks); *conte, raconter* (linked *compter*, to count)
	Erzählung (*Zahl.* number): that which is exposed detail by detail
	lay, *lai, leich* (Celtic, brief narrative poem to be sung)
novel (*novella*, what is new, cp.news, nouvelles – information	*roman* (narrative in Romance language)
	récit (re-citer, *citare*, method of calling witnesses & evidence)
	theatre (*theatron*, place of spectacle, from *theasthai*, to look)
	pièce, Stück: piece
	play (game, exercise, action)
	journal, diary (what is written day by day
	cinema (*kine-* motion, speed)
	film (matter)

Ambiguous
(the *what* given before the *how*)

epic:	*epos* : what is expressed in words / word
drama:	*drama* : action / performance
elegy:	*elegei* : funeral chant, lamentation / a genre, a metre
comedy:	*komos* : feast, gaiety + ode / with songs and dances
tragedy:	*tragos* : goat + ode, song / played during immolation in feasts to Bacchus
chronicle:	*chronos* : time, events in time / way of telling
newspaper:	news / paper, material

This list is only a sample, and I have kept to genres and metres only, but the same could be said, *a fortiori*, of more recent technical terms, precisely because they are still felt as technical (analepsis, flashback, long shot and so on). But clearly the list shows the natural development of all language from an original concrete, practical description towards more abstract and generalizing senses. Nevertheless it is interesting that such a chance poll should lean so predominantly towards the *how*: for even today I feel that all the words in the right-hand column still evoke a form rather than a content, this or that content occurring to us (perhaps simultaneously) by way of example. That is, even without calling upon the literary 'competence' some critics would make into an exact parallel of linguistic 'competence' (which has a very technical sense), surely the most naive reader knows that a sonnet is not a novel or a play or a film, and it is by the form that he knows this.

The same cannot be said of the more general literary names for movements and periods, since they came about in much later times than most of the above, and almost always express (is it by chance?) a content, an ideal, or even a mere temporal grouping: *the Middle Ages* and *Mediaeval, the Renaissance, Classicism* (from *classicus*, [superior] class), *Romanticism* (notion of returning to mediaeval Romance), *Realism, Naturalism, the psychological, the sociological novel, Symbolism, Surrealism, the Absurd*, etc. The rare exceptions are *baroque* (*barroca*. regular pearl) and its sequel *rococo* (French, 'perhaps a fanciful formation on the stem *rocaille*. pebble work', OED).

As for the poverty of later twentieth-century vocabulary in the naming of contemporary literature, it is well-known: the contemporary, when it was difficult of access or unfamiliar, was called simply *modern*, and then, when it was no longer either modern or unfamiliar, the label remained stuck to the period (now *Modernist*), or rather,

it was applied to all the works that survived, even those which were
not 'difficult' then: and this was followed by *anti-modern* and *postmodern*: or the *nouveau roman*, followed by the *nouveau nouveau roman*.
These terms have been much criticized as merely temporal, which
must lead to *anti-postmodern* or *neopostmodern* or *classical postmodernism*
(*post post? past post?*), or even now, *post-contemporary*. But they have
also been defended as more than just temporal (that is, filled with
description, mostly of content, sometimes of technique). Only Cristopher Nash (1988) and Mare Chénetier (1989) to my knowledge at
the time of writing, have refused the term 'postmodernism'. Nash
has troubled to find non-temporal terms: *cosmic* (realism), *anti-realist*
as a general term to set against that, with *neocosmic/anticosmic* as subdi-
visions. This at least shows what is at stake, but we are still very
much in content-categories, and this shows up in his chapter headings: *Shapes, Ideas, Substance, Shape vs Substance*. I shall return to these
problems in Chapter 14. Chénetier presents the American novel in
general from 1960 on, without any such labels, discussing specific
renewals technically. He does, however, condemn the term 'postmodern' (84–8), not only as poor (a *cache-manque*), but as confusing
(in 'post*modern*') an intellectual caesura which starts roughly with
Hegel and (in 'post*modernist*') an artistic movement which opens the
twentieth century (86).

It would seem then that the writer today can no longer have the
same type of consciousness of what he is doing. He can of course,
and often does, become an academic expert in the formal analysis
of genres (a notion often said to be exploded), but the dangers of
this are obvious, and I have discussed them in my first two chapters.
Or he can remain 'innocent' and trust his instinct, but here too
lies danger of technical naivety (see Ch. 2). For on the one hand
he has lost that assurance of a common *Zeitgeist*, that general security
of railway lines and roads that gave him a grand panorama of the
real while allowing him adventure on the sideroads and footpaths
and in the villages. Today it's the plane or the motorway. On the
other hand, he 'knows everything', the villages and footpaths are
accurately mapped.

Chaucer could mock gently at the rhetoricians while nevertheless
knowing them thoroughly. But all poets had an unconscious knowledge that enabled them (to repeat my example from Ch. 1) to write
varied and sometimes almost free but 'correct' iambic pentameters
without knowing the one and only rule they could not and did not
break. And then the iambic pentameter died, *outre-atlantique*, first

with Whitman, echoing the changed rhythms of the American language and the Bible, then with Pound ('to break the pentameter, that was the first heave', C.81), although the iambic rhythm natural to English dragged on in Eliot and others. These are the mysteries of creation, or rather, of craftsmanship learnt by doing. Similarly the great novelists of the past, while perfectly conscious of their techniques and even comically revealing them, also had an unconscious knowledge of 'mimesis', imitation of the 'real', which it seems it was enough simply to observe and reproduce in words in order to re-form it. But it was not at all 'easier' for them than it is for us: to practise seeing, for a lifetime, a living 'reality' (the 'truth') in order the better to transform it (since humankind cannot bear it) has always been and always will be the painful and splitting dilemma of the artist, the truth and the lies that already so tormented Plato. And the 'reality', the 'truth', changed with each period and generation. The difference is that today we cannot believe in truth any more: the more one practises looking for it beyond the appearances, the less it is there.

Writing today

To form in order to feign, while feigning that one doesn't form, that one 'captures', 'imitates' (but in the most elegant and 'natural' way possible), a Nature (a passion) pre-existent to language ... We have only lately become fully aware that what we talk of is identical to the discourse (see *mythos*, *epos*, *fabula*) we no longer dare to speak (on the one hand) and can't stop uttering (on the other).

This awareness has made us over-conscious, self-conscious, and it hurts, it makes fullness empty, it divides the atom which threatens to explode when brought together again. Once upon a time, out there, were the Gods, the Vices and Virtues, the Personifications, and the Gods and Personifications died. So then several times upon a time, out there, was Nature, and when Nature also revealed itself, at an ever-increasing pace, to be made in our mortal image, once upon another time, out there, was Reality, which also turned out to be discourse, languages, systems of significance, continuing their own negation, signifying nothing.

It is thus discourse that kills, the letter killeth as quote Hardy and Jude, discourse that becomes a substitute for the supposed real, which 'quite simply is' (Robbe-Grillet).

One individual solution has been silence: to stop writing, to plunge into the 'real' (Rimbaud); to die (Mayakovski) and so on. Another, quasi-collective and the most frequent, has been and still is, to continue 'as if': the real is still there, on the one hand, and it signifies: discourse, on the other hand, captures it, transparent as a window, or skilfully positioned like a camera: story, fabula, subjected.

Another solution, more difficult, more ambiguous, was 'the aesthetics of silence' that Susan Sontag spoke of already in 1966, or Steiner in other terms in 1958, yes, a quarter-century or more ago:

> ... art is foundering in the debilitating tide of what once seemed the crowning achievement of European thought: secular historical consciousness. In a little more than two centuries, the consciousness of history has transformed itself from a liberation, an opening of doors, blessed enlightenment, into an insupportable burden of self-consciousness. It's scarcely possible for the artist to write a word (or render an image or make a gesture) that doesn't remind him of something already achieved.
>
> (Sontag 1966, 14)

Later she cites Novalis who said that the astonishing and ridiculous mistake people make is to believe that they use words in relation to things, whereas the nature of language is to be its own subject. 'Novalis' statement may help to explain the apparent paradox: that in an era of the widespread advocacy of art's silence, an increasing number of works babble' (26–7). She distinguishes especially two styles of 'silence', the loud and the soft, but both are reaching

> to the same idea of art's absolute aspirations (by programmatic disavowals of art): they share the same disdain for 'meanings' established by bourgeois-rationalist culture, indeed for culture itself in the familiar sense. What is voiced by the Futurists, some of the Dada artists and Burroughs as a harsh despair and perverse vision of apocalypse is no less serious for being proclaimed in a polite voice and as a sequence of playful affirmation.
>
> (32–3)

I requote this much-quoted essay to emphasize that it has been going on a long time, this intolerable super-consciousness of mankind's discursive nature, further elaborated by Foucault, Derrida *et al*. And although Sontag was careful to say that 'The present prospect is that artists will go on abolishing art, only to resurrect it in a more retracted version', and Barth later followed up his famous essay 'The Literature of Exhaustion' with his equally famous 'The Literature of Replenishment' (1967; 1984), the same sorts of things continue to be said. And the more this super-consciousness lasts, the more the fictions proliferate (modernist, antimodernist, postmodernist, supramodernist ...), and the more the analyses and descriptions and declarations continue, those of diverse poststructuralisms which have had the merit and the temerity to ɲnveil the egologo (phallo) centrism of our reading presuppositions. One generation of literary academics creates another, which creates another, and from thesis to thesis some of us can't help wondering whether anyone else reads these texts, critical and fictional, criticofictional or fictocritical, outside that self-perpetuating and confraternal industry – at least what is left of such texts, for the next generations will soon be or already are wholly televisual. The eternal and instinctive desire to be told a story is already satisfied otherwise than through writing, and after all why not? The fabula had already migrated from the Greek epic to tragedy and then to romance, then again from the mediaeval epic to the metrical romance in the twelfth century, which turned into the prose romance until the fifteenth then 'story' migrated to the theatre in the sixteenth, then back to a sort of epic, before being reborn in the prose novel that seems to us so classical, permanent and eternal. But why should 'story' not have migrated again into the media, its 'realist' aspect into documentary and its fictional aspect into soap and comics, the novel having finally proved itself inept for the times, or, as Sarraute said more than forty years ago, always fifty years behind the other arts (1956: 1963)? After all, one important aspect of poetry has returned to its musical sources in popular song, and this is good.

In *Fabula 1* (1983), Jean-Claude Dupas tried to show (with the help of Foucault, Louis Dumont and Locke, and as Lionel Trilling and Ian Watt had done in different ways earlier), that certain fundamental breaks in the European consciousness at the Renaissance had created the conditions for the new individualism, the putting into question of the analogical (Foucault), of the hierarchizing spirit (Dumont), of subordination (Locke), and were also propitious to the development of the novel (my translation):

Since only the particular as unique origin of sensation is a source of ideas, only singularity is conceivable, and the individual is necessarily singular. In order to be, the character in the novel must be unique and not emblematic. It is not therefore through his representing a value or a class of individuals that the character brings about reflection, but through his singularity.

(26–7)

Yes, but the character in the novel has long become emblematic again (see Ch. 11): not only in 'neocosmic' fiction (science fiction and alternative world fiction), where this pertains to the genre, but in 'anticosmic' fiction also (and the two often overlap these days). Does one, can one, analyse the 'psychology' or the 'social background or status' or the 'feelings' or the 'conflicts of passion' (etc) of K, or HCE, or the simple pronouns of the *nouveau* (+ *nouveau*) *roman*? Can one, does one, speak even of the innumerable anti-heroes in the picaresque revival of the fifties, or of the characters in the traditional neorealist novel of today, as one spoke of Rastignac or Tess or Emma (Woodhouse or Bovary)?

The historical perspective (the fabula of history) gives us the impression that the rise and development of the novel occurred very smoothly, *sans histoire si j'ose dire*. Cervantes having fun with the romance of chivalry or Fielding later announcing triumphantly that he had created a new form. And because *les petits, les obscurs* have disappeared, everything seems very simple. And other more distant breaks, the long decline and decentralization of Rome, the 'barbarian' invasions and the long slow birth of vernacular literatures, not to mention formal literary (therefore also sociopolitical) changes, some already mentioned above, from the Middle Ages to the eighteenth century, all these breaks seem very evident seen from afar.

But when one is *inside* the effect of so many ruptures? Those that presided over the birth of the modern novel lasted after all from Copernicus to the Enlightenment, which itself ended in a great burst of regenerative nostalgia for the analogies of yore.

Today, precisely when that individualism so necessary to the character in the novel is fading away, when everything is happening so much faster than it did between Copernicus and the Enlightenment, other ruptures, as fundamental as those if not more so (and described often enough for me not to have to do it here), seem to preside over the 'death of the novel', so long announced and apparently now occurring, at least in its traditional form since any 'serious' fiction *claims* to be non-referential and deconstructive (I shall return to this in Ch. 14). And although the technical super-consciousness involved may well betray (once again) the mastery of the word over that about which one speaks (of the *sjuzhet* over the *fabula*, the *how* over the *what*), it may also engender renewal through the comic and the irreverential, as Barth has claimed and doubtless achieved in his works, together with many others of many different kinds in the 'anticosmic'/'neocosmic' movements. It is perhaps a regeneration of the novel, which I shall examine in the next few chapters, but in other ways we are often closer to poetry (itself also often proclaimed dead), but also, and often contrarily, away from stylistic concerns to problems of fictional representation denuded of all but the barest and even the poorest language: the novel is dead, long live the poem; the poem is dead, long live the text; and now: the text is dead, long live the fiction.

Déjà-vu

I am simplifying, naturally, for it is difficult to say, as *author*, exactly what it means to write fiction today. Having learnt writing by writing, rather than from theory, I often had a sensation of *déjà-vu*, though perhaps not yet known under this or that critical term, when I plunged into the new philosophies of *écriture* and declarations about metafiction, fiction as metatheorem, overtotalization, parody and all the rest that have accumulated since the sixties around the unfortunate term 'postmodernism'.

All then has been said, there is nothing new under the sun, not only because all is undecidable (or is it undeicidable?), but because, as well, we already know what each will say, each being no longer unique but returned to the emblematic, each a member of a class, a social, political or ideological group, each has this or that neurosis and therefore this or that reaction, reply. And even scenes are labelled, the happiness sequence, the chase sequence, the scene of violence, the marital scene, the love-scene, the high society scene, the scene of diplomatic intrigue, the office sequence, the work sequence, with its appropriate music and lighting. What can *la scène de l'écriture* do against all that?

And we know all on the how, at least in theory. The rhetoricians, the grammarians, the logicians, have retailed their Trivium over all the texts. We no longer speak thought, we think language. Just as exacerbated analysis kills love (which, like power, is at its apogee in silence), so the simple fabula of a situation (a life, a world), more or less political, social, psychoanalytical, idyllic, unhappy – in brief, ordinary – is subject to a discursive expansion rule, almost a rule of proliferation if it weren't a contradiction in terms, for proliferation is chaotic, cancerous, that is, obsessional, reflexive, autophagous.

As in all period-ends. The 'less and less so ostentatiously advanc-[ing] itself as more' (Sontag) has become, on the one hand, the mania for huge texts, self-indulgent texts (see Ch. 13), and, on the other, the controlled 'less' of a Beckett, and other 'minimalist' texts, the acceptance of non-interpretability, nevertheless interpreted *ad nauseam* by each and everyone, be it through instruction, constructivism or deconstruction.

And so here we are, many of us, authors, critics, teachers (*criticus*, which goes back to *krinein*, to judge; to *kritikos*, capable of judging, deciding: *kriteon* from *krino*, to separate, sort out, distinguish, judge – but also to interpret dreams – *ça fait rêver*), writing on the impossibility of writing, sorting out diverse writings on the impossibility of writing, distinguishing them, interpreting their non-interpretability, we are the judges of the impossible.

How then can we not suffer from paralysing over-consciousness, except by overcoming it and passing into either self-indulgence or silence?

So we feign to form fictions with figments, *sjuzhets* without a *fabula* which comes from *fari*, to speak. We count and recount what we have counted, we recite and cite ourselves in justice, we cut ourselves in pieces to play, we sing beside the note, out of tune with our para-audiovisual, we narrate therefore we know, we dramatize therefore perform, conform, transform, form without informing, in brief *ça cause* because *che cosa*?

11

Which way did they go? Thataways

It is a commonplace of contemporary criticism that the character in the novel, as known for generations from a type of criticism, a type of school-teaching and therefore of examination-question, from innumerable fictobiostudies and from the traditional way of reviewing that came out of all that, no longer exists. Some continue as if it did, but the problem is not really one of choice, of 'you go your way I'll go mine'. Nor is it that certain wicked authors have killed off all characters, or the possibility of characters, so that writers who continue in the old mode somehow can't produce convincing ones any more. It is that the whole concept of character in the novel has changed, and while some writers have noted the fact and mimed it or played with it, others have ignored it.

Character A to Z

Over twenty years ago, John Barth was already dissolving characters in 'Life-Story', a chapter of *Lost in the Funhouse* (1968, 117–21):

> D comes to suspect that the world is a novel, himself a fictional personage [...] since D is writing a fictional account of this conviction [...] Moreover E, hero of D's account, is said to be writing a similar account [...] If I'm going to be a fictional character G declared to himself [...] If he can only get K through his story I reflected grimly [...] Why could he not begin his story afresh et cetera? Y's wife came into the study.

Barth is doing several things here. First, the character has become an action (his action), in a Structuralist way, and as is in fact the case in the sort of folktale analysed by Propp (1928): D suspects, D is writing, E is writing a similar account, G declared to himself, I reflected. By the same token, Barth is representing the disappearance of character from the modern novel – the character has become mere letters, even if one of them is I, who may also be Y whose wife comes into the study. After all, the briefest epigram of metaphysical anguish could be said to be 'I – Why?' (and 'Why' has been asked just before). Also, there is a *mise en abîme*, E being the hero of D's novel and so on, all being in fact versions of I: a technique that has a venerable ancestry and is much re-exploited in postmodern fiction from Borges onwards.

Barth is also representing the creative process in this new denuded situation. Gone is the trepidation of a Henry James stepping warily around his complex creations. Gone too are the Jamesian ecstasies of the notebooks as the author pictures his characters, deftly adding stroke to stroke. Instead, we have a raging despair at the emptiness of D or E, mere supports for their own self-reflections and quickly replaced by G or K. They express all frustrated attempts at character-making and all versions of the author's various selves, lasting but a few seconds and presumably torn up and thrown into the waste-paper basket. The process perhaps reached its peak in Brautigan's *Trout Fishing in America* (1967), where the title phrase is used in every function from title via adjective to character: 'trout fishing in America terrorists', 'Dear Trout Fishing in America', and the reply signed, 'Your friend, Trout Fishing in America'. Or as theme turned deconstructively back into character: 'This is the autopsy of Trout Fishing in America, as if Trout Fishing in America had been Lord Byron and had died in Missolonghi, Greece, and afterwards never saw the shores of Idaho again, never saw Carrie Creek, Worsewick Hot Springs, Paradise Creek, Salt Creek and Duck Lake again' (50, 56, 63, 65). Since then, everyone has had a go. The characters of Pynchon have names that signify their state or activity, as in allegory, and in William Gass' *On Being Blue* (1976) the colour blue seems to have replaced both character and action.

Barth, in addition, is simultaneously parodying two complementary techniques, but one is vertical (the *mise en abîme*), the other horizontal in the sense that sequentially we have an absurd version of a technique typical of the late realistic novel, namely, defocalization of the hero (Hamon 1973), which has two main functions: first, to avoid the heroic or 'novelistic' (*le romanesque*), which ensured the reader's identification by a sustained focalization on the main character; second, to build up a portrait of society (however large or small), by focalizing on one character at a time, introducing A, then B, then C, then A again, then D, and so on. This defocalization reached its climax in the 1930s, in Huxley's *Point Counterpoint* for example, and it has become the most familiar cliché of the current traditional novel, and the main technique of films. In its most mechanical form, TV soap, we pass from couple to couple, hardly able to distinguish one drama from another or one serial from the next, or, for that matter, from the interjected commercials: two intense women in a kitchen discussing either infidelity or detergents. But clearly the *mise en abîme* is also a way of 'forgetting' the main character of one level when we plunge into the embedded story at the next level. The defocalization of the realist novel is 'parodied' (but see next chapter) in Pynchon's V, where we are never allowed to identify for more than a few paragraphs with any one of the innumerable characters or to grasp the real nature of the complicated quest.

Already in Barth's *Lost in the Funhouse*, in the chapter called 'Title', we see the blatant naming of a technique comically replacing the use of it: ' "Why do you suppose it is", she asked, long participial phrase of breathless variety characteristic of dialogue attributions in nineteenth-century fiction, "that literature people such as we talk like characters in a story?" ' (11).

'The novel that contains characters belongs well and truly to the past', Robbe-Grillet could say already in 1962 (transl. 1965, 60). And fourteen years later the critic Zavarzadeh could repeat of characterization: ' The "function" of this device [...] has become obsolete today' (1976, 30).

In fact the dissolution of character is not, except perhaps in some of its extreme forms, peculiar to 'postmodernism'. There, it is the final outcome of something that had begun much earlier – with Kafka's Joseph K, for example. Although still a character apparently complex and puzzling enough to elicit the countless reinterpretations of our trade, K (divested of even a surname) is merely a support for an emotional state and an asocial situation, as Nathalie Sarraute pointed out thirty years ago in *The Age of Suspicion* (1956; 1963). It is the circumstances which are puzzling and complex, not him. In a different vein, Nathaniel West's characters, and later some of Nabokov's, were already mechanical spokesmen of their states or actions, actants rather than actors, carriers of events rather than characters with psychological depth. Earlier, the Surrealists had twisted mimetic description into zanier language-games than anything found in 'postmodernism', and Djuna Barnes described a character by what she was not (*Ryder*, 1928, Ch. 17). As for the dazzling and better-known parodies in *Ulysses*, it is surely a moot point whether they partake in or dismantle the mimetic illusion. And by 1939 Flann O'Brien could write:

Characters should be interchangeable as between one book and another. The entire
corpus of existing literature should be regarded as a limbo from which discerning
authors could draw their characters as required, creating only when they failed to
find a suitable existing puppet. The modern novel should be largely a work of reference.

(At *Swim-Two-Birds*, 25)

For if a fictional character can be reduced to what he does (as in
folktale and romance), it is also true that he can be a result of what
he says and the way he speaks (as in drama). When the narrating
author kept a strong hold over his characters, counterpointing what
they said with his own discourse (see Chs. 5 to 7), characters seemed
full, 'rounded', 'real', 'alive', and only the 'flat' characters, as Forster
called them (1927), were merely given to be recognized by what
they said and the way they said it (Mrs Micawber or, say, a traditional butler). The more the novel tried to save itself, earlier this
century, by letting the character 'take over' (as the authorial cliché
goes), and just talk, the flatter the characters became: for this technique merely borrows from the theatre without the theatre's advantages (as Sarraute pointed out about Ivy Compton-Burnett, 1956).
Some characters, said McElroy more recently, 'are wholly fabricated
by the jargon they use' (1983, 84). And nothing dies more quickly
than merely mimed jargon: the author must transmute it if it is
to survive, as does McElroy himself (e.g. in *Plus*, 1976) or, for that
matter, Mark Twain with Huck's 'dialect'. Interestingly, when the
novel since the fifties privileged 'free' direct speech (see Ch. 5), it
was mostly (apart from Sarraute) the narrating author's voice that
was heard, not that of the quasi-inexistent characters, and the same
phenomenon is observable in the 'self-reflexive' American novel from
the sixties on.

Valéry's scornful sentence *La marquise sortit à cinq heures*, admired
by the Surrealists, epitomized the detailed social trivia of a typical
character's activities and consciousness in the novel, and was taken
up as a title by Claude Mauriac (1961; 1962). In the fifties it had
become a joke-phrase for the writers of the *nouveau roman* and the
nouvelle critique, which had turned against the novel of minute psychological and social analysis, the 'old myths of depth' as Robbe-Grillet
called them (1962, 45). Some think the character died for good then,
some date its death much further back, to Freud on dreams and
the case histories so much more convincing than any subsequent
ghosts of fiction.

For two centuries characters had reigned supreme in our imagina-
tions. Ostensibly we valued the way they were created, but above

all we identified with them and talked of them – Emma, Becky Sharp, Jean Valjean, Little Dorrit, Fabrice, Rastignac, Marcel, Leopold Bloom, or even Ulrich, the Man Without Qualities – as if we knew them better than we knew our friends and kin. This has been revealed to be a wholly fantasmatic process: characters are verbal structures, they are like our real-life relationships but have no semblance of a referent. More and more swollen with words, like stray phalluses they wander our minds, cut off from the body of the text – hence the endless character analysis of traditional criticism, which would be perfectly irrelevant to the characters of, say, Beckett; hence also our disappointment when we see these fantasized 'realist' characters incarnated by actors.

Nevertheless, for many critics the ultimate value of a novel depends on the author's ability to create characters as complex and convincing as real people. But the way this illusion was created and then, curiously, uncreated, so that it now lies in pieces at our feet like a disassembled toy, together with the novel as we commonly understand the term, deserves and has received serious consideration. We certainly do not feel we know, as we feel we know the characters of earlier novels, the mostly unnamed personages of Sarraute, Butor, Robbe-Grillet, or even the named but ambiguously existing creatures of the Beckett novels, or those great paranoiacs Pirate Prentice and Tyrone Slothrop of Pynchon's *Gravity's Rainbow*, and we are not meant to. The one 'postmodern' character I do feel I know is Borges' briefly textualized Pierre Menard (1962, 36–44) – but only as someone who is writing *Don Quixote* in the twentieth century, word for word the same as the sixteenth-century text. An emblem. The 'postmodern' / 'anticosmic' novel often seems to be at best a desperate parody of a dying genre, though some, like Barth, believe in regeneration through genre parody. The reasons are many, and have been much discussed, but I'll gather a few I think important.

Origins of dissolution

One is the dead hand of history. Sontag wrote about it in 'The Aesthetics of Silence' (1969, see Ch. 10, p. 162). Moreover, even history has become as inaccessible to us as the ontological it purports to relate; all our realities have been revealed to be products of our many systems of representation and, in particular, of our tropes, as Hayden White has suggested in his *Metahistory* and *Tropics of Discourse* (1973, 1978).

But 'living' history is also permanently falsified, not just by totalitarian systems that efface and reinterpret, but by liberal systems that exploit, and, in particular, that present it only as 'story' (revolutions, massacres etc.) and are consequently surprised by such events through chronic blindness to non-'story' elements that have long prepared them. The surprise then creates dramatization and wrong interpretation, and further blindness. We have been going through a more and more generalized crisis of representation at all levels: not only have our political systems, both totalitarian and democratic, become incapable of efficient political representation, but societies and their complexities are no longer imaged for us except through the distortions of media conventions. Perhaps it always was so, but less visibly and less fast, and today the 'representation crisis' even seems institutionalized for the profit of the culture-and-information purveyors who live on it. Whatever the extent of the process, our old beliefs in the 'truth' of people and events as represented has long collapsed, and we seem to live in a simulation-cabin that gives us detailed illusions of movement and control, all the while keeping us immobile and observed.

Dick Higgins has called our age 'post-cognitive' and McHale has taken this up and traced, even within the work of single writers, a change from epistemological to ontological concerns, producing what he calls 'an ontological flicker' in postmodern novels (see Ch. 2, p. 25, and Ch. 14).

This long representational crisis, with its inevitable advances and retreats, denials and desires, has in addition taken the very specific form of technical self-consciousness, and this not only at the level of high philosophy. If every script-writer knows the few deft touches needed to make a character convincing in one shot, so does the structuralist and poststructuralist critic. The character, Todorov told us (then in his pure structuralist period) is a function (that is an action, a verb: the one who receives, gives, transgresses, punishes etc.) (1969). The character, Roland Barthes then said (1970), is the convergence of selected semes upon a proper name. And Hamon (1977) went one still further in reductionism by comparing characters to signs, of which he found three main types:

(1) Referential signs, which refer to an exterior reality coded in institutionalized knowledge – referential characters (historical, allegorical, social etc.) immobilized by a culture.
(2) Deictic signs (the egocentric circumstantials of Russell or shifters of Jakobson) which refer to the situation of utterance – deictic characters that mark the

presence of the author, the reader, and their substitutes in the text.

(3) Anaphoric signs, which refer back to other disjoined signs in the spoken or written chain – anaphoric characters recognizable only within the system of the work and forming a network of reminders and interpreters.

In this semiotic superconsciousness, it would seem that 'postmodernism' has eliminated all but the egocentric circumstantials.

We have also seen the attempts (in Hardy, in Crane) to dissolve the boundaries between author and character and later attempts to get rid of the 'author as God' concept (see Ch. 5, but see also Ch. 14 on the return of this notion in 'postmodernism'); and how one of the main techniques for entering the consciousness of a character became *un*conscious, came to be misunderstood and misused to create implausibly 'narrating' characters, and how it disappeared (Ch. 5). Over-familiarity of technique is also responsible for the exploding of the mimetic illusion.

Besides an increased technical consciousness, we have also acquired an increased knowledge, provided by psychoanalysis and sociology, of what the novel's modes of representation are assumed to convey, so that these modes came to seem inadequate to this new complexity. This is linked to the bourgeois origin of the novel, which Ian Watt was the first to show (1957). The society that the novel was developed to study and depict has lost all solid basis, all stability, all belief in itself, our vision of it has broken into fragments. On the one hand, the individual has lost his central role and has been replaced by a collectivist mode of thought. On the other hand, the critics and philosophers of the deconstructionist movement have, since 1967, steadily subverted what was left of the mimetic and expressive theories of literature, killing the signified in favour of the signifier, the author in favour of the reader, and the fiction in favour of textuality as an activity, an endless dissemination, or even, for the Barthes of 1973 (*The Pleasure of the Text*), a *jouissance* of infinite codes. Meanwhile, Lacan had disintegrated the self into a play of selves.

People still behave, writers still write, novelists portray and satirize, but the society they refer to is no longer there, in the sense that there is no fixed or certain belief in it. Serious writers have lost their material. Or rather, this material has gone elsewhere: back to the novelist's original sources in documentary, journalism, chronicles, letters – but in their modern forms, such as the media and the human sciences, which supposedly do it better. Nonfiction has taken back all the sociology, the psychology and the philosophy that enriched the 'realist novel, while the poetry, the myth and the dream have also moved elsewhere, to pop and rock, for example, with their flashing lights and surrealist video-clips. Even dialogue, which the novel had learnt from sophisticated seventeenth- and eighteenth-century comedy, has long returned to the stage and screen, as has story. In 1958 (1967, 84ff.), George Steiner could speak already of a new nonfiction genre that would replace the novel, including works ranging from the high journalism of documentaries like Oscar Lewis' *The Children of Sanchez* (1961) to more fundamentally changed forms, perceptible in Blake and including Nietzsche, Kierkegaard, or Bloch's *Das Prinzip Hoffnung* (1938–59; 1969). Steiner even included Wittgenstein's *Tractatus* as a borderline case.

Another reason may lie in what Walter J. Ong (1982), perhaps simplistically, has called 'secondary orality'. In primary orality, he says, narratives are episodic and characters are what E. M. Forster (1927) called 'flat', as opposed to 'round'. Round characters, like Aristotle's well-made plot, could not occur before the advent of writing. We meet them first in the Greek tragedies, which their actors' written parts rendered more analysable and linear than the earlier, stereotyped oral and formulaic epics. A second technological revolution, that of print, widened and deepened our ability to analyse and present complex characters. And now, through the electronic media, we have entered a secondary orality, quite unlike the first since writing and print profoundly altered our minds, but it may alter us again no less profoundly.

Whether or not we agree with Father Ong and his predecessors (McLuhan 1962, Havelock 1963, 1976, 1982, Lord 1960), flat characters are coming back. They have been coming back for some time, through the comic strips and the hero/villain western or spy or gangster films, and they seem more real to the young than all the rounded, complex characters of our classic loves. It is Superman and Wonderwoman, Batman, the Schtrumpfs (Smurfs) and all the rest, that the new generations identify with.

Round characters seem to have vanished back into fact, into the news clips and the documentaries, retaining all their real-life opacity. The realist novel's window into their souls seems to have blacked out. The reader got bored perhaps, overwhelmed as he is with the daily horror of the world as global village or with endless interviews of spokesmen for every aspect of life and their expected answers, and he has come to prefer nonfiction or pure fantasy to realistic fiction, whose modes can no longer cope with the global village except by undermining the realism (Fuentes or Rushdie, for example). A real terrorist, an Islamic fanatic, a little girl sinking into the mud and dying under camera-eyes, are far more mysterious, opaque and fantasmatic than all our acutely observed and literate bourgeois tizzies.

So the human need for fictions has been channelled into the 'popular' genres, now earnestly studied in the universities. As Northrop Frye showed in *The Secular Scripture* (1976), there is always, in any culture, a 'secular' tradition on the fringe of the 'central myth' tradition – in our case Graeco-Judeo-Christian. The central tradition despises and excludes the secular tradition, except when it is itself exhausted. Then it returns to the secular and popular genres to find new vigour. And of course the characters in these popular genres are 'flat' characters, as in the folktale, and even in the more sophisticated mediaeval romances they are mere supports for this or that strength, weakness, passion, or, in their more serious interpretations, seasonal or other archetype. In science fiction, which many agree is a modern equivalent of romance, the characters are by genre-definition flat, and the best sci-fi critics maintain that realistic characterization is not its job: landscape as hero, said Mark Rose (1976), but Kingsley Amis had already gone one better (1960) and said: idea as hero.

It could thus be said of characters in both the 'postmodern' novel and the best science fiction (which today rejoins 'postmodernism') that they exist in any complexity only in so far as they represent ideas (paranoia, the writing author etc. or 'postmodernism'), rather than individuals with a civic status and a subtle social or psychological history. And even if such a history is given or implied, which is rare, it is contingent, it is not what is meant to interest the reader. Rounded individuation has become an addition, like the 'ornaments' of traditional rhetoric.

Another way of putting all this is to recall Frye's historical and cyclical theory of Modes (1957), based on the hero's power of action. He identified five Modes: myth, where the hero is a god; romance, where he is a man but with magic powers; high mimetic, where he is a man but a leader (who in the tragic version falls); low mimetic (the realist novel, domestic tragedy), where he is a man like us; and irony, where his power of action is less than ours, so that we watch his mistakes or, by Kafka's time, his disoriented torments. But when existence outbids fiction in the savagery of this ironic mode, fictions escape and return to myth – as happened in the modernist period of Pound, Eliot, Joyce. And now we would be back in romance. Or, as George Steiner put it (1958, 78–91), fiction is silent before the horrors of the mid twentieth century.

I would say rather that it is the realist mimetic tradition which is silent before these horrors and cannot cope with them, but that poetry (in the widest sense), being essentially non-mimetic, can, like various types of modern fantastic, cope with everything from the sublime to the horrific. And the best of 'postmodern' fiction has escaped into poetry.

It is not only the horror of political violence, however, but the loud clamour of sexuality which has killed the mimetically realized character, now gone detumescent. In *Language and Silence* (1958, 68–77) Steiner says: 'The novels being produced under the new code of total statement shout at their personages: strip, fornicate, perform this or that act of sexual perversion. So did the S.S. guards at rows of living men and women.' Yet French critics like Kristeva and Sollers have called this 'the experience of limits' (with reference to Bataille and others). Surely the mimetic fails here too, because referentially there *is* a limit as well as a severe limitation in variation to this type of activity. I do not myself consider the told orgies of sodomy and shit-swallowing and pee-drinking in Burroughs or certain scenes of *Gravity's Rainbow* to be high literary achievements. Moreover both the 'postmodern' novel and science fiction, like utopias, are regressively phallocratic for our age. It is as if a return to popular forms, or even a 'parody' of them, even via the intellectual cognition of utopian models, necessarily entailed the circulation of women as value-objects, which occurs both in those models and in the folktales of early cultures. I shall return to this problem in Chapters 15 and 16.

Resurrection?

Fictional character has died, or become flat, as had *deus ex machina*. We're left, perhaps, with the ghost in the *machina*.

La marquise revint à minuit. This was the title of an article by Philippe Muray in *L'infini* (1983), the review that replaced *Tel Quel*. Character, Muray noted, may well be coming back but, precisely, as a *revenant*, a ghost; and we must know it for what it is. Yet surely this knowing it for a ghost, a verbal construct, and the consequent loss of our innocence, of our passionate identifications, created the situation in the first place. Fragmented ectoplasms, pale copies of case-histories or of ancient archetypes, our characters are either documented records artificially animated or ghosts of past fictions and strip-cartoons. Nor do the repeated comic demystifications of the realistic procedures used to create characters cause any *marquise* to return, whether 'real' or as ghost. The long process of *déniaiserie* was necessary but perhaps costly.

There is, however, a sign of such conscious 'ghosts' in some later American fiction, where the native oral tradition of *Huckleberry Finn* has returned, and characters are again 'fabricated by their jargon' – in Ishmael Reed, Robert Coover, Joseph McElroy, in Stanley Elkin's non-innocent realism, in Raymond Carver's 'minimalist' realism, in some of the best 'ethnic' writers such as Toni Morrison or Grace Paley. Indeed, voice and the speech-act in general seems a far more vital, regenerating phenomenon in modern American fiction than in European or Latin American fiction, where characters speak little and it is on the contrary the author's commentary on his characters that has returned, for instance in Kundera, Fuentes, Eco, Rushdie. Pawić (1983, transl. 1989) has even written an entire novel as biographical dictionary entries, which are extraordinarily effective (see Chapter 12). Whether speech-act alone can bring character back to fiction remains to be seen. For there is also the danger of either self-indulgence (the many paranoiacs speaking) or tape-mimetism (Warhol's *a*, 1968, which *is* a transcribed tape of an endless weekend party in his house).

We are in transition, no doubt, like the unemployed waiting for the newly structured technological society. Realistic novels on the old techniques continue to get written and published, but fewer and fewer people buy them or read them, except for the best-sellers with the right admixture of voluptuousness and violence, sentimentality and sex, familiarity and fantasies. Serious writers have joined the poets as elitist outcasts and have retreated into self-reflexive, self-mocking forms – from the fabulated scholarship of Borges to the cosmicomics of Calvino, from Beckett's despairing hollow men to the choreography of mere pronouns in the *nouveau nouveau roman*, from Barthelme's mysterious stylizations of our cultural 'dreck' (his word for junk) to Brautigan's and Ishmael Reed's light funny ones, from the magic realism of a Márquez to the surrealistically achronological histories of a Fuentes, of a Rushdie, from Barth's anguished Menippean satires to Pynchon's disorienting symbolic quests for nothing at all – which use the techniques of the realistic novel to show that they can no longer be used for the same purposes (see Ch. 13). The dissolution of character is a conscious gambit of 'postmodernism' as it rejoins the techniques of science fiction. The move was, however, already implicit in Modernism.

Here, perhaps, lies our hope: a starting again, *ex* almost *nihilo*, so that narrative can again, as it once did, aspire to the condition of poetry. The novel must do things that cannot be done in the other media, or die. The impetus may come from two apparently contradictory sources, the electronic revolution and the feminist revolution.

And they are indeed contradictory. On the one hand, computer science seems to root our thought structures in the absolute limitation imposed by logical operations based on binary oppositions, whose positive and negative values are of course completely neutral and unprivileged, since they are mere electrical impulses. On the other hand, the more interesting feminists have been attracted by and are contributing to the deconstructionist movement in its many variations.

Now deconstruction is ultimately also based on polarities, such as speaking/writing, sound/silence, being/non-being, presence/absence, man/woman, conscious/unconscious, and has shown how in the logo-phonocentric metaphysics of presence that has ruled us for twenty-five centuries the first term is always somehow privileged, even when equilibrium is supposed. Inverting these polarities can have a dizzy effect, and induces fear, resistance. But could the ultimate effect not be re-equilibration, which should produce (and has produced) flights of creativity and word-game processes as enriching and magical as those produced by the incredibly complex flow-charts and numerical logical operators of computer-science?

To come back to earth, just as the flat characters of romance, through print and the far-reaching social developments connected with it, eventually became rounded and complex, so perhaps the electronic revolution, after first ushering in 'secondary orality' and super-efficiency at one level and the games and pre-programmed over-simplifications of popular culture at another, will as computer-memory more powerful than that afforded by writing, alter our minds and powers of analysis once again and enable us to create new dimensions in the deep-down logic of characters, as it has enabled engineers and architects, with the help of simulated images (and what is fiction if not controlled simulation), to design the most complex aircraft, spacecraft, satellites or even buildings today. I do not mean computers with human emotions or humanoids with computer brains.

As the relevant article in the *Science Fiction Encyclopaedia* says, science fiction has so far been disappointingly unimaginative in its treatment of computer science. I mean a completely different power of analysis arising from computer logic, but as unimaginable to us now as a Shakespearian character would have been to an oral-epic culture, a different way of thinking about and rendering the human character, of thinking about and rendering world phenomena, as revolutionary as the scientific spirit that slowly emerged out of the Renaissance and the Gutenberg Galaxy.

The second source, feminism, is more problematic, and I shall return to its more desolatingly problematic aspect in Chapter 15. But we should remember that it is in the novel that the feminine contribution to art was most allowed and able to flourish, for all the reasons analysed by Virginia Woolf in *A Room of One's Own* and by others since. Moreover, I believe that it is the feminine element in humankind that creates art, as was long represented by the Muse (but see Ch. 17 on this). Lacan (1973) argues that totalization, or the construction of a whole, is always based on exclusions and is therefore always on the masculine side in his division *tout/pas tout* (whole/non whole), the *pas tout* being on the feminine side. The desiring subject on the masculine side desires the *objet petit 'a', l'autre* (the object with a small 'o', the other), located on the feminine side – desiring it via the phallus (as psychic construct) and with a phallic enjoyment. But the desiring subject on the *pas tout*, feminine side has two directions of desire: toward the phallus and toward *l'Autre* with a capital A, the Unconscious, the Symbolic, the Infinite, God – the cause of the feminine element in anyone. But each must pass through the other.

This of course is another 'story' or scenario (see Chapters 1 to 3), but it might be more appropriate to our present situation than are those of Freud.

As Jean-Claude Milner (1978) argues, this scheme can apply to any totalizing, excluding system, such as science and, for him, linguistics. Thus the language of the linguists (*la langue*) totalizes and excludes, whereas *lalangue* (in one word) is non-totalizing and feminine: in it all substitutions and arborescences are possible. The linguist's desire for this *lalangue* operates via *la langue*, the linguistic system, just as in the psychic model the desiring subject passes through the phallus. By contrast, on the *pas tout*, feminine side, *lalangue*, having access to language as Symbolic can cause surplus pleasure and produce language as substance, or what is closest to the real, the poem.[1]

In this new psychology both men and women artists who have rejected the totalization, the *tout*, of traditional and even modernist art, and chosen the underdetermination and even opaqueness of the *pas tout* may clash in an enriching and strengthening way with the binary, superlogical and by definition excluding structures of the electronic revolution (which we cannot evade). But this must be a mating, not merely a clash, the *pas tout* and the *tout* must absorb and quicken each other, not merely refuse each other, as seems to be the case at the moment (see Ch. 15).

When women have passed the stage of what I call 'mere' feminism, however radically necessary, when they have ceased to feel obliged to pounce on phallocratic instances and to claim or sometimes shriek their specificity, perhaps they will turn their attention, as they did in the past and as most men are doing now, to the deep-down regeneration of the novel. This may take a long time, but it may also happen with incredible speed, like the electronic revolution itself. Meanwhile, perhaps we will have to be satisfied with self-conscious parody or documentaries on the one hand and, on the other, with Superman, Wonderwoman, Schtrumpfs, and the dwarfs, giants, monsters and magic monarchs of pseudo-scientific romance.

---

[1] Lacan's use of 'Symbolic' as here specifically concerned with the feminine side is not to be confused with Kristeva's opposition of 'Symbolic' (masculine) vs. 'Semiotic' or pre-symbolic (feminine), to which I shall return in Chapter 15.

12

Palimpsest history

The title of this chapter is adapted from a notion, by now familiar but particularly well-expressed in Salman Rushdie's novel *Shame*. The notion is that of history as itself a fiction, the expression is varied. First a short quote: 'All stories', he says as intruding author, 'are haunted by the ghosts of the stories they might have been' (116). And now a long-quote:

> Who commandeered the job of rewriting history? The immigrants, the *mohajris*. In what languages? Urdu and English, both imported tongues. It is possible to see the subsequent history of Pakistan as a duel between two layers of time, the obscured world forcing its way back through what-had-been-imposed. It is the true desire of every artist to impose his or her vision on the world; and Pakistan, the peeling, fragmenting palimpsest, increasingly at war with itself, may be described as a failure of the dreaming mind. Perhaps the pigments used were the wrong ones, impermanent, like Leonardo's; or perhaps the place was just *insufficiently imagined*, a picture full of irreconcilable elements, midriffbaring immigrant saris versus demure, indigenous Sindhi shalwar-kurtas, Urdu versus Punjabi, now versus then: a miracle that went wrong.
>
> As for me: I too, like all migrants, am a fantasist. I build imaginary countries and try to impose them on the ones that exist. I too, face the problem of history: what to retain, what to dump, how to hold on to what memory insists on relinquishing, how to deal with change.
>
> My story's palimpsest country has, I repeat, no name of its own.
>
> (*Shame*, 87–8)

A few lines later, however, he retells the apocryphal story of Napier who, having conquered Sind in what is now South Pakistan, 'sent back to England the guilty, one word message, "Peccavi"': *I have Sind*, and adds 'I'm tempted to name my looking-glass Pakistan in honour of this bilingual (and fictional, because never really uttered) pun. Let it be *Peccavistan*.' (88).

But earlier he had said, also as intruding author: 'But suppose this were a realistic novel! Just think what else I might have to put in.' There follows a long paragraph-full of real horrors, with real names, as well as real comic incidents, which ends: 'Imagine my difficulties!' And he goes on:

> By now, if I had been writing a book of this nature, it would have done me no
> good to protest that I was writing universally, not about Pakistan. The book would
> have been banned, dumped in the rubbish bin, burned. All that effort for nothing.
> Realism can break a writer's heart.
>
> Fortunately, however, I am only telling a sort of modern fairy-tale, so that's all
> right; nobody need get upset, or take anything I say too seriously. No drastic action
> need be taken either.
>
> What a relief!

The semi-conscious dramatic irony of this last passage is poignant.

For of course, all these quotations also apply, in advance of time,
to *The Satanic Verses* (1988), where two palimpsest countries, India
and England, and one palimpsest religion, Islam, are concerned;
and which belongs to a type of fiction that has lately burst on the
literary scene and thoroughly renewed the dying art of the novel.
Terra Nostra (1976), by Carlos Fuentes, and *Dictionary of the Khazars*
(1983) by Milorad Pavić, are other great examples. Some have called
this development 'magic realism'. I prefer to call it palimpsest history. It began, I believe, with John Barth's *The Sotweed Factor* (1960)
and with *A Hundred Years of Solitude* by Gabriel Garcia Márquez
(1967), Thomas Pynchon's *Gravity's Rainbow* (1973) and Robert
Coover's *The Public Burning* (1977). Eco's *The Name of the Rose* and
Foucault's Pendulum represent another variety. You will note that these
are all very big, very long books, and this in itself goes against the
trend for novels of some 80,000 words of social comedy or domestic
tragedy to which the neorealist tradition had accustomed us for so
long. But I'll return to that point later.

First I want to distinguish between various kinds of palimpsest
histories:

(1) the realistic historical novel, about which I shall say nothing;
(2) the totally imagined story, set in a historical period, in which magic unaccoun-
     tably intervenes (Barth, Márquez);
(3) the totally imagined story, set in a historical period, without magic but with
     so much time-dislocating philosophical, theological and literary allusion and
     implication that the effect is magical – here I am thinking of Eco; and, in
     a very different key, partly because the historical period is modern, of Kundera,
     esp. 1984, 1990);
(4) the zany reconstruction of a more familiar because closer period or event,
     with apparent magic which is, however, motivated through hallucination,
     such as the relations between Uncle Sam and Vice-President Nixon in *The
     Public Burning*, or the great preponderance of paranoiacs in Pynchon's *Gravity's
     Rainbow*.

Fifthly and lastly, the palimpsest history of a nation and creed, in which magic may or may not be involved but seems almost irrelevant – or shall we say almost natural – compared to the preposterousness of mankind as realistically described. This we find in *Terra Nostra*, *The Satanic Verses*, and *The Dictionary of the Khazars*, which I consider to be far more significant, more readable and truly renewing, than either *The Public Burning* or *Gravity's Rainbow* in my fourth category, with which they seem to have much in common. In fact they are more deeply linked, imaginatively if in different ways, to Márquez, Kundera and Eco, although they look superficially different: Márquez tells an imaginary story of a family travelling and settling, and doesn't bother much with history; while Eco's history, theology, theosophy and so forth are on the face of it scrupulously accurate. So are Kundera's.

You will have noticed that, if we except Coover and Pynchon, who to my mind do not fully succeed in renewing the novel in this palimpsest way, all the novels discussed are by writers foreign to the Anglo-American novel – for if Rushdie writes in English, and writes very well, renewing the language with Indian words and highly idiomatic expressions, he certainly claims to write as a migrant. The English novel has been dying for a long time, enclosed in its parochial and personal little narrated lives, and if American postmodernism has seemed at times to bring new vigour and a breath of fresh air, it is often still too concerned with the narcissistic relation of the author to his writing, which interests no one but himself. The reader, although frequently addressed, is only taken into account with reference to this narcissistic concern in a 'look-what-I'm-doing' relationship. Here I'm thinking particularly of John Barth, who also writes big novels, or of Gilbert Sorrentino's *Mulligan Stew*. But these have little to do with history, and more to do with either the form of the novel or the modern American Way of Life, or both.

I mentioned Eco's ostensible historical accuracy a moment ago. In contrast, consider the Khazars, a historical but vanished people, mock-reconstructed through biographical entries, in three parts (Christian, Judaic, Islamic), each of which believes the Khazars were converted to its own religion, characters recurring in different versions. Or consider Philip II of Spain in *Terra Nostra*, depicted as the son of Felipe el Hermoso, who died young, and Juana la Loca, still alive and participating. Now the son of Philip the Handsome and Joan the Mad was the Emperor Charles V. There is a curious fusion of the two. Although often called Felipe, he is mostly referred to as *el Señor*, which could apply to both, and at one point he says 'my name is also Philip' – which makes the reader wonder whether Charles V's second name was Philip. He is also shown as young Philip, forced by his father *el Señor* to take his *droit de cuissage* on a young peasant bride. But later he is said to be married to an English cousin called Isabel, which was not true of Philip II, whereas Charles V's queen was called Isabel, but Isabel of Portugal. This English Isabel he never touches, and although he knows she has lovers, he finally separates from her amicably and sends her back to England where she becomes the Virgin Queen Elizabeth. Now we know that one of Philip's four wives was English, but this was Mary Tudor.

Moreover, a constant theme of the novel is that *el Señor* has no heir, and indeed dies heirless, or is at least shown dying in a horrible way and lying still alive in his coffin as he watches the triptych behind the altar, which has curiously changed. Obviously Charles V had an heir, Philip II, and so did the historical Philip II, by his fourth and Austrian wife, an heir who later became Philip IV. Thus the only historical items are that he besieged a city in Flanders – though Ghent is never named – and that he built the Escorial – and that too is never named, only described. And Philip's retreat into this palace of the dead sometimes sounds curiously like Charles' retreat to the monastery at Yurta – which, however, he did not build – after his abdication.

A similar fusion or confusion occurs with the New World, to which one of the three triplets and supposed usurpers, who each have six toes and a red cross birthmark on their back, sails on a small boat with one companion, who is killed, and has long and magical adventures in pre-Spanish Mexico. When he returns, Philip refuses to believe in the existence of the Nuevo Mundo which, of course, has historically been well established by his time, since Charles V's empire was one on which, as all the schoolbooks say, the sun never set.

None of this impedes the reading, any more than does the reincarnation of some of the non-royal characters in modern times. Why? Not only because it is a rattling good story in its own right, as convincing as the real story. But also because it is a different view of the human condition and what it endures and springs from, of absolute power and its aberrations, of the way its leaders could discount the deaths of hundreds of workers to build monster palaces, or the deaths of thousands of innocents to build monster dreams, to establish the truth as they saw it. In a way it is what science-fiction theorists call an alternative world.

But science-fiction alternative worlds are either more or less modelled on this one, with some obvious differences required and accepted by the genre; or else they represent our familiar world with some parameter altered, by extraterrestrials or other scientifically impossible event. This is not an alternative world, it is alternative history. Palimpsest history. And there are, incidentally, one or two meditations or fantasies, by Philip especially, of palimpsest religion, that look remarkably heretical or even blasphemous, or at least what Christians would have called heresy or blasphemy in the past. But the Christian authorities have never objected to them. Perhaps they learnt from the Inquisition. Or, more likely, they don't read novels. But then, the condemners of Rushdie, like many of his defenders who speak only on principle and rarely of the book itself, don't seem to have read him either.

Which brings me back to *The Satanic Verses*. Possibly Rushdie had read *Terra Nostra*, since it also contains a character with six toes, though a minor one, and the millions of butterflies that flutter over the pilgrims on their way to the Arabian Sea seem to be inspired by the headdress of live butterflies over the head of the Aztec goddess. But this may be chance. Or allusion. My point is that, whether influenced or not, *The Satanic Verses* too, is palimpsest history.

Of course we should not be surprised that totalitarian governments, and not least theocratic governments, should, when someone draws their attention to such works, object to palimpsest history. It has happened over and over in the Soviet Union. Such governments are always busy rewriting history themselves and only *their* palimpsest is regarded as acceptable. And yet there is not a single passage in *The Satanic Verses* that cannot find echo in the Qur'an and qur'anic traditions and Islamic history. The notion of 'Mahound' always receiving messages that justify his double standard with regard to wives, for example, is expressed not by the narrator but by protesting characters in conquered 'Jahilia', and finds its echo in Mohammed's revelations:

Prophet. We have made lawful to you the wives to whom you have granted dowries and the slave-girls whom Allah has given you as booty; the daughters of your paternal and maternal uncles and of your paternal and maternal aunts who fled with you; and the other women who gave themselves to you and whom you wished to take in marriage. This privilege is yours alone, being granted to no other believer.

We well know the duties We have imposed on the faithful concerning their wives and slave-girls. We grant you this privilege that none may blame you. Allah is forgiving and merciful.

(288)

What an easy step in the light-fantastic to imagine that the twelve harlots in the Jahilia brothel should assume the names of the prophet's wives. But Rushdie has explained himself on this. My point is that throughout the book we have a different reading, a poetic, re-creative reading, of what is in the Qur'an. Even the incident of the Satanic Verses finds echo in another context, or rather, in no context at all, when out of the blue Mohammed is told: 'When We change one verse for another (Allah knows best what He reveals), they say: "You are an imposter". Indeed, most of them are ignorant men' (304).

And of course, as Rushdie has insisted, all these re-creative readings are rendered, though less clearly perhaps than univocal readers are used to, as the dreams of Gibreel Farishta, an Indian Muslim actor who often played parts of even Hindu gods in the type of Indian films called 'theologicals'. In other words, the different reading is motivated in much the same way as Pynchon's events are motivated by paranoia. Indeed the use of dreams are part of Rushdie's defence, but personally, and on a purely literary level, I think they are almost a pity, and prefer to read them as fictional facts: why should Gibreel, who falls from the exploded plane and survives, not also travel in time? His companion Saladin after all changes into Shaitan, with growing horns and a tail, and then is suddenly cured. These too are readings, in a way allegorical but also psychological, palimpsest religion. As seen and felt and reread by a modern sensibility. But as Eco says in one of his lectures (1988):

> Even if one says, as Valéry did, that *il n'y a pas de vrai sens d'un texte*, one has not yet decided on which of the three intentions [planned by the author, ignored by the author, decided by the reader] the infinity of interpretations depends. Mediaeval and Renaissance Kabbalists maintained that the Torah was open to infinite interpretations because it could be rewritten in infinite ways combining its letters, but such an infinity of readings (as well as of writings) – certainly dependent on the initiative of the reader – was nonetheless planned by the divine Author.
>
> To privilege the initiative of the reader does not necessarily mean to guarantee the infinity of readings. If one privileges the initiative of the reader, one must also consider the possibility of an active reader who decides to read a text univocally: it is a privilege of fundamentalists to read the Bible according to a single sense.
>
> (155)

This is certainly what happens with the Qur'an. Only the authorized exegetes are allowed to interpret. A mere author is just nowhere, indeed 'Mahound' is made to say in *The Satanic Verses* that he can see no difference between a poet and a whore. If in addition this author happens to be a non-believer he is even worse than nowhere, for the Qur'an says clearly that Allah chooses the believers and even misleads the unbelievers – a curious concept which reminds us of 'do not lead us into temptation', though the Pater Noster adds 'but deliver us from evil'. Not so the Qur'an, unless of course the non-believer repents and believes (for Allah is merciful): 'None can guide the people whom Allah leads astray. He leaves them blundering about in their wickedness' (256). As to possible new readings in time, Allah says after a similar passage about unbelievers not being helped: 'Such were the ways of Allah in days gone by: and you shall find that they remain unchanged' (272). Or again: 'Proclaim what is revealed to you in the Book of your Lord. None can change His words' (92) – except, as we saw, Allah Himself.

Interestingly, the unbelievers are several times shown as accusing Mohammed's revelations of being 'old fictitious tales' (29) or, on the Torah and the Qur'an: '"Two works of magic supporting one another. We will believe in neither of them"' (78). Islam seems to the non-Islamic reader totally anti-narrative. There are no stories in the Qur'an, except one or two brief exampla. This could be regarded as due to the anti-representation rule, if there were not also many bits of stories taken from the Torah (in the wide sense): Tell them about our servant Abraham, Allah says, or Moses, or Lot, or Job, David, Solomon, all the way to Elizabeth and Zachariah or Mary and Jesus. This is admirably syncretic, and the Israelites are called 'the people of the Book'. But the stories themselves are unrecognizable as stories; they are fragmented and repetitive, and occur as 'arguments' and 'signs', and 'proof' of Allah's truth. Apart from these, the Qur'an is amazingly static. There is no narrative line. It is a book of faith and ethics, that establishes a new humanism of a kind, and it proceeds by affirmation and injunction, threats of punishment, examples of destruction, and promises of reward. The story of Mohammed himself comes from other sources. I don't want to venture too far in this, as I am not an Islamist, and no doubt exegesis has different views. No doubt also that other Arabic, and especially Persian, traditions do have stories. My point is simply that from the Qur'an alone, it seems hardly surprising that its more rigid interpreters and followers would be incapable of conceiving, let alone understanding, this new fiction that is palimpsest history, palimpsest religion, or palimpsest history of man's spirituality.

And yet, to a modern sensibility (or at least to mine) – and if it is true, as many sociologists and other observers are saying, that the religious spirit is returning, the agonized doubts of both Gibreel and Saladin, as well as those of Philip II, speak more vividly to us today than can those of the self-centred, sex-centred, whisky-centred, sin-and-salvation-centred characters of Graham Greene, precisely because they are anchored in both ancient and modern history, with its migrations and regenerating mixtures.

I mentioned the sheer size of this type of book, and I would like to end on a more general point, that of knowledge. All the books I have mentioned are large partly because they are packed with specialized knowledge. Pynchon, as Frank Kermode pointed out recently, 'has an enormous amount of expert information – for instance, about technology, history and sexual perversion' (LRB 8/2/90, p. 3). So does Eco about theology and theosophy, literature, philosophy, mechanical engineering, computers etc.; so does Fuentes about the history of Spain and Mexico; so does Rushdie about Pakistan, India, Hinduism and Islam. Like the historian, these authors work very hard on their facts. So, incidentally, does the author of the more scientific kind of science-fiction.

Now knowledge has long been unfashionable in fiction. If I may make a personal digression here, this is particularly true of women writers, who are assumed to write only of their personal situations and problems, and I have often been blamed for parading my knowledge, although I have never seen this being regarded as a flaw in male writers; on the contrary. Nevertheless (end of personal digression), even as praise, a show of knowledge is usually regarded as irrelevant: Mr X shows an immense amount of knowledge of a, b, c, and the critic passes to theme, plot, characters and sometimes style, often in that order. What has been valued in this sociological and psychoanalytical century is personal experience and the successful expression of it. In the last resort a novel can be limited to this, can come straight out of heart and head, with at best a craftsmanly ability to organize it well, and write well.

Similarly the Structuralists devoted much analysis to showing how the classical realist novel produced its illusion of reality. Zola did enormous social research on mines and slaughterhouses, and distributed these items of knowledge, as Philippe Hamon has shown, comparing them to index cards, among various pretext-characters to impart, usually to an innocent learner-character, also existing for the purpose. And so on. These various techniques were invented to 'naturalize' culture. But this demystification of the realist illusion does not in fact alter the illusion. 'The nineteenth-century as we know it', said Oscar Wilde, 'is almost entirely an invention of Balzac.' Dickens too had to learn all about law and other spheres of knowledge, Tolstoy all about war, and Thomas Mann a little later all about medicine, music and so on. George Eliot – another knowledgeable novelist, though a woman – said it was not necessary for a writer to experience life in a workshop, the open door was enough. This is obviously true: the writer cannot do without imagination. Dostoevsky understood this. And mere homework is not enough either. But a great deal of this homework done by the classical realist was sociological, and eventually led, in the modern neorealist novel we are all familiar with, to slice-of-life novels about miners, doctors, football-players, admen and all the rest. Back to the personal experience of the writer in fact. Now personal experience is sadly limited. And the American postmodern attempt to break out of it rarely succeeds beyond fun-games with narrative conventions – a very restricted type of knowledge.

Naturally I am caricaturing a little, to make a point. Naturally I am not trying to say that the polyphonic palimpsest histories I have been discussing are the only great novels of the century, nor that there haven't been other types of highly imaginative novels before these. I am only saying that the novel's task is to do things which only the novel can do, things which the cinema, the theatre and television have to reduce and traduce considerably in adaptations, losing whole dimensions, precisely because they now do better some of what the classical realist novel used to do so well. The novel took its roots in historical documents and has always had an intimate link with history. But the novel's task, unlike that of history, is to stretch our intellectual, spiritual and imaginative horizons to breaking point. Because palimpsest histories do precisely that, mingling realism with the supernatural and history with spiritual and philosophical reinterpretation, they could be said to float half-way between the sacred books of our various heritages, which survive on the strength of the faiths they have created (and here I include Homer, who also survived on the absolute faith of the Renaissance in the validity of classical culture), and the endless exegesis and commentaries these sacred books create, which do not usually survive one another, each supplanting its predecessor according to the *Zeitgeist*, in much the same way as do the translations of Homer or the Russian classics. Pope's Homer is not the Homer of Butcher and Lang, nor is it as readable today as other poems by Pope. And the Homer of Butcher and Lang isn't anything like Robert Fitzgerald's. It may seem disrespectful to place *The Satanic*

Verses half-way between the sacred book that is the Qur'an and the very exegetes who execrate it, but I am here speaking only in literary terms, which may become clearer if I say that Homer is only partially historical, and greatly mythical, or that Fuentes' history of Spain is as interesting as the 'real' history sacralized at school, or Eco's Pendulum as the 'real' history of theosophy, or Pavić's Khazars as their almost non-existent history. And this is because they are palimpsest histories.

13

Illusions of parody

I would like to take up a problem I left unresolved in my book *A Rhetoric of the Unreal* (1981), namely the problem of parody. All the more so because Brian McHale, in *Postmodernist Fiction* (1987), a book I have already quoted and much admire, takes me to task on this problem. I shall not go into a private polemic with him, for in fact (to my surprise) we basically agree.

Parody and stylization

Christine Brooke-Rose has described Thomas Pynchon's *V* (1963) as a parody of classic realist fiction, and not a very satisfactory parody at that, since the crucial distance between the parody and the model being parodied is not scrupulously enough maintained. I disagree; by my reading, *V* is not a parody but a stylization, and not of classic realism but of modernist fiction – like *Molloy, La Jalousie, Lolita,* and other texts of stylized modernism.

(McHale, 21)

He goes on to say that I draw my distinction parody vs. stylization from Bakhtin, which is true, and I shall do so again. However, since I had in fact called Pynchon 'ostensibly parody, towards stylization' (p. 385), and since the techniques supposedly stylized are (as in many postmodern novels, see Ch. 14) those of the realistic novel *taken over* by Modernism and already parodied by Joyce (for example, defocalization of the hero, pushed to excess, or 'free indirect discourse'), McHale's objections seem a quibble of terms. Nor does it explain the extraordinary difference in tone between *Molloy, La Jalousie, Lolita* on the one hand and Pynchon's apparent dead realism on the other. Moreover, McHale's own enlightening analysis of the shift from 'epistemological' to 'ontological' concerns, not just in general but author by author and book by book, seems to agree with me: the dominant in *V* is still 'epistemological', reaches the boundary of the 'ontological' in *The Crying of Lot 49*, and only becomes fully 'ontological' in *Gravity's*

Rainbow. My problem remains, and I shall try to resolve it here, as it is important for the next chapter.

Many critics, I said in 1981, treated 'postmodern' literature as parody, for instance Mas'ud Zavarzadeh (1976), talking of metafiction, spoke of 'a parody of interpretation' an over-interpretation which 'creates a work of low message value, at the degree zero of interpretation, and so frees narrative from all anthropomorphic order-hunting and assures that there is nothing, as Barthelme says, between the lines but white space.' (40, Barthelme's *Snow White* 1967, 105).

But of course the term 'parody of interpretation' is already an interpretation, and since parody cannot exist unless the discourse parodied is heard behind the first discourse, it seemed to me difficult to assert that there can be nothing between the lines but white space. The word 'parody' over the ages, had come to mean many different things, and I wasn't sure of its use here.

My problem was that quite a few of these supposed parodies of interpretation, notably by Fowles, Coover and Pynchon, were technically so old-fashioned that I could only assume they had tipped over into, or been absorbed by, the model of the 'realist', totalizing novel they were parodying. And indeed I had rested that supposition on Bakhtin (1929; 1973), who had done a great deal, in his own way, to deconstruct classical rhetoric, and to clarify the various types of what he calls the dialogical, or the degrees to which another discourse is heard in the first. And for him *parody* appropriates, as object, an already existing discourse, but introduces into it an orientation diametrically opposed to its own. (This is presumably what McHale means when he improves on Bakhtin by saying that the 'dominant' [of the parodied text] is not preserved.) Whereas *imitation* appropriates an already existing discourse but takes it seriously.

Between the two Bakhtin places *stylization*, that 'slight shadow of objectivization' thrown upon a whole series of procedures used by the other discourse. The stylizer is careful not to confuse the voice of the other with his own (as does the imitator). He is also careful not to trigger off a clash between the two voices (as does the parodist). He simply lets the presence of another voice (another style) be heard behind his own.

But, says Bakhtin, stylization can tip over into imitation if the author, drawn into his model, destroys the distance and weakens the perception of the other style. For it is the distance that creates the convention. Thus, in parody, the deliberate perception of the other's discourse must be particularly marked and strong. And so the danger of tipping over into the model (into imitation) is great for the stylizer but in theory impossible for the parodist, where the two voices are not only distanced but confront each other with hostility, with opposite orientations that turn the discourse into an arena.

And yet, in the texts that preoccupied me, it was precisely those called parodies, and not the stylizations, that seemed to tip over into the model. Was this so, and if so, why?

The stylizations posed no problem. The long and sustained stylization of Barth's *The Sotweed Factor* (1961), of John Fowles' *The French Lieutenant's Woman* (1969), or that of Barthelme's *The Dead Father* (1975), 'The Glass Mountain' (*City Life* 1970), Coover's stories in *Pricksongs and Descants* (1969), or the hidden polemic, as Bakhtin would call it, at the centre of Gass's *Omensetter's Luck* (1966), in all of these, and in many different ways, the discourse neither disappears into the model nor introduces a clash.

What concerned me more were the supposed 'parodies of interpretation', or over-totalization (parody of the classical 'realist' *and* 'Modernist' novel). Many of these 'parodies' are implausible but technically realistic representations of the non-interpretability of the world, in other words, they fictionalize *the theme* of non-interpretability, but use the conventional narrative of 'realist' representation to do so. This presumably is where the 'clash', the 'opposite orientation' comes in, not in the type of discourse but in the content. And this of course is the everyday meaning of 'parody' as we know it from vaudeville or from newspaper competitions. But even there something happens to the style.

The novels I dealt with were Fowles' *The Magus* (1966), Coover's *The Origin of the Brunists* (1966) and *The Public Burning* (1977), Pynchon's *V* (1963) and *Gravity's Rainbow* (1973). I shall not summarize my arguments here but stick to the theoretical problem which was well represented, perhaps unconsciously, by Ernst Von Glasenfeld (1979), who had described *The Magus* as a pragmatic, ethical treatment of the modern constructivist theory of knowledge, admitting that it was in a way a very old-fashioned novel and comparing it with Alain-Fournier's *Le Grand Meaulnes*, but insisting that in the framework of the history of ideals, it belongs to the front of constructivist thought.

Whether it does or not, it certainly belongs to the type of novel that dramatizes an idea, however modern, with conventional means, thus allowing this type of form/content criticism. And so with Coover's *The Origin of the Brunists*, which McHale places firmly in the 'Modernist' (epistemological) phase and also links with Berger & Luckmann's *The Social Construction of Reality* (1966, McHale 19). So far then presumably he would agree with me. Like *The Magus* (and like *V*) it uses realist techniques in quest of a non-existent truth. It merely (though less than *V*) goes further towards realism in excessive defocalization.

As for *The Public Burning*, it is much closer to the generally accepted sense of parody in that in attacking oppressive myths it projects a Nixon who is himself aware of their mechanisms and uses them (international communism as 'Ghost' and Uncle Sam who talks to Nixon and allegorically – if graphically – sodomizes him as representative of historical consciousness). But apart from a remarkable mimesis of voice throughout (a realist technique) and the genre-mix of a mock-play at the centre (a dialogue between President Eisenhower and the prisoner Rosenberg, called Pres/Pris), these 'outrageous' themes are set forth in the same fatigued modes of realistic narrative used in *The Origin of the Brunists*. McHale tells us (21) that 'it resembles Fuentes' *Terra Nostra* in its (ab)use of the conventions of the historical novel for ontological purposes', which is true enough, but it does not resolve my problem since his reading is one of outrageous content whereas parody touches on style. Chénetier (1989) tells us that Coover 'masters all voices, and there is no voice so powerful that he does not undermine it with the interference of another' (381–2, my translation). This would indeed be 'parody', but he does not demonstrate it, nor have I found this frequent enough in these long novels (as opposed to Coover's shorter texts) to warrant the term 'parody'.

For *Gravity's Rainbow*, McHale is much more convincing than he was for *V*, in that he does not deal with it in his 'epistemology to ontology' chapter (Ch. 2) but in Chapter 3 'In the Zone', where he presents Foucault's notion of heterotopia', a zone of incongruous disorder (as in, for instance, Calvino's *Invisible Cities* or Angela Carter's *The Passion of New Eve* and others):

So far, Pynchon's zone would seem to be a realistic construct, closely corresponding to historical fact, and a far cry from the heterotopian empire of Calvino's great Khan. But the collapse of regimes and national boundaries, it turns out, is only the outward and visible sign of the collapse of *ontological* boundaries. As the novel unfolds, our world and the 'other world' mingle with increasing intimacy, hallucination and fantasies become real, metaphors become literal, the fictional worlds of the mass – the movies, the comic-books – thrust themselves into the midst of historical reality. The zone, in short, becomes plural.

(45)

By now, however, McHale has left the question of parody/styliz-
ation behind. Does the 'heteropian' reading make *Gravity's Rainbow*
a stylization (which on his own admission tips over into the model
since 'it would seem to be a realistic construct' *until* we see the collapse
of ontological boundaries (largely achieved 'epistemologically' via
paranoia and hallucinations, see McHale 1979)? Or does it make
it a parody (of the 'realistic construct'), which appropriates an existing discourse but introduces into it an orientation diametrically
opposed? In which case there should be no 'tipping over'. Indeed,
throughout the book, McHale uses 'parody' in the loose (non-Bakhti-
nian) modern sense as if he had forgotten his own argument.

Clearly McHale's reading is superior to mine, but does not resolve
my problem of style. The *theme* of non-interpretability was (to me)
blurred in the very over-interpretation, which uses the same clogging
techniques that go with interpretation in the 'realist' novel. Chénetier
calls Pynchon's novels *'des oeuvres-monde, d'exemplaires tentatives de maîtrise'*, as are those of Barth (108), which reading seems at the opposite
pole from Zavarzadeh's 'parody of interpretation' and parodic 'over-
totalization'.

My main question was this: if only the *theme* distinguishes parodied
realism from realism, how does the reader feel the difference (until
he gets to that 'other world', much much later) between interpretation and over-interpretation (or 'parody' of interpretation)? Why,
in other words, do we experience in these supposed parodies, so
much of the time, a tipping over into the model, which in principle
(according to Bakhtin) should happen only with stylization, the two
voices in parody being too hostile to each other for this to occur?

One easy answer would be terminological and trivial: we would
remain in the Bakhtinian analysis but we would call all these novels
stylizations, which *can* tip over, and we would reject the over-used
term 'parody'. This in effect is what McHale does for *V*.

This answer was easy but unsatisfying, precisely because there
are true stylizations in the Bakhtinian sense, and even by the same
authors (Pynchon and Coover), much shorter and more elegant,
which do *not* tip over, whereas these long novels which fictionalize
the theme of non-interpretability seemed to be something else.

My tentative answer then was to separate form and content (which
is what crude parody does) and to say: There is *parody* of interpretation, but *stylization* of the techniques of interpretation and totalization, and it is this stylization which tips over into imitation,
abolishing the distance and contaminating the parody, itself a precar-

ious balance of form and content. For *over* -interpretation, as a *technique*, is not sufficiently opposed to interpretation (it is merely an exaggeration of it) to prevent the discourse from tipping over into the technique of interpretation. Whereas the *thematic* orientation (the non-interpretability of the world) is in direct opposition to that of the model (the interpretability of the world).

That was the position I had reached in my book, and I added that there was of course no reason why we should not appreciate some of these novels literally, not as metafictions but as realistic and sometimes satirical fictionalizations of contemporary problems. And presumably many people do. But then there is no essential (generic) difference between them and other novels of this type before them, and of the best: Musil and Mann had also fictionalized contemporary philosophical problems, and so in other ways had Lawrence or Tolstoy or Balzac. The bag is too big. *The Magus* would then be a modern version of *A la recherche de l'absolu* or *Les Illusions perdues* and *Splendeurs et misères des courtisanes*, with Conchis as a sort of Herrera-Vautrin.

Palimpsests

Meanwhile Genette's book on parody and other types of what he calls hypertexts (the hypotext being the model) had appeared: *Palimpsestes – La Littérature au deuxième degré* (1982), and I thought that a different answer might come out of that.

For Genette the term 'parody' has come to mean satiric pastiche, as in 'parody of justice' or 'parody of the Western', and thus to duplicate the terms 'pastiche' and 'caricature'. He traces the history of the term. The most rigorous and minimal form of parody consists in taking a known text literally and giving it a new significance, by changing a few words, a letter even, as in the deformation of well-known proverbs, such as Prévert's *Martyre, c'est pourrir un peu* (for *Partir, c'est mourir un peu*) or *Partir, c'est crever un pneu*, or *Tant va la vache à lait qu'à la fin elle se mange* (for *Tant va la cruche à l'eau qu'à la fin elle se casse*). An English version of this would be my 'let the beast man wane' in *Amalgamemnon*.

These hypertexts are brief, since it's rarely possible to sustain the game for long. But this strict sense of 'parody', despite its survival in such Oulipian deformation, tends to disappear from the nineteenth-century critical consciousness, whereas *travestissement burlesque* (burlesque travesty) acquires the meaning of 'parody', and *pastiche*, imported from Italy in the eighteenth century, is more and more

used for the plain fact (whatever its function) of stylistic imitation.
So Genette renames *parody* as the minimal transformation of a
text, as in *Chapelain décoiffé* (Boileau *et al.*, calqued on *Le Cid*), where
the 'noble' text remains noble; and keeps *travestissement burlesque* for
the degrading type of transformation such as Scarron's *Le Virgile
travesti*, where the subject remains the same but the 'noble' style
becomes 'vulgar' (these are classical terms). And after an elegant
analysis of the possible permutations of noble and vulgar, he arrives
at a first broad division according to the *relation* between hyper and
hypotext – a relation of either *transformation* or of *imitation* (downward
in figure 1); and another division according to the *function* or *régime*
(ludic, satiric, serious – across in Table 1).

Tableau général des pratiques hypertextuelles

relation	régime ludique	satirique	sérieux
transformation	PARODIE *(Chapelain décoiffé)*	TRAVESTISSEMENT *(Virgile travesti)*	TRANSPOSITION *(le Docteur Faustus)*
imitation	PASTICHE *(l'Affaire Lemoine)*	CHARGE *(A la manière de ...)*	FORGERIE *(la Suite d'Homère)*

The ludic or playful function, he says, modifies the subject without
modifying the style, and in two ways:

(1) *transformation* (where he places *parody*): by conserving the noble text and applying it to a vulgar subject.
(2) *imitation*: by forging, through stylistic imitation, a new noble text (the epic
for instance), and applying it to a vulgar subject, as in Boileau's *Le lutrin*
or Pope's *The Rape of the Lock* (*pastiche héroi-comique* or mock-heroic).

Strict parody and pastiche have distinct textual practices: parody
adapts an existing text, pastiche imitates a style. But they have in
common the introduction of a 'vulgar' subject without touching the
'nobility' of the style, which they conserve with the text (in parody)
or restore via the stylistic imitation (in pastiche), for instance *L'Af-
faire Lemoine* and other mimetic productions of Proust (1971), or,
earlier, mock-heroic. Pastiche is thus essentially an imitation and
not a transformation.

Genette's entire book consists in discussing, with detailed examples, all the categories of this diagram, which of course are theoretical

and thus in practice can overlap or mix. But clearly what chiefly concerns me here is the first column. I shall therefore re-pose my question in Genettian terms: is a metafiction which 'parodies' (in the vague sense) the traditional novel a parody in Genette's sense?

At one level the answer is clearly no: the 'nobility' of the model (the totalizing novel, whether 'realist' or 'modernist', equivalent of the epic poem) is conserved and applied to a 'vulgar' subject (the non-interpretability of the world) – hence contrived plots, filtering through hallucinations and so on. Moreover, the hypotext is not a unique text transformed but a reforged one. The use of 'realist' narrative within the zanier strategies does not refer back to one novel but to a whole genre, and it is therefore like the forging of a new 'noble' text through stylistic imitation.

We are thus much nearer to heroicomic pastiche than to parody. And pastiche in Genette's system is *imitation* and not *transformation*. This, in Bakhtin's terms, might explain the 'tipping over'.

Nevertheless, there are problems. Is the non-interpretability of the world (or in McHale's terms, the ontological hesitation) already a 'vulgar' subject? And are there vulgar subjects today? Perhaps it would be merely the *means* towards non-interpretability, namely the contrived and zany plots, the violence, the paranoia, the drug-like hallucination, which would constitute the 'vulgar' subject?

More importantly, the pleasure of heroicomic pastiche depends largely on the consciousness of distance between heroic style and trivial subject, whereas the problem of these novels is precisely that this double consciousness becomes extremely blurred: the 'noble' style of the great traditional novel is too 'familiar' in practice, passes unnoticed, and the zany plots are not much zanier than life. The first point, familiarity of style, no doubt explains the success. The second point has been made by one of the 'moral' critics of 'post-modernism', Gerald Graff (and by myself, 1981), that reality has itself become unreal: 'In a paradoxical and fugitive way, mimetic theory remains alive, literature holds the mirror up to unreality' (1979, 179).[1]

But Genette comes to our rescue when he speaks of pastiche in more detail (88–95). In general, he says, the pastiche-writer has a scenario, a subject, which he casts into the style of his model.

---

[1] Quoted more fully in McHale, 219–20, where he answers the charge by showing that the 'unreality of reality' is not the only theme of 'postmodern' literature, which has other objects of representation, such as love and death. See Chapter 14 where I return to this.

But the subject-stage is not indispensable: a good pastiche-writer is capable of practising the style of his model without a scenario (all quotations in my translation):

> This dissymmetry illustrates the difference in structure between transformation and imitation: the parodist or travesty-writer takes a *text* and transforms it according to this or that formal constraint and this or that semantic intention, or transforms it uniformly and mechanically into another style.
>
> The pastiche-writer takes a *style* – an object less easy to grasp – and that style dictates his text.
>
> In other words, the parodist or travesty-writer has to do with a text, and the style is an accessory. Inversely the imitator has to do with a style, and the text is an accessory. His target is a style and the thematic motifs it may contain (the concept of style must here be taken in its widest sense; it is a *manner*, on the thematic level as on the formal level).

For example, *Le Lutrin* does not imitate a particular epic poem but the epic style in general.

Genette goes further (89–91). Pastiche, he says, 'does not imitate a text, for the simple reason [...] that it is impossible to imitate a text, or rather, one can imitate only a style, in other words, a genre'. And later:

> It is impossible, because too easy, and therefore insignificant, directly to imitate a text. One can imitate it only indirectly, by practising its idiolect in another text, and one can discern that idiolect only by treating the text as a model, that is, as a genre. This is why there can be pastiche only of genre, and why imitating a particular work, a particular author, a school, a period, a genre, are structurally identical operations – and why parody and travesty, which never go through this mode of transmission, can never be defined as imitations but only as transformations, punctual and systematic, imposed upon texts. A parody or a travesty always takes on one or several singular texts, never a genre. The widespread notion of *parody of genres* is a pure illusion [*chimère*] [...] One can parody only singular texts; one can imitate only a genre ... because to imitate is to generalize.

Later Genette returns to the problem with regard to the sixteenth-century anti-novel – *Don Quixote* in particular, often described as 'parody of romance' (generating thereby the first modern, or 'realist' novel). But the formula 'parody of romance' is impossible in Genette's scheme, and he adds that it is faulty even in its vaguer sense, 'for the good reason that Don Quixote is not a caricature of an errant knight but a madman who believes himself to be or wants to be an errant knight'.

There follows a minute analysis of various texts, among which is Sorel's *Le Berger extravagant* (where the central character believes himself to be a shepherd). This novel, which would be loosely described today as 'parody of the pastoral', is subtitled *anti-roman* (which is where Sartre took the term when he applied it to Nathalie Sarraute in his preface to *Martereau*). But as Genette points out, madness is the principal operator of this type of hypertextuality.

So here we are, getting nearer to the psychotic focalizers, the voyeurs, criminals, idiots, lost souls, drug addicts and paranoiacs who have transformed the twentieth-century novel (including Modernist). But Genette himself arrives at 'postmodernism' via the topic of generic reactivation – the picaresque, for instance, which reappeared in Mann's *Felix Krull* already in 1937 (long before its supposed revival in the British novel of the fifties).

He speaks in particular about Barth's *The Sotweed Factor* which, he says, 'is more complex: the writing is a period pastiche, but the thematic and narrative type has nothing of the picaresque'. After a brief consideration of this novel he alludes to Barth's article 'The Literature of Replenishment' (1984a), and his commentary is so delightful that I must quote it almost in full – whatever we may think of his choice of 'ancestors' (James, for instance, is hardly a 'postmodern' model):

> ... the frontier that Barth tries to draw between modern and postmodern literature seems very fragile. From Joyce or Thomas Mann to Borges, Nabokov, Calvino or Barth himself (and many other American writers such as Barthelme, Coover or Pynchon), a whole contemporary literature, which cannot be reduced to hypertextual practice but which turns to it with visible relish, can be defined by its refusal of norms or types inherited from the romantico-realist 19th century, and by a return to the 'pre-modern' (or prepostmodern?) ways of the 16th, 17th and 18th centuries [...] The Russian Formalists could have said: refusal of the father (Balzac, Dickens) and election of this or that uncle until then unknown (James, Melville, Caroll), of the grandfather (Fielding, Sterne, Diderot), or of the greatgrandfather (Ariosto, Cervantes, the baroque age). The turn of the father will perhaps come back, when the following generation will have exhausted the joys of postmodern baroquism [...] That postpostmodern age will then be a return to the charms, for us very discreet, of a Zola or a Theodore Dreiser. This leapfrog evolution is well known [...] but since its perpetual masterword is Verdi's joke, *Torniamo all'antico, sara un progresso*, it follows clearly that generic reactivation still has some good days before it, as has hypertextuality in general, which is one of its resources.
>
> (235–6)

These rigorous analyses of Genette do not of course answer my precise question, which I will recall: why does metafiction of the type that Zavarzadeh calls 'parody of interpretation' tip over so easily into its model?

Genette's work does however support my intuition, since it places this type of text (or its hypertextual elements) unhesitatingly under pastiche, which must be pastiche of style, of genre, and pastiche has a relationship of imitation to its 'hypogenre' (I coin the term, since there cannot be a singular hypotext), and not a relationship of transformation, as does parody. And it is imitation, according to Bakhtin, into which stylization tips over easily. These novels would be then, not parody but pastiche, which via stylization can so easily become imitation of the model.

I doubt whether *imitation* (or even *parody*) would mean the same thing for Bakhtin and Genette – the life of humanists would be too easy if, as in science, a term had the same value everywhere.

But it is in this double perspective (Bakhtin/Genette) that the texts in question could be analysed. Or rather, Bakhtin/Genette plus another return to Bakhtin.

Back to Bakhtin

In his theory of the dialogical, and more particularly in his analysis of types of discourse in Chapter 5 of his book on Dostoevski's polyphonic narrative (1929a), Bakhtin proposes a broad triple division of what he calls 'the word', by which he clearly means what we now call discourse. The first two are *monovocal*:

(1) *The word directly oriented on its object* as expression of the author's or speaker's last interpretive instance, that is, the author's omniscient or ironic commentary, which explains and labels the character.

(2) *the objectivized word*, that is, the discourse of the represented character, with dominance of sociological or dominance of individual features, but still subject to the author's control and final word.

His third category, where I will now remain, is the *bivocal* word of which he is so passionate an advocate, and of which he proposes three subgroups. The first two are:

(i) *convergent* voices – and here he places various types of *stylization* including a narrator's style, *Icherzählung*, and the non-objectivized discourse of the hero as partial spokesman for the author.

(ii) *divergent* voices – and here he places various types of *parody* including parodic narrative, parodic *Icherzählung* parody of the hero's discourse.

Now in both these first subgroups of bivocal discourse, when the objectivization decreases (when the other discourse is more active), there is a tendency to *fusion* of the convergent voices for subgroup (i), or to *separation* into two autonomous voices for subgroup (ii). In both cases we go back to the monovocal discourse of the first category (author's control). The last interpretive instance of the author is too powerful and attracts these two bivocal discourses.

In other words, contrary to Bakhtin's earlier and my own first presentation, it is *not* just stylization that can fall back into monovocal discourse but both stylization and parody. Moreover, when the objectivization decreases in the second category (divergent voices, including parody), the discourse, instead of splitting into two autonomous voices, can *also* pass into internal dialogization, that is, into his third subgroup:

> (iii) *active subgroup*, where the word of the other acts from the outside, and where Bakhtin places his hidden polemic.

This is the truly dialogical, where there can be no return to the monovocal. He calls it the active subgroup because another discourse (or several discourses) is/are reflected in a first discourse. The other discourse works upon the first (the one we're reading) from the outside. This group includes hidden polemic, confession with polemic colouring, any discourse with a 'sideglance' on another's discourse, and hidden dialogue.

It would then be possible to consider, and to analyse, these problematic long texts, or the active elements of them, not in categories such as stylization (first subgroup), or parody (second subgroup), both of which can tip back into monovocal and authorial discourse, but as truly dialogical texts of this third subgroup, in which other discourses are reflected from outside in a constant hidden polemic.

For this third group of Bakhtin's third category represents the really revolutionary aspects of his work and, as I said earlier, the deconstructive aspect, although he would not have used the term nor, perhaps, recognized the enterprise. In this active subgroup, many different forms of other discourses can be refracted, and many different degrees of their deforming influence are possible.

Hence my puzzlement, when reading some of these texts, but more especially those thematic dramatizations I have been dealing with, together with the constant appellation of 'parody'. They are indeed post-Dostoevskian, yet much less clearly so, for they are not what they seem, neither interpretations nor parody of interpretation. The very uncertainty in the status of the discourse, in the ontology of the world presented, and, at best (for instance in Gass or Barthelme or later Coover, rather than in early Coover or early Pynchon), the very hidden nature of the sideglance on other discourses, the very secrecy of the inner polemic, gives us illusions of parody that are truer (that is, more chimerical) than Genette perhaps intended in his dispute over nomenclature, when he called parody of genre *une chimère de parodie*.

14

Illusions of anti-realism

If I have been cautious so far with the word 'realism', 'anti-realism' *a fortiori* carries worse risks. But much good work has been done on definitions in the past fifteen years, the most useful to me having been *Narcissistic Narrative – The Metafictional Paradox* by Linda Hutcheon (1980), *Postmodernist Fiction*, by Brian McHale (1987) and *World-Games–The Tradition of Anti-Realist Revolt*, by Cristopher Nash (1987), who themselves cite many others, and from whom I shall be quoting liberally. This chapter is a reconsideration and confrontation of their discussions from the viewpoint of a critic who is also a practising writer.

Realism

In the last chapter I quoted Graff, and part of McHale's reply, on the mimetism of 'postmodern' fiction, the argument being that the unreal reality it presents is in fact 'not a fiction but an element in which we live' (Graff 1979,179). Similarly Newman says that 'the vaunted fragmentation of art is no longer an aesthetic choice; it is simply a cultural aspect of the economic and social fabric' (1984, 183, both quoted McHale, 219–20).

McHale's reply to 'these serious charges' is, first to point out the critics' *parti-pris*, but in addition, since as he admits this is not a rebuttal, to show that 'postmodernism' does in fact *imitate* (my italics) something other than 'the unreality that modern reality has become', that is,

postmodernism may be unrealistic, but anti-realism is not its sole object of representation. Indeed the favoured themes to which it returns obsessively are about as deeply coloured with 'traditional' literary values as anyone could wish. What could be more traditional than love and death?

(220)

Love, in this argument, is chiefly 'represented' through the love/hate relationship between author and reader, in other words through metalepsis (transgressing narrative levels), either aggressively or pleasingly; and death through the literary 'topos' of the death of the author, of the 'narrative voice' in the text (227–32). In other words, both use the very self-reflexivity (self-love) of the text, because of the ontological transgressions involved.

This is an excellent technical analysis. Nash and other critics have provided many similar examples, without necessarily admitting the 'representation'. Nevertheless, McHale's argument seems to me partly to be conceding Graff's point, since it limits 'postmodernism' (a) to imitation after all, (b) to over-general, and as he says 'traditional' themes, and (c) to a very localized, often facetious treatment of the author/reader relationship and the much vaunted self-reflexivity of the text. It should also be added that any address to the reader must be made in 'discourse' (direct speech-forms), since the narrative sentence is of its nature 'ignorant of an audience' (see Ch. 5, p. 74). Even Hawthorne's contorted allusions to the reader in 'The Custom House' are made in the third person and in the universal present tense used for general statements, which break narrative flow (see Ch. 4). But once all novels are using direct speech forms rather than 'narrative sentences', or at least a preponderance of such forms, as is the case of 'avant-garde' writing since the fifties, the author is free to address the reader with only a minimal metalepsis. Far too much is being made of such devices.

More to the point, McHale reminds us that nostalgics for unproblematic mimesis are legion, notably Robert Alter's notion that 'the attacks on mimesis ultimately depend on defining experience out of existence' (1978, 233) and his 'witty parable of the tiger' (the real as opposed to the paper one). I'm not sure that the parable is all that witty, for it has been made in various forms by naive realists since the eighteenth century. But McHale's reply is incisive:

The best answer might be formulated in terms of the by-now widely familiar poetics of the Russian literary theorist Mixail Baxtin [... who] reminds us how little the novel has historically been concerned with real world tigers, and how much it has been concerned with *human* and *social* reality – reality that is first and foremost linguistic and discursive, reality experienced in and through discourse.

(165)

In *World-Games*, Cristopher Nash has dropped the term 'postmodern' and adopts 'anti-realism' on the grounds that anti-realism has flourished at other times. The term (like 'metafiction', which however is more restrictive) has the great advantage of not being *also* and so overtly a period term.[1] On the other hand, the term 'anti-realist' is itself fraught with dangers, most of which Nash avoids, and I'll come to one of these in a moment. Nash defines Realism as *cosmic*, or concerned with the world familiar to us, outside the world of the book, pre-existent; and Anti-realism as either *neocosmic* (alternative worlds) or *anticosmic*, that is anti the type of cosmos posited by the Realist movement. Nash thus fruitfully brings together two genres generally and until fairly recently kept apart, science fiction and 'postmodern' fiction.[2]

The disadvantage of the term 'anti-realist' is the obverse of its advantage: there have been anti-realist movements in all periods, but conversely it has often been argued (depending on how one defines realism) that all literature is 'realist' in the trivial sense that language is by definition representational, though this is too often forgotten. Hutcheon reminds us of this several times: 'In all fiction language is representational, but of a fictional other world, a complete and coherent "heterocosm"' (7). 'The most extreme autonomous universes of fantasy are still referential; if they were not the reader could not imagine their existence. This has always been the case' (77). Or, much more technically on military officers writing to Claude Simon to say that they recognized their experience in *La Route des Flandres*, and Ricardou's comment that such people confuse, as does traditional realism, the signified and the referent:

In fact the signified of the literary language is the same as that of ordinary language [e.g. the signifier *dog* evokes an image (dog)]; it is the nature of the *referent* that has changed. The people he mentions confuse not signified and referent, but real and fictive referents [...] At this *langue* [system] level fictive referents are not real because they are non-existent in empirical reality. On the level of *parole* [usage] this issue is more complex. Referents can again be real, as in most ordinary language usage [table, honesty] or fictive (physical or not). Here, however, they are fictive either because they are lies (false referents) or because the objects are imagined. It is this latter instance that is of interest here [...] In the literary text there are no such things as real referents for the reader: all are fictive [table, honesty, unicorn, the latter doubly so]. The *reader* accepts this once he accepts the fact that what he is reading is an imaginative construct. That the *author* may or may not have had real referents in mind can never be determined with certainty.

(93–4)

[1] See Chabot (1988) for yet another attack (after my own, 1981) on 'postmodernism' as 'a period concept', and Hassan's reply that it is a period concept *and* other things. Hutcheon prefers 'metafiction'. I take no sides here, and use all three in quotes, according to the author I am discussing.

[2] As I had in 1981, indeed many 'anti-realists' or 'postmodernists' practise both, as I do. McHale too, has an interesting chapter on the return (contrary to Todorov's theory) of the fantastic, with subheadings 'The science-fictionalization of postmodernism' and 'The postmodernization of science fiction' (65–72).

All this is obvious to literary theorists, but is worth repeating in view of the number of critics who continue to cite with approval examples of 'illusion-breaking devices' of the type 'these characters aren't real, I'm inventing them as I go along' which, in the supposed 'love/hate' between author and reader, seems patronizingly insulting (even soap-watchers do nowadays know that the characters are actors, who can be written out of the script or even be changed). But to return to the more historical aspects of 'realism', Nash, after quoting Sontag (to the effect that every writer from Homer to Robbe-Grillet thinks he is a realist, 1967, 154–3, Nash 4), continues:

> Among those seeking a more refined combination of these propositions, it's asserted that if Realism *were* to be defined it would have to be called a mode that is not simply *about* reality but *mimes* it – but this 'mimesis' (as made famous in modern times by Auerbach) is to be found virtually everywhere, from the Bible and Homer to early Latin and mediaeval texts and Shakespeare, and thus cannot be *located*. It's 'a perennial mode', says J. P. Stern.
>
> (1973, Nash 4)

Anti-realists, in fact, are

> thinking only about one kind of realism. That of the fiction of a particular movement in Europe and the Americas in the nineteenth and twentieth centuries. The fact is that no one denies this [...] Anti-Realists of all sorts positively express in a variety of ways the opinion that the right target of *their* objections to what has happened in the history of imaginative writing is not 'realism' in any all-encompassing sense, but a delimitable literary *convention* [...] It's in this sense that Stern, too, has felt free to say that 'realism hasn't been the dominant mode of writing during most periods in the history of literature' and that 'there is no assurance that there will be realism tomorrow'.
>
> (157, Nash 5–6)

Mimesis is everywhere, yet Realism has not been the dominant mode. Nash proceeds to sort out these apparently contradictory statements (contradictory to those who think mimesis and realism are the same thing), but what is important is the insistence on the revolt against specific and fatigued *conventions*, as has occurred throughout the ages and always in the name of a new and better realism. Even Scholes says of 'metafictional' writers: 'I believe I see in the writers I have called fabulators the way toward a new reality' (1969, 416). It is true, however, that there have been parallel revolts, not against conventions but as to content, and this may have confused the issue, revolts within 'realism', extending the previously accepted range of *what* to imitate, as in the periodic rebellions against the Classical proscription of 'low' subjects, or in the 'psychological' novel (reality inside), or the working-class novel, the franker-sex-than-before novel, the Black novel, the homosexual novel, the feminist novel, the novel 'about' footballers, miners, female orgasms, which are somehow considered 'more real'.

The point about the *conventions*, however, is that they arise from underlying suppositions, and those that underlie nineteenth-century Realism are not only of a determinable world, pre-existent, external to the fiction and governed by coherent rules, but that its data are verifiable, and can be materially transcribed, objectively despite subjective perceptions, and presented as probable according to general experience, in an illusionist and declarative mode, to make a world the reader will recognize and which is rationally paraphrasable (summarized from Nash, 8–9, itself largely based on Hamon 1973, reformalized by me, 1981).[3] And these premises have continued to this day, at least in journalistic reviewing, though Hutcheon places them higher and calls these assumptions 'a block in literary theory' (42), a 'reification of a period concept' to cover all literature, a failure of novel criticism to realize that, as Kermode says, 'The history of the novel is the history of forms, rejected or modified by parody, manifesto, neglect, as absurd' (1966, 129–30, Hutcheon, 40).

'Anti-realism', then, for Nash, is everything that goes against these suppositions: the invention of other worlds (neocosmic) and (for anti-cosmic) the breaking, in all the innumerable ways described by him, by McHale, by Hutcheon and other critics, of the illusionist mode, and notably of the 'probabilistic' mode. For later, when dealing with Plato's 'pointless duplication of the world' argument (which he attributes to Johnson), he distinguishes between 'illusionist' in general and 'probabilistic' in particular, by specifying the necessity

that fiction be willing and ready to break with probabilistically mimetic illusion, in at least one of two ways. As a still illusionistic mode it may feel free to pretend [...] that there's more than everyday-life-in-the-world to feel and think about. Or, as an anti-illusionist mode, it may unfold and explore [...] the one thing fictional

---

[3] I am not sure that the last feature (aboutness), on which Nash insists quite a bit, isn't applicable to any narrative in the sense that one must be able to describe a book briefly or criticism would collapse. Most 'anti-realist' books can be and are summarized in this way, and I summarized my own in Chapter 1, either for content (*about* a simultaneous interpreter, *about* a man who dies) or technically (*about* the future tense, *about* the theory of the novel). But then perhaps I am not an 'anti-realist'.

illusions can't cope with: the fictionality of fiction itself, and all that it's 'composed of'.

(46)

It may be 'the one thing' but it has its own limitations as we'll see. He also reminds us that although 'the Realist impulse in its *broad outlines* exists side by side with its alternatives' in any era, 'what makes it and narrative in the novel *come together* in the nineteenth century has to do with historical forces [...] that no longer cohere' (32). And he asks the very pertinent question:

Yet by what oversight can anti-Realists have let slip by the whole Modernist movement? Or to be more accurate, why should one large group of them these days in fact be frequently called not 'post-Realists' but 'post-Modernists'? [...] The truth is that 'post-Modernists' acclaim Modernists among their favourite influences, and we can find them objecting to Modernism only in terms of those characteristics which it shares with Realism as I've described it.

(38)

And after insisting that the leading figures of Modernist fiction 'intelligibly' fall well within the principles of Realism and 'that Modernists have not, as Modernists, ever participated, at the level of fundamental issues, in the "struggle against" Realism' (33), he reminds us that it's Modernism that gives us the words for realistic processes such as exploring subjectivity 'as an object' or 'objectivizing the abstract': for example the *objective correlative* 'which, while it's anti-Naturalistically transcendentalist, invokes that very cosmic faith which realism aims to promote', or the *epiphany*, the *archetypal symbol* (35, my italics).

It is useful to be reminded just how persistent Realism is – and, I would argue, necessarily so. For both the 'neocosmic' and the 'anti-cosmic' ('ontological' for McHale) depend a great deal not only on all language being representational, but also on the very Realist presupposition described above. As I have shown elsewhere (1981), Science Fiction uses realist techniques to create new worlds, and clearly so does the Fantastic in Todorov's sense (1972). As to 'anti-realism', breaking rules of any kind, formal or epistemological, depends on the rules being known or felt. As McHale says: 'much postmodernist fiction continues to cast a "shadow", to use Roland Barthes' expression: it continues to have "a *bit* of ideology, a *bit* of representation, a *bit* of subject". Indeed, it is precisely by preserving a *bit* of representation that postmodernist fiction can mount its challenge to representation' (75, Barthes 1973; 1975, 32).

And McHale is constantly observing, after his analyses, that 'postmodernist fiction turns out to be mimetic after all' (38, sim. 39, 169, 182–6, 219). But the reality mimed 'is plural' (39). Sukenick and B. S. Johnson are being mimetic when larger and larger gaps represent breakdown and increasing vacuity (183). Concrete prose contains 'iconic' designs (184). We even get (several times) the objective correlative: 'Here spacing is the objective correlative, not just of a destabilized fictional ontology, but also of carnivalesque revolution' (182). The mind boggles a bit at this critical fusion of Modernism and Postmodernism in a theory that tries to distinguish them, but it would support Nash as quoted above (as well as my reply to McHale about *V* parodying/stylizing Realism, not Modernism). But all these instances support my general point here: realism of a kind is essential to all fictional modes.

Linda Hutcheon had already expressed this very clearly, defining metafiction as mimesis of imaginative *process* (which also grows out of Modernist psychological realism), as opposed to mimesis as *product* (5). Mimesis of the imaginative process breaks the Realist notion of language as a neutral, transparent window on the world and the author as silent. He is not only not silent but has become, in the more 'narcissist' narratives, loudly self-indulgent. In a parallel way, the old 'intentional fallacy' in criticism returned as *not* a fallacy, and this is to be expected once the novel turns away from 'narrative sentences' to 'discourse' (speech modes), since any message in the communication model must have an addresser as well as an addressee. Indeed Rorty has even suggested that the 'author's intention' should be considered as equivalent to the 'external object' of science (1985, discussed for other aspects in Ch. 1, see also Mansell 1988 for rebuttal).

Mimesis of process also enables Hutcheon to insist that the reader is continually taken into account (as he cannot be in the traditional Narrative Sentence, except by passing into 'speech' modes, see Ch. 5, p. 96). This happens either *overtly* (the illusion-breaking conventions are thematized and often pointed out to him), or *covertly* (they are actualized, and the reader is assumed to know them). 'In both overt and covert forms [...] this focus [on the *writing* process] does not *shift*, so much as *broaden*, to include a parallel process of equal importance to the text's actualization – that of *reading*' (27). Or again, on one specific convention actualized, the power/inadequacy of language:

What is new perhaps in the metafictional use of this linguistic theme is that new role of acknowledgement and active involvement that is textually pointed out to the reader. The act of reading is no longer safe, comfortable, unproblematic.[4]

Theory and criticism

Nash notes that among the many objections to attempts at defining realism, the most insistent is that 'to define the thing is to bring together works that are not the same', and he adds that it is the advocates of realism who so energetically make this objection, while remaining 'the most liberal practitioners of the "lumping together" activity' (5). Later he says much the same of the anti-realists, who are 'inclined to commit all the sins those uncomfortable with the term [realism] dread most. They fail to escape the charge of over-simplification, of "lumping together" (7).

So everybody lumps. My concern, however, is not so much the lumping under broad labels if it is a stage and convenience of method, as the failure to distinguish different examples of a feature described as belonging to that broadly labelled group. In many studies of 'post-modernism', the mere naming of a feature (device, strategy, topos) seems sufficient, followed, at best, with one or a few examples, at worst with a list of names. In the latter case, the reader has either to know all the writers' texts extremely well, or to take the statement on trust.[5] And the mere naming of a feature does not enable the critic to distinguish between different uses of these features, either in function or quality. The latter of course entails value-judgments, which in theory don't belong to theory.

For the exclusion of value-judgment is perfectly conscious. In Chapter 2 I commented on one effect of theory upon criticism in that theory stops at recognizing, naming and describing a structure (a device, strategy). Evaluation was for 'traditional' criticism and

---

[4] Hutcheon also has an excellent chapter on the more extreme anti-representation positions of the *Tel Quel* group in France and *Gruppo 63* in Italy (late sixties), notably Kristeva and Sollers: against auto-representation, and for the generative word-play on the pure signifier. The intent was 'to go beyond mimesis – even a diegetic or linguistically self-reflecting version of it' (135). Kristeva even regarded the 'product' aspect of Roussel's *Impressions d'Afrique* as 'auto-representation, and therefore still novelistic, mimetic' (135–6, Kristeva 1968, 59–83). This 'outer limit' was not in fact followed by novelists and even Sollers seems to have turned his back on his *Tel Quel* days.

[5] I may cite my own work, but only because I do know it all: I have several times found myself figuring in a list of authors using a feature I don't in fact use, or not figuring for a feature I do use (I don't mean in a book which omits me altogether but in books that don't). This doesn't bother me, but my knowledge does make me doubt the validity of the method.

discarded. The trouble with that is that evaluation has only gone superficially, banished from 'serious' criticism but covertly there in the sense that selecting structures and devices implies approval. Indeed, as certain concepts and practices deriving from them became at one moment or another unfashionable, it has been amusing to see how quickly critics learnt to turn their phrases differently ('the aim of the text', 'the reader infers', and so on) even when the thing said betrays older dispensations. As I remarked in Chapter 2, to talk of 'strategies' implies 'intention', whether that of 'the text' or 'the author' is left vague.

If author-intention is both covertly and overtly back, evaluation is still officially taboo, or at least not practised. Perhaps, like narratology, it got swallowed into story, the story of this or that theory. The result is that what gets evaluated is not novels (they got 'described' and at best 'interpreted', which means *a priori* that they are worth interpreting), but theories of novels.[6] And the labels behind which the theories sometimes proceed can look, in grosser cases, like demarking one's territory, the way male animals do.

But labels are rarely enough. As McHale well puts it for his own study:

A philosophical thematics specifying the ontology of postmodern texts, will only tell us that there *is* foregrounding [of ontological concerns], it will not tell us how this foregrounding has been accomplished, what strategies have been deployed.

(27)

But naturally the same objection can be made to the mere naming of a strategy. For my difficulty here is of the same order as the difficulties about parody which I tried to sort out in the last chapter: that it doesn't seem enough simply to call something (a sentence, a passage, a text) a parody, or a stylization, or even a strategy (say, an illusion-breaking device), if the effect on a reasonably sophisticated reader (me) is quite simply of brilliant skill and humour in one case and facility or even shoddy writing in another. Yet no one ever says: the use of this 'strategy' is banal, clumsy, too insistent (or whatever). Or rather, those who might do so are said to be

---

[6] It interested me that for the only two instances in *A Rhetoric of the Unreal* where I ventured upon evaluative criticism of *texts*, I have been taken to task by two of the three critics discussed in this chapter: McHale for Pynchon (see Ch. 14) and Nash for Tolkien (the realistic techniques that weigh down the Marvellous). But Nash likewise admits my points and simply says that the realist techniques are part of the 'cosmic intention' which neocosmic shares with realism. This I never denied, and even emphasized, but it was part of the problem, a question of degree and effect, not of intention. In other words, evaluation, *verboten*, evidently.

aesthetically prejudiced (against 'postmodernism'), nostalgic for stable structures or stable moral values or art as illusion and so on.

There's a lot in this, and those who defend 'anti-realism' must not weaken their case, they must restrict themselves to describing, explaining, persuading. Which can produce a pretty gormless and pedagogic criticism: everything teacher mentions is good.

I shall take one brief 'device' to illustrate the process. In 'Worlds under Erasure' (Ch. 7), McHale describes the device of uncreating, or ontologically destabilizing a thing or person just created, as in Derrida's *sous rature*, where the item cancelled is still legible beneath the crossing out. No examples of actual crossing out are given, but Maurice Roche does this admirably, even with incorporated proof-corrections (priez pour nous, saigner etc., *Circus* 1972, and others, see Brooke-Rose 1981, 335).

Similarly the item can be affirmed then verbally denied, as in Beckett's 'you must go on, I can't go on, I'll go on' (*The Unnamable*, end). This McHale would regard as still 'epistemological', that is motivated through a character, but soon it is taken over by the narrating author, as in (McHale's examples) Robbe-Grillet's 'No' or 'Retake' (*Projet pour une révolution à New York*, 1970) or Clarence Major's 'I erase him' (*Reflex and Bone Structure*, 1975) and Pynchon's 'Of course it happened. Of course it didn't happen' (*Gravity's Rainbow*, 1973). A more subtle example (mine) is Barth's 'one of his mistresses whereof he had none entered his brown study' (with pun on 'brown', *Lost in the Funhouse*, 1968). Or the artifice of creation can be more overtly bared: 'These people aren't real, I'm making them up as I go along' (Sorrentino, *Imaginative Qualities of Things*, 1971); 'Perhaps tomorrow I will invent Chicago and Jesus Christ and the history of the moon. Just as I have invented you, dear reader, while lying here in the afternoon sun' (Coover, *Pricksongs and Descants*, 1969). Or it can be bared through the literalization of a cliché (McHale's example): 'She had no private life whatsoever. God knows where she went in her privacy' (Spark 1957). Briefer and wittier I feel (and considerably earlier) than his other example of Pynchon's 'spectacular literalization of "suffers a breakdown", "goes to pieces"' for Slothrop in *Gravity's Rainbow* (McHale, 105), which seems to me heavy.

If even in such a simple technique as 'decreating' the examples, though each striking on first acquaintance if the technique itself is unfamiliar, show such variability of tone, no wonder there is such label-bemused admiration with regard to entire passages or entire novels which, even if long quotations are given, by definition escape labels, whether towards the good (richer than) or towards the bad (poorer than).

More developed than these simple sentences is the topos of author-as-god, the character his creature. It is an ancient topos, but it has been exploited into constant play, to the point of becoming a commonplace. Borges used it delicately and briefly. Flann O'Brien used it wittily in *At Swim-Two-Birds* (see Ch. 11, p. 170). The idea returns in Sukenick's *The Death of the Novel* (in which his real-life wife appears as a character and vanishes):

> What I need is a bunch of friends who would be willing to become my characters for a whole story. Maybe I can hire someone. Somebody ought to start a character rental service.
>
> (1969, 85)

O'Brien's idea is stolen but altered (characters from 'real' life, not books, renting instead of borrowing, but of course the 'real-life' character *becomes* fiction), and it's wittily brief. But what about Sorrentino's *Mulligan Stew* (1979), in which not only O'Brien's 'author' Dermot Trellis becomes a (dishonest) author-character, but his Anthony Lamont becomes the main 'author' of the book, with constant personal troubles and increasing paranoia, who creates Martin Halpin who befriends Ned Beaumont (out of Dashiel Hammett), both of whom find themselves inside for ever rewritten stories? Admittedly the book is dedicated 'To the memory of Brian O'Nolan [Flann O'Brien]' and is clearly a tribute. It also contains marvellous things, notably (in-joke) a list of refusal-phrases for the use of publishers (and in fact used by publishers both inside and outside the story) or, more eerily and out of Ingarden's theory of textual 'gaps', the discovery that a house has no bathroom or kitchen, or on the contrary that this or that door has appeared, or even a whole town. Sorrentino is not only 'laying bare' the novelist's structures – and this is very pleasurable, but massively collecting together all the clichés of the trade – and this does become tiresome, however 'intended'. Moreover, the entire novel is based on this one idea, which is not developed except through the fictive novelist's deeply uninteresting paranoia, but exuberantly (heavily) repeated. This I suppose would come under the label 'hypertrophy', like his lists of titles of books on the shelves, that go on for pages (one skips; one should *not* have to skip in a 'postmodern' novel, which by definition plays with textuality).

Much has been made of exuberance in American (as opposed to European) 'postmodern' fiction, but when used in illusion-breaking devices, often with exclamation marks, it breaks the illusion-breaking.

Furthermore, and this is a far more important point, why has 'postmodernism' taken over this old (and Modernist) topos of author as God v. his creature and flogged it to death, when we have long been in a critical world that has strongly shifted to the act of reading, however much of a return 'author-intention' tries to make? Clearly a character is created by the author, so that making him conscious of that fact is transgressing ontological barriers. But this consciousness exists metaphorically in Dostoevski's more extreme dialogism, and the literal transgression was exploited in the theatre as long ago as Pirandello (because, Nash suggests, the barrier there is a physical and visible one, whereas in the novel it first has to be created to be transgressed), and has become a commonplace of film, music-hall, television and even commercials. As usual the novel is fifty years behind the other arts (Sarraute 1956). For if it is a truism that no character can exist without his author, it would be more philosophically interesting today, with the loss of novel-reading, to explore the notion that, even more clearly, no character can exist (whatever his relationship to his author) unless he is read.

Metafictional authors have in fact been aware of this, as Linda Hutcheon notes: 'Metafiction, however, seems aware of the fact that it (like all fiction of course) has *no* existence apart from that consti-tuted by the inward act of reading which counterpoints the external act of writing' (28). She gives no examples except, later, from Coover (quoted p. 213) and from Barthelme's *Snow White* (1967) where the reader is asked to fill in questionnaire-type questions about the story (and so is assumed to be there), or from Barth's *Lost in the Funhouse* (1968), which after over twenty years continues to be one of the most interesting of all his 'postmodern' texts, described by Hutcheon as:

a set of meditations on the act of reading (and listening) as life-granting [...] In 'Title' the reader is constantly asked to fill in the blanks. He is requested by the narrator to acknowledge his complicity in both the fictional creation *and* the self-consciousness about it. 'You tell me it's self-defeating to talk about it instead of just up and doing it, but to acknowledge what I'm doing while doing it is exactly the point'. The writer is reader too, and must face this knowledge, as does the narrator of 'Life Story': 'don't you think he knows who gives his creatures their lives and deaths? Do they exist except as he or others read their words?'

(143)

But Barth never gets beyond talking about it, and falls back almost at once on the writer/writing relation, appealing to the encoded or intradiegetic reader. More subtle but still not quite actualizing the problem is her other example, Calvino's covert treatment in his *Ti con zero* stories: 'Taking the human reader into account, Qfwfq tries to explain his pre-human state as constantly striving to perceive new forms of nature by assembling sensations which allow a visual or aural image to form' (77). But we are still in the writer's *process*. And of course Hutcheon, like all reader-oriented critics, thoroughly explores the reader's complicity in 'deciphering' the techniques, but that is not quite what I mean. She admits that the writer has little control over the 'real' [as opposed to the intradiegetic 'implied', or even dramatized, apostrophized, reader], and that is indeed the difficulty: the character as created or uncreated by the 'real' reader (who corresponds to the 'real' author and who can be, like the 'real' author, variously surrogated within a fiction), remains to be explored.[7]

The reader only comes into metafiction intradiegetically, either 'overtly', in the old author/reader relationship of dear-readerism, or 'covertly, in the many demands that are made upon him to decipher, fill in, co-write.

In many American metafictions, we can get long chunks of 'realistic' description or franker-sex dialogue that could come straight from any average fiction or thriller ('parody'? It reads too self-indulgently mimetic for that), and this is no doubt the point: we are naturally not meant to 'identify'. But how long can a supposedly sophisticated reader (the one appealed to) take 'slice-of-life' writing before another 'device' comes to uncreate it? Quite long, as Fowles shows so skilfully in *The French Lieutenant's Woman* (1969), but then, his stylized recreation of Victorian writing (we even get Hardy's hypothetical observer) is exquisite in itself, either because the reader is himself 'caught up' (identifies) and therefore 'caught out', or because he is not caught out.

There is clearly a question of quality of imagination here. Banality and self-indulgence are surely never a value. The parallel with realistic writing is obvious: how to 'represent' a bore, an idiot, a dull character, without being oneself boring and dull. That takes art, even in classical realism.

---

[7] Cp. Pavić 1989, where the reader, though given much work, is declared dead in the dedication, or 1990, where he becomes a character.

One often has the impression that the famous renewal in some American postmodernism is achieved entirely through anti-illusionist devices, self-reflexive 'strategies' and topoi, by now pretty fatigued, rather than through language itself finding and forming a renewed and renewing content, as in, say, Beckett, Borges, Calvino, Robbe-Grillet, Sarraute, Pinget, Spark, Marquez, Barthelme, Brautigan, Reed, and no doubt quite a few others, all of whom, whether one likes what they do or not, have what used to be called a distinctive tone, a sense one had, on reading them, that it had become impossible to write 'as before'.

Now strategies and devices and topoi are part of the *agencement*, the organization of narrative, exactly in the same way as were the traditional strategies of fiction analysed by Genette (1972). Indeed it is chiefly what comes under his heading *Voice*, and notably metalepsis, that 'postmodernism' explores. But over and above this *agencement* is the actual language of the text, or how these strategies are in any one case incarnated. We have already seen how 'free indirect discourse' (Represented Speech and Thought, see Ch. 5), which comes under *Distance* in Genette, can date a text, as can its disappearance. And since the strategies are themselves overdone and imitated from author to author, I sometimes feel that there is, in some postmodern writing, a certain 'vulgarity' (in the classical sense, see Ch. 13) of both 'style' and 'subject', that undermines the surface brilliance, but above all, that fails to 'transform' both the language of the novel and the 'world' it presents.

Subrealism/Hyperrealism

I would like to end this chapter with a brief consideration of certain *post* 'postmodern' texts, which are never cited in works on 'postmodernism' because they are not 'metafictions' and use no iconoclastic illusion-breaking devices or word-play, and yet in their own way are every bit as 'anti-realist' and 'ontological' as those constantly discussed.

The first group is what Olga Scherer has studied under the term *subrealism*, coined by her in relation to *surrealism* (1983; 1986). Surrealism (I summarize and translate) eventually spread beyond the boundaries set by the school itself, and was absorbed by Western avant-garde creativity, based above all on an immediate writing 'I' and the presence of *états d'âme*, sensations, motivations, all inevitably represented, in however fragmented a way. Inversely, subrealist discourse tries to tell, at all costs, an untellable story:

untellable from the lack of adequate semantic links in the real model [...] which
is governed by relations that are obscure, hidden, arbitrary even, and thus non-existent
for a mentality that supposes itself normal, innocent or simply acting in good faith
[...] The author pretends not to believe in the unbelievable aspect of life's spectacle,
and not to be aware that he is constantly trying, without success, to fill in these
semantic gaps, through means that are well-proven but inadequate, which he draws
from traditional fiction.

(1983, 15)

This pretending not to believe the unbelievable aspect of the real
and not to be aware of semantic gaps recalls (for me) the eighteenth-
century *roman philosophique*, but I may have misunderstood. The link
with Kafka and Gogol (notably *The Nose*) is clear and Scherer makes
it. But above all it is a reaction against avant-garde movements
of the post-dialogical (post-Dostoevskian) kind. She calls it neo-
monological, that is, not a simple monologism as still practised
despite the Dostoevskian revolution. On the contrary, while aware
of it and wishing to preserve its main principle (author-conscious-
ness), this type of work

tries to lessen its effects which, when pushed to extreme [as discussed in the previous
section], can paralyse the relics of the already minimal link between words and things.
To recuperate a minimum of represented real, it wants to weaken the hyperbolised
function of the signifier and give back to fiction its epic foundations.

(1986, 32–3)

However, it reveals no preoccupation with regard to socialist realism
which, being non-credible anyway, is a minimal threat compared
to the exaggerations of Western post-dialogism [that is, *nouveau nouveau* to 'postmodern'], including especially word-play on the signifier,
and more especially, I presume, the 'pure generative word-play' as
advocated by *Tel Quel* (see n. 4, p. 211).[8]

Moreover, subrealism can use the supernatural, and in this it is
linked to magic realism, but the constraints are strict: (1) it must
remain non-allegorical; (2) it must avoid all effect of SF; (3) if it
occurs as a dream or hallucination (rare) this must be clearly
denoted; (4) it must be articulated directly upon the social. In fact

---

[8] She cites mine in *Amalgamemnon* (1984) and those of Maurice Roche in *Compact*
(1966) and *Camar(a)de* (1981), and although I would deny that word-play is
non-mimetic, I admit that it has its limits, and it is true that both Roche and
I, in different ways, have turned to other modes.

the fourth and prescriptive condition depends on the first three: 'free of allegory, SF and onirism, the supernatural slides automatically towards the social and becomes a hyperbolised psychosociological phenomenon' (1986, 37). It becomes, in fact, what she calls *le sursocial*, an anecdote, a *Witz*, which absorbs the supernatural.

For these and other reasons, Scherer believes that this kind of novel is being written only in societies deprived of political freedoms, and her examples are Tadeusz Konwicki's *Polish Complex* and *The Little Apocalypse* (1981) and his pseudo-journal *Moonrises and Moonsets* (1982), Kazimierz Brandys, *Months* (1981–2), Milan Kundera's *The Book of Laughter and Forgetting* (1978) or Josef Skvorecky's *Miracle in Bohemia* (1978). Whether this external constraint on the genre is a true one would remain to be seen (see Group 2 below, Hofmann). I am not sure for example whether she would include Kundera's later books or those of Rushdie as discussed in Chapter 13, all written in freedom but about unfree circumstances. She herself has discovered an Algerian writer who fills these conditions, Rachid Mimouni (*Le Fleuve détourné*, 1982, *Tombéza*, 1984) – but perhaps Algeria is/was not free either. In *Le Fleuve détourné*, for example, a young soldier and sole survivor of a bombing of his camp by the French Air Force during the Algerian War of Independence, returns to his village where he had been counted as dead on the admin registers. He will never prove his aliveness. Advised to consult his commander (who was killed in the bombing) he finds the grave. The commander slowly wakes, slowly remembers the soldier, thanks him for the tobacco, but says he can do nothing. The dialogue is totally natural, and ends:

I'm sorry, I can't tell you anything, even less advise you. Don't go and believe the dead know much. Not the least secret. Sunk in obscurity. Worms gnaw on our flesh. A cloud of invisible microbes are busy on our bones. Then we'll be nothing. The living must lose this mania for making us depositaries of the secret of human life. I'm sorry, I can't tell you anything. I was glad to see you. Thanks for the tobacco.

(1982, 82)

The second group could be (and perhaps has been) called hyper-realism, for it shares with it (and with 'subrealism'), not only an apparent return to realism, with its refusal of commentary and authorial complicity, but also a refusal of the authorial chitchat, obsession with illusion-breaking devices and other 'extravagances of mid-century avant-garde' (Scherer on 'sub-realism'). However, the American school called Minimalist (Raymond Carver and disciples such as

Ann Beattie, Jayne Ann Phillips, Frederic Barthelme and others)
is ambiguous in a way which the texts of my second ('hyper-realist')
group are not. For if, in both, language is no longer transparent
and dupes no one, this can and does, in the American school, lead
in two different (and very American) directions: the old complicity
is in practice back (with the facilities this entails); and, since day
to day reality can only be made amazing through media intensifica-
tion, the language tends towards not just opacity but also strained
baroque (with the self-indulgence this entails), whereas in the texts
of my second group the intensity of language is highly controlled
and produces the very 'ontological flicker' that McHale attributes
to his illusion-breaking fictions. These texts in fact seem to me closely
linked to Olga Scherer's 'subrealism'.

For what could be more 'realist' in style and presentation than
Georges Perec's *La Vie, mode d'emploi* (1972), in which a house and
each of its many tenants are described, with map attached, in a
diegesis so anecdotal, so condensed, so intense and cyclical and yet
so totally pointless, that the 'ontological flicker' is undoubtedly felt,
and a good deal less ostentatiously ('overtly') than in many of the
often archly self-conscious examples found in McHale and others,
and yet more incisively than in the various 'condominium' stories,
of which, 'The Condominium' in Stanley Elkin's *Searches and Seizures*
(1973), is the best known. The same 'ontological flicker' is produced,
though in a very different way in *La disparition* (1969, mentioned
in Ch. 1), written without the letter *e*, the 'disappearance' of which
'character' (print, signifier) very covertly figures the disappearances
of characters (fictive, signified) in the text.

This constraint, in addition, produces a strange style, since all
the masculine nouns must be introduced either with the indefinite
article *un* or in zero-grade, the latter rare in French except in prepositional locutions (an article-less noun is a purely abstract lexical entry,
unlike English which has zero-grade for abstractions and plurals,
see Brooke-Rose 1958); while the feminine nouns must on the contrary all be introduced by *la*, and be preponderantly abstracts (but
ending in *-ion* not in *ité*). This is certainly playing with the signifier,
but in a deadpan realistic style, the constraint also leading to rare
words, words in foreign languages or in Latin, and the result plunges
the reader into a strange duality, forcing him both to believe and
not to believe what he is reading. This is true of all Perec's books,
each time for different reasons.

Less well-known perhaps, but equally bizarre and full of 'ontological flicker', are the odd narratives of Gert Hofmann: *Gespräch über Balzacs Pferd* (1981), *Auf der Turm* (1982), and *Unsere Eroberung* (1984). The *Gespräch* consists of four stories, one about Lenz (the 'mad' writer that Buechner had already 'brought to life' as a younger man), going back to Riga to find his respectable merchant father, and the total breakdown of communication between them; another about Balzac in the Paris catacombs, another about Casanova, and the fourth about the German poet Robert Walser on his Swiss island. Despite the ostensible fictionalization of 'real' characters, each story is weirder and less 'biographical' than the other.

As for *Auf der Turm*, it seemed to me such a perfect example of Scherer's 'subrealism' that I thought it would enlarge her 'lack of political freedom' constraint. It tells of a German tourist couple stranded by car-trouble in a Sicilian village and at the mercy of a local guide who has staged and invented incredible and horrific tourist sights (since the village has none) that climax in a boy leaping to his death from a tower to entertain them. Of course the 'lack of freedom' is here the lack of economic freedom of the local population, but the situation is slowly and ruthlessly reversed, the two tourists ('a mentality that supposes itself normal, innocent or simply acting in good faith' – Scherer, quoted p. 218) more and more helpless in the hands of the guide. *Unsere Eroberung* tells the adventures of a German boy of fourteen and a mentally retarded friend in a small town on the day of the Allied Victory. They go out in search of food for their mother, but also hope to see Americans, especially black ones. They never do see them, but have 'real' yet incredible experiences in an old slaughter-house, in the house of a widow who gives them the suit of her dead soldier-husband, much too large, and so on, all this, too, in a highly stylized yet dead-pan narrative tone that gives the reader the same strange effect of both getting thoroughly involved and not believing a word of it.

Hofmann's stories are 'realistic' but impossible, or rather, just possible, miming in a highly formal style the unreality of our real, the result being total ontological instability on the one hand, and possibly 'subrealism' on the other.

I mention Perec and Hofmann – and no doubt others might belong here – to emphasize that the 'revolt' was not against 'realism' but against the conventions of one historical type of realism called Realism and the no longer tenable presuppositions that went with it; that there are many more interesting things to write about than the writer's difficulties with representation; and that there are many

realisms available to the unavoidable representative nature of language. We can explore them in rich and varied ways, instead of
constantly bashing at the fatigued conventions themselves, a bashing
which is in danger of itself becoming a fatigued convention.

15

A womb of one's own?

As a useful transition to the next section, which deals with women and women's writing in general, I would like to continue in the thrust of the last chapter with a brief consideration of women in 'postmodernism', where similar problems arise, but are sometimes made worse by some of the feminists themselves.

Women and the 'avant-garde'

In a perceptive article entitled 'Male Signature, Female Aesthetic: The Gender Politics of Experimental Writing' (Friedman & Fuchs 1988, 72–81), Marianne DeKoven confronts the problem of women's experimental fiction head on. She notes that manifestos for avant-garde and feminist stylistic practice 'often sound remarkably alike without knowing that they do or taking cognizance of one another in any way'. Already in 'For the Etruscans' (1980), Rachel Blau Duplessis and members of 'Workshop 9' had noted that 'any list of the characteristics of postmodernism would at the same time be a list of the traits of women's writing' (151, quoted DeKoven 73). The few recognitions of affinities are all formulated by women and, moreover, feminist critics like Kristeva and Cixous have both defined *écriture féminine* as an eruption of the feminine pre-Oedipal, or pre-symbolic (which Kristeva calls 'the semiotic') into avant-garde *masculine* writing, from Mallarmé, Lautréamont to Joyce and Artaud for Kristeva (1980, 165), or, for Cixous, Genet, one of the 'rare exceptions' to the rule that 'there has not yet been any writing that inscribes femininity' (1976, 98, quoted DeKoven 72). In other words, *écriture féminine* is the male avant-garde.

DeKoven notes that although feminists are 'free to choose from among the best of what culture has to offer, discarding the misogynist, female-deleting tendencies within particular literary movements', some (my italics, to stress the astonishing lateness and admission of derivation) 'have *recently* come to see that the arguments developed by the modernist avant-garde are relevant to their own struggle to develop a radical aesthetic [. . .] and have *discovered* that avant-garde practice *can be adapted* to their purposes' (73–4). But it is a one-way traffic:

The [. . .] canonized postmodernists, surfictionists, magic realists, anti-realists, meta-fictionists and fabulators, virtually all of whom are male (as are the critics) do not seem to need to rejoice in their similarity to Stein, Woolf, H. D., Barnes, Nin, Sontag, Wittig, Duras, Sarraute. Or Cixous.

(73–4)

The extreme misogyny of 'male modernism' (by which she clearly means both Modernism and Post-) has often been noted (Gilbert & Gubar, Fraser and others). But DeKoven also blames the feminists:

The Anglo-American literary feminist hostility or indifference to avant-garde may not be merely a repudiation of male supremacy tradition. Feminist critics and writers are also frequently suspicious of the (putative) cultural marginality of the avant-garde: afraid that claiming other outsiders as allies will make their position even shakier.

Even when feminists claim for women a privileged, transgressive marginality it seems necessary also to claim sole occupancy of that margin. Women must *be* difference.

(76)

She then explains this 'oft-attacked essentialism' as dictated by the necessity of political fact, dealing notably with Mary Jacobus' insistence ('Is There a Woman in this Text', 1982, as paraphrased by DeKoven) on this political fact:

we must appropriate avant-garde/experimental style, call it écriture féminine, connect it simultaneously to an exclusively feminine Other of discourse [. . .] and suppress again the question of a possible theoretical historical convergence of a female and avant-garde traditions [. . .] suppress altogether our knowledge of the existence of the avant-garde tradition and hypothesise écriture féminine as if it were an entirely new literary practice. If we allow écriture féminine a history, that history begins with Stein, H. D., Woolf: many analyses of those foremothers, as well as of contemporary women writers, simply relabel their work écriture féminine, as if there were no male writers who used the same stylistic practices.

(DeKoven 77–8)

Whether read as complaint about political fact or as description of a programme, the views here summarized by DeKoven seem both silly and paranoiac to me. DeKoven comments:

The invisibility of the avant-garde tradition to most exponents of écriture féminine/ female aesthetic/women's writing is superseded only by the monumental male exclusivity of the avant-garde, particularly in American postmodernism. I say 'superseded' rather than 'equaled' because the avant-garde is the repressed of écriture féminine, cropping up sporadically in a context of belittlement, repudiation, or flaws/holes/gaps in the critical argument. To the male avant-garde, however, écriture féminine, women's writing as a category, simply do not exist.

(78)

She asks, pertinently: 'Why is experimental writing, a demonstrably anti-patriarchal practice, so exclusively dominated by men at a time when women writers are doing extremely well in traditional, culturally hegemonic literary forms?' Part of the answer, she says, 'is that women *are* writing experimentally but getting little or no recognition for it' and secondly that 'the female gendered signature is *simply too subversive* to be recognized by the hegemonic institutions such as academy or mainstream publishing' (78).

I am not sure about this last reason, which would have been more convincing with at least one analysed example, but I'll return to this. DeKoven goes on to say that

the question we should be asking is not how experimental writing by women, even though it looks like and describes itself similarly to experimental writing by men, is really profoundly different [...] Feminist analysis of experimental stylistics, rather than pretending either that the avant-garde tradition doesn't exist or that it is the same thing as écriture féminine, should acknowledge the anti-patriarchal potential of form in historical, male-signed avant-garde writing, but at the same time acknowledge the self-cancelling counter-move of that writing towards male supremacism and misogyny. We cannot claim allegiance naively, in particular, with contemporary American postmodernism, allegiance that postmodernism (with a few exceptions) would not even notice let alone bother to repudiate.

(78)

And later:

Since we (feminist critics, women experimental writers) are the ones who are in danger of being silenced, it behooves us to articulate our language clearly: to establish ourselves as an 'ambiguously nonhegemonic group' *in relation to male avant-garde hegemony*, simultaneously within it and subversive of it.

(79)

I wholly concur. Clearly the silencing of women critics and writers, and especially of women experimental writers, is true, is constant, and is done by ignoring them or, more often than might be supposed, by stealing from them without acknowledgement. I have experienced both myself and simply put up with it. Nevertheless I have always been deeply suspicious of all movements and labels which create

blind obsessions. A writer, man or woman, is essentially alone, and
will be 'good' or 'bad' independently of sex or origin. This view
is condemned by some feminists as the 'androgynous-great-mind
stance', but it is fundamentally a sound one, however ill used (see
Ch. 17). And if the misogyny situation is indeed as described by
DeKoven and many others, there are, fortunately and as she says,
exceptions. Of the three books on 'postmodernism' I discussed in
the last chapter, Brian McHale does indeed omit some women who
could illustrate his theories (notably Doris Lessing's science fiction –
though one must allow for personal taste and not regard every
omission as sexist). But he discusses and quotes Muriel Spark, Angela
Carter, Brigid Brophy, Monique Wittig and myself quite independently of our sex. Cristopher Nash has only me (and only *Thru*,
although his theory includes science fiction), but he too does not
feel he has to specify that I am a woman. It is Linda Hutcheon,
a woman, whose (merely passing) references to women novelists
are only: Jane Austen, Agatha Christie, Iris Murdoch, Hélène Cixous
and (less passing) Virginia Woolf (of course). That is, her only 'postmodern' writer is Cixous (for *Tombe*, which 'presents the act of writing
as an erotic activity', 33). But things are changing, however slowly,
and only indirectly through feminism, much more directly through
specific women writers.

More encouraging from this statistical perspective is Chénetier's
book on modern American fiction since the sixties (1989). It has
a bibliographical guide which exceeds the number of writers mentioned or discussed in the book. The distribution of names is as
follows (percentages rounded upwards):

	Guide	*Book*	*Presented as innovative*
Men	265	169 (75% of Guide)	74 (28% of Guide) (43% of Book)
Women	114	51 (45% of Guide)	21 (18% of Guide) (41% of Book)
	(under $\frac{1}{2}$ of men)	(under $\frac{1}{3}$ of men)	(under $\frac{1}{3}$ of men)

In other words, although far fewer women are mentioned than
men (which may reflect the publishing situation), there are many
more than the usual one per cent or so; and of the men and women
mentioned in the book, forty-three per cent of the men and forty-one
per cent of the women are presented as innovative – almost equal
(as it should be since the book is about renewal). This 'almost equal'

treatment is a spectacular improvement over other books on the same topic.

This is, however, an exception, and there *is* a deleting problem. I shall return to it in Chapter 17.

As for the refusal to acknowledge male forbears, surely revenge for similar male malpractice is not a sound strategy, even from a feminist viewpoint. Yet this refusal is often found, notably in the very book where DeKoven's brilliant essay appears, *together with* opposite attempts to hook on features of this or that feminine experimental writing to the better-known male postmodernist writing. This means that the Introduction presents both as feminine features, even on the same page, but without any apparent awareness of the contradiction (see p. 231 below). Whichever policy they adopt, feminists should at least watch their critical slidings and not try to have it both ways.

And why should such features not exist in both masculine and feminine writing? This was after all the point of the Kristeva and Cixous theories. Surely what matters is the way they are used, their quality in any one instance. The answer, it seems, is that such an acknowledgement would contradict the feminist thesis of specificity, of difference.

Specificity

What is this feminine specificity? Perry Nodelman, in an essay on Joyce Carol Oates' *Bellefleur* in the same collection (Friedman & Fuchs 1988, 250–63), reminds us that Oates has criticized followers of Nabokov and Borges for being solipsistic and Beckett for refining man ' "out of existence in a recognizable world [. . .] doomed to exist within the confines of his own skull, to babble endlessly about the very process of babbling" ' (*New Heaven* 89, 95, quoted Nodelman 251). He goes on to assert that masculine innovators disrupt and fragmentize story to assert their authority over their material. Now fragmentation and disruption is often claimed (and in this book too) as specifically feminine. But Nodelman makes the point that 'interestingly, literary experimentation involving women, either as characters in novels or as literary commentators [?], tends to be characterized as anything but fragmented' (252). This does not mean that it is logical and linear, on the contrary, for he opposes fragmentation and disruption to *flow*, though surely 'flow' can be disrupted, and is. I wonder also whether 'literary commentators' could just 'flow' (at least as 'flow' is further described by Nodelman with quotations from Cixous and Kristeva, see below) and get their articles published, but I'll return to this point. The model, however, seems to be male:

> Feminist critics often cite the monologue that James Joyce gives to Molly Bloom at the end of *Ulysses* as an example of writing unrepressed by the usual masculine assumptions about structure, and Joyce Carol Oates sees Molly's soliloquy as an attack on masculine authority [...] Julia Kristeva characterizes feminism itself as a flowing stream: 'by demanding recognition of an irreducible identity, without equal in the opposite sex and, as such, exploded, plural, fluid, in a certain way non-identical, this feminism situates itself outside the linear time of identities which communicate through projection and revendication' ['Woman's Time', *Signs 7*, 1981, 13–35]. Speaking of her own writing, Hélène Cixous says 'I too, overflow [...] Time and again I, too, have felt so full of luminous torrents that I could burst' [*The Laugh of the Medusa*, transl. 1976, 246].
>
> (Nodelman 252)

For Cixous in fact, 'a feminine text goes on and on and at a certain moment the volume comes to an end but the writing continues [...] The quest for origins, illustrated by Oedipus, doesn't haunt a feminine unconscious. Rather it's the beginning, or beginnings [...] not promptly with the phallus in order to close with the phallus, but starting on all sides at once' ('Castration or Decapitation?' *Signs 7*, 41–55, p.53).

The basic idea, then, is that of *flow*, indeed the words *flux, flow, fluidity* return again and again, together with the notion of circular structure, open endings, avoidance of climax. Nodelman puts it very precisely:

> Conventional fiction mirrors the conventional male orgasmic pattern, and conventional innovative fiction merely confirms the significance of that pattern by defiantly disrupting it in something like an act of self-centered masturbatory exhibitionism; but fiction might be both innovative and feminine if it mirrored the conventional female orgasmic pattern [...] Rather than disrupt the representational and sequential aspects of story by putting technique in the foreground and emphasizing the artist's 'gymnastic expertise' over plot, feminine innovation would have to evoke both a recognizable and consistent reality and maintain a pleasurable flow of continuous events; but to avoid the pressure of the masculine pattern, it could not allow that flow to be dominated by the climactic end it might be seen to be moving toward.
>
> (253)

And this, his essay sets out to demonstrate, is what Joyce Carol Oates does in *Bellefleur*. The theory is mimetic, and fits the book.

Feminine specificity, then, apart from simply representing feminine characters and their viewpoint, sensibility and psyche (just as Realism represented those of other previously oppressed elements of humankind), seems to consist of circular structures, open endings, non-linearity and, for some, disruption of structures. But these have all been used by men, though this is explained away as femininity erupting first in male writing. There remains *flow*, eternal beginnings from all sides at once as opposed to quests for origins, flow and chaos, which Cixous neatly calls *chaosmos*. 'Foremothers' are Dorothy Richardson and, more succinctly, Anais Nin and what has been called after her 'the music of the womb' which is a more graphic name for *écriture féminine* as described by Kristeva and Cixous. Why then do these not acknowledge her, or Richardson, but prefer to find *écriture féminine* in men? Presumably because they do not find them 'good enough', striking or telling enough, for their case. For the 'striking' model is indeed Molly Bloom's soliloquy, though in another sense this is highly controlled and purposeful, like all the other 'parodic' uses of different styles in *Ulysses*.

However,

'Modernity', in the name of which French male [?] theorists are claiming the feminine for themselves, has, in essence, declared its identity with Molly Bloom rather than Stephen Dedalus – a profound shift in identification that carries the potential for the reorganization of the dominant conceptual structures of the West [...] This feminine has been written by men, but perhaps more relevant to the reconciliation of feminism and modernity, it has also been written by women. It is time, indeed, to read Molly not only as she has been written by Joyce and his brothers, but also as she has written herself from Gertrude Stein to Kathy Acker.

(Friedman & Fuchs, Introduction, 42)

True. There remains, however, as in the last chapter, the question of quality and degree ('male' control? Or just artistic control?). Molly's soliloquy is one chapter, and the last. If it becomes a whole book, pure flow is hardly exempt from Oates' accusation of solipsism for men. And in fact Nodelman does a kind of *volte face* and divorces 'flow' from story-telling: 'But such flowing feminine writing is not necessarily story-telling [...] Verena Andermatt suggests that the "amniotic flow" of Cixous' texts is equally divorced from the conventional structure of narrative [...] This is pure flow divorced from narrative: it describes events without structure, just as conventional masculine innovation offers structure divorced from events: but in its absence of structural order it is not exactly fiction in any way we might recognize' (252).

This last sentence (by Nodelman, not Andermatt) sounds like the usual objection to *all* innovative fiction, so can be discounted as argument. But the formulations are both too generalizing and too neat. One even wonders whether Nodelman has read Cixous' fictions in the original, which are subtly controlled and intellectual. (In the feminist debate, only her two theoretical texts are ever quoted, never her creative work, which includes deeply innovative plays and a film scenario.) In fact, having opposed flow to mere disruption and fragmentation, he now discards it (which, if he believes his description of it, is just as well) in his desire to show that Oates falls into none of these traps.

For we may well ask, from a feminist viewpoint, why this 'semiotic'/'amniotic' flux is recognized by two leading women feminists yet apparently denied in women's writing up to that point (except Cixous' own, presumably). Obviously the creative process is deeply linked with erotic ones, and I shall take up the ill-logic of male creative metaphors in Chapter 17. Here I simply want to ask two questions: first, if the psychological and intellectual creative process is so intricately bound with physical and pleasurable activities, why should it be a female specificity as a *process*? Or rather, why should the female share of this not be (as indeed it has been) imaginatively and even mimetically used by men, just as the male aspect is and has been imaginatively used and developed by women, or both by both? And second, are flux and chaos in fact what feminists should defend? The first question will be dealt with in Chapter 17. The second is no doubt controversial and I shall simply state my position while fully admitting that others can be and are defended.

The semiotic, the amniotic, the semidiotic

Are flux and chaos in fact what feminists should defend? And, as corollary, are they entitled to defend it?

I do not deny for a moment that control and mastery, logic and reason, the will to power over natural and primitive forces have produced the terrifying and often ludicrously illogical world in which we live. But women have not exactly refused the benefits of comfort and civilization that go with that male world. Moreover, early feminist arguments, now apparently discarded, were passionately devoted to claiming and showing that women can be every bit as brainy, as logical and rational as men, which qualities imply control, discipline, mastery and the will to power, and it is largely thanks to these forbears that today's feminists are in the posts and positions they occupy today. But it could also be argued that even repressed and 'primitive' women need to develop control and a high degree of organization, a logic of their own. Naturally I do not advocate this kind of repression and logic of resignation, but the present and constant emphasis on certain structures as 'masculine' and others as 'feminine' is a gross over-simplification, which flourishes only at the cost of much sliding and a good deal of loose thinking. Perhaps that *is* the point? Loose thinking as a feminine specificity?

But if this loose thinking is merely contingent, the main question remains: are flux and chaos really what civilization with all its ills actually needs? I have been to feminist workshops and heard, among sound good sense, earnest papers on 'primitive' perceptions as the salvation of humankind, on 'feminine' images (caves, water etc.) in women's poetry as if they occurred nowhere else, and I have read, here and there, many papers which, alas, exemplified the supposed female lack of logic but not, in any creative sense, the music of the womb, which concept is rarely developed but simply repeated or, at worst, used to justify flat self-indulgence or hypertrophy – that is, when examples are given and not just paraphrased or externally described and theorized about. In just this one book of essays (Friedman & Fuchs 1988, the most recent book on these problems at the time of writing), we find many contradictions and incoherences, normal in a collection by diverse hands, but typical also of a confused and confusing situation.

A good case is made, for example, by the editors in their Introduction, for 'meganovels' such as Marguerite Young's *Miss Macintosh My Darling* (1965), 'nearly 1,200 pages long', to receive the same attention as Barth's *Letters* (1979) or Pynchon's *Gravity's Rainbow* (1973), while other essays pretend that male forebears don't exist. Moreover, the case is made on Frederick Karl's argument that the apparent disorder of these sprawling works [Barth, Pynchon] are 'vast, intricate *systems* [my italics] of coherence' the 'unity' of *Gravity's Rainbow* being attributed to Pynchon's borrowing from chemistry and that of *Letters* to its epistolary 'system' which absorbs the 'systems' of Barth's earlier works, as well as on other criteria: 'dense prose, accretion or amassing of fictional materials rather than continuous development, a narrow, sometimes skewed view of a given society, and a sense of incompletion despite enormous length. Young's novel has all these and more' (Karl 1985, 251–3, 258, F & F, 34).

This is not only what I have called 'hooking on' a woman writer to male postmodernism (via a male critic), but it also claims coherence and 'system' (à la New Criticism), while many essays in the rest of the book, and indeed other parts of the Introduction, insist

on the writing of the womb, the 'process of de-evolution, of deciviliz-
ing, what Joan Kirkby calls "a gradual erosion of hierarchical social
structure into a state of dissolution"' (Intro. 39), or on the plot
being in disarray in *Nightwood* 'because Barnes employs a quest narrative that – because it is obsolete – her characters cannot sustain
[...] and through this process Barnes dislocates the form and indicts
the ideology of master narrative' (19); while a novel by Nin in another
essay on the contrary 'derives its leisurely organic structure from the
archetype of the journey' (167). Is a quest not a journey? But then
perhaps it was not regarded as male, masterful and obsolete in the
thirties. Similarly Dorothy Richardson's views are paraphrased in
one essay, apparently in approval:

> Women hardly ever 'know', so their reliance on instinctual life makes them more
> real, more alive, more *authentic* than men. Those women who do trouble to 'know'
> are absurd; they are not really women, but imitation men.
>
> (F & F 87)

Why should instinct be 'more real' than thought, or imagination,
or other fantasmatic activity? And is this kind of woman what feminists want to be? If so, how can they even get to the point of even
finding and paraphrasing such views without 'knowledge'?

There are also examples of inept critical statements, perhaps due
to the music of the womb invading the criticism:

> It is clear that H. D.'s seemingly 'different' prose (though very like prose by Woolf,
> Richardson and Stein) [!], carries many implications about her sense of herself as
> both writer and woman.
>
> (151)

> The 'music of the womb' is radical in three distinctive ways. First and most obvious
> [...] Nin was unveiling and exploring *themes* that few women except Colette had
> taken on [examples] *Technically as well*, Nin's earliest published works were boldly
> experimental [examples]. What unites these works, making them cohere as a unified
> oeuvre is *'the music of the womb'*: their musicality [...] and their devoted excavation
> and articulation of women's experience.
>
> (162)

In this last quotation I have used italics to show that only *two*
'distinctive ways' are given, unless the third is 'the music of the
womb', which was the original generic. Does this kind of writing
try to mime the fact that 'women hardly ever know' and rely on
instinct? Is it an indictment or a failed imitation of 'male' abstract
thinking? The best experimental women writers are not served by
this kind of praise.

The 'pre-symbolic' (or 'semiotic' in Kristeva's sense) must, like any other ontic, go through the symbolic to be perceptible at all, just as anti-realism cannot do without these or those structures of realism or anti-representation without representation. It is, as always, a question of the dominant, and above all of quality in any one case, not of vague generalizations and special pleadings disguised as theory.

The twentieth century in general, from the Surrealists and much misunderstanding of Freud onwards, has tended to enthrone the Unconscious as the latest substitute for dogmatic truth, rather than as a language to understand, a language to come to terms with and to explore, exploit, imaginatively. The Unconscious (or the pre-Symbolic) by definition is inaccessible, like the ontic, except through conscious effort and analysis, which automatically means structuring and schematizing and rehandling, to which all perception is subservient: we already rehandle a dream the moment we try to capture it and write it down. The Unconscious as Truth, the 'music of the womb' as 'more real'. Feminism is belatedly repeating the same gesture, and I am not at all sure how 'subversive' it really is, on its wombish own.

Flux and chaos and primitive perceptions, for all their undoubted vitality and necessity as a means of achieving tolerance, integration, wholeness, are nevertheless at the moment more in danger of threatening all that we hold dear in civilization today. Moreover, control and logic (etc.), as well as 'symbolic' rather than purely 'semiotic' expression can hardly be said to be absent from the best and most incisive feminist criticism – it couldn't make its points without them. Cixous and Kristeva, who seem to be the highest feminist reference, are the two most highly qualified, intellectual, and intelligent literary women in France. Feminist critics usually hold jobs in academia, with all its internecine power-struggles, and presumably they partake in those, using 'male' structures. Naturally there is still unfairness and difficulty, but to compete they presumably do not turn to the music of the womb, but to tough preparation for tough examinations, dissertations, conference papers, publications. It seems to me unacceptable to live in these relative sinecures and continue to talk about the desirability of flux, chaos and pre-Oedipal sensibility. It reminds me of 1968 demagogues who refused to prepare students for the *concours* of the *agrégation* (regarded as part of the *ancien régime* power structure) while all themselves *agrégés*. Apart from the moral aspect (an old one, intellectuals talking to the left and living to the right), it transforms this supposedly so important and all-engulfing but so far repressed 'specificity' into a new object of scientific (hence male) study, and thus creates a deep divide between critical writing and the creative process, which is exceedingly anti-postmodern (see Ch. 2) and even reactionary.

It seems to me that 'specificity' in creation is an individual, not a sexual, racial or class phenomenon. Marc Chénetier, for instance, in his excellent book on new American fiction from the sixties on (1989, 370) makes the well argued point that the most efficient feminist writers are not the strident (Marge Piercy) or the simplistic (Marilyn French), but those who distance themselves from such 'ratified' [*homologué*] discourse, by the 'grace and vigour of their poetics' (Marianne Hauser, Toni Morrison or Marilynne Robinson), by 'creatively mingling genres' (Maxine Hong Kingston, Leslie Marmon Silko, Alice Walker or Louise Erdrich), or by 'basing their critical irony on a (sometimes metafictional) perspective of dominant discourse' (Joanna Russ, Grace Paley, Ntozake Shange). None of these characteristics, he adds, is specific to their sex. And 'ironically it is to the older generation of contemporary women that we must turn for literary works that are convincing from a feminist point of view which hardly interests them: Marianne Hauser, Ursula Molinaro and Georgiana Peacher, in their discretion, have done more for "écriture féminine" than the mediatized "specialists" of this struggle' (my translation; see also 'A la recherche de l'Arlésienne', Chénetier 1986, for fuller treatment of feminine specificity).

Of course each writer will write about what he/she knows most deeply, from suffering or joy or any other experience, and of course this will produce differences, but differences right cross the ideological board, differences in subject, treatment and tone that will vary from writer to writer, whatever species they belong to. Ultimately the writer survives as writer, not as black, Indian, Chinese, female, miner, all of whom first need to learn to read and write (with all the various technical and philosophical sophistications all writing implies) at least minimally to organize their ideas. Art is above all an ordering, however widely this may be interpreted and carnivalesquely inverted in various periods. Flux and chaos, like anything else in the cosmos, can be used in art, but they are not themselves art. A womb of one's own? Why?

PART IV

Things?

16

Woman as semiotic object

There have been a few delightful moments, during my desultory and decidedly non-expert readings in semiotics, when the subject made me laugh out loud instead of terrorizing, or, same thing perhaps, boring me stupid.

Elementary structures

One of them occurred early on when I read 'The Interaction of Semiotic Constraints' by A. J. Greimas and François Rastier (1968), where the logical rectangle of contraries and contradictories which Greimas adopts as deep structure of his narrative grammar and which is said to represent 'the elementary structure of significance', is used to show how the model works when semantically invested in, for example, sexual relations. The first model is the *social* one (model A), in which the Culture/Nature opposition subsumes, on the one hand, permitted sexual relations (Culture) and, on the other, excluded ones (Nature) (see Fig. 8).

A.

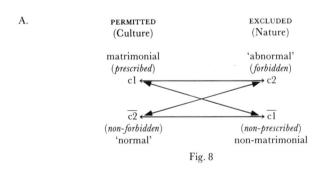

PERMITTED　　　　　　EXCLUDED
(Culture)　　　　　　(Nature)

matrimonial　　　　　'abnormal'
(*prescribed*)　　　　(*forbidden*)
c_1　　　　　　　　　c_2

$\overline{c_2}$　　　　　　　　$\overline{c_1}$
(*non-forbidden*)　　　(*non-prescribed*)
'normal'　　　　　　non-matrimonial

Fig. 8

Further semantic investment (more particular) then gave, 'for traditional French society':

c1 *prescribed*	c2 *forbidden*
conjugal love	incest, homosexuality
c2 *non-forbidden*	c1 *non-prescribed*
male adultery	female adultery

(141–5)

Thus the old double standard, lingua in sheer semiotic cheek, is made sexplicit as an 'elementary structure of significance'. The model does not attempt to account for systems in which both marriage and incest are prescribed (for instance, Egyptian dynasties), presumably regarded as exceptional.

Two further models are then given: B, *economic* (e1 profitable/ e2 harmful; e1 non-profitable / e2 non-profitable) where the 'non-profitable' falls conveniently on the position of 'female adultery' and the 'non-harmful' on that of 'male adultery'; and C, *individual* or *personal* (p1 desired / p2 feared; p1 non-desired / p2 non-feared), where the 'non-desired' falls conveniently on the position of 'female adultery' and the 'non-feared' on that of 'male adultery' (144–6).

These two models, when articulated with the first, allow for sixteen different kinds of sexual relationships – surely a poor generating model – of which some are balanced, some weakly conflictual and some strongly conflictual. For example, the relations of Balzac's Père Rigou with his servant are 'non-forbidden, desired, non-harmful; those of the servant with Père Rigou are non-prescribed, feared and non-profitable; there is therefore conflict, however the relations are expressed'. These semiotic situations are said to 'help us define "romantic insatisfaction"' and perfect love is said to be the manifestation of the relations from two groups of permutations:

(1) *prescribed A + prescribed B* [matrimonial + profitable];
    forbidden A + forbidden B [forbidden + harmful]
(2) *prescribed A + non-forbidden B* [matrimonial + non-harmful i.e. male adultery]:
    prescribed B + non-forbidden A [profitable + non-harmful i.e. male adultery]

I wonder whether these formulae for perfect love have been programmed into the computers of matrimonial agencies instead of tastes, ages and social situations. I know they have been programmed into male and female consciousnesses for thousands of years, and are not likely to be truly effaced in the mere few centuries since women began to try and think of other possibilities for themselves. For of course many things have changed, and the double standard in adultery is no longer and perhaps never was what women have been protesting about – after all they managed to ignore it throughout history. What they protest about is the constant displacement of the double standard into every other aspect of life, and in such insidious ways that it has not always been, and is still not always easy to bring up into consciousness. Feminist studies have pinpointed so many that I shall not do so here, but it is important to understand the original structure of which these are displacements.

For the double standard in adultery goes back to the natural physical fact, so insupportable in patrilineal societies, that *pater semper incertus est*, and that therefore the only method of being *certus* is social: lock up your wives or hedge them about with equivalent taboos, lies and terrors; men could sow as many bastards as they had women but woe to the women who bore them.

This archaic inherited situation is at the back of all women's minds, and afforded me another moment of semiotic delight with Greimas' actual proposals for a narrative grammar (1970), when the same logical rectangle is used to explain a narrative sequence as 'a topological representation of the circulation of value-objects between deixes' (177, my translation) (see Fig. 9).

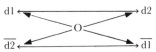

'Thus the circulation of values, interpreted as a sequence of transfers of value-objects, can follow two itineraries:

(1) $F (d1 \rightarrow O \rightarrow \overline{d1}) \longrightarrow F (\overline{d1} \rightarrow O \rightarrow d2)$
which, in the particular case of Propp's Russian tales can be interpreted: society (d1) suffers a lack, the traitor $(\overline{d1})$ ravishes the king's daughter (O) [= object] and transfers her elsewhere (d2).

(2) $F (\overline{d2}) \rightarrow O \rightarrow d2) \longrightarrow F (\overline{d2} \rightarrow O \rightarrow d1)$
which means: the hero $(\overline{d2})$ finds somewhere (d2) the king's daughter (O) and gives her back to her parents (d1).'

Fig. 9

'And if the king's daughter, settling a pillow by her head or throwing off a shawl, and turning toward the window should say, That is not it at all, that is not what I meant at all ...' (quotation from my novel *Thru*, 89–90, a narrative about narratology, where pen in cheek and cheek in pen I adapted *Prufrock* and juxtaposed it with the above passage from Greimas).

It would seem, then, that in the 'elementary structure of significance' even the king's daughter does not escape woman's fate as object of exchange, which Lévi-Strauss has shown lies at the basis of social organization (1949).

Token silence

Another good semiotic moment came when Lévi-Strauss returned to the topic ten years later (1958, trans. 1963) and wondered whether we might not achieve insight into the origin of language via the marriage-regulations that represent 'a much more crude and archaic complex' in communication. Poets, he says, are the only ones who know that words were once values as well as signs, and women are considered by the social group as 'values of the most essential kind', although we do not understand how these values became integrated into systems endowed with a significant function:

> This ambiguity [values and signs] is clearly manifested in the reactions of persons who [re 1949 analysis] have had against it the charge of 'anti-feminism', because women are referred to as objects. Of course it may be disturbing to some to have women conceived as mere parts of a meaningful system [note the sliding from 'objects' to 'parts of a meaningful system', which applies to men too, so that it all seems less sexist, although men created the system]. However, one should keep in mind that the process by which phonemes and words have lost – even though in an illusory manner – their character of value, to become reduced to pure signs, will never lead to the same results in matters concerning women [because women lost their character of value in no illusory manner?]. For words do not speak, while women do: as producers of signs, women can never be reduced to the status of symbols or tokens [So, why were they?].
>
> (1963, 61)

It is of course as woman that I have inserted the quibbling polemic – purposely confusing values and signs – into Lévi-Strauss' discourse, since he kindly allows me to speak in order not to be reduced to a token. For surely it would have been enough for Lévi-Strauss to say he was describing primitive structures (against which women have been fighting and which they therefore have to recognize), to answer the more superficial feminist objections. Instead, he gets unnecessarily tied up.

I am naturally not arguing against his descriptions of the facts in the societies studied, any more than I was denying the facts described by Greimas' structure. I am merely noting a certain relish in those facts shown by the semioticians and, here, an amusing speciousness and bad faith in the argument used in defence, which even attributes the 'ambiguity' (that is, confusion of values with signs, as in my polemic) to the reactions of those who protest, when the whole problem is that the confusion is inherent to the system, which allows the necessary circulation of women as 'essential values' to degenerate into a negotiated exchange of women as value-objects, that is, tokens, signs. And since signs *do* 'speak', if only through the 'symptom-signifier', the system was doomed from the start, or rather, had to depend for aeons on women's silence, on the repression of their signified into the unconscious.

Such women who did 'speak' their signified were usually castigated as too close to both nature and truth for comfort, in other words, as witches, and in more 'scientific' times as hysterics (see Cixous and Clément 1975) – indeed the very word *hysteria*, from *ustera*, uterus, womb, is misogynous (see Rousselle 1983, Ch. 4, 'Virginité et hystérie' for the early medical history of the word).

It is also interesting that female oracles (the prophetess or pythoness) were on the one hand reduced by legends of their origins to 'twittering birds' (Herodotus Bk 2, 1954 Penguin, 152), and on the other hand taken over, very early, by male gods, that is to say reduced to priestesses of Zeus, Apollo etc., speaking in their name, so that kings and leaders could nevertheless continue to consult them with respectability. As for the priestess of Athene at the oracle of Pedasus, she was said to grow a beard at impending disaster (Herodotus, Bk 1, 1954, 112). And did not soothsayers see the sooth they said in *entrails* of birds (no longer twittering)? Indeed, I have always found it comical – and rarely, if at all, treated, that both Judaism and Christianity (and indirectly Islam) should have as Genesis the story of woman's *scientific* curiosity, not only as to the Knowledge of Good and Evil but also, surely, to see if the great patriarchal prophecy/threat would be fulfilled, if the theory would fit the facts, for which daring, rapidly transformed into Original Sin, she was scapegoated into bearing not only children in pain (Nature) but the consequences for ever (Culture), the story in effect 'motivating' the already existing 'consequences'.

Lévi-Strauss goes on to argue that it is precisely because women are not reducible to tokens that the position of women as actually found in this system of communication between men may give us an image of the type of relationship that might have existed between human beings and their words at a very early period in the development of language:

As in the case of women, the original impulse which compelled men to exchange words must be sought for in that split representation that pertains to the symbolic function. For, since certain terms are simultaneously perceived as having a value both for the speaker and the listener, the only way to resolve this contradiction is in the exchange of complementary values, to which all social existence is reduced.

(62)

Yes, but why such an uncomplimentary deal in the 'exchange of complementary values'? for what is valorized by the system is men, not women, and even today's society is still far more cruel to unattractive women than it is to unattractive men, who can still consider the offer of marriage and name as a signal honour to be bestowed, and women still on the whole go along with that. It is as if, in the comparison with language, only the terms used by the men had any value, both the speaker and the listener in the system being men.

Lévi-Strauss adds that these speculations may be judged utopian: by utopia does he mean the possibility of research into the topic words/women as objects of exchange (a dangerous desire) or does he mean the close link between such objects as a utopian ideal? Men have peopled their heavens either with objects erotic *ad aeternam* or with sexless angels, and their utopias have never imagined much of a role for women – nor indeed for poets. Perhaps that is not perchance? Erotics is a silent art, and angels are imagined as communicating without words. Well, let's talk about women's words preventing her reduction to a token.

'Silence in woman is like speech in man'

The old comedy theme of the mute woman (*The Devil and his Dame*, Jonson's *Epicoene or The Silent Woman*, Molière's *Médecin malgré lui*, and others), whose torrent of words is let loose by marriage or love-philtre, certainly reveals a male fantasy of the dream woman as dumb. Jean-Paul Debax, in 'Et voilà pourquoi votre femme est muette' (1980) analyses this phenomenon as essentially one of power. For man to exercise his sovereignty nothing must arise as equivalent to his word (or his beating stick) that maintains her in obedience, so the male imagination constructs a mute ideal, a 'quality' in woman, which can be expressed as a wish or regret (Sganarelle, *MML*.II.iii), or as dream, or as an actual virtue (*The Devil and his Dame*), or else the fantasy becomes actual situation in the theatre (my translation):

To reduce woman to silence is to reduce her to powerlessness; that is how the masculine will to castrate operates [Debax' note: It operates literally in *Titus Andronicus*: Lavinia's tongue is cut off, as are her hands, a symbol of total powerlessness]. Thus – perhaps because of this – women's will to revolt necessarily passes through the use of language, the tongue [*la langue*]. Language, the tongue, is woman's weapon.

(Debax, 33)

Debax reminds us that the letting loose or 'liberation' of the tongue always occurs at the moment of marriage:

The young girl's muteness figures her virginity, her ignorance of sexual commerce, or her fear before the act. Marriage – or union – reveals her sex (masculine viewpoint). According to the dominant masculine theory her self-affirmation should stop there, and she should acquire speech only to abandon it at once. If she continues to make herself heard she becomes a 'shrew', she becomes guilty of 'amazonian impudence' [*Epicoene*]. Marian [in *Devil*] challenges this ["Tis better to be a shrew, Sir, than a sheep']. This defiance is the response to intolerance; for man only one authority is conceivable, his own, one sex, his own, one discourse therefore, his own. Sir John Daw [in *Epicoene*] gives the credo of this anti-feminism in doggerel verses one must quote to appreciate their full flavour:

Silence in woman, is like speech in man
  Deny't who can
  Nor is't a tale
That female vice should be a virtue male.
Or masculine vice a female virtue be.

Thus the trick is played: a difference of behaviour, of sex, of appearance etc., is interpreted in terms of an opposition of contraries: if man is strong woman is weak; if man speaks woman must be silent. So was created an image of woman in negativity to that which man was forging of himself. We are at the heart of the dynamism of racism.

(34–5)

We are also back with Greimas and his contraries / contradictories: before union, speech (male) vs. silence (female): after union, non-silence (male) vs. non-speech (female) – a clear displacement of the original double standard on adultery, which had its reasons. Certainly the obverse image to that of the silent woman is that of the nagging wife, the scold, later the *castratrice* who must be fled, silenced or abolished somehow, just as the 'lying' or awkwardly truth-telling poets must be excluded from the Republic. Nobody asks, of course, why a sweet silent woman should become a scold at all through marriage.

It is no doubt the mootest of moot points whether women are what they are because of men or vice versa. The 'nag' image is usually post-marriage and therefore conceived, unconsciously, as a result of it. Perhaps however it is also calqued on the mother, who teaches men language in the first place and scolds them in words, though girls, who have the same experience, do not seem to have that calque in their attitude to language.

George Steiner (who would hate to be considered a semiotician)
takes up the problem from a more subtle angle in the first chapter
of *After Babel* (1975), in which he contends that all communication
is translation, both diachronically (language changing much faster
than we feel it changing) and synchronically. And as to the latter,
he marvellously discusses the different 'languages' of represser/
repressed (classes, adults/children, men/women). On men/women
he reminds us that 'the headings of mutual reproach are immemorial.
In every known culture, men have accused women of being garrulous'
(41), then he asks if they are, in fact, 'more spendthrift of language'
(which is a nice way of putting it). He tries, gallantly, to relate
men's undoubted conviction of this to ancient perceptions of sexual
contrast:

> The alleged outpouring of women's speech, the rank flow of words, may be a symbolic
> restatement of men's apprehensive, often ignorant awareness of the menstrual cycle.
> In masculine satire, the obscure currents and secretions of woman's physiology are
> an obsessive theme.
>
> (42)

But here too there seems to be an unconscious double standard,
not commented on, men's secretion (less mysterious, less secret)
being super-valorized. It is interesting that Steiner deals with the
cognate idea – men's professions of delight in sweet and low registers,
and of course in silence – *after* their terror of the word-torrent, as
if the fantasy of silence were something to dream of in vain as against
the awful reality, instead of, as is more likely, something imposed
by man in the first place, and found, to his delight, in the young
girl brought up to that end. Obviously Steiner knows this:

> The motif of the woman or maiden who says very little, in whom silence is a symbolic
> counterpart to chasteness and sacrificial grace, lends a unique pathos to the Antigone
> of *Oedipus at Colonus* or Euripides' Alcestis. A male god has cruelly possessed Cassandra
> and the speech that pours out of her is his; she seems almost remote from it, broken.
> Though addressed to an inanimate form, Keats' 'unravished bride of quietness' pre-
> cisely renders the antique association of feminine quality and sparseness of speech.
> These values crystallize in Coriolanus' salute to Virgilia: 'My gracious silence, hail!'
> The line is magical in its music and suggestion, but also in its dramatic shrewdness.
> Shakespeare precisely conveys the idiom of the man, of a personage brimful with
> overweening masculinity. No woman would so greet her beloved.
>
> (42–3)

But Steiner also gives voice to women (inevitably via men). Women,
he says, have not been slow to answer, and Elvira's

Non lo lasciar piu dir;

Il labbro è mentitor . . .

has rung down through history. Men are deceivers ever. They use speech to conceal the true, sexually aggressive function of their lips and tongues. Women know the change in a man's voice, the crowding of cadence, the heightened fluency triggered off by sexual excitement. They have also heard, perennially, how a man's speech flattens, how its intonations dull after orgasm. In feminine speech-mythology, man is not only an erotic liar; he is an incorrigible braggart. Women's lore and secret mock record him as an eternal *miles gloriosus*, a self-trumpeter who uses language to cover up his sexual or professional fiascos, his infantile needs, his inability to withstand physical pain.

(43)

He tells us that of course the grounds of differentiation are largely economic and social, that 'sexual speech variations evolve because of the division of labour, the fabric of obligation and leisure within the same community is different for men and for women' (in some languages women even have a slightly different grammar and vocabulary), and women are excluded from most male forms of communication. And he tells us that two great artists in particular, Racine and Mozart, had the extraordinary ability to render that crisis in sexual identity and communication between men and women (44–5). The tone-discrimination (between Susanna and the Countess in *Figaro*) 'is made even more precise and more dramatically different from that which characterizes male voices by the "bisexual" role of Cherubino. The Count's page is a graphic example of Lévi-Strauss' contention that women and words are analogous media of exchange in the grammar of social life'. Stendhal, Steiner tells us, carefully studied Mozart's operas and this can be seen in 'the depth and fairness of his treatment of the speech-worlds of men and women in Fabrice and la Sanseverina in *La Chartreuse de Parme*'. Today, he adds, when there is sexual frankness as never before, such fairness is, paradoxically, rarer. It is not as 'translators' that women novelists and poets excel, but as 'declaimers of their own, long-stifled tongue' (44–5).

'Values of the most essential kind'

Curiously, although agreeing with Lévi-Strauss, whilst admitting elsewhere that 'anthropology – itself a term charged with masculine assumptions – distorts evidence as does the white traveller's edge of power over his native informant' (44), Steiner epigraphs his book with an interesting quotation from Heidegger:

Man acts as if he were the shaper and master of language, while it is language which remains mistress of man. When this relation of dominance is inverted, man succumbs to strange contrivances. Language then becomes a means of expression. Where it is expression, language can degenerate to mere impression (to mere print). Even where the use of language is no more than this, it is good that one should still be careful in one's speech. But this alone can never extricate us from the reversal, from the confusion of the true relation of dominance as between language and man. For in fact it is language that speaks [. . .]

('. . . Dichterisch Wohnet der Mensch . . .')

It would seem, then, that man thinks he shapes and masters and exchanges words and women, while all the time language is shaping and mastering him (and women), so that his exchanges and controls and double standards must be as mutable as language itself. Perhaps that is what man cannot stand, to think he is in control and can shape his dream, and to discover that he cannot, that his dream 'speaks' otherwise and controls him? Perhaps (more playfully), women so took it out of men in those mythical Mother-Goddess days (mythical as 'Old Religion' but also because ethnologists apparently now agree that matriarchy never existed – or is that another male plot?), that men in their phylogenetic system never forgave them. And are we now, alas, in for an equally long period during which women, in their post-consciousness torrent of abuse, will never forgive men for the use men made of them since those mythical times? there is no answer to that question except time. Meanwhile, perhaps we should be grateful for being told that, like words, we have always been considered as values 'of the most essential kind'. As for instance in:

I am not surprised that with so many people and so many beasts the rivers sometimes failed to provide enough water: what does surprise me is that the food never gave out, for I reckon that if no more than a quart of meal was the total ration for one man, the total daily consumption would have amounted to 110,340 bushels – and this without counting what was consumed by women, eunuchs, pack-animals and dogs.

(Herodotus, 1954, 507)

Well at least food was consumed. After all, women and pack-animals are useful and must be kept alive. Ah, men will say, but those were just testicle-emptiers, *le repos du guerrier*, we do not treat our lady-loves like that. Of course. The blanket bodily transfer of women as value-objects in complex social systems has a highly privileged status compared to that of garbage-cans accompanying armies. But it remained a commerce. The social exchange of women was for property, pleasure, release, *and* procreation, which had to be patri-

lineal. Similarly other developments, towards more grace in the winning, on the one hand, and harder bargaining in the buying (higher
dowries) on the other, are mere displacements and refinements. And
there are displacements within such displacements, as systems of
exchange became more sophisticated or simply more conscious: winning a woman through prowess or with six camels easily becomes
winning her through prowess with money or prowess with words,
both objects of exchange. But women's amorous discourse was traditionally silent (gestures, looks, tricks and 'wiles'), or else like
Chaucer's Criseyde needed a Pandarus, while Shakespeare's highly
articulate, witty and verbally autonomous girls in love are disguised
as boys.

Today we seem to have an almost complete inversion in the ideal
of the strong silent man of films and the free forward girl, but it
could be superficial, a fashion merely inverting a dead code, and
women well-versed in types of amorous discourse often get the
impression that a man brings out this or that type as he might bring
out a wallet, and men versed in women's wiles must have the same
impression, but the other way round, of a contract passed. (I am
talking of dominant cultural images, not individual cases, which
can vary in subtle ways.) Nevertheless, any reticence or objections
a woman might voice are still silenced, not only as before, by the
power of a man's desire as expressed in his discourse (amounting
to 'I want it so you must want it'), but, supreme irony of sexual
freedom, by accusations of prudery, frigidity, repression, abnorma-
lity, anything rather than acceptance that he is not desired: where
'virtue' was once sought for and praised, as a token in the language
of negotiation, men have learnt to use the very freedom won by
woman to replace that token. Then, having 'won' her, and assuming
he wants to 'keep' her, he still tends towards two types of possessive
behaviour: the Pygmalion urge (to form her to his own desires, and
ceasing his love should she herself take wing), or the demolition
enterprise (using his very love to prevent her, in innumerable ways
and whatever his verbal assurances, from achieving any kind of self-
expression). Should she protest, he then withdraws into silence,
which at this point becomes his strength, a wall against which women
beat in vain ('making a scene'). That is surely when she becomes
a frustrated scold. Women's silence, traditionally, is initial, first out
of fear, then out of guilt; man's silence is final, first out of guilt,
then out of fear. A perfect chiasmus, traces of which undoubtedly
remain in most sexual situations today, starting as game, ending

as war. Some endure them as war others learn to play them as game throughout.

And the game is also a language-game, in both signs and tokens, *pace* Lévi-Strauss. In almost every sentence we betray the deep-rootedness of those 'elementary structures of significance'. I remember when Umberto Eco, in a seminar at New York University in 1976, gave an example of coreferential ambiguity:

> (1) John sleeps with his wife twice a week, so does Bill.

I pointed out that the ambiguity was socially determined rather than syntactic, and that there was no ambiguity at all in:

> (2) John mows his lawn once a week, so does Bill.
> (3) John washes the dishes on Sundays, so does Bill.
> (4) John takes his son to school twice a week, so does Bill.

And so on. Umberto Eco was delighted, put the whole problem in his book (1979, Intro.), and quoted me in a footnote, for which I thank him. Interestingly however, he invents a completely new sentence:

> Christine Brooke-Rose (personal communication) suggests that no ambiguity would arise were the sentence /Charles walks his dog twice a day. So does John/. It means that in (7) [(1) here] one of the first moves of the interpreter is to evoke the intertextual frame 'adulterine triangle', since thousands of texts record such a situation. On the contrary, no text (as far as one remembers) records the story of a morbid passion of two men for the same dog, and it is enough to activate the common frame 'walking *his own* pet'. Thus no ambiguity arises.
>
> (41, n. 12)

Ye-es. I find it odd, all the same, that this charming semiotician should alter my several examples for the one possibility in which man – and woman for that matter – is particularly possessive, namely a dog, a pet, a substitute (dumb) companion. It is surely not a question of 'morbid passion' for the *same* dog (though relations to pets *can* be morbid), or even of passion *tout court*, but of a dog as toy, as object-alive, like a woman. And precisely because of that I for one *can* read the sentence as ambiguous, not in the sense of passion or rivalry, as in adultery, but in the sense of a possession shared between friends, as in wife-sharing (where often no passion is involved).

All the sentences are in fact intertextually sensitive, but not with the same intertext: in (2) a lawn is a proud possession for show, but mowing is a chore, so Bill would hardly share it regularly (and in any case a lawn need only be mown once a week); in (3) washing dishes is also a chore. Both are cliché situations, objects of jokes, and clear as such. In (4) a son is not a possession, an acquisition, which can be shared as a relationship. And in all three the frequency adverbial alone clears the ambiguity pragmatically, which it does not in (1), nor (really) in Eco's dog-sentence.

I am of course quibbling again, to take up my prerogative as speaking value not token. Perhaps the real counter-example should have been:

(5) Sue sleeps with her husband twice a week, so does Mary.

Is it ambiguous? As ambiguous as (1)? Or not *quite*? And if it is, would it have been so in the nineteenth century, as surely (1) would have been? Or perhaps the test-sentence should have been:

(6) The Sultana plays with her eunuch twice a week, and so does the princess Fatima.

Or even:

(7) The sergeant beats his pack-animal every five minutes, and so does the corporal.

A corporal ending indeed. At any rate, I cannot help wondering whether semiotics is not a peculiarly reactionary discipline, and semioticians unconsciously nostalgic for nice, deep, ancient, phallo-cratic, elementary structures of significance.

17

Illiterations

To be an 'experimental' woman writer is one thing. To write about the situation of 'experimental' women writers is quite another. This will not be a description of specific writers, least of all myself, and their difficulties, but a general, lightly deconstructing speculation on ancient prejudices – and what are prejudices but ill iterations of untenable positions in the face of change? And what can protests against these be but themselves ill iterations?

To be an 'experimental' woman writer

Three words. Three difficulties. *To be a woman*: vast and vastly written up. *To be a woman writer*: narrower but proportionately ditto.

Assuming that most of the problems described by Elaine Showalter (1971) – and many other studies since – for nineteenth-century writers have disappeared, and that the sexes, like classes and races, have on the face of it the same chances, there are nevertheless different types and levels of critical attention, on a sliding-scale that can be subsumed in the general opposition *canonical/non-canonical* (or ephemeral). And as Kermode (1979) has shown, only the canonical is deemed worthy of serious attention. Inside the canon interpretation multiplies wildly, while outside it a text does not exist. I would add, the pressure of the canonic is such that the self-allotted task of interpretation is to transform into qualities elements which, in a non-canonic work, would be considered as serious flaws, and this process of canonization has been more consistently applied to masculine works than to the few feminine entries.

In theory the canonic/non-canonic opposition applies to all writers and thus cuts across the sexual or any other opposition. In practice a canon is very much a masculine notion, a priesthood (not to be polluted), a club, a sacred male preserve; and yet a second matrix, as Norman O. Brown said of clubs and societies (1966). Or a heroic father–son struggle in Harold Bloom's terms. But a body, a corpus, something owned. And not only a male preserve but that of a privileged caste. For women are only one part, however large, of an originally much larger exclusion: that of barbarians and slaves, or, later, other races and the 'lower' classes from peasants to modern workers, who were long considered incapable of any art worth the dignity of attention, indeed of any education towards it or towards anything else, even as late as Hardy's Jude.

Nevertheless male outsiders enter the canon more easily than women do, for reasons much deeper than those of caste. At the individual level, white males of outside origin have long been able to enter a canon, chiefly because of a long (canonic) tradition of the poet as visiting rhapsode, travelling minstrel, outsider. That is how a canon is formed and slowly altered. At the collective level, the canon also absorbs. In *The Secular Scripture* (1975) Northrop Frye speaks of the central 'mythic' tradition of any one culture (in our case the Graeco-Judeo-Christian), which excludes the parallel (popular) or 'secular' art forms, until in moments of exhaustion it has to turn to them for replenishment and renewed vigour (for instance today, SF, comics and so on).

But women's writing does not seem ever to have that role of 'tonic' or outside remedy, nor does it today (cp. Ch. 15). On the contrary, it has also turned to popular forms for replenishment, just as male writing has (e.g. Kathy Acker and her 'punk' style, or, for oral traditions, some 'ethnic' writers such as Toni Morrison, Maxine Hong Kingsley, Leslie Marmon Silko and others). Even with the 're-reading' by the feminists of a whole new area of women's literature previously relegated to oblivion (see Kolodny 1975), it is still possible for Nancy K. Miller to write: 'This new mapping of a parallel geography does not, of course, resolve the oxymoron of marginality: how is it that women, a statistical majority in our culture, perform as a "literary subculture"'? (1981, 38). And a sub-culture, I would add, *without* the fashionable status and envigorating role described above.

Traditionally then, this notion of a canon, of a central tradition around the central myth, which is essentially male, priestly and caste-bound, underlies types and levels of critical attention, so that despite the various and increasing waves of emancipation since the nineteenth century, certain relics remain, ill iterations in the unconscious of society.

It is thus one thing for a woman to have only the usual or no difficulties in getting published today, in acquiring a fashionable

success or at least getting well-known enough to continue being published, but quite another thing for a woman writer, with equivalent
speed and given the usual ups and downs, to enter a canon. One
need only mention names like (in order of difficulty) Barbara Pym,
Jean Rhys, Christina Stead, Ivy Compton-Burnett, Isak Dinesen,
Nathalie Sarraute, who all received the accolade of serious recognition late in life. Or Kate Chopin or Edith Wharton, both dismissed
as imitators, who are now being 're-read' and understood long after
their death.

Or Gertrude Stein, or Djuna Barnes, who are only now receiving
serious critical attention. For of course it is yet a third thing for
a woman to be genuinely welcomed and attended to as an 'experimental' writer. This is caught up in a second opposition, that of tradition
and innovation. But let us first go back to a more deeply buried
concept.

To be a creator

Barely a decade ago, Anthony Burgess wrote an article in the *Observer*
('Grunts from a Sexist Pig', 21/6/81), in reaction to receiving a Pink
Pig Award from the Women in Publishing Group 'for outstanding
contributions to sexism'. The article is mildly amusing and even
occasionally sensible and fair, until Burgess brings out – in all seriousness – the hoary old chestnut that

Women have never been denied professional musical instruction – indeed, they used
to be encouraged to have it – but they have not yet produced a Mozart or a Beethoven.
I am told by feminists that all this will change some day, when women have learned
how to create like *women* composers, a thing men have prevented their doing in the
past.

He says this is nonsense and would be denied by composers like
Thea Musgrave and the late Dame Ethel Smyth [whom, however,
one rarely hears spoken of seriously]. Now Burgess may well be
right to poke fun at the notion of composing as *women* composers
(see Ch. 15). But to hear the ancient argument about Mozart and
Beethoven (or Michelangelo or Shakespeare) repeated so late in the
day is discouraging. He goes on: 'Freud, bewildered, said "What
does a woman *want*?"' and insists that this question has not been
answered, despite the writings of (here a long list, with amazing
omissions, of feminist names from Kate Millett and Simone de
Beauvoir all the way back to Mary Wollstonecraft 'and the great
Virginia herself').

That such unimaginative assertions can still be made after some twenty years of deconstruction (of Freud among others) and other investigations, would alone justify my title. All this has been much researched and written about. It takes centuries, generations of artists being allowed and expected to practise their art and to show themselves practising it, rather than just looking pretty at a spinet as an asset on the marriage market (composing being for brother Wolfgang), for a Mozart or a Michelangelo or a Shakespeare to emerge. Even today the prejudice against women painters, sculptors and composers runs deeper than that against women writers, for precisely the reasons described by 'the great Virginia herself'.

But where do these judgments come from if not from the canon? Jane Austen is perfect, but of course she is not Shakespeare. Nor for that matter is Thackeray or Trollope. What does it mean? Burgess himself is very careful to welcome the republication by Virago of 'the masterpiece of Dorothy Richardson'. Does he really mean that? Or is it really 'only' a mistresspiece? In which case I would *personally* agree with him but would have the courage to say so: there are secondary works of historical interest in both masculine and feminine writing. And indeed his evaluation is wholly in relation to Joyce (though it is already much to recognize her as 'anticipating' him), and used more to defend himself than to praise her:

> In considering [...] the masterpiece of Dorothy Richardson I did not say that here we had a great work of women's literature, but rather here we had a great work which anticipated some of the innovations of James Joyce. I should have stressed that this was a work by a woman, but the womanly aspect of the thing didn't seem to me to be important. I believe that the sex of an author is irrelevant because any good writer contains both sexes.

I leave aside the question of whether innovations picked up by a later writer in themselves make a work less (to me) self-indulgent and tedious (or even whether the later writer might not also have been so considered had he not been a man) – since these are questions of literary evaluation which do not belong here. Burgess certainly wants to soften the enemy by calling Richardson's novel a 'masterpiece', but at once must anger one sect at least by his 'androgynous-great-mind' argument. An impeccable stance on the face of it – and indeed it has been mine in this book, but it is not that of the out-and-out feminist (see Ch. 15). It goes back to Coleridge, and of course to 'the great Virginia herself' (Woolf 1929, Ch. 6), who however adds:

Coleridge certainly did not mean, when he said that a great mind is androgynous, that it is a mind that has any special sympathy with women; a mind that takes up their cause or devotes itself to their interpretation.

The androgynous-great-mind stance is what some feminists con-demn as 'humanist' rather than 'feminist', while for others it is the only possible option, providing it is understood properly and not used as a pig-snout mask.

Meanwhile, back to the canon: would anyone now seriously dis-pute the major status of writers such as Jane Austen, George Eliot, or Emily Dickinson? Probably not. For of course, they are safely dead.

One useful analogy: the nineteenth-century gentleman who would live by the classics (in dead languages), or sometimes study ancient Arabic or Persian or Hebrew, yet show no interest in contemporary equivalents – indeed there couldn't *be* equivalents, oral or written – and would despise any living representative of those cultures as wogs and Jews.

Another useful analogy: the performing arts, where the artists are necessarily alive, but die with their art (or did before the modern media). Thus men did not feel threatened in their real creativity, that is to say, in their desired posterity, and for this reason the per-forming arts (the living word) have often been considered as vaguely inferior to the creative arts. For although the *work* involved is as great for performing artists, they merely transmit, perform, interpret, the verbal artefact that has been 'created' by the 'real' artist, who alone possesses that mysterious quality called *genius*.[1]

The performing arts require ability, talent, hard work, but genius? No! The contradiction is found already in Plato, who devalues the mere performance and interpretation of the rhapsode in the *Ion,* yet elsewhere devalues writing as against the voice (see 'La Pharmacie de Platon', Derrida 1972a).

The work/genius opposition goes back at least to Longinus, in

---

[1] It is not by chance that women were admitted into the performing arts, late but much earlier than in the creative ones (and for that reason were treated as *demi-mondaines*, belonging not to *the* world but to a half-world use by men). Nor is it by chance that even today one can still hear the opinion, unwittingly echoed from the Thirties, and from the same type of man, of the same generation as those who say there have been no women Mozarts, that Jews are brilliant performers and interpreters but not creators.

what is basically a nature/culture opposition (*On the Sublime*, Ch. 2). The privilege is on genius (nature), with work (culture) as both a curb and a spur.

Genius is the tutelary god or demon that makes the artist. The poet may have his Muse (pre-Hellenic *Montya,* from Indo-European *mon-, men-, mn-* to remember), daughter of Zeus (supreme power) and Mnemosyne (Memory), but she merely presides or inspires, that is, jogs, or, as Beauty, she is both his inspiration and his aim. This notion goes back to an oral tradition, since writing is supposed to kill Memory, but later poets steeped in the classics never seemed to notice the contradiction and went on invoking the Muse, possibly as a dead Letter, and in fact representing the bisexual nature of creativity.

The really mysterious creative force, however, is genius: direct contact with the gods. Plato called it divine madness, Longinus called it ecstasy, the eighteenth-century Genius, the Romantics Imagination but also Genius. And whatever the name it belongs to man.

Gender, genre, genius, genesis: all come from the same Indo-European root **gen* to beget / to be born. Only man begets, woman bears and travails: genius vs. work.

Burgess turns this into a back-handed compliment: 'I believe that artistic creativity is a male surrogate for biological activity, and that if women do so well in literature it may be that literature is, as Virginia Woolf said, closer to gossip than to art'.

A male surrogate for *bearing*? Or for *begetting*? Both are biological activities. But the metaphors of literary paternity are very curious indeed. On the one hand, 'the text's author is a father, a progenitor, an aesthetic patriarch whose pen is an instrument of generative power like his penis' (Gilbert & Gubar 1979, 7). On the other, genius belongs to men in a strangely passive role. He is possessed. He is pregnant. The metaphor for literary works as begotten children and their production as childbirth is older than the pen/penis begetting metaphor. As Elaine Showalter (1981, 188) reminds us (quoting Gilbert & Gubar, Nina Auerbach, Tillotson, Ellmann), the eighteenth and nineteenth centuries are full of gestation metaphors, and Joyce echoes them.

In fact they go back to Plato, for whom the speeches of Phaedrus and Lysias are their sons (never of course their daughters), indeed any speech (logos) was a son.

But a quaint, motherless son. For what gets occulted in all this is the woman, just as the real producer, the worker or small farmer, gets occulted by the rise of capitalism.[2]

In the *Symposium* it is Diotima, the only woman allowed into the dialogues but *in absentia*, who has given Socrates the apparently extraordinary revelation that the purpose of love is procreation *in beauty*. For what purpose? For immortality (206e, 207a). And she rapidly moves on (in the account of Socrates) to those who have fecundity of *soul* (men, 209a), who will look for the beautiful object (a boy) and educate him, and at whose contact they will give birth to that with which they have long been pregnant (209c).

Why does Plato put this nonsense into a woman's mouth, via Socrates? Precisely because she is a woman and knows about 'real' childbirth, the literal half of the metaphor, which gives such a solid, physical basis to her figurative sliding, that is, to the meaning Plato wants. The fecund male, though procreating through 'contact' with Beauty (boy or Muse) is already long pregnant, quite independently of this contact. He has been touched with divine madness, with genius. The Muse (or boy), contrary to some feminist analysis, is never a mother in this, but a memory-jogger or an 'ideal'. In practice she is merely a titillating hand-maiden, a stage on the Platonic ladder, at most a gorgeous midwife.

Thus in the earliest texts that echo down and influence the European literary tradition, even to modern times (e.g. Pound), men have simply appropriated childbirth as a painless metaphor, a *bearing* over, a mater phor artistic creation. A Muse may or may not preside, but genius begets *and* travails. The woman in this does neither. Indeed when women did start writing, the ancient metaphor was all too easily reversed: her books were produced *instead of* children, as surrogates, in the absence of the all-essential male.

For men have always had it both ways: the begetting *and* the travail (the travail which, as 'work' belongs to culture, but which as bearing and 'labour' belongs to nature); the genius *and* the work (the genius which is itself both passive possession and authoritative production), the penis *and* the womb. Man has in fact appropriated,

---

[2] This is only incidental to my argument. Cp. Derrida (1972a, 91–5) who reminds us that the father is 'also: a *chief*, a *capital*, and a *possession* [*un bien*]. *Pater* in Greek means all that' (my translation, his italics). Rabaté (1986, 191) takes this up with reference to Pound: 'The questions of generation and usury appear from the start as inextricably confused, for interest is the "offspring", the "son" of money.'

to represent his relation to truth or God, both aspects of woman's role in relation to man: the being made fecund and the travail. This in addition to begetting. It is his *supplément*: he, as God, begets a work upon himself; he, as poet, is made fecund and labours. But on a safe, metaphoric level: he would never actually die in childbirth.

How perfectly logical, then, in this long tradition, that women should have no role at all in artistic creativity. The double connotation of 'womb' as both birth and death has been split, men appropriating the birth process and leaving its death connotations to the woman. Just as writing is death, the outside *pharmakon*. Obviously then, woman cannot be included in that 'tonic' aspect of 'secular' culture to which the central male tradition now and again turns when exhausted. All she can be is beautiful, and hence not understand beauty.[3]

Can women then, traditionally, never be in that 'masculine' role of creativity, have they ever been supposed to have that privileged, direct contact with the gods, that goes by the name of genius?

The only institutional example seems to be the ancient prophetesses, who might be supposed to be directly inspired from the gods in their oracles. Yet they uttered their 'sibylline' oracles uncomprehendingly in the name of the male gods (see Ch. 16, p. 241). They merely transmitted blindly, they were the hidden spokespersons for the gods, and rulers consulted Apollo or Zeus, not his priestess.

Woman cannot have direct access to truth, or to the divine madness of the poet, and *do* something rational with it: *her* divine madness is from the devil, she is a witch, or its modern equivalent, a hysteric.[4]

If as in the rare case of the sibyl she *has* access to the 'fecundation', she is automatically deprived of the understanding necessary for the 'travail'. The Church's present resistance to women priests is

---

[3] In *Mademoiselle de Maupin* (1835), by Théophile Gautier, the beauty-seeking d'Albert writes to his friend that women understand no more of poetry than do cabbages or roses, which is natural since they are themselves poetry: the flute cannot understand the tune played on it (1966, 206). And Mademoiselle de Maupin herself (disguised as a man) obligingly echoes these views. Women (she writes to *her* friend) are usually deprived of the feeling for beauty, because they possess beauty, and since self-knowledge is the most difficult knowledge they naturally understand nothing of it (301–2, my rendering). Cp. Pound to H.D.: 'You are a poem though your poem's naught' (H.D., *End to Torment* 1979, 12).

[4] Cp. Hawthorne to his publisher, praising a contemporary woman 'domestic' writer, Fanny Fern, author of *Ruth Hall*: 'The woman writes as if the devil was in her; and that is the only condition under which a woman ever writes anything worth reading. Generally women write as emasculated men ... ' (Ticknor 1913: 141–2, quoted by Voloshin 1976).

no different, whatever the specious (canonic) arguments given, such as lack of biblical authority or inversely patristic authority against: *taceat mulier in ecclesia.* The true reason is the same time-honoured, self-assigned prerogative: the divine and metaphoric power of producing one thing out of another thing through the word is deeply felt as a male power. The priest, who with the Holy Spirit produces Christ the Body (the Logos), parallels the poet, who with his genius begets and labours to produce not only metaphors (Aristotle: a sign of genius) but motherless sons. Interestingly, the resistance to women priests corresponds exactly to the varying versions of transubstantiation from full metaphor (the bread *is* the Body) to a mere symbol: the Roman Catholic Church says no, never; the Anglican is in agonized compromise, the Lutheran and other Protestant Churches have mostly accepted.

It is thus almost normal, if such a contorted logic can be considered 'normal', that beneath an apparent general acceptance and praise of women in literature and the arts, there should still lie in men's unconscious, and therefore in that of society the deep phallocratic fear of women as memory, as birth, as death, of writing as the death of memory, and hence as birth and death, leading to the total occultation of women from the writing process and the resulting but equally deep conviction that women cannot be 'great' artists of 'genius' or even serious 'creators' with a possible posterity. As men can. As a few exceptional women have been, but they were influenced by men and they are dead, their posterity has been accommodated, it is not a new and threatening future posterity. Moreover, women writers can only write disguised autobiography, that is, 'life', but consigned to death because (a) not male life and (b) not 'creative'.[5]

And yet, in artistic creation, by anyone whatever and given the necessary initial conditions, life and death are shared by all, and the begetting is also the travail and vice versa.

---

[5] See Kolodny 1975, 77, even on a successful feminist author, about reviewers and TV hosts insisting that Erica Jong reveal the 'autobiographical underpinnings' of her novel *Fear of Flying*, so that, 'by attributing its narrative to autobiophy, the inherently sexist view might be maintained that women's productions are attributable to something less than fully conscious artistic invention'. The observation is just, and men who use autobiography are seldom so plagued, or are tacitly assumed to have 'transmuted' it. A few pages later, however, Kolodny seems to contradict herself when she insists on feminine experience: 'To cavalierly label Kate Chopin's Edna as immoral, or Joan Didion's Maria as mad [...] is to ignore the possibility that the *worlds they inhabit may in fact be real, or true*, and for them the only worlds available' [italics mine]. Feminists cannot have it both ways, or at least Kolodny should define 'real' and 'true'.

To be an experimental writer

I am aware that in this return to my main topic, the sudden juxtaposition of 'experimental' writing with 'genius' may seem to be equating
the two. In fact I don't even like the word 'genius' and have only
been using it to point up a deep-lying contradiction. Clearly there
can be trivial as well as truly innovative experiment, just as there
can be trivial as well as important writing in wholly familiar forms.
I shall not here define Greatness, or the Sublime, or Imagination,
or Literature. But I should perhaps try to define 'experiment'.

I have so far put the word in quotes, because it seems to mean
so many different things. What is 'experimental' art, or an 'experimental' novel? Is it a *genre*?

People often talk as if it were, although most experiment either
widens the concept of a particular genre or explodes the notion of
genre altogether. Yet a writer, or a group of writers, is put into
that category, as if it were equivalent to Science Fiction, the Fantastic,
Romance, Realism.

For Zola, the father of a certain kind of Realism, the 'experimental
novel' meant a novel which had been carefully researched and backed
by 'experiment' in the scientific sense of verification (of slaughterhouses, mines, peasant life), or what we now call documentary. The
narrative voice had to be objective, impartial, 'scientific'. In other
words, a new kind, or school, of Realism, called Naturalism, almost
a new genre.

For Hardy it meant, as we saw (according to Boumelha's interesting readings), experiment away from Naturalism, the 'search for
a form' revolving round the problem of female characters, provoking
'an uncertainty of genre and tone which unsettles the fictional modes
in a disturbing and often provocative manner'. But the 'experiment'
in question turns out to be (for me) chiefly Hardy's odd but by
no means novel manipulation of viewpoint and a curious 'blend'
of traditional forms for different purposes (see Ch. 7). If this is 'experimental', then every writer who develops his art is experimental, and
there is indeed a sense in which every writer is. But at least Boumelha
is genuinely concerned with formal experiments as they are related
to the themes of the 'New Woman' fiction of the nineties. Today,
on the other hand, the word 'experimental' is often used by feminists
to designate new feminist *themes*, that come out of feminine 'experience' (as opposed to 'experience' of mines and slaughterhouses),
whether or not these create new modes or structures.

Conversely, in the Formalist and then the Structuralist periods, the underlying opposition was often felt to be Realism *versus* Experiment, that is, a complete reversal, with the privilege of seriousness on the 'experimental' side, since the presuppositions of Realism were being thoroughly requestioned. It is often forgotten that the *nouveau roman*, when it burst out in the fifties *against* the traditional realistic novel, first acquired the label *nouveau réalisme*, and was linked to phenomenology, just as earlier literary 'revolutions' had been made in the name of a greater realism (see Ch. 14). Only later did it come to be seen as, and further developed into, a much more complex poetics, linked to 'postmodernism', but this was because of its radical changes in the *form* of the novel.

So 'experiment', although part of the tradition/innovation opposition, was caught up in that of realism/formalism – which itself had meant different things from Hegel on: for Hegel (and for the Marxists after him) 'formalist' meant superficial (Preface to *Phenomenology of Mind*), but for the Russian Formalists (much condemned by the Soviet regime at the time) it meant rigorous attention to literary structures and conventions, in other words, poetics. Thus 'experiment' is often regarded as 'merely' formal, tinkering with technique (conceived quite logically as something external in just the way Plato considered writing as external), tinkering with the signifier irrespective of the signified, the 'content', the 'truth', the 'real', and other such idealist concepts; the implication being that the real exists independently of our systems of looking at it, and even that such tinkering is not accompanied by any valid 'content' at all, let alone 'value'. Baudelaire was complaining of this already in 1861 in his essay on Gautier.[6]

Years ago (1956) Nathalie Sarraute reversed the realist/formalist opposition and said that the true realists were those who look so hard at reality that they see it in a new way and so have to work equally hard to invent new forms to capture that new reality, whereas the formalists were the diluters, who come along afterwards and take these now more familiar forms, pouring into them the familiarized reality anyone can see. Sarraute's reversal in a way goes back to Hegel (formalism as superficial), for it calls the imitators formalists and the innovators realists. But such a reversal, although expressed

---

[6] 'Among the innumerable prejudices of which France is so proud is the common notion, naturally found heading the precepts of vulgar criticism, namely that a work which is *too well* written *must* be lacking in feeling' ([1868] 1921, 266, my translation and italics).

in terms of an older dispensation (forms to capture a pre-existing reality), is basically sound, for it insists on the link between innovation and a completely different way of looking, which is after all another way of defining genius, for example in science. Today one would push it much further and say, not that new ways of looking necessitate new forms, but that experiment with new forms produces new ways of looking, produces, in fact, the very story (or 'reality' or 'truth') that it is supposed to reproduce, or, to put it in deconstructive terms, repeats an absent story (see Brooks 1977, Hillis Miller 1976, Chase 1979, Culler 1980).

Both aspects of the opposition, whichever way one takes it, are as necessary to the continuity of art as they are to that of life. Both occur in all art forms across the spectrum of genres and subgenres, both can be practised and achieved by men and women of all origins. And the prejudice against the unfamiliar affects all who experiment.

To be an experimental woman writer

Nevertheless women writers, not safely dead, who at any one living moment are trying to 'look in new ways' or 'reread' and therefore rewrite their world, are rarely treated on the same level of seriousness as their male counterparts. They can get published, they can even get good reviews. But they will be more easily forgotten between books and mysteriously absent from general situation surveys or critical books about contemporary literature, even about contemporary 'experimental' (or, for now, 'postmodern') novels. They will not ultimately be taken up by the more attentive critics. Even 'the great Virginia herself', who had the best possible environment in the Bloomsbury Group to be so taken up, and her own publishing firm, who was called a 'genius' by her husband and friends, not only became ill with agony over the reception of every book by the then predominantly male literary scene, but was not fully and widely appreciated until well after her death. And she is the 'best' case, the token case. Similarly Nathalie Sarraute, another token case, was nearly sixty years old when she won recognition, at the time of the *nouveau roman* and thanks to the label, although her writing was and remains quite distinct from that of its male representatives.

It does seem, in other words, not only more difficult for a woman *experimental* writer to be accepted than for a woman writer (which corresponds to the male situation of experimental writer vs. writer), but also peculiarly more difficult for a *woman* experimental writer to be accepted than for a *male* experimental writer. She may, if young, get caught up in a 'movement', like Djuna Barnes, like H.D., like Laura Riding, as someone's mistress, and then be forgotten, or if old, she may be 'admitted' into a group, under a label, but never be quite as seriously considered as the men in that group.

Perhaps one of the safest ways of dismissing a woman experimental writer is to stick a label on her, if possible that of a male group that is getting or (better still) used to get all the attention. Fluttering around a canon. The implication is clear: a woman writer must either use traditional forms or, if she dare experiment, she must be imitating an already old model. Indeed, the only two advantages of 'movements' are (1) for the writers, to promote themselves (hence they are usually men), and (2) for the critics, to serve as useful boxes to put authors into. But women are rarely considered seriously as part of a movement when it is 'in vogue', and then they are damned with the label when it no longer is, when they can safely be considered as minor elements of it.

It may well be that women writers do not like new 'movements' and still shrink from declaring all over the place how revolutionary they are. Political women, and hence feminists, have had this courage. But, as well as 'muted' women (Ardener, see below), many artists, male or female (rightly or wrongly), evade the overtly political, and it seems to me that the combination of woman + artist + experimental means so much hard work and heartbreak and isolation that there must be little time or energy for crying out loud.

And here we come back to the canon, in the form of another ancient opposition within the idea of belonging: traditionally, men belong to groups, to society (the matrix, the canon). Women belong to men. And in so far as women, emancipating themselves, also behave in the same way, they are said to be imitating men (and so to belong to them again). All emancipation apparently has to pass that way, just as it has to pass through a 'separatist' stage to find its strength and identity. But every individual needs a mixture of withdrawal and belonging. And it seems to me that the woman artist needs more withdrawal and less belonging. She needs to withdraw, either from the man she is with who may be consciously or unconsciously punishing her for or otherwise stifling her creativity; or from society (ditto). She will try less hard to belong, because she needs it less deeply. Thus she will tend to belong neither to a man nor to society. At best she will belong to what Ardener calls the 'wild' zone, as described by Elaine Showalter (1981).

Showalter gives Ardener's diagram of the 'muted' and the 'dominant' group as one circle over another, the 'muted' circle shifted
slightly to the right (whereas in Victorian society the 'woman's
sphere' was conceived as separate and smaller). (See Fig. 10).

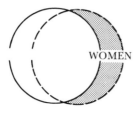

Fig. 10

Showalter points out that spatially and experientially each group
has a crescent-shaped zone inaccessible to the other, but that 'meta-
physically, or in terms of consciousness', the wild zone

> has no corresponding male space since all male consciousness is within the circle
> of the dominant structure and thus accessible to or structured by language. In this
> sense, the 'wild' is always imaginary: from the male point of view, it may simply
> be the projection of the unconscious. In terms of cultural anthropology, women know
> what the male crescent is like, even if they have never seen it, because it becomes
> the subject of legend (like the wilderness). But men do not know what is in the
> wild.
>
> (200)

If this is so, there are not only very few truly experimental writers
of the 'wild' zone (to my knowledge only Angela Carter and Hélène
Cixous at her least self-indulgent succeed here, though my knowledge
may be limited), but in theory they must also know, and accept,
that they cannot enter the canon (unless of course men were to open
their minds, and abolish the notion of canon). Except, perhaps, a
female canon.

But then, the very notion of a female canon (the new geography)
is a contradiction in terms. Feminists have not quite faced that problem, as we saw in Chapter 15, but I cannot deal further with this
huge issue here, beyond noting the danger: not only can the new
boldness of feminist themes seem in itself sufficient renewal (the
wild zone perhaps turned into a new chunk of reality to be sold),
it can also help to create the stamp, the label 'feminist writer' or
even 'woman writer'. As I have suggested, one safe way not to

recognize innovative women is to shove them under a label, and one such label is 'woman writer'. Women may feel that the dismissive aspect comes from men, but I am not so sure. Naturally it must be comforting to be backed and hailed by a sisterhood (a female canon) but that sisterhood is, with some few exceptions, generally so busy on feminist 'themes', on defining a 'feminist aesthetic' and on discovering or reinterpreting women authors of the past (rather as the Deconstructionist School in America paid little attention to the deconstructing 'postmodern' literature all around them), that it has no time to notice or to make an effort to understand, let alone to back, an unfamiliar (experimental) woman writer who does not necessarily write on, or only on, such themes, but whose discourse is, in Elaine Showalter's phrase (1981), 'a double-voiced discourse, containing a "dominant" and a "muted" story, what Gilbert and Gubar in *The Madwoman in the Attic* call a palimpsest'. If the 'wild' zone writer is inaccessible to most male readers, she is at least appreciated by feminists. The 'double-voiced' writer (unless he is a man) antagonizes both, she is in the sea between two continents.

In his book *On Deconstruction* (1983), Jonathan Culler has a chapter called 'reading as a Woman', where he quotes Shoshana Felman (1975): 'Is "speaking as a woman" determined by some biological condition or by a strategic, theoretical position, by anatomy or by culture?' And he applies this to the divided structure of woman's reading: women can read, and have read, as men, and have learnt to identify with a masculine experience presented as the human one. Today, women face this problem, and 'try to bring a new experience of reading for both men and women, a reading that questions the literary and political assumptions on which their reading has been based'.

It would seem, then, that the androgyny that some men have claimed for *all good* writers at the *creative* end has willy nilly been acquired by women at the *receiving* end, but not by men, who rarely identify with women characters as women do with male ones. Whatever the case, it would surely be a good thing if more men learnt to read as women (even the wild zone), so that the bisexual effort, which they have metaphorically appropriated at the creative end, should not remain so wholly on the women's side at the receiver's end. Both should read as both, just as both should write as both. And one of the ways in which this delightful bisexualism should occur is in a more open and intelligent attitude to experiment of all kinds by women.

18

Ill wit and good humour

This chapter is more a light-hearted meditation on women and comic writing than a scholarly analysis, more the pursuit of an intuition, which may be wrong, than an exhaustive investigation. This is because, although I do not think the intuition is wrong, I do think that comedy tends to be killed by exhaustive analysis.

Soap-bubble or 'text-object'

In Umberto Eco's best-selling novel *The Name of the Rose* (1980), the solution to all those monkish murders lies in the library's secret possession of Aristotle's lost work on comedy – which is of course fictionally lost again as the monastery burns. This is superbly self-referential comedy, based on both knowledge of rhetoric in general and on the absence of a specific rhetoric of comedy. But I have often wondered whether that supposed loss of Aristotle's supposed work on comedy does not in fact represent the undesirability of theorizing about comedy or analysing it. I don't mean that theorizing about comedy is impossible, merely that it seems more murderous of it. Of course, there are rules, but rules have to do with craftsmanship and production. It seems, however, a peculiar contradiction in terms to analyse what makes us laugh. From Schopenhauer to Freud and beyond, laughter, or the joke, or whatever we call it, seems more like a soap-bubble than an analysable 'text-object'. Whereas human passions treated on a grand scale or the sadness of the human condition, from classical tragedy through domestic tragedy to the modern weepy, seem somehow more conducive to analysis. But of course, to say that something is unanalysable smacks of old-fashioned idealism, or even, as I. A. Richards put it over sixty years ago, of mystery mongering.

The difficulty of theorizing about laughter, as in Schopenhauer or Kierkegaard or Bergson (to the latter two of whom I shall turn below), is the very generality of theory, despite examples, compared to the apparently unique specificity of comic situations – an illusion of course. For this is partly due to the very social nature of laughter, compared to the essential solitariness of suffering, even when witnessed or shared – unless of course suffering is presented as comic. We have all experienced trying to retell a funny situation to someone who wasn't there. It only works as part of a new social situation, a re-enacting in fact, a re-creation. And naturally this aspect, so clear in the theatre, even varying from one performance to another, poses particular problems in the novel, the reading of which is normally a solitary activity.

The theatre obviously disposes of many comic elements not available to the novelist – gestures, facial expressions, timing, costume, props – in other words the combined talents of actor and producer. The novelist has *only* language. And although he shares its natural riches with the dramatist, his equivalent for the different reception (re-creation) according to different audiences can only be the different readings, which he can only experience from brief and scattered individual reactions if at all. Such individual reaction can happen in the theatre too, but it is submerged by the social situation – as for example the splendid scene in the Greek film *Never on Sunday*, when the call girl, played by Melina Mercouri, finds herself in an ancient amphitheatre where classical tragedy is being played, which she finds irresistibly funny. On a simpler level, every music hall audience knows that parodies (in Genette's sense) of famous extracts from tragedies can be a source of comedy. In this sense, comedy is perhaps simply a displacement of things taken seriously in one social context, to another social context. But this seems insufficient, and particularly so in relation to another problem.

Why no women?

To these two generalities – the difficulty of theorizing about what is funny and the essentially social dimension of laughter, I would like to suggest a third, which is the apparent – and if true, extremely strange – exclusion of women from the comic canon.

By this I do not mean that there have been no comic women writers or that women writers are never funny – how could anyone say that within an English tradition that starts with Jane Austen? Nor am I presupposing an authoritarian exclusion of comic women writers, as opposed to others, by men.

No. I mean that, relative to men, women comic writers seem rare.
I would look at it this way: women are now officially accepted as
equal in every ex-male domain, from the arts to politics, from news-
caster to sports commentator to city expert. But this has not happened at the same speed. Doctors came long before sports
commentators for instance, and even now there are still pockets of
resistance where a fifty-year-old discourse is still heard – the domain
of engineers for example. I would like to suggest that, within the
art of writing, where women (with varying difficulties) were accepted
much earlier than in the other arts, there are still pockets of unconscious non-acceptance. Experiment is one, which I discussed in the
last chapter. Comic writing may be another, but here the non-acceptance is complex enough to have created, in fact, a curious kind
of *self*-exclusion by women.

For the general picture is of a tradition of women's writing which
first flourishes in the aristocratic imitations of courtly literature from
the twelfth to the sixteenth centuries in France, continues more 'seriously' with *La Princesse de Clèves*, but also with a crop of seventeenth
and eighteenth-century ladies more or less regarded as blue-stockings
or *femmes savantes*, if not *précieuses ridicules*, then blossoms to an unex-
pectedly balanced serio-comic perfection in Jane Austen, to be followed, grandly enough, by passionate romance (Mme de Stael) or
passionate Gothic, domestic tragedy and portraits of society in the
work of the Brontës, George Sand, George Eliot or Mrs Gaskell.
All excellent writers, full of irony, but hardly comic writers.

Why, in other words, was women's writing, when allowed to flourish at all, so serious? The New Women protest novels of the eighties
and nineties, which partly influenced Hardy, the stories of great
romance or the streams of personal consciousness, all these poured
out in profusion. And it is chiefly a certain kind of irony – acutely
observed social nuances noted with wit and malice and gentle mockery – in other words what is already highly developed in Jane Austen
– that flourishes in the twentieth century, from the popular detective
story of an Agatha Christie to the passionate thresholds of consciousness of a Virginia Woolf. In the modern domestic novel there is
much pleasure of recognition but little outright laughter. Such comic
writers as did emerge seemed to develop as brilliant journalists rather
than as novelists: Dorothy Parker is the archetype (and she died
forgotten and wretched). Even today a great deal of specifically feminist writing of the type that refuses to 'conquer' or 'imitate' any
male domain tends to manifest itself as free but deadly earnest

descriptions of sex and expressions of flowing feelings (so in fact imitating earlier male freedoms) – free, sometimes highly experimental and poetic, opening up new horizons, but rarely funny, except perhaps unconsciously. There must be exceptions, and I am perhaps deliberately exaggerating to stress the impression I have – but I do have it – that between Jane Austen and Muriel Spark or, in different veins, Angela Carter and Kathy Acker, there is very little that would stand up to, say, the comedy of Dickens or Jerome K. Jerome or P. G. Wodehouse or even Edgar Anstey (to cite as many different registers as possible). Or, in modern times, to anyone from Evelyn Waugh to Kingsley Amis, from Joyce to Barth or Ishmael Reed.

This is extremely peculiar and surprising, since the comic spirit is perhaps the only successful weapon in any struggle for equality, far more efficient than complaint, aggression or segregation, and one, moreover, that men are far more afraid of. Why did women not turn to it in larger numbers and develop it more sharply? Other oppressed groups did and do still – Jewish humour and the humour of Black writing for instance – and both are sophisticated enough to include self-mockery, which feminist writing rarely does.

If this self-exclusion from the comic canon is true, it would, I think, be linked very directly to the social nature of the comic and, less obviously, to the difficulty of theorizing about the comic, in the sense that theorizing about women's writing has proved far more difficult and quicksandy than most Feminist critics would probably admit, as we have seen (Ch.15).

What makes women laugh – or not laugh?

The social aspect, like all social things including communication, has two facets, that of inception, and that of reception, and the latter (what makes people laugh) thoroughly conditions the former (comic creation), which is why I shall look mostly at what makes people laugh, for, as we shall see, it almost explains the strange situation. Here is a personal anecdote.

At a 1986 Conference, during an excursion, the bus had to brake violently for a car, which happened to have a woman driver. My companion, who admittedly was Germanic but belonged to my generation (and sometimes I wonder whether men move less quickly with the times than women do) immediately launched into the story of the statue of Boadicea on Westminster Bridge who, with the reins in her right hand, is driving her chariot in that direction but with her other arm outstretched to the left. The predictable punch-line was 'how like a woman, to signal one way and go off the other way'. I smiled politely, for I had first heard this joke some forty years earlier, and teased his trivial (and inaccurate) sexism. His reaction was interesting: Okay you're right, it's a very old joke. But it belongs to an old tradition, in which a bad woman driver is funny, a bad man driver is not.

Conversely that same month, there was an article in *The Women's Review* about slapstick, which observed that a man falling over is funny, a woman falling over is not. In other words, in audience reception, comic situations are sexually determined: women do not spontaneously laugh at jokes about women drivers or at sex-jokes except when trying to imitate and join males.

Historically, women have never been expected or allowed to be more than, at very best, witty in a society salon, that is, to add charm and general agreeability to an occasion, the icing on the cake, the spice to the dish – and it is interesting that I can only think of cooking metaphors. And even pepperpot charm would be restricted to a high-society milieu at certain relatively libertine periods – the Renaissance, the English Restoration, the eighteenth century, the English Regency or the nineteenth-century *fin de siècle*. It is difficult to imagine either a Puritan or a Victorian wife or daughter being allowed to make jokes at the husband's or the father's, or indeed anyone's, expense. For good humour is nearly always ill wit, at someone's expense even if it is one's own (the safest). Being funny, like talking too much or appearing intelligent, wasn't done, except perhaps by a mistress or a scarlet whore. And this was precisely during the period that women novelists at last emerged as other than aristocratic or blue-stocking exceptions.

This excluding attitude was partly due to the social protectiveness of men, in other words, to decorum. Women should not make themselves ridiculous, or vulgar, just as women should not fall over. But behind the decorum lies something deeper. It seems to me precisely because humour is such an efficient weapon, and feared by men, that it had to be either evaded by women or used very covertly. Even today, when in a quarrel a man laughs at something said by his companion, she tends to be disoriented or cowed, whereas when the woman laughs, the man's reaction tends to be fury or silent exit. For I believe that the situation of women in history is more complexly determined than that of classes or races, because although that of classes or races can be complicated by sex, it is not itself sexual but political and social, whereas that of women is itself sexual and can be complicated by power urges and social conditions. The slave or the oppressed worker does not love his oppressor in the same way as the woman may love her man, and be afraid to lose him. The slave fears his master and longs for freedom, whereas women's attitude to 'freedom' was for a long time, and often still is, much more ambiguous, with many even against it, and historically many conservative backlashes (like today's 'post'-feminism) may mean that every new start has to go back a bit.

'Feminists have no sense of humour, as Wayne Booth has shown.' This sentence is from an essay by Nancy K. Miller (1986) on 'Rereading as a Woman', where she retells 'a celebrated moment at a symposium organized by *Critical Inquiry* in 1981 on "The Politics of Interpretation"' when Wayne Booth, 'then President of the MLA, came out as a male feminist'. I quote the relevant bit she gives from Booth with the Rabelais recall:

When I read, as a young man, the account of how Panurge got his revenge on the Lady of Paris (as you recall, he punishes her for turning him down by sprinkling her gown with the pulverized genitals of a bitch in heat, then withdraws to watch gleefully the spectacle of the assembled male dogs of Paris pissing on her from head to toe), I was transported with delighted laughter; and when I later read Rabelais aloud to my young wife, as she did the ironing (!), she could easily tell that I expected her to be as fully transported as I was. Of course she did find a lot of it funny, a great deal of it is very funny. But now, reading passages like that, when everything I know about the work as a whole suggests that my earlier response was closer to the spirit of the work itself, I draw back and start thinking rather than laughing, taking a different kind of pleasure with a *somewhat* diminished text.

(1985, 292; Booth, *Critical Inquiry* 9/1, 1982, 68)

The tone of regret, at having something taken away from him by a more feminist-sensitive reading, is a revelation in itself. Could feminism be an *impoverishment?* But sex-jokes, of which the above is an extreme example, are not the only comic situations which are sexually determined. This has not been greatly written about, but if we go back, first, to Bergson on laughter (*Le Rire*, 1900; 1984. Transl. 1911), we find that his analysis unwittingly explains this sexual determination.

Things

Bergson does not define the comic. His theory is that there is a vitality in the human organism, which is highly flexible, creative, alive, but that humans constantly fall back into lifeless matter, which behaves mechanically, inflexibly, killing the creativity of the 'life-force'. Laughter is the safeguard that wakes us up when we drop into the merely mechanical, behave mechanically, inflexibly. It has to be *people*: an object as such, or a landscape, isn't funny, unless connected to a human being or a human reaction. But humans behaving like things are the basic source of laughter. And inversely so are mechanical objects animated like humans (the jack-in-the-box, the marionette) sources of laughter (1984, 53).

Later Bergson further elaborates this opposition of life versus lifeless mechanism: life changes, the mechanical repeats itself; life is irreversible (or has irreversible series), the mechanical is reversible: life needs a minimum of individuality and self-containment, mechanical series are liable to reciprocal interference. These three elements, repetition, inversion and reciprocal interference of series (say plot and sub-plot) are the mainstay of comedy in Bergson's mechanical theory of laughter (67–8). He further applies all this to language, for instance when language clogs thought or when clichés or dead metaphors are brought to life and so on (99ff.). However, there is an interesting constraint: laughter is a corrective to all behaviour due to inflexibility, but as corrective it always contains 'an unavowed intention to humiliate' and requires a degree of cruelty: rather than sympathy.

Naturally I am not suggesting that women could have been aware of all these elements, but the elements do explain, in negative counter-foil, why women did not willingly go in for rousting comedy, but rather more for the wry smile or irony. Why should women, so long considered as things, and trained to react in a dutifully mechanical way, laugh at the thingness of people and the thingness of language they were themselves so inextricably a part of? Why should they, caught up in the irreversibility of life, amuse themselves with mechanically reversible situations and reciprocally interacting sequences? Why should they throw themselves into a genre which makes laughter incompatible with sympathetic understanding?

And yet, the inflexibility and rigidity of much masculine behaviour towards them and towards the politics of life, family and power could have given them splendid material. It did so, but more comfortably through gentle irony and emotional sympathy than through rumbustious or even sophisticated comedy.

Irony, humour, comedy

If what makes people laugh (reception) has an almost direct bearing
on inception, so do generally received ideas of comedy as a genre,
of humour as a faculty.

The traditional ideas about comedy were that it is 'low', whereas
tragedy is 'high'; that it is clever and cold and suggests superiority
whereas tragedy is emotional and profoundly understanding; and
that it has a happy ending. Clearly women were not expected to be
'low', or 'clever', and as to 'happy endings', women certainly used
them, but they are not specific to comedy. In the novel (where men
used them too) they can be either sentimental, that is, not warranted
by the elements of the story (see end of Ch. 7, p. 121, for example,
the ending of *Middlemarch*), but they can also be wryly happy endings,
such as Jane Eyre finally marrying Rochester but blind and maimed,
in other words castrated (for if some might argue that this savage
irony is unconscious for the author, it certainly cannot be for us).

For Kierkegaard (1946), there were three spheres of existence,
the aesthetic, the ethical and the religious. Between them are two
buffer zones, irony and humour. This scheme could be represented
as follows:

Although the religious is inaccessible to comic apprehension,
humour seems to be closer to the religious because Kierkegaard
thought that prayer, though expressing the highest pathos, is ultimately comical. And one could hardly expect nineteenth-century women
to go along with that. He also thought it was a regression to childhood, though earlier he had said that the comical is a mark of maturity.

Michael Silk (1988) who discusses Kierkegaard's ideas but with
a different purpose from mine (to show that comedy is autonomous
and not a proper opposition to tragedy), tries to reconcile the various
contradictions and unclarities, but these do not concern me here.
I simply want to take the negative calque of these ideas, as with
Bergson, and show how they could explain women's self-exclusion
from 'humour' (comedy) as opposed to 'irony': women have always
felt at home between the aesthetic and the ethical, but less so between
the ethical and the religious. Their religion (in the eighteenth and
nineteenth centuries) does not seem to have been a very profound

affair, but more of a social *bienséance* (between the aesthetic and the ethical), and even an atheist like George Eliot was still 'concerned' with religion, but in a serious, philosophical and ethical way. Women's upbringing would quite prevent them from jesting with the Almighty. As to 'maturity' and 'regression to childhood' ('a startling anticipation of Freud's infantilism' as Silk says, 22), both are present in humour, but the infantilism seems more prevalent in the general idea people have of humour (men's jokes, the frivolous, the trivial), and since women seem to have been considered either as more mature (the mother-figure) or as child-wives, it is easy to imagine a double standard situation in which men's jokes, however regressive, were regarded as mature, and women's jokes, when made at all, as infantile.

There are also a few other persistent notions about humour and comedy and laughter which would exclude women: that comic laughter comes from ridicule and implies superiority (already in Hobbes, quoted by Silk who links this with Freud's aggressive element 'which turns pathos to bathos, tragedy to comedy' – 13); laughter is Satanic (Baudelaire): it degrades and materializes (Bakhtin); comedy is more materialistic than tragedy (Brecht, all these cited for other purposes by Silk). And the comic is of course intimately linked with performance, from which women were in fact excluded. All these images of the comic, which must have floated around as *idées reçues* long before they were expressed, go a long way to explain the strong preference women writers have shown for, on the one hand, serious topics, and on the other, for irony.

This 'negative' reading of what has been said on laughter and comedy may have suggested a false picture of women as utterly cowed, angelic, non-aggressive, withdrawn, profoundly understanding and so on. I hope it is not necessary to insist that I am talking about images of comedy, and ideal images that women must have had of themselves, as reflected by the expectations of society, and not of individual women with their angers and private cruelties. Much of what I describe has long disappeared, and I am talking of ancient structures, which, like all ancient structures, have left an inheritance, not only in the reception of women writers who are in fact funny, but also, perhaps, in women writers themselves. For, as I said in Chapter 17, just as a young girl could exhibit her skills at the spinet or pretty watercolours as extra accomplishments on the marriage market, but was never, never expected to compose or paint a fresco, similarly, when a woman did become a writer, she was benignly expected not only to imitate the male canon but within that to confine herself to familiar forms and to the domestic scenes she knew best. I would add, similarly again, that she was not expected to risk her precious person and become any kind of clown, certainly not on stage, but not even when safely hidden from view in the pages of a book. High comedy seems in a way the last bastion for women writers truly to conquer, not as exceptions but as the norm, like doctors, financial experts, and, why not, engineers. But:

Perhaps not?

Some critics have suggested (Jean Paul for instance) that the comic writer does not in any way distort the real but sees it that way (as mad). If this is true, then women were hardly trained to do this, but to accept the world as not only masculine but as sane and normal because masculine. Even if it is not true (and it belongs to the notion that the world is pre-existent and merely 'seen' by the writer, rather than created by him), comedy still requires not only a certain hardness of heart but an ability to 'see' at least aspects of the world as abnormal. It requires a degree of independent judgment that women took decades to develop.

Indeed, it may well be that women writers should *not* merely try to 'catch up' and develop the comic spirit as evolved by men over centuries: since the whole world is now 'seen' by all to be ab-'normal', it may well be classical comedy that has died, and not, as everyone thought, tragedy, or even the novel: for it is true that comedy as commonly understood in the theatre-world is chiefly limited to boulevard, that is, to outrageous caricatures of the middle class in its most fixed image of inflexibility (which, because it is mechanical, women can write today as well as men). And those fixed images of the middle class are dead and gone – which is why they are popular.

But that's another story. The different 'view' of the world needed for high comedy, and apparently not acquired by women, might, however, also explain the lack of success (broadly speaking) of women in 'postmodern' experiment, where outrageous humour is one of the chief ingredients on the male side.

19

An allegory of aesthetics

A few years ago I was asked for an essay on 'my aesthetics' for a review partly devoted to my work. One of the editors put the word in scare-quotes as if sensing there might be a problem. There was, apart from the quasi-impossibility of writing in critical terms about oneself. In fact there were two main problems: one derived (perhaps naively) from the inherent or at least the original meaning of aesthetics, which is clearly a matter of reception (so how can an author write about that?); the other, more complex, deriving from the 'modern' use of the word from the Enlightenment on. At the time, I only responded to the first, and decided I could only write about the supposed 'difficulty' of my work – and the resulting essay was certainly not among those I have wanted to rehandle for this book.

Since then, however, I have thought more about the second problem, particularly in relation to the strange feminist use of the word 'aesthetics' in phrases like 'the search for a feminist aesthetic(s)' or this or that writer's 'aesthetic(s)'. What does it mean, and why are feminists using it?

Aesthetikos

But first a brief return to the first problem: 'aesthetics' is not a concept an author can apply to him or herself (and therefore he or she cannot be asked about it or make declarations about it). According to the Oxford Dictionary the word was 'misapplied' by Baumgarten to 'criticism of taste', and used in three senses: (1) received by the senses, (2) of or pertaining to the appreciation or criticism of the beautiful, (3) having or showing refined taste. Strictly, then, it can only be used of effect, therefore by critics.

The word, however, comes from *aesthetikos*, of or pertaining to *aisthera*, things perceptible by the senses, things material, as opposed to *noera*, things thinkable or immaterial. But this opposition is very early blurred: *aisthesis* meant the faculty of perceiving through the senses, hence sensation (in Euripides), *and* the faculty of perceiving through the intellect (in Theocritus and Plato). The same happens with the verb *aisthanomai* (to perceive through sight/hearing; to understand). This presumably, in the later use of the word, would still apply to how one views a work of art and not to how one creates it or what one's 'aims' and 'intentions' are (which is usually the purpose of such interviews or requests to writers, often from critics who don't know what to say of the work themselves).

So this shift from sense to intellect seems to have been followed, in modern times, by a shift from reception-aesthetics to 'inception-aesthetics'.[1] The two are not unconnected: it is notoriously difficult to explain how one 'feels' about a work of art, and obviously the same applies to one's 'aims'; feelings are supposedly in the text, but perceptions, how one perceives the world (in other words themes, content, ideas) are much easier to describe. But I am not at all sure whether this is what feminists mean.

Power

The second problem is far more interesting, for 'aesthetics' seems to have returned in a more or less consciously political sense, at least I assume the choice of the word by feminists is political. I have certainly never seen talk of a male writer's 'aesthetics'. And although some feminists use it as a merely new fashionable word and interpret it (wrongly) as a personal declaration of intention (as described above), others seem to use it as English equivalent of *écriture féminine* (though this term is also transposed but without italics, see Ch. 15). In other words, with political implications. But I wonder whether it is used in full awareness of its peculiar modern history, which is extremely complex. This history has been very ably but also bizarrely summarized by Terry Eagleton (1988, 327–38), so bizarrely that it amounts to an Eagleton 'story', a highly political story, which has on the one hand considerably clarified my own ideas, and on the other considerably increased my puzzlement. I

---

[1] In the subtitle of Blau Duplessis (1980) the two are apparently equated: 'For the Etruscans: Sexual Difference and Artistic Production – The Debate Over a Female Aesthetic'. Also, some consider postmodernism as anti-aesthetic, see Foster 1983.

shall therefore further summarize him here, but by quoting freely since his language is more political than mine can be, with comments which I hope will bring the feminist aspect into focus (and this is not of course Eagleton's purpose, as we shall see). He backs his statements with sources I shall not give here, since they are all available in the article.

Eagleton describes aesthetics as 'a whole apparatus of power in the field of culture', firmly in place a whole century before modern hermeneutics, and which determined 'not the power and effects of particular readings but the political meaning and function of "culture" as such'. It is 'effectively synonymous with a shift in the very concept of power, which we can characterize as a transition to the notion of hegemony' (which he describes as 'ruling and informing from within'). And secondly, 'it has little enough to do with art' (327).

Aesthetics was 'born as a discourse of the body', the vital distinction for Baumgarten being 'not between life and art but between the material and the immaterial'. The vast territory of our sensate life had suddenly to be somehow recouped philosophically. For Baumgarten aesthetics 'mediates between the generalities of reason and the particulars of sense', but 'in a confused mode'. Thus it was 'the "sister" of logic, a kind of inferior feminine analogue of reason, at the level of material life'. But necessary: 'only by such a concrete logic will the ruling class be able to understand its own history; for history, like the body, is a matter of sensuous particulars, in no sense merely derivable from rational principles' (328).

Schiller's project was also 'to soften Kant's imperious tyranny of reason in the direction of social hegemony' (328). 'It is easier [...] for reason to repress sensuous Nature if it has already been busy eroding and subliming it from the inside and this is the task of the aesthetic.' The program installs 'manners' and 'Manners means the meticulous disciplining of the body which converts morality to style, aestheticizing virtue and so deconstructing the opposition between the proper and the pleasurable' (329). 'The moment when moral actions can be classified as "agreeable" or "disagreeable" marks a certain mature point of evolution in the history of a ruling class' (330).

Thus all conflicts must be transformed into 'new kinds of spontaneous social practice, which in a kind of creative repression or amnesia can afford to forget the very laws they obey' (329). And again: 'What matters in aesthetics is not art but this whole project of

reconstructing the human subject from inside.' But 'if aesthetics is
every bit as coercive as the most barbaric law [...] this is not the
way it feels' (330). And that, one might add, is fortunate for the
modern feminist project of 'reconstructing the human subject from
inside', since the original project sounds insidiously repressive. And
surely feminists cannot admit to that?

The best example of 'lawfulness without a law is the English Constitution, at once ineluctable and unformalizable'. And, 'if one
wanted to give a name to the single most important nineteenth-
century instrument of the kind of hegemony in question, one which
never ceases to grasp universal reason in concrete particular style,
uniting within its own depth, an economy of abstraction with the
effect of spontaneous experience, one might do worse than propose
the realist novel' (330).

Aesthetics as sexist?

So far so good. But Eagleton has a peculiar allegorically sexist concept
of the aesthetic, I hope reproduced 'tongue-in-cheek' from his
sources, yet apparently made his without comment or disowning
quotes. We have already seen aesthetics as an 'inferior' sister to
logic (re Baumgarten). He continues:

If beauty is a consensual power, then the sublime – that which crushes us into admiring
submission – is coercive. The distinction between the beautiful and the sublime is
in part one between woman and man and partly that between what Louis Althusser
has called the ideological and the repressive state apparatus.

(330)

In other words, if the metaphoric parallel structure here functions
as it should, ideology is 'feminine'.

How then reconcile beauty and the sublime? He is now talking
about Burke:

As enervated feminine beauty must be regularly stiffened by a masculine sublime
whose terrors must be instantly defused, in an endless rhythm of erection and detumescence. The law is male but hegemony is a woman and the aesthetic would be their
felicitous marriage. For Burke, the revolutionaries who seek to 'strip all the decent
drapery of life' from political power, de-aesthetize it, are in danger of exposing the
phallus of this transvestite law, which decks itself out as a woman. Power will thus
cease to be aestheticized and what will grapple us to it will be less our affections
[as in hegemony] than the gallows.

(331)

Thus a Law that engages our intimate affections is a woman (although Law is 'male', but 'hegemony' female) and 'will have the laxness of the other', while a Law that 'inspires filial fear' will 'spur us to oedipal resentment' (330). I assume that the 'rhythm of erection and detumescence' etc. are Eagleton's and not Burke's, but at no point does he distinguish between paraphrase and interpretation. It would seem, from this argument, that power has been 'aestheticized', presumably by 'female' aesthetics, and 'decently draped', and will be de-aestheticized by revolutionary males. Eagleton goes on to argue that the bourgeoisie's problem is 'that their obsession with freedom is incompatible with feeling at home in the world. Bourgeois ideology [female if the earlier parallel structure is correct] thus continually violates one of the central functions of ideology in general, which is to make the subject feel that the world is not an altogether inhospitable place' (331). Unless Eagleton's sense of language has gone haywire, it would seem that a female (allegorical) force can rape one of its own functions.

For Kant, all adjustments are made through the contemplation of that pure form of cognition which is aesthetics:

> The aesthetic is simply the state in which common knowledge in the very act of reaching out to its object, suddenly arrests and rounds upon itself, forgetting its referent for a magical moment and attending instead, in a wondering flash of self-estrangement, to the miraculously convenient way in which its innermost structure seems geared to the comprehension of the real [...] Not *what* we know but *that* we know [...] and this is to say that for Kant the aesthetic is nothing less than, in a precise Lacanian sense, the Imaginary [...] The Kantian subject of taste who misperceives as a quality of the aesthetic representation what is in fact a delightful projection of its own powers and who projects onto a blind, mechanical universe a figure of idealized unity, is in effect the infantile narcissism of the Lacanian mirror-phase.
>
> (331–2)

And if human beings are to feel comfortable enough in Kant's rational world 'to act as moral agents, there must be somewhere in reality some image of that ethical purposiveness which [in Kant's world ...] falls outside representation and is not available as a sensuous, which is to say, an ideological [i.e. female], force. That image is the aesthetic [i.e. female, inferior sister to logic], in which a mutual mirroring of ego and world is allowed to occur'. But it should not 'domesticate and naturalize the subject too much', and this is the function of the sublime [male]' (332).

The Allegory of Reading allegory

The bourgeois dilemma is 'that its very atomizing individualism and competitiveness threatens to destroy the ideological [presumably female] solidarity necessary to its reproduction', that is, if values are derived from the marketplace [presumably male] we end with the worst kinds, and values though related to social practice are so related 'by their contradictory dislocation from it'. So 'solidarity needs a third realm, the universal subjectivity of the aesthetic' (for 'the Imaginary of the aesthetic is universal rather than individual subjectivity') (332). And the 'universal' is a result of the rational, that is the masculine in this story. The Allegory of Reading this allegory of aesthetics is becoming as blurred and multi-levelled as *Piers Plowman*.

Paradoxically, 'it is in the most apparently frail, private and intangible of our feelings that we blend most harmoniously with one another' – a doctrine that Eagleton calls both 'astonishingly optimistic and bitterly pessimistic':

On the one hand: 'How marvellous that consensual intersubjectivity [hegemony, feminine] can be found installed in the very inwardness of the subject!' On the other hand: 'How sickeningly precarious human unity must be, if one can finally root in nothing more resilient than the vagaries of aesthetic judgment!'

(333)

That is, in the 'frail' and female.

'Aesthetic pleasure cannot be *compelled*', he says later, returning to the coercive aspect, 'and yet somehow it is, for all that [...] The ethico-aesthetic subject – the subject of bourgeois hegemony – is the one who, in Kant's phrase, gives the law to itself and who thus lives its necessary freedom' (333). And the problem with such freedom (for Kant) 'is that it is entirely noumenal. It cannot be *represented* and is thus at root anti-aesthetic' (334).

The problem also dogged Hegel, but Eagleton shows that Hegel 'gravely underestimates the ideological force of sensuous representation'. Nevertheless, by shifting 'the whole concept of culture away from its aesthetic to its every day or anthropological sense', he effects a 'vital transition from ideology to hegemony' [both apparently female in Eagleton's representations] (334). And he reconciles 'the conflict between the bourgeoisie's drive for freedom and its desire for an expressive unity with the world', solving

this problem at one stroke by projecting subjectivity into the object itself: why fear to unite with a world which is itself free subjectivity? If Hegel assigns the aesthetic a lowly status, it is in part because, in uniting subject and object in this way, he has already secretly aestheticized the whole of reality.

(335)

For British empiricism, which was 'all along too aesthetic for its own good', the problem was not that of 'an aesthetic supplement to eke out' rationalism (as it was for the German rationalists), but on the contrary

how to drag itself free of the clammy embrace of the sensuously immediate to rise to something a little more conceptually dignified. The answer of the British 'moral sense' theorists was that there was really no need. The 'moral sense' is that spontaneous, well-nigh somatic impulse which links us in the very textures of our sensibilities to some providential whole.

(335)

A sort of ideological defeat, Eagleton comments: 'incapable of extrapolating its desired harmony from the anarchy of the market-place, the bourgeoisie are forced to root it instead in the stubborn self-evidence of the gut' [presumably female and 'frail'? or 'stubborn' and male?]. But in another sense 'it provides a powerful *ideological* riposte to an arid Enlightenment rationality' (335). 'The aesthetic for a Shaftesbury or a Hutcheson is no more than a name for the political unconscious [...] The beautiful is just political order lived in the body' (360). Nevertheless, for the rationalists, 'virtue [...] is thereby reduced to a matter of taste, and ethical ideology accordingly subverted' (336). Is 'ethical' ideology here 'male', subverted by the aesthetic (female), or does 'ideology' remain female as before?

And there is a greater risk:

The aesthetic begins as a supplement to reason, but we have learnt from Derrida that it is in the manner of such lowly [here female] supplements to supplant what they are meant to subserve. What if it were the case that not only morality but cognition itself were somehow 'aesthetic'? [...] The name for this subversive claim in Britain is David Hume, who, not content with reducing morality to a species of sentiment, threatens to collapse knowledge to fictional hypothesis, belief to intensified feeling, the continuity of the subject to a fiction, causality to an imaginative construct and history to a kind of infinite intertextuality.

(336)

This is a good description of our present situation and Eagleton has 'traced a kind of circle':

Reason, having spun off the subaltern discourse of aesthetics, now finds itself threatened with being swallowed up by it. The rational and the sensuous, far from obediently reproducing one another's inmost structure à la Baumgarten, have ended up in Hume wholly at odds.

(336)

Not only at odds, but with the 'male' rationalism thoroughly threatened by the 'female' aesthetic that will swallow it up like an unleashed sea. No wonder feminists have taken up the word! Yet is it wise? Presumably Eagleton is 'representing' images in his sources, yet he takes them over as his own:

> What, after all, to paraphrase Nietzsche, if experience were a woman? What if it were that slippery, tantalizing, elusive thing which plays fast and loose with the concept, the eternally labile which is gone as soon as grasped? At once intimate and unreliable, precious and precarious, indubitable and indeterminate, the very realm the aesthetic addresses itself to would seem to have all the duplicity of the female.
>
> (336)

Or, on the other side: 'Men are deceivers ever' (see Ch. 16, 245). But here the steady 'putting down' of aesthetics as female, enervated, frail, unreliable and so on suddenly veers right down to the male terror of being engulfed, swallowed, by all this 'frailty'. *Nous y voilà*! However, this extraordinary rhetoric, with its clichés and *idées fixes*, serves only to lead us back to the more seriously political:

> If this is the case, then the only possibility would seem to be to go back to where you started and think everything through again, this time from the basis of the body. It is exactly this which the two greatest aestheticians, Marx and Freud, will try to do: Marx with the laboring body, Freud with the desiring one. To think everything through again in terms of the body: this, surely, will have to be the logical next stage of the aesthetic.
>
> (337)

Whose body? Which body 'labors' and which body 'desires'? And thinking things through again from the basis of the body is, precisely, what some of the more sophisticated feminists have done and are doing, notably Cixous and Kristeva, with some of the more unfortunate derivative results we saw in Chapter 15. Perhaps the threatened swallowing act Eagleton mentions is what Marianne DeKoven meant when she said that 'the female gendered signature is *simply too subversive* to be recognized by the hegemonic institutions such as academy or mainstream publishing' (see p. 225) – though here 'hegemony' seems to be masculine!

All the same, the promise in Eagleton is peculiar: for these philosophers were surely not considering women at all when they spoke of the sensate, but of their own, masculine sensuousness. Nor is the body exclusively female, *pace* the feminists, and the 'slippery ... unreliable ... precarious ... indeterminable ... duplicity' not to mention 'infantile narcissism' belong as much to the masculine as to the feminine psyche.

Feminists, then, should perhaps beware, when they use the term 'aesthetics' or 'feminist aesthetics', of its history and of all its manifold implications, not only of 'inferior sisterhood', 'enervated', 'frail', 'unreliable', 'lowly' and so on (as opposed to the 'dignified' rational, which they prefer to call 'master-structures' and such), but also of the insidious power and coercion contained in the concept, even if, as Eagleton says, 'that is not the way it feels'. It is not only 'not concerned with art' but it implies a de-moralizing of ethics into the agreeable and disagreeable. For Kant it is even 'at root anti-aesthetic'. Is that really what feminists want when they use the word? And even the notion of 'hegemony', which somehow gives birth to or goes with the aesthetic, is double-faced: for hegemony can become one with dictatorship when in fact directed from above, using the 'political unconscious' of the masses and producing a 'consensus from within' that has been skilfully manoeuvred or coerced. And 'aesthetics' can sometimes 'feel like' that.

References

Alain-Fournier, H., 1913. *Le Grand Meaulnes*; transl. Frank Davison, *The Lost Domain*, London, Oxford University Press 1959.

Alter, Robert, 1978. 'Mimesis and the Motive for Fiction', *Triquarterly* 42, Spring 1978, 228–49.

Amis, Kingsley, 1960. *New Maps of Hell*, London and New York, Harcourt Brace.

Andermatt, Verena, 1979. 'Hélène Cixous and the Uncovery of a Feminine Language', *Women in Literature*, 7, 31–48.

Ardener, Edwin, 1977. 'Belief and the Problem of Women' in *Perceiving Women*, ed. Shirley Ardener, London and New York, Malaby 1975, 1–27.

Auden, W. H., 1948. *The Age of Anxiety*, London, Faber & Faber.

Auerbach, Erich, 1946. *Mimesis – The Representation of Reality in Western Literature* (orig. Berne); transl. Willard R. Trask, Princeton, N.J., Princeton University Press 1953 et seq.

Auerbach, Nina, 1980. 'Review of Gilbert & Gubar, *The Madwoman in the Attic*', *Victorian Studies* 23, 506.

Austin, J. L., 1962. *How To Do Things with Words*, Oxford, Oxford University Press. Oxford Paperback 1971.

Bakhtin, Mikhail, 1929a. *Problems of Dostoevky's Poetics*; ed. and transl. Caryl Emerson with an Introduction by Wayne C. Booth, Manchester University Press 1984.

(1929b). *Marxism and the Philosophy of Language*, published, under the name of V. N. Voloshinov; transl. L. L. Matejka & I. R. Tiburnik (under Voloshinov), New York, Seminar Press 1979.

Balzac, Honoré de, (1834). *A la recherche de l'absolu*, Paris, Garnier-Flammarion.

(1837). *Illusions perdues*, Paris, Garnier-Flammarion 1966.

(1839). *Le Chef d'oeuvre inconnu*, Paris, Garnier-Flammarion 1981.

(1844). *Splendeurs et misères des courtisanes*, Paris, Garnier-Flammarion 1968.

Banfield, Ann, 1982. *Unspeakable Sentences*, London, Routledge & Kegan Paul.

Barnes, Djuna, (1928). *Ryder*, New York, St Martin's Press 1956.

(1936). *Nightwood*, New York, New Directions 1961.

Barth, John, 1961. *The Sot-Weed Factor*, London, Secker & Warburg.

1967. 'The Literature of Exhaustion', *Atlantic Monthly* 220, Boston, 29–34.

1968. *Lost in the Funhouse*, Harmondsworth, Penguin 1972.

1979. *Letters*, Frogmore, St Albans, Granada paperback 1981.

1984a. 'The Literature of Replenishment', *Atlantic* 245, 65–71.

1984b. *The Friday Book: Essays and Other Non-Fiction*. New York, Putnam.

Barthelme, Donald, 1967. *Snow White*, New York, Bantham.

1970. *City Life*, New York, Farrar Strauss, Pocket Book 1976.

1975. *The Dead Father*, New York, Farrar Strauss, Pocket Book 1978.

Barthes, Roland, 1966. 'Introduction à l'analyse des récits', *Communications* 8, 1–27, Paris, Seuil; transl. 'Introduction to the Structural Analysis of Narrative', in *Image, Music, Text*, New York, Hill & Wang 1977, 74–124.

1970. *S/Z*, Paris, Seuil; transl. R. Howard, New York, Hill & Wang 1974.

1973. *Le Plaisir du texte*, Paris, Seuil; transl. *The Pleasure of the Text*, New York, Hill & Wang 1975.

Baskett, Sam S., 1961. 'The (Complete) Scarlet Letter', in Hawthorne 1961, pp. 321–8.

Baudelaire, Charles, 1868. *L'Art romantique*, ed. E. Raynaud, Paris, Garnier 1921.

Baym, Nina, 1961. 'The Romantic *malgré lui*: Hawthorne in "The Custom-House"', in Hawthorne 1961, pp. 279–86.

Beardsley, see Wimsatt

Beckett, Samuel, 1953. *L'Innommable*, Paris, Editions de Minuit; transl. 1958, author, *The Unnamable*, London, Calder & Boyars.

Beer, Gillian, 1979. 'Beyond Determinism – George Eliot and Virginia Woolf', in *Women Writing and Writing about Women*, ed. Mary Jacobus, London, Croom Helm; New York, Barnes and Noble, pp. 80–99.

Benveniste, Emile, 1966. *Problèmes de linguistique générale*, Paris, Gallimard; transl. Elizabeth Meek, *Problems in General Linguistics*, Coral Gables, University of Florida Press.

Berger, Peter L. and Luckmann, Thomas, 1966. *The Social Construction of Reality: A Treatise in the Sociology of Knowledge*, Garden City, Doubleday.

Bergson, Henri, (1900). *Le Rire, essai sur la signification du comique, Oeuvres*, 4th ed. 1984, pp. 381–485, Paris, Presses Universitaires de France; transl. C. Brereton and F. Rothwell, *Laughter, an Essay in the Meaning of the Comic*, London, Macmillan 1911.

Binder, Henry (ed.), 1982. *The Red Badge of Courage*, by Stephen Crane, newly edited from Crane's original manuscript, New York, Norton.

Blau Duplessis, 1980. Rachel (and members of Workshop 9), 'For the Etruscans: Sexual Difference and Artistic Production – The Debate Over a Female Aesthetic' in Eisenstein and Jardine, pp. 128–56.

Bloch, Ernst, 1959. *Das Prinzip Hoffnung*, Frankfurt-am-Main, Suhrkampf; *The Principle of Hope*, transl. Neville Plaice, Stephen Plaice and Paul Knight, Oxford, Basil Blackwell 1986.

Bloom, Harold, 1973. *The Anxiety of Influence*, New York, Oxford University Press.

1975. *A Map of Misreading*, New York, Oxford University Press.

1977. 'Coda: Poetic Crossing' in *Wallace Stevens: The Poems of our Climate*, Ithaca, Cornell University Press, pp. 375–406.

Boileau, M. Despréaux, (1672). *Le Lutrin, Oeuvres complètes*, Paris, Pléiade.

Boileau, Racine, *et al.* (1664). *Chapelain décoiffé*, in Boileau, *Oeuvres complètes*, Paris, Pléiade, pp. 292ff.

Booth, Wayne C., 1961. *The Rhetoric of Fiction*, Chicago, Chicago University Press.

1982. 'Freedom of Interpretation: Bakhtin and the Challenge of Feminist Criticism', in *Critical Inquiry* 9–1, 45–76.

Borges, José-Luis, (1956). 'Pierre Menard, Author of Don Quixote', in *Ficciones*, Buenos Aires, Emecé Editores, and London, Weidenfeld & Nicolson 1962; as *Fictions*, London, Calder 1965.

Boumelha, Penny, 1982. *Thomas Hardy and Women: Sexual Ideology and Form*, Totowa,

N. J., Barnes & Noble / Sussex, Harvester.

Bove, Paul A., 1980. *Deconstructive Poetics: Heidegger and Modern American Poetry*, New York, Columbia University Press.

Brandys, Kazimierz, (1977). *A Question of Reality*, transl. from French Isabel Barzun, London, Blond and Briggs, 1981 (originally pub. New York, Scribner 1980).

    A Warsaw Diary 1978–1981, transl. from Polish Richard Lourie, London, Chatto and Windus 1984.

    (1981–2), *Miesiące*, Paris, Kultura; transl. Thérèse Douchy, *Les Mois*, Paris, Gallimard 1984.

Brautigan, Richard, 1967. *Trout Fishing in America*, New York, Dell.

Brooke-Rose, Christine, 1958. *A Grammar of Metaphor*, London, Secker & Warburg.

    1964. *Out*, a novel, London, Michael Joseph.

    1966. *Such*, a novel, London, Michael Joseph.

    1968. *Between*, a novel, London, Michael Joseph.

    1971. *A ZBC of Ezra Pound*, London, Faber & Faber/Berkeley, California University Press.

    1975. *Thru*, a novel, London, Hamish Hamilton.

    1977. 'The Squirm of the True: An Essay on Non-Methodology', *PTL* 1/2: 265–94, repr. in 1981.

    1981. *A Rhetoric of the Unreal*, Cambridge, Cambridge University Press.

    1984. *Amalgamemnon*, Manchester, Carcanet.

    1986. *Xorandor*, Manchester, Carcanet.

    1990. *Verbivore*, Manchester, Carcanet.

Brooks, Cleanth, and W. K. Wimsatt, 1957. *Literary Criticism – A Short History*, London, Routledge & Kegan Paul.

Brooks, Peter, 1977. 'Freud's Master Plot: Questions of Narrative', in *Yale French Studies* 55, 280–300.

    1980. 'Repetition, Repression and Return: *Great Expectations* and the Study of Plot', *New Literary History* 11/3, 503–26.

    1984. *Reading for the Plot*, New York, Knopf, Oxford, Oxford University Press.

Brown, Norman O., 1966. *Love's Body*, New York, Random House.

Brownell, W. C., (1909). *American Prose Masters*, New York, Scribner's Sons, pp. 96–103, reprinted as 'This New England Faust', in Hawthorne 1961, pp. 291–3.

Burgess, Anthony, 1962, *A Clockwork Orange*, London, Heinemann.

    1981. 'Grunts from a Sexist Pig', *The Observer*, June 21, 37.

Butler, Lance St John (ed.), 1977a. *Thomas Hardy after Fifty Years*, London, Macmillan.

    1977b. 'How It Is for Thomas Hardy', in 1977a: 116–25.

Butor, Michel, 1967. *La Modification*, Paris, Editions de Minuit, 1980.

Calvino, Italo, 1967. *Ti con zero*, Torino, Einaudi.

    1978. *Le citta invisibili*, Turin, Einaudi, 1972; transl. William Weaver, *Invisible Cities* New York, Harcourt Brace.

Camus, Albert, 1942. *L'Etranger*, Paris, Gallimard; transl. Stuart Gilbert, *The Stranger*, New York, A. A. Knopf 1946.

Carter, Angela, 1977, *The Passion of New Eve*, London, Gollancz.

Cervantes, Miguel de, (1604–14). *Don Quijote de la Mancha*, Coleccion Austral, Madrid, Espasa-Calpe 1940; transl. J. M. Cohen, *Don Quixote*, Harmondsworth, Penguin Classics 1950.

Chabot, C. Barry, 1988. 'The Problem of the Postmodern', *New Literary History* 20/1,

1–20.

Chase, Cynthia, 1979. 'The Deconstruction of Elephants: Double Reading of *Daniel Deronda*', *PMLA* 93, 215–27.

Chénetier, Marc, 1986. ' "A la recherche de l'Arlésienne": l'écriture féminine dans la fiction américaine contemporaine', *Revue française d'études américaines*, November, 415–35.

1989. *Au-delà du soupçon – la nouvelle fiction américaine de 1960 à nos jours*, Paris, Seuil.

Cixous, Hélène, & Catherine Clément, 1975. *La Jeune Née*, Paris, Union générale d'éditions.

Cixous, Hélène, 1976. 'The Laugh of the Medusa', transl. Keith & Paula Cohen, *Signs* 1, 875–93.

1981. 'Castration or Decapitation?', transl. Annette Kuhn, *Signs* 7, 41–55.

Clément, Catherine, see Cixous.

Coover, Robert, 1966. *The Origin of the Brunists*, New York, Viking, Bantam Books 1978.

1969. *Pricksongs and Descants*, New York, Dutton.

1977. *The Public Burning*, New York, Viking, Bantam 1978.

Cox, James M., 1975. '*The Scarlet Letter*: Through the Old Manse and the Custom-House', *Virginia Quarterly Review* 51, 432–47.

Crane, Stephen, (1895). *The Red Badge of Courage*, newly ed. from Crane's original MS, Henry Binder, New York, Norton 1982.

1976. *The Red Badge of Courage* (Appleton Text) ed, Sculley Bradley *et al.*, Norton Critical Edition, New York, Norton.

Culler, Jonathan, 1980. 'Fabula and Sjuzhet in the Analysis of Narrative: Some American Discussions', *Poetics Today* 1/3, 27–37.

1983. *On Deconstruction – Theory and Criticism after Structuralism*, London, Routledge & Kegan Paul.

Darras, Jacques, 1985. Cantos 42–51 and 62–71 in Pound 1985.

Debax, Jean-Paul, 1980. 'Et voilà pourquoi votre femme est muette', in *Caliban XVII*, Tome XVI, Fasc.1, Université de Toulouse le Mirail, 23–7.

Debray-Genette, Raymonde, 1984. 'Some Functions of Figures in Novelistic Description', in *Poetics Today* 5/3 (*Representation in Modern Fiction*), 677–88.

DeKoven, Marianne, 1988. 'Male Signature, Female Aesthetic: The Gender Politics of Experimental Writing', in Friedmann & Fuchs 1988, pp. 72–81.

Deleuze, Gilles, 1969a. *Différence et répétition*, Paris, Presses Universitaires de France.

1969b. *Logique du Sens*, Paris, Editions de Minuit.

1976. *Rhizome*, Paris, Editions de Minuit.

de Man, Paul, 1979. *Allegories of Reading*, New Haven, Conn., Yale University Press; 'Rhetoric of Persuasion (Nietzsche)' at pp. 119–31.

Derrida, Jacques, 1967a. 'Freud et la scène de l'écriture', in 1967b, pp. 293–340.

1967b. *L'Écriture et la différence*, Paris, Seuil; transl. *Writing and Difference*, Chicago University Press 1978.

1972a. 'La Pharmacie de Platon', in 1972b, pp. 91–5.

1972b. *La Dissémination*, Paris, Seuil; transl. *Dissemination*, Chicago University Press 1982.

1972c. 'Le Supplément de copule', in 1972e, pp. 209–46.

1972d. 'La Mythologie blanche: la métaphore dans le texte philosophique', in 1972e, pp. 247–324.

1972e. *Marges de la philosophie*, Paris, Editions de Minuit; transl. *Margins of*

Philosophy, Chicago, Chicago University Press 1982.

1975. 'Le Facteur de vérité' in *La Carte postale: de Socrate à Freud et au-delà*, Paris, Flammarion; transl. 'The Purveyor of Truth', *Yale French Studies* 52 (1975), 31–114; and in *The Postcard*, Chicago, Chicago University Press 1984.

1977a. 'Signature événement contexte', *Glyph* 1, 172–97; transl. in *Margins*, see 1972e.

    1977b. *Limited Inc*, Suppl. to *Glyph* 2, 1977, 162–254 (response to Searle's reply in *Glyph* 1, see Searle).

Doolittle, Hilda (H. D.), 1979. *A Memoir of Ezra Pound*, ed. Norman Holmes Pearson & Michael King, New York, New Directions.

Dujardin, Edouard, (1887). *Les Lauriers sont coupés*, in *La Revue indépendante*, republ. 1925 with preface Valéry Larbaud, Paris, Albert Messein 1925.

Dupas, Jean-Claude, 1983. 'Transformation de la fiction et fiction de la rupture', in *Fabula* 1, Presses Universitaires de Lille, 9–32.

Eagleton, Terry, 1988. 'The Ideology of the Aesthetic', *Poetics Today* 9/2, 327–38.

Eakin, Paul J., 1971. 'Hawthorne's Imagination and the Structure of "The Custom-House"', *American Literature* 43, 346–58.

Eco, Umberto, 1979. *The Role of the Reader – Explorations in the Semiotics of Texts*, Bloomington, Indiana, Indiana University Press.

    1980. *Il nome della Rosa*, Milano, Fabbri-Bompiani; transl. William Weaver, *The Name of the Rose*, London, Secker & Warburg, New York, Harcourt Brace Jovanovich 1983.

    1988. 'Intentio Lectoris – The State of the Art', in *Differentia* 2, Spring 1988, 147–68.

    1989. *Il pendolo di Foucault*, Milan, Bompiani; *Foucault's Pendulum*, London, Secker & Warburg 1989.

Eisenstein, Hester, and Jardine, Alice J. (eds.), 1980. *The Future of Difference*, Boston, Hall.

Eliot, Valerie (ed.), 1971. *T. S. Eliot: The Waste Land – a facsimile and transcript of the original drafts and fragments including the annotations of Ezra Pound*, London, Faber & Faber.

Empsom, William, 1930. *Seven Types of Ambiguity*, London, Chatto & Windus, rev. ed. 1947.

    1951. *The Structure of Complex Words*, London, Chatto & Windus.

Felman, Shoshana, 1975. 'Women and Madness: The Critical Phallacy', *Diacritics* 5, 2–10.

    1977. 'Turning the Screw of Interpretation', *Yale French Studies* 55–6, 94–207.

    1978. *La Folie et la chose littéraire*, Paris, Seuil.

    1980. *Le Scandale du corps parlant*, Paris, Seuil.

    1987. 'The Case of Poe: Applications/Implications of Psychoanalysis', in *Jacques Lacan and the Adventure of Insight – Psychoanalysis in Contemporary, Culture*, Cambridge, Mass., Harvard University Press, pp. 27–51.

Fish, Stanley, 1970. 'Literature in the Reader: Affective Stylistics', *New Literary History* 2/1: 123–62; 1980b, pp. 21–67.

    1980a. 'How to Recognise a Poem When You See One', in 1980b, pp. 322–37.

    1980b. *Is There a Text in this Class?* Cambridge, Mass., Harvard University Press.

Forster, E. M., 1927. *Aspects of the Novel*, London, Arnold.

Foster, Hal (ed.), 1983. *The Anti-Aesthetic – Essays on Post-modern Culture*, Bay Press, Port Townsend, Washington.

Fowles, John, 1966. *The Magus*, London, Cape; Frogmore, Triad/Panther 1978.

    1969. *The French Lieutenant's Woman*. London. Cape; Triad/Panther 1977.

Freud, Sigmund, (1900) 1955a. *The Interpretation of Dreams*, in *The Standard Edition of the Complete Psychological Works (SE)*. London. Hogarth Press, Vols. 4–5.

(1920) 1955b. 'Beyond the Pleasure Principle'. *SE*, Vol.18, 3–66.

(1915) 1957. 'Repression', *SE*, Vol.14, 46–58.

(1923) 1961a. 'The Ego and the Id', *SE*, Vol.18, 3–66.

(1925) 1961b. 'A Note upon the "Mystic Writing Pad"', *SE*, Vol.19, 227–34.

(1885) 1966. 'Project for a Scientific Psychology', *SE*, Vol.1, 283–94.

Friedman, Ellen, 1988. 'Breaking the Master Narrative: Jean Rhys', *Wide Sargasso Sea*, in Friedman & Fuchs, pp. 117–28.

Friedman, Ellen & Fuchs, Miriam (eds.), 1988. *Breaking the Sequence – Women's Experimental Fiction*. Princeton, N. J. Princeton University Press.

Frye, Northrop, 1957. *Anatomy of Criticism*, Princeton University Press, Reprinted in Paperback by Atheneum, New York 1965.

1976. *The Secular Scripture*, Cambridge, Mass., Harvard University Press.

Fuchs, Miriam, see Friedman.

Fuentes, Carlos, 1978. *Terra Nostra*, Barcelona, Seix Barral, 1975; transl. Margaret Sayers Peden *Terra Nostra*, New York, Farrar, Straus, Giroux 1976; London, Secker and Warburg 1977.

Gass, William, 1966. *Omensetter's Luck*, New York, New American Library.

1976. *On Being Blue*, Boston, David R. Godine.

Gautier, Théophile, (1834). *Mademoiselle de Maupin*, ed. Geneviève van den Bogaert, Paris, Garnier 1966.

Genette, Gérard, 1972. 'Discours du récit', in *Figures III*, Paris, Seuil; transl. Jane E. Lewin, *Narrative Discourse*. Ithaca, Cornell University Press 1980.

1982, *Palimpsestes*, Paris, Seuil.

1983. *Nouveau discours du récit*, Paris, Seuil.

Gilbert, Sandra, and Gubar, Susan, 1979. *The Madwoman in the Attic: The Woman Writer in the Nineteenth-Century Literary Imagination*, New Haven. Yale University Press.

Gittings, Robert, 1975. *Young Thomas Hardy*, London, Heinemann.

Glasenfeld, Ernst Von, 1979. 'Reflections on John Fowles' *The Magus* and the Construction of Reality', *Georgia Review*, Summer, 444–8.

Goode, John, 1979. 'Sue Bridehead and the New Woman', in Jacobus 1979, pp. 100–13.

Graff, Gerald, 1979. *Literature against Itself: Literary Ideas in Modern Society*, Chicago, Chicago University Press.

Greimas, A. J. and Rastier, François, 1968. 'The Interaction of Semiotic Constraints' in *Yale French Studies* 41, 86–105.

Gubar, Susan (see also Gilbert, Sandra), 1981. '"The Blank Page" and the Issues of Female Creativity', *Critical Inquiry* 8/2: 243–53.

Gumbrecht, Hans Ulrich 1988. '"Phoenix from the Ashes" or: From Canon to Classic', *New Literary History* 20/1 :141–63.

Halle, Morris, and Keyser, S. J. 1970. *English Stress: Its Form, Its Growth and Its Role in Verse*, New York, Harper and Row 1971.

Hamburger, Käte, 1957. *Die Logik der Dichtung*, Stuttgart; transl. Marilyn Rose, *The Logic of Literature*. Bloomington & London, Indiana University Press 1973.

Hamon, Philippe, 1973. 'Un discours contraint', *Poétique* 16, Paris, Seuil: 411–45; reprinted in *Littérature et réalité*, Paris, Seuil 1982, pp. 119–81.

1977, 'Pour un statut sémiologique du personnage', in *Poétique du récit*, Paris, Seuil, 411–45.

Hardy, Thomas, (1895). *Jude the Obscure*, Oxford University Press 1985.

Hassan, Ihab, 1971. *The Dismemberment of Orpheus – Toward a Postmodern Literature*, Oxford University Press, repr. Madison, Wisconsin University Press 1982.

    1975. *Paracriticisms*, Urbana, University of Illinois Press.

    1980. *The Right Promethean Fire*, Urbana, University of Illinois Press.

    1988. 'On the Problem of the Postmodern' (reply to Chabot), *New Literary History* 20/1, 21–2.

Havelock, Eric A., 1963. *Preface to Plato*, Cambridge, Mass, Belknap Press of Harvard University Press.

    1976. *Origins of Western Literacy*, Toronto, Ontario Institute for Studies in Education.

Hawthorne, Nathaniel, (1849–50). 1978 *The Scarlet Letter*, Norton Critical Edition, New York, W. W. Norton & Co. 1961, 2nd ed. 1978.

    1932. *The American Notebooks 1841–1852*, ed. R. Stewart, New Haven, Yale University Press.

Hegel, G. W., (1807). *The Phenomenology of Mind*, transl. J. B. Baillie, New York, Harper 1867.

Herodotus, 1972. *The Histories*, transl. Aubrey de Selincourt 1954, rev. A. R. Burn, Harmondsworth, Penguin 1972.

Hesse, Eva, 1956. *Ezra Pound: Pisaner Cantos*, transl. Hesse, rev. 1969, Zurich, Arche Verlag.

    1964. *Cantos I-XXX*, Zurich, Arche Verlag.

    1975. *Letzte Texte – Entwurfe und Fragmente zu Cantos CX-CXX*, Zurich, Arche Verlag.

Higgins, Dick, 1978. *A Dialectic of Centuries: Notes Towards a Theory of the New Arts*, New York & Barton Ve, Printed Editions.

    1984. *Horizons: The Poetics and Theory of the Intermedia*. Carbondale & Edwardsville, South Illinois University Press.

Hirsch, E. D. 1967. *Validity in Interpretation*, New Haven, Yale University Press.

Hofmann, Gert, 1981, *Gespräch über Balsacs Pferd*, Salzburg & Wein, Residenz Verlag; München, Deutscher Taschenbuch Verlag 1984.

    1982. *Auf der Turm*, Darmstadt, Luchterhand; transl. Christopher Middleton, *The Spectacle at the Tower*, London, Carcanet 1987.

    1984. *Unsere Eroberung*, Darmstadt, Luchterhand; transl. Christopher Middleton, *Our Conquest* London, Carcanet 1987.

    1986. *Der Blindensturz*, Darmstadt, Luchterhand.

Honek, R. P. and Hoffman, R. R., 1980. *Cognition and Figurative Language*, Hillsdale, N.J., Lawrence Erlbaum Associates 1980.

Hutcheon, Linda, 1980. *Narcissistic Narrative – The Metafictional Paradox*, New York & London, Methuen.

Huxley, Aldous, 1928. *Point Counterpoint*, New York, Harper & Bros. Perrennial Classic Paperback. Harper & Row 1965.

Ingarden, Roman (1931). *The Literary Work of Art*, transl. G. G. Grabowicz, Evanston, Ill., Northwestern University Press 1973.

Ingham, Patricia, 1985. 'Introduction', *Jude the Obscure*, Oxford University Press, pp. i-xxxii.

Jacobus, Mary, 1979. *Women Writing and Writing about Women*, London, Helen Croom, New York, Barnes & Noble.

    1982. 'Is There a Woman in This Text?' *New Literary History* 14, 117–41.

Jakobson, Roman, 1960. 'Closing Statement: Linguistics and Poetics' in *Style in Language*. ed. T. Sebeok, Cambridge. MIT Press, pp. 350–77.

James, Henry, 1879. *Hawthorne*, ed. J. Morley, London, Macmillan & Co. 1879.

Jameson, Frederic, 1980. 'Balzac et le problème du sujet', in Le Huenon & Perron (eds.), *Le roman de Balzac*, Montréal, Didier.

Jardine, Alice A., see Eisenstein.

Johnson, Barbara, 1980. *The Critical Difference – Essays in the Contemporary Rhetoric of Reading*, Baltimore, Johns Hopkins University Press.

1987. *A World of Difference*, Baltimore, Johns Hopkins University Press.

Johnson, Mark, 1980. 'A Philosophical Perspective on the Problem of Metaphor' in R. P. Honeck & R. R. Hoffman (eds.), *Cognition and Figurative Language*, Hillsdale, N. J., pp. 47–67.

Josipovici, Gabriel, 1971. 'Letter into Hieroglyph', in Hawthorne 1978, pp. 421–8, reprinted from *The World and the Book*, Basingstoke & Stanford Ca, Macmillan & Stanford University Press, pp. 155–78.

Joyce, James, (1922), *Ulysses*, London, Faber & Faber, Penguin Books 1968.

(1939). *Finnegans Wake*, London, Faber & Faber, Paperback 1975.

Karl, Frederick, 1985. 'American Fictions: The Mega-Novel', *Conjunctions* 7, 248–60.

Kermode, Frank, 1966. *The Sense of an Ending*, New York, Oxford University Press.

1979. *The Genesis of Secrecy*, Cambridge, Mass., Harvard University Press.

Keyser, see Halle.

Kierkegaard, Sören, (1846). *Concluding Unscientific Postscript*, transl. D. F. Swanson and W. Lowrie, Princeton, N. J., Princeton University Press 1941.

Kiparsky, Paul, (1977). 'The Rhythmic Structure of English Verse', *Linguistic Inquiry* 8, 189–247.

Kirkby, Joan, 1986. 'Is There Life After Art? The Metaphysics of Marilynne Robinson's *Housekeeping*', *Tulsa Studies in Women's Literature* 5, 91–109.

Kolodny, Annette, 1975, 'Some Notes on Defining a Feminist Literary Criticism', *Critical Inquiry* 2/1, 75–92.

1976. 'The Feminist as Literary Critic', *Critical Inquiry* 2/4, 821–32.

Konwicki, Tadeusz, 1979, *Mała apokalipsa*; transl. *La Petite Apocalypse*, Paris, Laffont 1981; transl. R. Laurie, *A Minor Apocalypse*, London, Faber & Faber 1983.

Kristeva, Julia, 1968. 'La Productivité dite texte', *Communications* 11, Paris, Seuil, 59–83.

1977. 'Hérétique de l'amour', *Tel Quel* 74, reprinted as 'Stabat Mater', *Histoires d'amour*, Paris, Denoel 1983; transl. *Poetics Today* 6/1–2, 1985, 133–52.

Kummings, D., 1971. 'Hawthorne's "The Custom-House" and the Conditions of Fiction in America', *CEA Critic* 33, ii, 15–18.

Kundera, Milan, 1978. *The Book of Laughter and Forgetting*, transl. Michael Henry Hein, London, Faber & Faber 1982, New York, Penguin 1981.

1984, 1987. *L'Insoutenable légéreté de l'être*, transl. François Kerel 1984, revised with author 1987, Paris, Gallimard.

1990. *L'Immortalité*, transl. Eva Bloch and author, Paris, Gallimard.

Kuroda, S-Y., 1973. 'Where Epistemology, Style and Grammar Meet: A Case Study from the Japanese', in P. Kiparsky & S. Anderson (eds.) *A Festschrift for Morris Halle*, New York, Holt, Rhinehart & Wilson, pp. 377–91.

1976. 'Reflections on the Foundations of Narrative Theory from a Linguistic Point of View', T. Van Dijk (ed.) *Pragmatics of Language and Literature*, Amsterdam & New York, North Holland, pp. 108–40.

Lacan, Jacques, 1966. *Ecrits*, Paris, Seuil.

1973. *Le Séminaire 1972–73: Livre XX. Encore*, Paris, Seuil.

Lecercle, Jean-Jacques, 1985. *Philosophy through the Looking-Glass*, London, Hutchinson.

Leclaire, Serge, 1968. *Psychanalyser*, Paris, Seuil.

　1972. 'Les Mots du psychotique', *Change* 12, Paris, Seghers/Laffont, pp. 116–32.

Le Huenon, Roland, and Perron, Paul, 1984. 'Reflections on Balzacian Models of Representation', *Poetics Today* 5/4, 711–28.

Leitch, Vincent B., 1983. *Deconstructive Criticism: An Advanced Introduction*, New York, Columbia University Press.

Lévi-Strauss, Claude, 1949. *Les Structures élémentaires de la parenté*, Paris, Presses Universitaires de France.

　(1958). *Structural Anthropology*, transl. Claire Jacobson & Brooke Grundfest Schoepf, New York, Basic Books 1963.

Lewis, Oscar, 1961, *The Children of Sanchez: autobiography of a Mexican family*, London, Secker and Warburg 1962.

Lodge, David, 1977a. *Modes of Modern Writing*, London, Arnold.

　1977b. 'Thomas Hardy as a Cinematic Novelist', in Butler 1977a, pp. 78–89.

Lord, Albert B., 1960. *The Singer of Tales*, Cambridge, Mass, Harvard University Press.

Lyotard, Jean-François, 1979. *La Condition postmoderne*, Paris, Editions de Minuit.

　1988. *La Postmoderne expliqué aux enfants*, Paris, Editions Galilée.

Major, Clarence, 1975. *Reflex and Bone Structure*, New York, Fiction Collective.

di Manno, Yves, 1985. Cantos 52–61 in Pound 1985.

Mansell, Darrel, 1988. 'The Difference between a Lump and a Text', *Poetics Today* 9/4, 791–805.

Márquez, Gabriel Garcia, *Cien Años de Soledad*, Buenos Aires, Editorial Sudamericana SA; transl. Gregory Rabassa, New York, Harper & Row 1970.

Matthiessen, F. O., 1941. *American Renaissance Art and Expression in the Age of Emerson and Whitman*, Oxford, Oxford University Press.

Mauriac, Claude, 1961. *La Marquise sortit à cinq heures*. Paris; transl. R. Howard. *The Marquise Went Out at Five*, London, Calder and Boyars 1966.

McCall, Dan, 1967. 'The Design of Hawthorne's "The Custom-House" ', *Nineteenth-Century Fiction* 21, 349–85.

McElroy, Joseph, 1983. *Anything Can Happen*, Illinois University Press.

McHale, Brian, 1978. 'Free Indirect Discourse: A Survey of Recent Accounts', *PTL* 3/2, 249–87.

　1979. 'Modernist Reading, Postmodern Text: The Case of *Gravity's Rainbow*', *Poetics Today* 1/1–2, 85–110.

　1983. 'Unspeakable Sentences, Unnatural Acts – Linguistics and Poetics Revisited', *Poetics Today* 4/1, 17–45.

　1987. *Postmodernist Fiction*, London, Methuen.

　1988. 'Telling Postmodernist Stories', *Poetics Today* 9/3, 545–71.

McLuhan, Marshal, 1962. *The Gutenberg Galaxy: The Making of Typographic Man*, Toronto, University of Toronto Press.

McShane, Frank, 1962. 'The House of the Dead: Hawthorne's Custom-House and *The Scarlet Letter*', *New England Quarterly* 35, 93–101.

Mikriammos, Philippe, 1985. Cantos 1–41 in Pound 1985.

Miller, J. Hillis, 1976. 'Ariadne's Thread: Repetition and the Narrative Line', *Critical Inquiry* 3/1, 57–77.

　1982. *Fiction and Repetition*, Cambridge, Mass., Harvard University Press.

Miller, Nancy K. 1981. 'Emphasis Added: Plots and Plausibility in Women's Fiction', *PMLA* 96, 36–48.

1986. 'Rereading as a Woman: The Body in Practice', in Suleiman 1986, republ. as book from Special Number of *Poetics Today* 6, 1985, 254–62.

Milner, Jean-Claude, 1978. *L'Amour de la langue*, Paris, Seuil.

Mimouni, Rachid, 1982. *Le Fleuve détourné*, Paris, Laffont.

1984. *Tombéza*, Paris, Laffont.

Muray, Philippe, 1983. 'La Marquise revint à minuit', *L'Infini* 2, Paris, Denoel, pp. 26–38.

Nash, Cristopher, 1987. *World Games – The Tradition of Anti-Realist Revolt*, London, Methuen.

Newman, Charles, 1984. 'The Post-modern Aura: The Art of Fiction in an Age of Inflation', *Salmagundi* 63–4, 3–199.

Nietzsche, Frederick, (1922). *Gesammelte Werke*, Munich, Musarion Verlag.

1968. *The Will to Power*, ed. & transl. W. Kaufman, New York, Random House, Vintage Books.

1970. *Werke Kritische Gesamtausgabe*, Giorgio Colli & Mazzino Montinari (eds.), Berlin, de Gruyter.

Nin, Anaïs, 1967. *The Diary of Anaïs Nin 1934–39*, ed. Gunther Stuhlmann, New York, Harcourt Brace.

Nodelman, Perry, 1988. 'The Sense of Unending: Joyce Carol Oates's *Bellefleur* as an Experiment in Feminine Storytelling', in Friedman & Fuchs, pp. 250–64.

Oates, Joyce Carol, 1972. 'Whose Side Are You On?', *NYTBR*, June 4, p. 63.

1974. *New Heaven, New Earth: The Visionary Experience in Literature*, New York, Vanguard.

1981. *Bellefleur*, New York, Warner.

O'Brien, Flann (Brian O'Nolan), (1939). *At Swim-Two-Birds*, London, Longman & Green; Harmondsworth, Penguin 1967.

Ong, Walter J., 1982. *Orality and Literacy – The Technologizing of the Word*, London, Methuen.

Paris, Jean, 1978. *Lisible/Visible – Essais de critique générative*, Paris, Seghers/Laffont.

1986. *Balzac*, Paris, Balland.

Pawel, Thomas, 1988a. *Le Mirage linguistique*, Paris, Editions de Minuit.

1988b. 'Formalism in Narrative Semiotics', *Poetics Today* 9/3, 593–606.

Pavić, Milorad, (1984). *Dictionary of the Khazars: A Lexicon Novel in 100,000 Words*, transl. Christine Pribicevic-Zoric, London, Hamish Hamilton 1989.

(1988) *Paysage peint avec duthé*, transl. Harita and Francis Wybrands, Paris, Belfond 1990.

Perec, Georges, 1969. *La Disparition*, Paris, Denoel.

1972. *Les Revenentes*, Paris, Julliard.

1975. *W ou le souvenir d'enfance*, Paris, Denoel.

1978. *La Vie, mode d'emploi*, Paris, Hachette.

Perron, Paul, see Le Huenon.

Pope, Alexander, (1712). 'The Rape of the Lock', *Poetical Works*, ed. Herbert Davis, Oxford, Oxford University Press, pp. 86–109.

Pound, Ezra, 1975. *The Cantos of Ezra Pound*, London, Faber & Faber.

1985. *Les Cantos*, transl. Jacques Darras, Yves di Manno, Philippe Mikriammos, Denis Roche, François Sauzey, Paris, Flammarion.

Pratt, Mary Louise, 1986. 'Ideology and Speech Act Theory', *Poetics Today* 7/1, 59–72.

Propp, Vladimir, (1928). *Morphology of the Folktale*, transl. L. Scott, rev. 1968 Louis A. Wagner, Austin, University of Texas Press.

Proust, Marcel, 1971. *Contre Sainte-Beuve, Pastiches et Mélanges, Essais et Articles*, Paris, Pléiade.

Pynchon, Thomas, 1963. *V*, New York, Lippincott; Bantam Paperback 1964.

1966. *The Crying of Lot 49*, New York, Lippincott, Bantam Paperback 1974.

1973. *Gravity's Rainbow*, New York, Viking, Bantam 1974.

Quin, Ann, 1964. *Berg*, New York, Scribner's.

1969. *Passages*, London, Calder.

Quine, W. V. 1976. 'Quantifiers and Propositional Attitudes', *The Ways of Paradox and other Essays*, Cambridge, Mass., Harvard, University Press.

Qur'an, The, 1956. *The Koran*, translated N. J. Dawood, Penguin Classics.

Rabaté, Jean-Michel, 1986. *Language, Sexuality and Ideology in Ezra Pound's Cantos*, London. Macmillan.

de Rachewiltz, Mary, 1985. *Ezra Pound – I Cantos, a cura di Mary de Rachewiltz*, Milan, Mondadori.

Rastier, François, see Greimas.

Rees, Nigel (ed.) 1983. *A Year of Graffiti*, London, Unwin Paperbacks.

Rehder, R. M. 1977. 'The Form of Hardy's Novels' in Butler 1977a, pp. 13–27.

Ricardou, Jean, 1972. *Nouveau roman: hier et aujourd'hui 2*, Paris, Union générale d'éditions 10/18.

Richard, Claude, 1985. 'The Character of Fiction as Physical System of Quantity and Quality in *The Floating Opera*', *Delta* 21, Presses Universitaires de Montpellier, pp. 17–29.

Richards, I. A., 1929. *Practical Criticism – A Study of Literary Judgment*, London, Routledge & Kegan Paul.

Richardson, Dorothy Miller, (1938). *Pilgrimage*, London, Dent, New York, Knopf, republ. Dent & Knopf 1967; London, Virago 1979.

Ricoeur, Paul, 1971. *Hermeneutics and the Human Sciences*, ed. and trans. John B. Thompson, Cambridge, Cambridge University Press 1981, pp. 145–64.

1983. *Temps et récit I*, Paris, Seuil.

1984. *Temps et récit II*, Paris, Seuil.

Robbe-Grillet, Alain, 1959. *Dans le labyrinthe*, Paris, Editions de Minuit; transl. C. Brooke-Rose, *In the Labyrinth*, London, Calder 1967.

1962. *Pour un nouveau roman*, Paris, Editions de Minuit; transl. Barbara Wright, London. Calder & Boyars 1965.

Roche, Denis, 1985. Cantos 74–84 (*Pisan*) and 85–95 (*Rock-Drill*) in Pound 1985.

Roche, Maurice, 1966. *Compact*, Paris, Seuil.

1972. *Circus*, Paris, Seuil.

1976. *Mémoire*, Paris, Belfond.

1981. *Camar(a)de*, Paris, Arthaud.

Ronen, Ruth, 1988. 'Completing the Incompleteness of Fictional Entities', *Poetics Today* 9/3, 497–514.

Rorty, Richard, 1979. *Philosophy and the Mirror of Nature*, Princeton. NJ, Princeton University Press.

1982. *Consequences of Pragmatism*, Minneapolis, University of Minnesota Press.

1985. 'Texts and Lumps', *New Literary History* 17/1 1–16.

Rose, Mark (ed.) 1976. *Science Fiction: A Collection of Critical Essays*, Englewood Cliffs, N.J., Prentice Hall.

Ross, John, 1970. 'On Declarative Sentences' in R. Jacobs & Rosenbaum (eds.), *Readings in Transformational Grammar*, Waltham, Mass., Ginn & Co.

Roussel, Raymond, 1910. *Impressions d'Afrique*, Paris, Alphonse Lemerle; repub. J.-J. Pauvert 1963; transl. R. Heppenstall, London, Calder & Boyars 1966.

Rousselle, Aline, 1983. *Porneia – De la maîtrise du corps à la privation sensorielle, IIe-IVe siècles de l'ère chrétienne*, Paris, Presses Universitaires de France.

Rudolf, Anthony, 1988. *Gilette or The Unknown Masterpiece*, by Honoré de Balzac, transl. and introd. A. Rudolf, London, Menard Press.

Rushdie, Salman, 1985. *Shame*, London, Jonathan Cape.

1988 *The Satanic Verses*, London, Penguin-Viking.

Sampson, George, 1942. 'Prose and Poetry: Sir Thomas North to Michael Drayton', Ch. 4, Section 16 of the *Concise Cambridge History of English Literature*, Cambridge, Cambridge University Press, pp. 217–23.

Sarraute, Nathalie, 1956. *L'Ere du soupçon: essais sur le roman*. Paris, Gallimard; transl. Maria Jolas, *The Age of Suspicion*, London, Calder & Boyars 1963.

Sauzey, François, 1985. Cantos 96–109 and 110–17, in Pound 1985.

Scarron, Paul, (1648–9). *Virgile travesti*, ed. Victor Fournel, Paris, Delahaye 1858.

Scherer, Olga, 1983. 'Qu'est-ce que le sous-réalisme?', *TLE* 3, Paris, Presses Universitaires de Vincennes, pp. 5–32.

1986. 'Aspects du sous-réalisme', *TLE* 4, Paris, Presses Universitaires de Vincennes, pp. 31–44.

Scholes, Robert, 1969. 'On Realism and Genre', *Novel* 2, Spring 1969, pp. 269–71.

Searle, John, 1968. *Speech-Acts: An Essay in the Philosophy of Language*, Cambridge, Cambridge University Press.

1977. 'Reiterating the Difference: A Reply to Derrida', *Glyph* 1, 198–208.

Shelley, P. (1840). *A Defence of Poetry*, in *The Complete Works of Percy Bysshe Shelley*, ed. Roger Ingpen and Walter E. Peck, London 1930, 7, p. 135.

Showalter, Elaine, 1971. 'Women Writers and the Double Standard', *Women in Sexist Society*, ed. V. Gornick & B. K. Moran, New York, Basic Books, pp. 323–43.

1981. 'Feminist Criticism in the Wilderness', *Critical Inquiry* 8/2, 179–205.

Sidney, Sir Philip, (1595). 'An Apology for Poetry', in *Selected Poetry and Prose*, ed. D. Kelstone, New York, New American Library 1970.

Silk, Michael, 1988. 'The Anatomy of Comedy', *Comparative Criticism* 10, Cambridge University Press, pp. 3–37.

Simon, Claude, 1960. *La Route des Flandres*, Paris, Editions de Minuit; transl. R. Howard, *The Flanders Road*, with an Introduction by John Fletcher, London, Cape, 1982.

Skvorecky, Joseph, 1972. *Mirakl*; transl. from Czech Claudia Amelot, *Miracle en Bohème*, Paris, Gallimard 1978.

Sontag, Susan, 1967. *Against Interpretation*, London, Secker & Warburg.

1969. *Styles of Radical Will*, London, Secker & Warburg.

Sorel, Charles (1627). *Le Berger extravagant*, with Introduction by H. D. Bechade; originally published in 3 vols., Paris 1627–8. Facsimile reprint: Geneva, Slatkine 1972.

Sorrentino, Gilbert, 1971. *Imaginative Qualities of Things*, New York, New Directions.

1980. *Mulligan Stew*, London, Marion Boyars/Picador 1981.

Spark, Muriel, 1957. *The Comforters*, London, Macmillan.

Stanzel, F. K. 1979. *Theorie des Erzählens*, Göttingen, Vandenhoeck & Ruprecht; transl. Charlotte Goedsche, *A Theory of Narrative*, Cambridge University Press 1984, Paperback 1986.

Stein, Gertrude, 1937. *Four in America*, New Haven, Yale University Press.

Steiner, George, 1958. *Language and Silence*, Toronto, repr. 1960 to 67, New York, Atheneum Paperback 1982.

1975. *After Babel*, New York & London, Oxford, Oxford University Press.

Stern, J. P., 1973. *On Realism*. London, Routledge & Kegan Paul 1973.

Stevick, Philip, 1988. 'Voices in the Head: Style and Consciousness in the Fiction of Ann Quin', Friedman & Fuchs, pp. 232–9.

Stouck, David, 1971. 'The Surveyor of "The Custom-House": A Narrator for *The Scarlet Letter*', *The Centennial Review* 15, 309–29.

Sukenick, Ronald, 1969. 'The Death of the Novel' in *The Death of the Novel and Other Stories*, New York, The Dial Press.

Suleiman, Susan, 1986. *The Female Body in Western Culture – Contemporary Perspectives*, Cambridge Mass., Harvard University Press; orig. special number of *Poetics Today*, 6/1–2, 1985.

Tillotson, Kathleen, 1961. *Novels of the Eighteen-forties*, Oxford, Clarendon Press.

Todorov, Tzvetan, 1969. *La Grammaire du Décameron*, The Hague, Mouton.

1970. *Introduction à la littérature fantastique*, Paris, Seuil; transl. R. Howard, *The Fantastic – A Structural Approach to a Literary Genre*, Ithaca, Cornell University Press 1975.

Twain, Mark, (1885). *Adventures of Huckleberry Finn*, Norton Critical ed., New York, Norton 1977.

Van Deusen, Marshall, 1961. 'Narrative Tone in "The Custom-House" and *The Scarlet Letter*', in Hawthorne 1978, pp. 264–8.

Voloshin, Beverly, 1976. 'A Historical Note on Women's Fiction: A Reply to Annette Kolodny', *Critical Inquiry* 2/4, 817–20.

Voloshinov, V. N., see Bakhtin.

Watt, Ian, 1957. *The Rise of the Novel*, London, Chatto & Windus: Harmondsworth, Peregrine Books 1963.

White, Hayden, 1973. *Metahistory: The Historical Imagination in Nineteenth-Century Europe*, Baltimore, Johns Hopkins University Press.

1974. 'The Historical Text as Literary Artefact', *Clio* III, 3, 277–303.

1978. *Tropics of Discourse: Essays in Cultural Criticism*, Baltimore, Johns Hopkins University Press.

Wilde, Alan, 1981. *Horizons of Assent: Modernism, Postmodernism and the Ironic Imagination*, Baltimore & London, Johns Hopkins University Press.

Wimsatt, W. K. (see also Brooks. Cleanth), 1954. *The Verbal Icon*, University of Kentucky Press; London, Methuen 1970.

Wimsatt, W. K., and Beardsley, Monroe C., 1946. 'The Intentional Fallacy', *Sewanee Review* 54, and in Wimsatt 1954, pp. 3–18.

1949. 'The Affective Fallacy', *Sewanee Review* 57, and in Wimsatt 1954, pp. 21–39.

Wittgenstein, Ludwig, J. J., 1922. *Tractatus Logico-Philosophicus*: The German text of 'Logisch-philosophische Abhandlung' with a new translation by D. F. Pears and B. F. McGuinness, and with the Introduction by B. Russell, London, Routledge & Kegan Paul 1961.

Woolf, Virginia, 1929. *A Room of One's Own*, London, Hogarth Press; New York. Harcourt Brace 1957, Panther Books, Granada 1977.

Young, Marguerite, 1965. *Miss Macintosh, My Darling*, New York, Scribner's.

Zavarzadeh, Mas'ud, 1976. *The Mythopoeic Reality – the Postwar American Nonfiction Novel*, Urbana, University of Illinois Press.

Ziff, Larzer, 1958. 'The Ethical Dimension of "The Custom-House"', *Modern Language Notes* 73, 338–44.

Index